Praise for *Sin in the Second City*

"Poetic . . . Abbott describes the Levee's characters . . . in such detail that it's easy to mistake this meticulously researched history for literary fiction." —*The New York Times Book Review*

"Described with scrupulous concern for historical accuracy . . . an immensely readable book." —*The Wall Street Journal*

"Assiduously researched . . . Even this book's minutiae . . . makes for good storytelling." —*The New York Times*

"[A] satisfyingly lurid tale . . . Karen Abbott has pioneered sizzle history. . . . Change the hemlines, add 100 years, and the book could be filed under current affairs." —*USA Today*

"A colorful history of old Chicago that reads like a novel . . . [a] compelling and eloquent story." —*The Atlanta Journal-Constitution*

"Gorgeously detailed." —New York *Daily News*

"At last, a history book you can bring to the beach."
—*The Philadelphia Inquirer*

"Once upon a time, Chicago had a world-class bordello called The Everleigh Club. Author Karen Abbott brings the opulent place and its raunchy era alive in a book that just might become this year's *The Devil in the White City*." —*Chicago Tribune Magazine* (cover story)

SIN IN THE SECOND CITY

Sin in the Second City

Madams, Ministers, Playboys,
and the
Battle for America's Soul

Karen Abbott

RANDOM HOUSE TRADE PAPERBACKS 🏠 NEW YORK

2008 Random House Trade Paperback Edition

Copyright © 2007 by Karen Abbott
Reading group guide copyright © 2008 by Random House, Inc.

Published in the United States by Random House Trade Paperbacks, an imprint
of The Random House Publishing Group, a division of
Random House, Inc., New York.

RANDOM HOUSE TRADE PAPERBACKS and colophon are trademarks of
Random House, Inc.

Originally published in hardcover in the United States by Random House,
an imprint of The Random House Publishing Group, a division of
Random House, Inc., in 2007.

LIBRARY OF CONGRESS CATALOGING-IN-PUBLICATION DATA
Abbott, Karen.
Sin in the Second City : madams, ministers, playboys, and the battle for America's
soul / Karen Abbott.
p. cm.
Includes bibliographical references and index.
ISBN 978-0-8129-7599-4
1. Prostitution—Illinois—Chicago. 2. Brothels—Illinois—Chicago.
3. Everleigh Club. 4. Everleigh, Ada. 5. Everleigh, Minna. I. Title.
HQ146.C4A23 2007
306.7409773'1109041—dc22
2006051878

Printed in the United States of America

www.atrandom.com

4 6 8 9 7 5

Book design by Stephanie Huntwork

FOR LAURA DITTMAR, MY SCARLET SISTER

Contents

PART THREE

FIGHTING FOR THE PROTECTION OF OUR GIRLS

State Street in Chicago, circa 1907.

THE GIRLS WHO DISAPPEARED

In 1905, a woman named Katherine Filak said her first and final good-bye to the red-roofed cottages and soaring church spires of Ljubljana, Slovenia, and boarded a boat to America. Twenty-one years old and a devout Catholic, she prayed about what lay ahead: work as a domestic and abuse from strange neighborhood men, who tricked her into reciting English curse words. She raised six children, my grandmother among them, and experienced a heartbreak not uncommon to immigrants at the turn of the last century. A sibling who accompanied her on the trip from Europe ventured to Chicago and was never seen again.

This sibling's disappearance became her lone defining trait—my great-grandmother, I'm told, refused to speak of her—and over time I've imagined this lost relative's face, retraced unknown steps, filled in the blanks of her life by probing the city that might have taken it. Chicago in that year experienced a particularly brutal crime wave; not since a mild-mannered killer stalked the grounds of the 1893 World's Fair had its citizens experienced such fear. "A reign of terror is upon the city," declared the *Tribune*. "No city in time of peace ever held so high a place in the category of crime-ridden, terrorized, murder-breeding cities as is now held by Chicago."

The daily tallies of muggings, rapes, and homicides were troublesome enough, but a new threat—unfamiliar, and therefore especially menacing—prepared to creep through Chicago. Young girls stepped from trains into a city steeped in smoke and sin—a "stormy, husky, brawling" city, as Carl Sandburg so affectionately wrote—and vanished without warning or word. Stories abounded, growing more detailed and honed with each retelling. Predatory men met these girls at depots. They professed love at first sight, promised work and shelter and protection. Instead these girls were drugged, robbed of their virtue by professional rapists, sold to Levee madams, and dead within five years.

Most of the brothels in the city's thriving vice district were indeed wicked, block upon block of dingy, anonymous, twenty-five-cent cribs, but one, in remarkably short order, became as well known as Chicago itself. In these pages I tell the story of the Everleigh Club and its iconic madams, their libertine clients and bitter rivalries, and their battle to preserve the empire they so lovingly built. I want to stress that this is a work of nonfiction; every character I describe lived and breathed, if not necessarily thrived, on the Levee's mean streets. Anything that appears in quotation marks, dialogue or otherwise, comes from a book, archival collection, article, journal, or government report.

Before opening their world-famous Club, the Everleigh sisters, too, were girls who disappeared, and they reconstructed their histories at a time when America was updating its own. To that end, this book is also about identity, both personal and collective, and the struggle inherent in deciding how much of the old should accompany us as we rush, headlong, into the new.

KAREN ABBOTT

Chicago, a gaudy circus beginning with
the two-bit whore in the alley crib.

—THEODORE DREISER

CAST OF CHARACTERS

THE MADAMS

MINNA EVERLEIGH: The outspoken co-proprietor of the Everleigh Club handled promotion, disciplined courtesans, and mingled in the parlors with her "boys."

ADA EVERLEIGH: The quiet, elder Everleigh sister interviewed prospective courtesans, balanced the books, and was considered the brains of the operation.

VIC SHAW: The established queen of the Levee until the Everleighs' arrival resented the sisters' success and did everything in her power to ruin them.

ZOE MILLARD: A prominent madam in Vic Shaw's league who shared her dislike for the Everleigh sisters.

THE LORDS OF THE LEVEE

BATHHOUSE JOHN COUGHLIN: This powerful alderman of Chicago's First Ward ordered graft payments, threw an annual ball for denizens of the Levee, and wrote famously awful poetry.

HINKY DINK KENNA: Bathhouse John's diminutive, quiet First Ward partner, his shrewd political machinations kept Chicago's Democratic machine running smoothly and profitably.

IKE BLOOM: The clownish yet menacing owner of the notorious Freiberg's Dance Hall, he organized graft payments on behalf of the aldermen and was a frequent visitor to the Everleigh Club.

ED AND LOUIS WEISS: The Everleighs' neighbors on either side hatched several schemes to lure clients away from the Club—and ultimately became the sisters' greatest threat.

BIG JIM COLOSIMO: A prominent First Ward henchman and brothel keeper, Big Jim was the predecessor to Al Capone. He was also a close friend of the Everleigh sisters despite the fact that he ran an interstate white slavery ring.

MAURICE VAN BEVER: Influential French brothel keeper and Big Jim's partner in the white slavery ring.

THE MINISTERS

ERNEST BELL: A reverend who opened his Midnight Mission in 1904, he preached against segregated vice districts and held nightly open-air sermons outside the Everleigh Club.

MELBOURNE BOYNTON: The pastor of the Lexington Avenue Baptist Church and one of Bell's main "saints" helped to escalate the war against the Levee district.

DEAN SUMNER: Head of the flock at the Episcopal Cathedral of Saints Peter and Paul and chairman of the Chicago Vice Commission.

THE POLITICIANS

CLIFFORD ROE: The young, ambitious Chicago state's attorney used a note tossed from a brothel window to launch America's obsession with white slavery—and his own career.

EDWIN SIMS: The U.S. district attorney in Chicago entered the fray by raiding French brothels in the Levee and persuaded the federal government to take action.

JAMES R. MANN: A U.S. congressman and sponsor of the White Slave Traffic Act, otherwise known as the Mann Act.

MAYOR EDWARD DUNNE: Chicago's Democratic mayor from 1905 to 1907, Dunne faced the public's growing anxiety about dance halls, nickel theaters, saloons, and the "social evil."

MAYOR FRED BUSSE: Dunne's successor, a Republican who served from 1907 to 1911, was sympathetic to saloon keepers, and was eager to stay on good terms with Hinky Dink and Bathhouse John.

MAYOR CARTER HARRISON II: The son of Chicago's favorite mayor, Harrison, a Democrat, succeeded Busse in 1911 and planned to protect the Levee district—a task that proved more difficult than he expected.

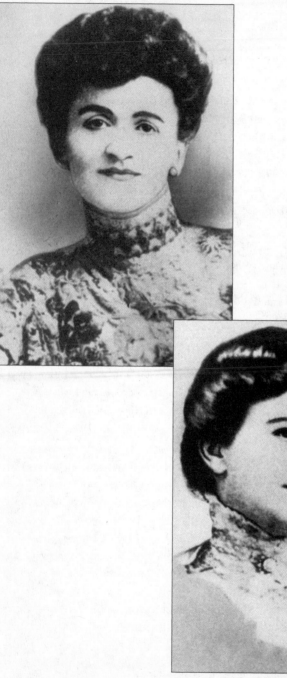

Minna (left) and
Ada Everleigh.

ANGELS OF THE LINE
1905

As soon as the bullet pierced Marshall Field Jr.—the only son and heir of Marshall Field, founder of the splendorous department store, the man who famously said, "Give the lady what she wants"—Chicago made the story even bigger than it really was. Amplifying things, good or bad, was what Chicago did best.

In the days following November 22, 1905, rumors about the shooting spun through the city's streets. The fruit cart vendors whispered to the newsboys who shouted to the hansom drivers who murmured to the society women who were overheard by servants who gossiped with bartenders who bantered with pimps and whores and drunks. Did they hear the wound was just like the one that killed President McKinley? Tore through his abdomen, caught a corner of the liver, grazed the stomach, and skidded to a halt outside the spinal cord—lucky for Marshall Junior. He was in his bedroom at the Prairie Avenue mansion, home alone with his son and the hired help, when a hollow boom split the air. A cry followed, thin and drawn out like taffy.

The family nurse and the butler scaled the stairs in flying jumps and found him slumped in a chair, wan face seeking cover in the curve of his shoulder. Goodness, the blood—it was everywhere. Veining across his shirt, fissuring down the wall. His automatic revolver came to rest on the tip of his shoe. He tried to straighten, treaded the air as if it were a lolling wave. "I shot myself," Marshall Junior said. "Accidentally."

But it couldn't have been an accident. Who really believed that Field dropped his gun, and that the trigger could slam an armchair with sufficient force to explode a cartridge? A reporter at the *Chicago Daily News* said it was impossible—he took an identical, unloaded revolver and hurled it several times to the floor. Not once did the thing go off. Marshall Junior must have pointed the gun at himself; it was the only way. And a suicide attempt made sense. He had suffered a nervous breakdown the year prior, in 1904—this act could be a decisive sequel.

No, what *really* happened was sadder than suicide, more pitiful than a nervous breakdown: Field had sneaked off to the Levee district for a tryst at the Everleigh Club. So what if he was married, the father of three—he had money and status and power, and men with those things always went to the Everleigh Club. A prostitute shot him, maybe in the Gold Room or the Japanese Parlor or beneath the glass chandeliers suspended like stalactites from the ceiling. Later, as the sun deserted the sky and the streets gripped the fog, those Scarlet Sisters, Minna and Ada Everleigh, ordered his unconscious body smuggled out and planted in his home.

Those Scarlet Sisters heard all about their alleged hand in the incident, how they stood idly by while one of their harlots blasted the poor man, then directed the covert removal of his bloody body.

"We are a funeral parlor," Ada Everleigh said, "instead of a resort."

Her younger sister, Minna, gave a blunt, trumpet-burst laugh. Ada parsed her words as if they were in limited supply, but damned if she didn't load each one before it left her mouth.

The Chicago rumor mill operated as predictably as the Everleighs' regular clients; no matter how gossip began, or where it twisted and turned, it ended up, invariably, at the doorstep of 2131–2133 South Dearborn Street. Nonsense, every bit of it. The sisters had decided long ago to permit no stains, blood or otherwise, on their house.

Neither would the Everleighs add their own voices to the din. Discretion paid—but also had its price.

Even Chicago's newspapers kept their distance from the speculation for fear that Marshall Field Sr. would pull his advertising dollars. He certainly wouldn't appreciate reports that his son, currently lying in critical condition at Mercy Hospital, had visited a whorehouse, even one as dignified as the Everleigh Club. Still, journalists staked out the sisters all week, trying to score something—anything—that would be safe to print. Minna and Ada waited in the front parlor, expecting yet another newsman.

All thirty Everleigh Club harlots remained upstairs in their boudoirs, preparing for the night ahead, running razors under their arms, down and between their legs—clients didn't have a smooth woman at home. They packed themselves with sponges, made certain they had enough douche, checked cabinets for the little black pills that, along with three days of hot baths, usually "brought a girl around" from any unwanted condition. They yanked and tied one another's corsets, buttoned up gowns made of slippery silk, unrolled black stockings over long legs. Hair was wound tight with pins or left to fall in tousled waves, depending on the preference of their regulars. A dab of gasoline—the newest fad in perfume, if you couldn't afford an automobile—behind the ears, across the wrists and ankles, between the breasts. Eyes rimmed in black and lashes painted, standing stiffer than the prongs of a fork. Each courtesan had a name chosen by her peers. Once she entered this life—*the* life—she discarded all remnants of the one she'd left behind.

Minna navigated the silk couches, the easy chairs, and the grand piano, the statues of Greek goddesses peering through exotic palms, the bronze effigies of Cupid and Psyche, the imported rugs that swallowed footsteps. She had an odd walk, a sort of caterpillar bend and hump, pause and catch up, as the poet Edgar Lee Masters, a friend and frequent client, described it. She came to rest before a wide-paneled window and swallowed, her throat squeezing behind a brooch of diamonds thick as a clenched fist. Holding back the curtain, she surveyed Dearborn Street.

Arc lamps stretched up and out, unfurling bold ribbons of light. The air was thick and yellow, as if the varnish manufacturer on the next block had slathered his product across the sky. Visibility was reduced to the next street, or the next corner, or sometimes just the next step. No matter: Minna didn't have to see the Levee district to know what it was up to.

Panders, an underworld term that served as both verb and noun, were outfitted in dandy ties and jaunty hats, lurking in corners and alleys. Eugene Hustion and his wife, Lottie, the "King and Queen of the Cokies," weighed thirty pounds of cocaine and half as much morphine. Soon their salesmen would make the rounds. Funny thing was, Minna knew, Lottie was a college graduate who spoke five languages, and in her spare time composed music and painted portraits.

Down the street, at the House of All Nations, johns lined up at the $2 and $5 entrances—too bad the suckers didn't know that the same girls worked both sides. Blind men cranked hurdy-gurdies, spinning tangled reams of melody. The air reeked of sweat and blood and swine entrails, drifting up from the Union Stock Yards just a few blocks southwest. Mickey Finn hawked his eponymous "Special" at his Dearborn Street bar. Merry Widdo Kiddo, the famous peep-show girl, warmed up her booth, breasts twirling like pinwheels behind the glass. Levee piano players— "professors," they were called—cracked their knuckles before plucking out the hiccuped notes of ragtime.

Minna watched a figure turn the corner of 21st Street onto Dearborn and waited for the solemn gong of the bell. She patted the dark, frizzed coil of hair at the nape of her neck and reached for the door. From knuckle to wrist to elbow, waist to bodice to neck, she was ablaze in jewels. Diamonds played with the parlor light, tossing tiny rainbows against the wall.

"How *is* my boy?" she said, her customary greeting for every caller.

The boy this time was Frank Carson of the *Chicago Inter Ocean*, a once respected newspaper that had declined in recent years. Minna invited him inside with a slow-motion sweep of her arm. He was no stranger to the Everleigh Club; every reporter in the city knew its phone number, Calumet 412, by heart.

Carson saw precisely what the Everleighs wished him to see, and knew what they wished him to know. Both sisters had a prim, close-lipped smile, genuine but guarded, as if a full-on grin risked conveying complexities best left unmined. The younger one, Minna, was the talker. She spoke in clipped, staccato sentences, shooting words from her mouth—it was so *good* to see her boy, it had been far too long since his last visit, he should stop by more often. She broke occasionally for a frenetic drag of a gold-tipped, perfumed cigarette. Ada stood next to her sister, quiet. Her eyes were darker, her hair lighter, her figure fuller. Her hands were wind-chill cold.

Frank Carson knew they ran a clean place with clean girls; their house doctor never forged the reports. He knew that Sunday was "Beau Night" at the Everleigh Club, when girls were permitted to see their sweethearts, to accept flowers and hold hands, to experience all the thrills of dating as if they lived in homes. He knew there had been a shooting at the Club two years earlier, an unfortunate incident that was no fault of the sisters'. He knew the Everleighs brought a bit of decency to a profession rife with shame.

He knew Prince Henry of Prussia had visited the Club three years earlier and sipped champagne from a courtesan's shoe. He knew they had the ear and respect of the most powerful men not only in the Levee district, but in the entire city: Big Jim Colosimo, Ike Bloom, Bathhouse John, and Hinky Dink Kenna. He'd heard they'd come up from Virginia or Kentucky or a farm someplace in Indiana—Minna insisted that their southern accents were part of an act. They'd been married, the story went, to vicious, violent men. He knew a fellow Chicago journalist, Jack Lait, declared the sisters were "to pleasure what Christ was to Christianity."

What the reporter didn't know was how avidly the sisters, generally speaking, disliked his gender.

Minna took charge, ordering her boy to please sit and make himself comfortable. Yes—on that silk divan. She and Ada settled across from him. Edmund, the butler, appeared with a flute of champagne, which Carson downed in one zealous gulp. Minna signaled to keep the bubbly coming.

Carson asked what they knew he would ask. If Marshall Field Jr. had indeed ventured into the Levee on the night before he was shot, where else would a man of his stature go but to the Everleigh Club?

Minna and Ada smiled but said nothing.

Had Field, as one nurse alleged, been pierced by a paper knife and not a bullet?

The sisters replied that they had no idea.

If the Everleighs really had no involvement in or knowledge of the tragedy, why not dispel the rumors and just say so?

Edmund arrived on cue, offered their guest another drink. Carson, like all the others, left with a giddy champagne buzz but no story.

But Marshall Field Jr. wasn't dead yet, not in any sense of the word.

Chicago was changing. Every day it awoke a new city. Its leading citizens no longer recognized it as the place that had raised them.

The stream of immigration that flowed in the 1890s became a deluge during the first decade of the new century. More arrived every day from Italy and Germany, France and China, Russia and Greece, bringing with them their odd customs and habits, their peculiar religions and strange tongues. They joined the thousands that had descended during the 1893 World's Fair, disreputable men and women who stayed long after the Ferris wheel was dismantled and Buffalo Bill skipped town. Together these interlopers built their own cities within the city, block after block of gambling parlors and opium dens and brothels where inmates dangled bare breasts from windows and did unspeakable things with animals. What depravity went on inside a dive named the Bucket of Blood? Did a street called Bed Bug Row belong in a town like Chicago?

The horrors were spreading to respectable neighborhoods and solid homes. Young women were no longer content to sit with suitors on front porches or in parlors. Ten months earlier, in January 1905, a teenage girl from a good family guzzled a mug of chloroform and died on the floor of 33rd Street's American Dance Hall. There were whispers about syndicates of evil men, foreign men, who lured girls to the city, drugged and raped them at "clearinghouses," and sold them for $50 to enterprising madams.

Advertisements in newspapers seeking secretaries and clerks and leads for musical productions were best read skeptically. The taxi driver could deliver a girl straight to evil's door. The nickel theaters were moral suicide. Not even the ice-cream parlors were safe. If things continued as they were, the Levee district would corner Chicago and swallow it whole, this fine, proud city that wielded its triumphs like a scepter and wore its reputation like a crown. Surely the rest of America would not be far behind.

The Marshall Field Jr. shooting was a seismic boom with aftershocks that rattled the Everleigh Club. The sisters would be hit from both sides, the law and the outlaws, two diametrically opposed groups who disdained them for precisely the same reason. The Club was the gleaming symbol of the Levee district, shining too brightly on those who operated best in the dark.

"They were the Angels of the Line," wrote journalist Charles Washburn, twenty-five years after the war over the Levee, "and, as angels, hated and persecuted."

But on that fall night, as Minna Everleigh watched the reporter disappear into the murk of Dearborn Street, she did not fret about what trouble might come, or who would be behind it. She and Ada had work to do: keep books, prepare the courtesans, and greet their boys, watching each man admire the seesaw sway of a girl's rear as he followed her up the stairs. Would he like a warm bath, or something scrumptious from the Pullman Buffet, or a favor far too naughty to say aloud?

They ran the most successful—and respected—whorehouse in America and had no reason, yet, to believe that would ever change.

PART ONE

The
Scarlet Sisters
Everleigh

1899–1905

STRIPED SKUNK
AND WILD ONIONS

South Dearborn Street. (The Everleigh Club is at near right.)

*An amusing city, Chicago, any way you look at it. I'm
afraid we are in for the time of our lives.*

—THE EVERLEIGH SISTERS

In the winter of 1899, a train clattered toward Chicago, fat coils of
smoke whipping the sky. Minna and Ada Everleigh sat together in a
Pullman Palace car, sipping wine served by porters wearing white
jackets and gloves. Velvet curtains framed the windows, and thick rugs ab-
sorbed the curved heels of their boots. The sisters checked their reflections
in bevel-edged French mirrors, reclined on Marshall Field's most luxurious
bedsheets, ate in a dining car where woodcock and prairie chicken were
presented on tables set with Belgian linen and expensive English china.
The train, lit entirely by electricity, was fitted with a new contraption—
"vestibules," accordion-shaped passageways that connected the cars, shutting out the fumes and wind. The air inside their car hung heavy and
whisper quiet, but the sisters were restless, giddy with plans: They would
build upon what they had learned as madams in Omaha, Nebraska, and
create the finest brothel in history.

Their grandiose scheme could be expected in an era when consumers,
whether seeking a car or company for the night, were becoming royalty.
The world was, for the first time, a market where every need could be met,
every idea coaxed to fruition. Two brothers named Wright were experi-
menting with the idea of human flight. Druggists stocked $1 bottles of
Hibbard's Herb Extract, a "wonderful cure" that soothed "itching, burning, and smarting" and cured "Female Weakness." *McClure's Magazine*
marveled at how Marconi's wireless sent messages "at will through space."
The country's first major automobile show would take place on New Year's
Day. The economy fine-tuned itself as mass production replaced craft production—an admirable feat, but the precise inverse of what the Everleigh
sisters had in mind. A man would pay and pay well to feel as though each
of his parts, considered alone, was greater than his total.

Obsession with self-fulfillment began to mold the national ethos, a concept Theodore Dreiser explored in his soon-to-be-published *Sister Carrie*. Country girl Carrie Meeber, walking past posh Chicago department stores, feels keenly her "individual shortcomings of dress and that shadow of manner which she thought must hang about her and make clear to all who and what she was."

Chicago in particular had taken municipal confidence to new levels; the blustery talk of civic leaders—and not Chicago's weather—had inspired the "Windy City" moniker. Eight years before *New York Sun* editor Charles Dana popularized the nickname during the battle to host the 1893 World's Columbian Exposition, it appeared in the *Cleveland Gazette*, headlining an article about Chicago politics.

The city's boosters had always been more persuasive than most. After the Great Fire of 1871, propagandist William Bross traveled to New York. "Go to Chicago now!" he commanded. "Young men, hurry there! Old men, send your sons! Women, send your husbands! You will never again have such a chance to make money!" His prediction that Chicago would have a population of 1 million by 1900 came true ten years earlier, and by the time the Everleighs arrived, nearly 1.7 million people called the city home. Visitors were equally impressed by the city's tireless ambition. "She outgrows her prophecies faster than she can make them," Mark Twain wrote of Chicago. "She is always a novelty; for she is never the Chicago you saw when you passed through the last time."

The Everleighs vowed to continue this perfectionism and constant reinvention, a nineteenth-century amalgamation of Martha Stewart and Madonna. Over dinner in the Pullman car, the sisters concocted backstories for themselves suffused with glamour and drama. They were southern debutantes from outside of Louisville, Kentucky, with a wealthy lawyer father, a doting mother, and finishing school pedigrees. After marrying two men—make them brothers—who turned brutish and physically abusive, the sisters escaped and ran far away, ending up in Omaha, Nebraska. Their entrée into the madam business was a fortuitous accident, two proper Victorian ladies who decided that creating a fantasy for others was better than pretending to live in one.

Preternaturally savvy about the importance of marketing and image, the sisters also lied about their ages. Ada, thirty-five, would pass for twenty-three; and Minna, thirty-three, became twenty-one again.

During the previous year, 1898, when the Everleighs decided to move their burgeoning careers as madams from Omaha to a busier town, they scoured red-light districts across the country in search of the best fit. In these waning days of the Victorian era, every significant American city, along with many smaller ones, had a designated neighborhood where prostitution, though technically illegal, was practiced openly; "segregation" was a term that referred primarily to sex rather than race. Here men were free to indulge sexually without sullying their homes or offending the fragile sensibilities of their wives.

"Respectable women, it was held," the *Chicago Tribune* mused years later in an article that compared the Everleighs with Al Capone, "were safer from rape and other crimes if open prostitution was maintained and ordered as an outlet for the lusts of men."

But the Everleighs had their own notions of prostitution and its role in society. In a good resort, they reasoned, one free from the sorrier aspects of the trade, a harlot was more than an unwitting conduit for virtue. An employee in a business, she was an investment and should be treated as such, receiving nutritious meals, a thorough education, expert medical care, and generous wages. In their house, a courtesan would make a living as viable as—and more lucrative than—those earned by the thousands of young girls seeking work in cities as stenographers and sweatshop seamstresses, department store clerks and domestics. The sisters wanted to uplift the profession, remove its stain and stigma, argue that a girl can't lose her social standing if she stands level with those poised to judge her.

Traveling to major and minor cities alike, the sisters gathered ideas and consulted with each locale's most prominent madams. They sought a distinguished town with class and style that lacked a preeminent parlor house. Theirs would be "the most celebrated banging shop in the world," although clients, naturally, would never hear such language.

"Frisco Tessie" Wall, in San Francisco's Barbary Coast, ran a decent business but was too old school, in the sisters' opinion; and Nell Kimball, with her philosophical musings, was downright depressing. Like many madams, Kimball kept someone on staff to "work over" her courtesans if they got out of line. "A drunk is no good as a whore," she advised. "You can't hide her breath, and she doesn't do her work in style. Hookers are mean but sentimental. They cry over dogs, kittens, kids, novels, sad songs. I never cared much for a girl who came to work in a house because it was fun for her. There was a screw loose somewheres."

Walking the district, the sisters noticed that the harlots of each bordello, from Tessie's place to the lowest "cow yard," kept business cards on hand and distributed them at every opportunity. Most featured, simply, the name of a girl and the house to which she belonged, but some women chose to be infinitely more descriptive:

BIG MATILDA

THREE HUNDRED POUNDS OF BLACK PASSION

HOURS: ALL HOURS

RATES: 50C EACH: THREE FOR ONE DOLLAR

The sisters threw away the cards and shook their heads. They believed in advertising, but also in subtlety.

On to New Orleans. The famed Storyville district offered Belle Anderson's mirrored rooms and expert dancers, and Madam Lulu White's opulent bordello on the corner of Basin and Bienville streets. The city's Blue Book, a catalog that listed every house, its specialties and "stock," offered a kind description of White's establishment:

"Nowhere in this country will you find a more popular personage than Madame White, who is noted as being the handsomest octoroon in America . . . her mansion possesses some of the most costly oil paintings in the Southern country. Her mirror parlor is also a dream. There's always something new at Lulu White's that will interest you. 'Good time' is her motto."

A lively place, New Orleans, but the district overall wasn't to their liking—did they really want to operate up the street from a hall called the Funky Butt?

St. Louis was tolerable, but Babe Connors, a revered black madam who ran a brothel called The Palace, monopolized the city. In her house, the great Polish artist Ignace Paderewski once sat down at the piano, and a cadre of Republican politicians wrote their national platform. A large woman with a round, rambling body, she had a smile that gripped her face. Her teeth, the Everleighs were delighted to discover, were inlaid with diamonds. Tacky but fabulous. Madam Connors took Belle Anderson's mirror innovations one step further, installing an entire floor of reflective glass in her parlor. Minna made a mental note—wherever they settled, mirrored rooms would definitely be part of the décor.

New York City, with its hectic Tenderloin district, was marvelous, but Madam Rosie Hertz, the so-called godmother for prostitutes in the city, had already cornered the elite clientele, running several sporting houses on the Lower East Side while living on a moneyed block in Brooklyn. Rose Hicks dominated Philadelphia, "Lucky" Warren ruled Cincinnati, and Annie Chambers claimed Kansas City. Minnie Stevens in Boston and Belle Stewart in Pittsburgh had plenty of "wick dipping" going on, as the saying went, but their districts, too, were well below Everleigh standards.

Washington, D.C., with its bustling "Division," was a possibility. During the Civil War, John Wilkes Booth was a reputed regular in the district, favoring a sporting house on Ohio Avenue. The sisters checked into the Willard Hotel and looked up Cleo Maitland. This madam was an old-timer, they'd heard, and could offer some sound advice.

Madam Maitland operated in a brick row house on D Street, posing as a landlady, with several girls living with her as female "boarders." She welcomed the Everleighs inside her brothel, kissing their cheeks with dry, puckered lips. Her face was a topographic map, intricately rumpled and lined, but she sat spryly and alert while Minna talked. They'd finished their research, Minna explained, but had yet to find an appropriate city, one with plenty of wealthy men but no superior houses.

The madam had the answer. Chicago, Illinois! she said. An abundance of millionaires, a well-protected red-light district, and not one dominant brothel; the city's best madam, Carrie Watson, had retired to the suburbs a few years earlier. Madam Maitland even knew of the perfect building: two adjoining three-story mansions with fifty rooms, built for $125,000 just before the World's Columbian Exposition. The brothel's current proprietor, Effie Hankins, wanted to retire and had told Madam Maitland to keep an eye out for a possible buyer.

"See Effie," the old madam urged, escorting the sisters out. "She'll listen."

The engine bell began its raucous clamor, and the train windows offered a brilliantly vile panorama: slaughterhouses, steel mills, factories, silos, coal piles that doused the sky with black. "She-caw-go!

She-caw-go!" the brakeman called, and the train sputtered to a stop beneath a long roof made of glass and steel. A porter took the sisters' gloved hands in his and helped them down the stairs, where a hansom cab waited. Dodging insulated ice wagons, streetcars, and droves of private carriages, the Everleighs' hansom pulled up to 2131–2133 South Dearborn Street.

The imposing stone mansion boasted two mahogany staircases that spiraled gently upward. Broad windows dotted the façade, greedily inhaling the light, topped by strips of molding curved like haughty frowns. The place stood like a peacock amid pigeons.

Madam Hankins welcomed the sisters inside and told them to take their time, look around. Minna could see the brothel needed work—the 2133 side wasn't yet habitable, and both buildings would benefit from plusher rugs, fresh paint, art, statues, books, and mirrors, of course—but it was *right*. The feel of that staircase under her palm, so solid and heavy, was like gripping a piece of permanence.

"It's home to me and all I have," Madam Hankins said, poking teary eyes with a handkerchief. "For fifty-five thousand dollars it is yours even though I hate to part with it." She turned, tucked two fingers inside her mouth, and blew a shrill whistle. "Come, girls," she called, "let my guests see how nice you look."

Her harlots obliged, heels scuffing the floor as they trudged into a listless single file. The scent of cheap perfume soaked the parlor. Flesh bulged in all the wrong places. And their faces . . . Three words registered in Minna's mind: sloppy, uncouth, hardened. These harlots simply wouldn't do—not for the prices she and Ada planned to charge. With all due respect to Madam Hankins, these girls looked as if they'd logged more miles than the Chicago Limited.

"Thanks," Minna said, and Madam Hankins shooed the harlots away. "How much for the rent?"

"Five hundred a month . . . not high when you consider there are two buildings."

They struck a deal. The sisters advanced $20,000 and agreed to pay the remaining $35,000 within half a year, plus the subsequent $500 monthly fee.

"We have catered only to the best people," Madam Hankins insisted, shaking each sister's hand.

"Oh, yeah," Minna replied, voice rimmed with sarcasm.

She felt Ada's elbow poke her side, a clear warning to watch what she said. She knew Ada worried that her candor would one day bring them trouble.

The Everleighs took long carriage rides through their new city, peering from behind dark curtains, knees touching. Chicago was a city of superlatives, at once both spectacular and foul. Native Americans, after noting the presence of wild leeks in the watershed, began calling the city's river "Chicagoua." The word, aptly enough, reflected both the indigenous vegetation and its rank smell, also translating to "striped skunk."

The streets were flat and stretched without end. In the Loop, named for the pulley system that turned cable cars around the city's center, a dense forest of buildings stretched skyward, eclipsing the sun. Turn on Washington, and they saw the Herald Building, designed by the famous architects Daniel Burnham and John Root, with windows that arched upward and met like the hands of a man in prayer. On North Clark Street stood the Chicago-Clark Building, topped by turrets that speared the sky. Society ladies strolled down State Street, hats of every shape and color blooming from heads, a riotous country garden in motion.

The lake was a kaleidoscope of majestic blues and greens, the river rat-infested filth. A twenty-eight-mile-long canal would soon reverse its flow, sending the waste from Chicago's tenements, factories, and slaughter-houses downstream (over objections from St. Louis) instead of into Lake Michigan, which had caused devastating outbreaks of cholera. The din was omnipresent and relentless: horses' hooves clopped, elevated trains clattered, streetcars screeched, newsboys and peddlers shouted, all against the restless backdrop of ragtime.

William Archer, a Scottish critic who traveled throughout the United States, captured Chicago's dichotomy. "Walking in Dearborn Street or Adams Street of a cloudy afternoon, you think yourself in a frowning and fuliginous city of Dis," he wrote. "Driving along Lake Shore to Lincoln Park in the flush of sunset, you wonder that the dwellers in this street of palaces should trouble their heads about Naples or Venice."

The sisters' driver detoured through the red-light districts, up and down streets littered with abandoned hansoms. At night they shook, as streetwalkers entertained their tricks inside. Messenger boys scurried, the cold turning their breath to steam, fetching makeup or booze or chop suey for whatever whorehouse hired them, delivering Western Union telegrams to the demimondes. Minna pictured how she and Ada would elevate the district, transform their profession from an accident of circumstances to a genuine calling.

Even in its frontier days, Chicago oozed vice rooted in liquor and gambling, with prostitutes and pimps following closely behind, tailed in turn by the hoodlums, pickpockets, burglars, con men, ropers, and dopers. The Levee district, according to Chicago lore, was so called due to the large influx of Southerners (with their raunchy river-town ways) during the Civil War. The town's board of trustees, as early as 1835, imposed a fine of $25 upon any person convicted of operating a bordello. But the dive keepers merely shrugged and continued about their business.

A mere three years later, brothels lined Wells Street—shoddy, lowbrow establishments, but the genesis of the largest red-light region in United States history. The Great Fire of 1871 left seventy-three miles of streets in charred ruins and almost one hundred thousand people homeless, but Chicago knew its priorities. During the first eight months of 1872, the city granted 2,218 saloon licenses—approximately 1 to every 150 citizens. The vice districts, slung like a tawdry necklace across the city's South Side, were more brazen than ever. Junkies shot one another up with "guns"—hypodermic needles—in the middle of drugstore aisles. Women lounged stark naked against doorways, calling out obscene suggestions to passersby. And the competition grew fiercer as hundreds of newcomers settled in the red-light district every week.

The sex trade even enjoyed its own weekly newspaper throughout the late 1870s and early 1880s, a sort of Page Six forebear that cheekily chronicled the comings and goings of madams and sporting girls. It covered fashion, personal peccadilloes, drinking habits, and long-running feuds:

"Black-eyed Amy, of 478 State," one edition warned, "you had better let up on your foolishness with that married man, F., or you will think a freight train has run over you. DO YOU HEAR?"

By the time Chicago garnered international attention as the host of the 1893 World's Fair, the city's vice neighborhoods had cultivated distinct personalities. There was Little Cheyenne, a nod to the town in Wyoming, which at the time was considered a very depraved place. (Cheyenne returned the favor by calling their vice district "Little Chicago.") A six-foot, 220-pound black woman named Hattie Briggs ruled Little Cheyenne. Hattie was feared, not necessarily for her size and color, but for something she gave off: an unseen, wild-rooted purpose that circled the air around her. Wearing a flowing scarlet coat, she robbed male customers by slamming their heads against a wall until they were too dazed to resist.

Little Cheyenne and other vice neighborhoods observed strict rules about race and even ethnicity. A guide to neighborhood brothels titled *The Sporting and Club House Directory* offered separate, pointed entries for "French Houses" ("everybody knows what a 'French' house is," the editor wrote, "and we need offer no further explanation") and "Colored Houses." Upscale black madams like Vina Fields employed blond-haired black prostitutes who serviced only white men, and Madam Lillian Richardson emphasized that her brothel was "the least public colored house in the city." Little Cheyenne was also home to Carrie Watson's elegant house on Clark Street, which for years enjoyed worldwide fame despite the fact that its only advertising was courtesy of the resident parrot. Housed inside a gilded cage near the entrance, the avian pimp squawked, "Carrie Watson. Come in, gentlemen," in emphatic repetition.

The Everleighs had heard of Madam Watson. They knew she was once revered by Chicago leaders and left alone by the police. Most important, she'd affected the right attitude. "Miss Carrie Watson says she would be willing to reform," one red-light newspaper reported, "but she can't think of any sins she has been guilty of." The sisters intended to pick up exactly where the legend left off—and improve on every one of her contributions to the trade.

The line of brothels and dives on State Street, from Van Buren to 22nd, was known as Satan's Mile. Kitty Adams, better known as "the Terror of State Street," hailed from Satan's Mile and in the span of seven years robbed more than one hundred men. She and her partner, Jennie Clark, were arrested in August 1896 for slugging an old man and fishing $5 from his pocket. The Honorable Judge James Groggin, who presided over the case, acquitted the women, issuing a celebrated ruling that any man who ventured into the district deserved whatever he got.

Custom House Place, the adjacent area, earned an international reputation during the World's Fair. Its most infamous attractions were dives called "panel houses." The walls in these resorts were punched full of holes, placed strategically behind chairs where the johns hung their pants. As one harlot distracted a trick in bed, another would slip her hand through the crack and snatch his wallet.

Number 144 Custom House Place was operated by Madam Mary Hastings, one of the pioneers of what was known in Europe—and soon in America—as "white slavery." During frequent trips to neighboring cities, she extolled the virtues of Chicago and its high-paying jobs, returning with gullible young girls aged thirteen to seventeen. She took the girls' clothing and locked them in a room with six professional rapists. Once "broken in," the girls were sold to other madams for $50 to $300 each, depending on age and appearance. The eminent British journalist William T. Stead visited Hastings's brothel while researching *If Christ Came to Chicago*, his damning 1894 screed about sin in the Second City.

The Everleighs vowed never to deal with pimps, desperate parents selling off children, panders, and white slavers. If you treated girls well, they would come begging for admittance. A prospective Everleigh courtesan must prove she's eighteen in order to earn an interview, understand exactly what the job entailed, and know she's free to leave anytime, for any reason, without penalty.

Riding through Custom House Place, the sisters noted it was still a busy district, even six years after the World's Fair. Mayor Carter Harrison II had ordered all brothels on Clark Street, the neighborhood's main thoroughfare, to evacuate, citing complaints from citizens who took the new trolley car to and from work. The majority of madams and saloon keepers defied the edict and stayed put, others migrated to the West Side, and the rest, very gradually, packed up their furnishings, piano professors, and harlots to transfer south, settling into the growing vice district around Dearborn and 22nd streets. This latter contingent constituted the sisters' new neighbors and competitors, though none of them looked like much of a threat.

The California, across the street from the Everleighs' building, was one of the roughest resorts in the district. Operated by a three-hundred-pound bruiser named "Blubber" Bob Gray and his wife, the California offered thirty girls whose uniforms consisted of high-button shoes and sheer chemises that barely brushed their bottoms. Most nights, they appeared naked at windows or in the doorway, gyrating and pointing between their legs.

"Pick a baby, boys!" the madam yelled at her clients. "Don't get glued to your seats!"

She charged a dollar, but 50 cents would do if a man could prove by turning out his pockets that he had nothing more. Here, as in other bordellos, harlots "rolled" their clients, slipping a dose of morphine into his wine or beer and robbing him while he was passed out cold. The sisters added additional rules to their list: no knockout powders, no thieving, no drugs of any kind.

On Armour Avenue stood a notorious resort called the Bucket of Blood—the sisters shuddered to think what passed for entertainment behind its walls. Flogging, they supposed—all the rage in the lower dives and another activity they would not tolerate. Farther down the block, a brutal resort blithely called the Why Not? operated near Japanese and Chinese whorehouses that also catered only to white men. The sisters heard that the "Orientals," unable to bear the frigid Chicago climate, practiced their profession during the winter months clad in long woolen underwear.

Two brothers, Ed and Louis Weiss, both of whom seemed inordinately curious about what the sisters were up to, flanked the Everleighs' place on either side. Finally, there was a tight clique of upscale brothel keepers, led by one Madam Vic Shaw, who considered their resorts the Levee's finest attractions. True, their houses came closest to Everleigh standards—but in the sisters' opinion, not nearly close enough.

Amateurs, all of them, and not worth another moment of the Everleighs' time.

ANOTHER
UNCLE TOM'S CABIN

"MY GOD! IF ONLY I COULD GET OUT OF HERE"
The midnight shriek of a young girl in the vice district of a large city, heard by two worthy men, started a crusade which resulted in closing up the dens of shame in that city.

Stead was a man we are sorry not to have known. He
was just a little before our time. So broad-minded.

—MINNA EVERLEIGH

Before the Everleigh sisters so optimistically decided to improve their industry, and to apply a dignified sheen to its public image, a group of reformers in England embarked on a similar campaign of their own. Chief among them was William T. Stead, who, along with fellow activist Josephine Butler, wanted to raise England's age of consent for girls from thirteen to sixteen. The campaign needed, as Stead put it, its own *Uncle Tom's Cabin*.

In 1885, nine years before he published *If Christ Came to Chicago,* Stead, prepared to assume the role of Harriet Beecher Stowe, descended upon London's underworld. Recalling a letter Butler received from Victor Hugo—"The slavery of black women is abolished in America," it read, "but the slavery of white women continues in Europe"—Stead set out to find a story so sensational that Parliament would be forced to act. A story that would redirect the debate over prostitution, shifting the focus from the courtesan to those who profited from her work. A story that would recast her role in society from that of necessary evil to exploited victim—a "white slave."

He found the story in the case of Eliza "Lily" Armstrong, a thirteen-year-old girl living in a west London slum with her alcoholic mother, Elizabeth. Destitute, Elizabeth agreed to sell Lily to a woman, working in concert with Stead, for the sum of £5—£3 down and £2 after her virginity had been professionally certified. Stead, meanwhile, acting the part of the "purchaser," waited in a predetermined brothel for Lily to arrive.

"The poor child," Stead wrote, "was full of delight at going to her new situation, and clung affectionately to the keeper who was taking her away—where, she knew not. The first thing to be done after the child was fairly severed from home was to secure the certificate of virginity."

Stead's cohort took Lily to a midwife, who confirmed the girl's chastity and produced a small vial of chloroform to "dull the pain."

"This," the midwife advised, "is the best. My clients find this much the most effective."

The brothel was the next stop. The madam admitted Lily without question, ordered the girl to undress, and injected chloroform into her arm. A few moments later, Stead entered the room.

"And the child's voice was heard crying, in accents of terror," he later reported, " 'There's a man's in the room; oh, take me home!' "

Stead crept away. Lily's cries, he insisted, were proof he'd "had his way" with her. Police rescued the girl and placed her in the care of the Salvation Army.

In July 1885, Stead's "The Maiden Tribute of Modern Babylon" was published in the *Pall Mall Gazette*. Crowds gathered in front of the paper's offices, clamoring for copies. One and a half million unauthorized reprints were circulated. Thousands rioted. Virgins clad in white marched through Hyde Park, demanding passage of the Criminal Law Amendment Act, which proposed to raise the age of consent. It was passed in August. Stead kept his triumph—and himself—in the public eye when, in October, he was sent to prison for three months on a procuring charge. He relished his martyrdom, even publishing a pamphlet titled "My First Imprisonment."

Across the Atlantic, American reformers took careful note.

GETTING
EVERLEIGHED

The alcove of the Blue Bedroom at the Everleigh Club.

They tell me you are wicked and I believe them,
for I have seen your painted women under the gas lamps
luring the farm boys.

—CARL SANDBURG, "Chicago"

The Everleigh sisters were perhaps the first cathouse proprietors to apply the inverse formula for success: The more difficult it is to gain entry to an establishment, the greater the number of people who vie to do so. Minna told no one about their grand opening, planned for February 1, 1900. No free passes for critics, no advertisements in newspapers, no engraved invitations to Mayor Carter Harrison II or members of the city council, no klieg lights sweeping garish streaks across Dearborn Street. Their notoriety would come gracefully, like a red carpet slowly unfurled—leave the fireworks for those who cast no spark of their own.

Besides, Minna knew Chicago was preoccupied with other news, especially the brutal temperature, eight below zero. Telephone operators for the city's police stations experienced difficulty transmitting or receiving messages over the wires. Batteries in the patrol boxes had iced over, making communication almost impossible. Forget trying to take a streetcar anywhere. Horse carcasses turned up on corners, sometimes in pairs or groups, like capsized carousels. Several homeless people froze, splayed in rag doll poses across the slush and ice.

But inside the double mansion on South Dearborn Street, Minna and Ada bustled about, warm beneath their gowns, silk whispering with each step. It was a cataclysmic night in their lives—more important than their success in Omaha, more gratifying than leaving their pasts in the South. The past few months had been grueling and frantic; they'd had to dispose of Madam Hankins's tacky old furnishings and even shabbier girls.

Ada had taken charge of recruiting. She notified the harlots who worked their brothel in Omaha, and word spread quickly through the underworld pipeline. A few theater acquaintances expressed interest, too—

after all, acting and whoring drew from that same facet of the psyche that allowed the body to be in one place, and the mind another.

She soon had a long list of eager prospects, and set up one-on-one interviews.

"I talk with each applicant myself," Ada later explained. "She must have worked somewhere else before coming here. We do not like amateurs. Inexperienced girls and young widows are too prone to accept offers of marriage and leave. We always have a waiting list. To get in a girl must have a pretty face and figure, must be in perfect health, must look well in evening clothes. If she is addicted to drugs or to drink, we do not want her. There is no problem in keeping the Club filled."

The elder Everleigh grilled every candidate, measuring hips and busts and waists, hoisting up sleeves to check for needle tracks. After deciding on the final roster—the most luscious collages of curves and hair and tinkling laughter a man could ever meet—she sent them to Minna for proper instruction and lessons.

Minna embraced Honoré de Balzac's philosophy—"Pleasure," he wrote in 1834, "is like certain drugs; to continue to obtain the same results one must double the dose, and death or brutalization is contained in the last one"—and she stressed to her girls that contemplation of devilment was more satisfying than the act itself. In an establishment like the Everleigh Club, she advised, a girl could get away with a sly smile and a coy aside, like "Wait until I know you better." Temper the instinct to rush a man, to exploit his baser fantasies. Flirtations and banter could begin in any of the parlors, but a girl must have a deft touch once she escorted a man upstairs.

There was also the matter of appearance. Minna forbade Everleigh girls to wear those tawdry negligees that passed for standard uniforms in other houses. How would that look, after the girls had so judiciously studied the poetry of Arthur Symons and Ernest Dowson and Longfellow? No, they would wear elegant, full-length evening gowns and all the jewelry they owned, as long as it wasn't gaudy. Only Minna could pull off such excess.

Minna knew that most of them had come up from the lower classes (save the occasional exception, like Valerie, a doctor's daughter), so such thorough tutoring was necessary. Their harlots, and others in brothels across the country, usually chose this life—the sporting life—out of pragmatism, not adventure. Many girls were desperately poor, burdened with

supporting parents, siblings, and children. They had been juvenile delin-
quents and tossed out of the home, and the $35 per week that one made as
a whore—even in a low-class resort—far exceeded the $6 she could earn in
a factory.

Girls who turned to prostitution often suffered the death or desertion of
one or both parents at an early age; witnessed their mothers cohabiting with
a series of strange men; fell victim to incest, alcoholism, tuberculosis, de-
pression. For some, the sporting life was simply the family business, an inherited proclivity. The sisters' acquaintance Madam Nell Kimball recalled
the sage advice of her aunt Letty, a retired courtesan: "Every girl, if only
she knew it, is sitting on her fortune." Others were reared in brothels and
knew no other life. One courtesan in New Orleans was the daughter of a
prostitute and her former trick. Before the girl's fifth birthday, she learned
how to prepare opium and wash off her mother's clients. At seven, she
began selling sexual acts herself. Her virginity was auctioned off for $7.75.

"I ain't ashamed of what I did," she reasoned, "because I didn't have
much to do with it. I knew it'd be good if I could say how awful it was and
like crime don't pay, but to me it seems just like anything else—like a kid
whose father owns a grocery store. He helps him in the store. Well my
mother didn't sell groceries."

Their husbands left them or lost their jobs; society frowned upon a wife
working outside the home, but there was no other choice. Many young
girls were abandoned by family owing to suspicions of promiscuity and
then decided to hell with it, why not charge a man for the privilege? Sex
work wasn't so different from marriage anyway, they reasoned. "It is not
adequate to define a prostitute simply as a woman who sells her body,"
Havelock Ellis would soon write. "That is done every day by women who
become wives in order to gain a home and a livelihood." At least a sporting
girl got paid to take orders and perform.

Some women joined the life not out of financial necessity, but from a
desire for upward mobility, the Victorian version of bling—fine hats,
gowns, shoes, pricey baubles, a brand-new bicycle. A nineteen-year-old
Polish factory worker in Chicago told authorities that she had sex with men
at work in exchange for clothing, and proudly showed off a collection of
twenty pairs of silk stockings. "I got to get out of this place and meet some
guy, and marry him before my folks get wise," she added. "If my father
knew he'd kill me."

And returning to "respectable" work after a stint in prostitution was often more difficult than deciding to enter the life in the first place. A Philadelphia prostitute named Maimie Pinzer, who had lost the sight in one eye from a syphilitic infection, found that few jobs were available to a half-blind unskilled woman.

"I spent 3 days in despair," she wrote to a friend, "thinking of ditching it all and taking up again the life of least resistance."

Minna sympathized with the young women who were clamoring to work for the Club. High turnover was common in the business, but she vowed that each girl they hired would be spoiled, not degraded. After all, she and Ada, their own pasts dotted with deaths and disappointments, so easily could have been statistics on the other side of the equation.

I n between interviews and tutoring, the sisters grappled with prosaic but necessary details, like hiring black servants to replace Hankins's staff. Butler Edmund and housekeepers Julia Yancy and Etta Wright signed on, and the sisters even contracted with a French designer to create couture gowns for the courtesans. The esteemed Dr. Maurice Rosenberg agreed to perform regular medical examinations on the girls, a practice often forged or skipped altogether in lesser houses. The more resourceful prostitutes stocked up on quack doctors' tonics and creams, including a red mouth-wash laced with alcohol and morphine.

Redecorating projects progressed, but the sisters' grand vision wouldn't be complete without a gold piano. It would be the *pièce de résistance* in a parlor done entirely in the most precious of metals—the Gold Room. They turned to William Wallace Kimball, whose Kimball Piano Company was the largest manufacturer in the country. When Kimball recognized the Everleighs' address, as any man would, he dismissed their story about a "private conservatory of music"—who ever heard of such a thing at 22nd and Dearborn, in the heart of the South Side Levee?—and declined to sell the sisters a piano, gold or otherwise. A dealer in New York was happy to accommodate.

Piano professors came to audition on the glittering new $15,000 marvel, which Ada cooed over as if it were a sleeping newborn. The professor would complement three string orchestras comprising violins, cellos, and harps. One candidate, Vanderpool Vanderpool, wearing wildly wavy hair and a tuxedo that actually fit, performed a boisterous tune the sisters had loved since its release in 1898. They sang along with the refrain:

She was bred in Old Kentucky
where the meadow grass is blue, there's the sunshine of the country
in her face and manner, too,
she was bred in old Kentucky, take her, boy, you're mighty lucky,
when you marry a girl like Sue.

That was that: "Van Van" was their man.

Two private suites reflected their personal styles. Ada's was plain and serene, Minna's a cacophony of color. For a canopy, Minna picked an enormous eight-by-twelve-foot mirror—she would never bed a client, but she *was* a madam, after all. Her favorite feature was the floor-to-ceiling shelves, crammed with books bound in thick, fragrant leather. One day she would write her own.

Even before choosing Chicago as the ideal city, the sisters had lengthy debates about what to call their next brothel. They knew it would be highly inappropriate to use their given surname, Simms, since they still had family throughout the South. In Omaha, they'd gone by Everly—in honor, they claimed, of their grandmother's signature closing on her letters, "Everly Yours." It had a nice ring, but this new house required something extra, a certain aristocratic twist.

Inspiration finally hit, and they turned the "ly" into "leigh," just like Sir Walter Raleigh. Fitting, especially since the writer had spent some time in the American South.

And one of America's bawdiest idioms was born.

"I have always considered their choice of their professional name to be a marvelous 'play on words,' " wrote the sisters' great-niece, "which being a member of the family I could easily relate to their sense of humor." "The double entendre was intended," agreed one Chicago historian. The phrase likely evolved from, of all things, the Bible—several passages use "lie with" as a euphemism for sex—but in the decades after the sisters christened their Club, their legacy assumed the credit. *I'm getting Everleighed tonight*, eminent men from around the country reportedly boasted. A simple declaration that said many things at once, was under-

stood only by a privileged few—and, ultimately, was shortened and vul-
garized.

I n the days leading up to the grand opening, the sisters encouraged the
courtesans to strike a balance between comfort—this was their new
home, after all—and discipline. Minna ordered breakfast to be served daily
at two in the afternoon. After the Club was launched, she suspected these
meals should reflect the previous night's indulgences and consist only of a
soothing glass of iced clam juice with a side of aspirin. But for those who
were inclined to eat, the spread offered eggs, kidney sauté, clam cakes with
bacon, planked white fish, shad roe, breast of chicken with ham under
glass, buttered toast, and Turkish coffee.

Minna ordered the girls to consume plenty of baked apples, applesauce,
sliced oranges, stewed fruits, and, most frequently, iced canned tomatoes.
She watched approvingly as they downed the entire contents in quick,
wince-inducing gulps. Come now, she cajoled, it's not that bad—they'll be
thankful when old age crept upon them. Their hair would remain soft, their
skin unlined.

The harlots ate again at 6:00 p.m. If they kept to this schedule, they
would have plenty of time to primp and polish before the nightly festivities. These were raucous gatherings, with loud, rude jokes that made them
all slap the table out of laughter, china jostling, silverware hopping. Petty
quarrels and jealousies erupted, especially among the girls who'd become
lovers. Such relationships were common in brothels, Minna and Ada knew.
For many of the harlots, the Club was the first place they'd felt genuine affection, camaraderie, or security. But the spats, fortunately, were short-
lived. They were a close group, a good group, each passing on tips and
wisdom collected during her time in the trade—even if such folklore
didn't apply to a place like the Everleigh Club:

It's bad luck for a man to come in and then leave without spending, the
girls advised one another. To remove the curse from the house, spit on the
trick's back. A harlot should never use her real name—best to forget it altogether the minute she joins a house. Never bring a cat inside the resort;
it's plain bad luck. But setting wine out on the sidewalk or straightening a
parlor mirror will make the men come running. If the first customer of the

night passes over a girl, her luck will be bad for a long time. And when a harlot goes down on a trick, she mustn't swallow—that stuff causes an upset stomach and rotten teeth.

After a day of preparations and tutoring, Minna and Ada retired to another dining room, the Pullman Buffet. Carved out of mahogany, it was a splendid replica of a Pullman train car—just like the one they had traveled in during their journey to Chicago. The expert kitchen staff handled requests as well as any professor. Minna preferred chicken, and Ada liked vegetables. Both had a fondness for cheese and ice cream, which they ate as often as four times a day.

While they dined, the sisters finalized the rules for the Club's daily operations. Southern dishes and mannerisms and courtesies prevailed: Fruits, salted pecans, bonbons, cigarettes, cigars, and liqueurs would be available in every parlor, all night long. They must be strict, Minna insisted. After the first night, prospective customers could gain entry only with a solid letter of referral. Out-of-town visitors to Chicago had to prove their identity and financial standing. No sightseers or slumming parties allowed, but the sisters would make exceptions for a few colorful local rogues who paid their bills and kept their lewdness in check—at least until they climbed the stairs.

Banish anyone who spent less than $50, which was technically an entrance fee. Elsewhere in Chicago, a man could enjoy a three-course meal for 50 cents, but dinner in the Pullman Buffet started at $50 per plate. It would behoove them to open an account with Chicago's Chapin & Gore, allotting a budget of $2,000 to $5,000 a month for imported spirits. Wine would be sold in the parlors for $12 a bottle and in the bedrooms for $15, but beer and hard liquor weren't available at any price. Servants would press a gentleman's suit while he was being entertained, and money would not be mentioned until his party was over. All transactions would be handled discreetly, by check—cash was considered crass. When a client looked over his bank statement, he would find his check endorsed by the "Utopia Novelty Company."

On February 1, 1900, before the doors opened at 8:00 p.m., Minna ordered her courtesans to line up.

"Be polite, patient and forget what you are here for," she said. A diamond clasp, shaped like a butterfly, gripped her throat. She had grown tremendously fond of the insects, of how their short lives revolved wholly around the process of change. "Gentlemen are only gentlemen when properly introduced. We shall see that each girl is properly presented to each guest. No lining up for selection as in other houses. There shall be no cry, 'In the parlor, girls' when visitors arrive. Be patient is all I ask. And remember that the Everleigh Club has no time for the rough element, the clerk on a holiday or a man without a checkbook."

The girls clucked, shifted their weight, fidgeted beneath mountainous gowns.

"It's going to be difficult, at first, I know," Minna continued. She walked slowly up and down the line, a commander instructing her troops, arms folded, heels clacking. "It means, briefly, that your language will have to be ladylike and that you will forgo the entreaties you had used in the past. You have the whole night before you, and one fifty-dollar client is more desirable than five ten-dollar ones. Less wear and tear. You will thank me for this advice in later years. Your youth and beauty are all you have. Preserve it. Stay respectable by all means. We know men better than you do. Don't rush 'em or roll 'em. We will permit no monkeyshines, no knock-out drops, no robberies, no crimes of any description. We'll supply the clients, you amuse them in a way they've never been amused before. Give, but give interestingly and with mystery. I want you girls to be proud that you are in the Everleigh Club. That is all. Now spruce up and look your best."

From then on, Minna would refer to their girls as "butterflies." And she had an idea: On special occasions, why not import swarms of the insects and release them in the conversation parlors to flutter and float among the guests?

I nitially, some of the butterfly girls doubted the sisters, whispering behind their backs that the $50-minimum rule was absurd. "Just a bluff," one harlot sneered before the Club's doors opened for the first time. "Who is going to pay fifty dollars for a good time? I've heard of southern hospitality, but not at these prices."

At 8:00 p.m., several men sought admittance, but neither their credentials nor their wallets were sufficiently impressive. One look and Minna could tell they didn't belong: eyes shifty, hands shaking, feet restless. Before she could give them the boot, Ada told them, kindly, that they were at the wrong house.

Moments later, a group of actors stood, shivering, by the entrance. They worked at the Alhambra Theater, currently offering a play called *The City of New York*. A few of the girls had slipped out during the afternoon for a matinee, were "thrilled by the leading men," and had invited them to the premiere of their resort, opening under new management. More evidence that the harlots doubted the sisters' standards, since an actor's salary averaged just $40 per week. These men, too, were politely advised to seek their kicks elsewhere in the Levee.

Then came a group of Texas cattlemen who passed muster handily and spent $300 within a few hours. Madam Cleo Maitland, who so helpfully referred their building, sent flowers, as did a U.S. senator who knew the sisters from Omaha. A few friends from their theatrical troupe sent telegrams full of good wishes. Ike Bloom, a powerful Levee district leader known as "the King of the Brothels," came by early to pay his respects and promised the sisters he'd be in touch. Minna asked Ada if she could perhaps take a break—traffic was ebbing, and she had some reading to do.

Minna took her copy of the *Chicago Daily News* to the Gold Room. One headline in particular caught her eye: RITES FOR P. D. ARMOUR, JR. The young son of the famous Chicago meatpacker had died suddenly in San Francisco five days earlier, and his body had finally arrived home for funeral services. His father, Philip Danforth Armour Sr., was so upset by his heir's untimely death that he couldn't receive the body at the train station. Masses of men whose lives were connected to the great Armour enterprise filed past a coffin buried beneath a vast tumbling of flowers. Burial was at the prestigious Graceland Cemetery.

Minna was so engrossed in the article that she didn't notice a harlot tiptoeing up behind her. The girl backed away quietly and found her fellow courtesans.

"We've got her all wrong," she whispered, impressed. "Minna knows the swells all right. I caught her reading about the Armour funeral and she acted like she had known him. She's been holding out on us."

Ten minutes later, a loyal servant who had overheard the girls' chatter cornered Minna and relayed the conversation. The madam laughed, a screeching peal that orbited the room.

"I never heard of Armour until today," Minna confided. "Don't tell anyone I told you."

She and Ada had great fun and satisfaction tallying the opening night proceeds. The gross business was about $1,000, a resounding success for a Thursday evening, and from then on the courtesans could expect to pocket more than $100 per week.

Come Friday, no one posed further questions or made snide asides. One hundred dollars a week was an unthinkable salary in other houses.

Besides, the Everleigh butterflies were exhausted.

THE DEMON OF LUST
LIES IN WAIT

THE FIRST STEP

Ice cream parlors of the city and fruit stores combined, largely run by foreigners, are the places where scores of girls have taken their first step downward. Does her mother know the character of the place and the man she is with?

> *There are no good girls gone wrong,*
> *just bad girls found out.*
> —MAE WEST

In January 1886, as William Stead neared the end of his prison sentence for purchasing thirteen-year-old Lily Armstrong, a magazine titled *The Philanthropist* made its debut. The editors, all members of the New York Committee for the Prevention of the State Regulation of Vice—which had, over the years, defeated four proposals to legalize prostitution in that city—picked up where their British counterparts left off, printing Josephine Butler's impassioned defense of her friend.

"You may believe it or not as you please," Butler warned, "but I think we are living on the top of an inferno, walking about on a volcano which may burst at any moment and destroy us. . . . Mr. Stead tore aside the curtain and revealed the abyss of crime and misery."

Despite lurid narratives about virgins for sale, purity campaigns in Europe would hold Americans' attention for only so long. Trying a new tack, *The Philanthropist* editors shifted the focus to American victims. An article titled "The Traffic in Young Girls" warned of "an organized agency, by which, from rural districts and other cities, honest girls are lured to Chicago with expectation of work, and are then lost forever to friends, honor and hope . . . in one shape or another the demon of lust lies in wait at every door."

Still, not even a ripple of reaction among the American public. The editors continued to search for a story as dramatic as Stead's own "Maiden Tribute." They found it in January 1887, when authorities raided a Michigan lumber camp and arrested a group of nine women on prostitution charges.

Eight of the women accepted their prison sentences without protest, but one spun a salacious tale of torture and forced captivity. She thought she was going to the camp for work, making $14 a week plus "extras," but when she arrived her bosses locked her in a cage. Thirteen vicious bulldogs served as her constant guards. She was bound and gang-raped, her virtue forever lost. Few believed the den keepers' assertions that *all* of the women, including this alleged white slave, knew full well what they had been hired to do at the lumber camps—a job description that made no mention of cutting trees. The public was so moved by the woman's story that she was pardoned and released from jail.

Newspapers across the country seized the story, and *The Philanthropist* followed every twist and turn, underscoring its relevance to the average American. "These atrocities are committed against the womanhood of our country," declared one editorial, written by a Woman's Christian Temperance Union leader. The WCTU, founded thirteen years earlier in 1874, protested alcohol partly because women, already disenfranchised, were also barred from saloons, where ward leaders mingled and men argued about politics. White slavery gave women a chance to insert themselves into political discourse; America's women would best know how to protect America's girls. "When we see the condition of things in which the foreigner of the North," the editorial continued, "because all of the den keepers without exception are either foreigners or of foreign extraction, and have not been long in this country—when these foreigners of the North work as they do for the enslavement of our American girls . . . what shall we say of this condition of things?"

As a result of the scandal, Michigan lawmakers passed a bill that increased fines for owning a brothel, reformers raised troubling suspicions about immigrants, and America's sporting girls learned a valuable lesson in nuance: People reviled prostitutes, but pitied white slaves.

LOVELY
LITTLE LIES

Ada (left)
and Minna
in Omaha,
1895.

Before the Everleigh sisters could build the foremost brothel in United States history, they first had to raze their own pasts. They scattered their earliest years in disparate directions—absolutes, lies, and a litany of maybes—trying on identities the way men in lesser houses tried on whores, picking over a lineup before selecting the prettiest one.

First, the absolutes:

Ada and Minna Everleigh were born Ada and Minna Simms in February 1864 and July 1866, respectively, in rural Greene County, Virginia. From birth, they favored each other's company to that of anyone else, and promised they would die for each other. Ada, Minna insisted, was "ninety-nine percent more worthy than I am." They owned their connection, wholly and fiercely; it was the one thing that made them what they were while obscuring what they'd been.

The sisters were striking girls, with patrician features and deftly turned bones. Minna was bold and brash, quirky and quick, and slept in whenever she could. She was Lilliputian in stature, barely five feet two and just 106 pounds. She read constantly, preferring tomes about psychology or history or culture. Sex subjects and love stories were for girls who didn't know any better.

"I am absolutely a freethinker," Minna told novelist Irving Wallace in 1945, when she was seventy-nine years old (and still lying about her age). She and Ada were living under the name Lester in New York City, and her talks with Wallace would be the last interviews she ever granted. She was writing her own book at the time, titled *Poets, Prophets and Gods*. "No nursery stories for me," Minna added. "My book would be heresy."

Ada (who sometimes spelled her name "Aida") was guarded and reticent, more comfortable offering silent support to Minna's words rather than chiming in with her own. Minna was the aggressor, the general who would direct their every mission; Ada was the defender and the patient, cautious aide. She had, Wallace recalled, "a voice much younger than Minna's, a voice soft-spoken and well-modulated and faintly Southern. . . . This was Aida Everleigh, and she was charming."

Small but sturdily arranged, Ada monitored her figure so she never weighed more than 135 pounds. She, unlike the wiry Minna, benefited from a corset and used it to full advantage, flaunting her curves with fitted, tasteful gowns. Ada deliberately crafted a public persona—the southern belle with the simple, discreet charm—but saved her true personality for Minna alone.

The sisters' forebears were devout Episcopalians who emigrated from County Donegal, Ireland, in 1661, settled in north-central Virginia, and anglicized their surname to "Early." Jeremiah Early, a great-great-great-grandfather, bought a sprawling plantation that traced the foothills of the Blue Ridge Mountains. Their great-grandfather James Early served as a captain in the Revolutionary War and, in 1809, augmented the family's landholdings with the purchase of nearly two thousand acres along Buck Mountain Creek. John Early, a great-uncle, acquired another thousand acres in Albemarle County, an area that today is known as Earlysville. Among the sisters' ancestors are a presidential elector, state senators, congressmen, and one of the first settlers of Fredericksburg, Virginia; sheriffs, magistrates, lawyers, doctors, and surgeons; a man who gained a county-wide reputation as a "tall tale teller"; a U.S. registrar in bankruptcy; and a descendant of Andrew Jackson. Their family crest is, fittingly, a hand clenching a jeweled brass ring.

The sisters' father, Montgomery Simms, was born in 1834 in Greene County, Virginia, one of eight children of Lucy Thompson Early and James Simms, the county sheriff and a farmer. Twenty slaves cultivated wheat, hay, potatoes, and tobacco on the family plantation. At age twenty, Montgomery attended law school at the University of Virginia, leaving after one year. In that pre–bar exam era, a year of study qualified one to practice law. Montgomery was working in Charlottesville, Virginia, when he married his first cousin, Virginia "Jennie" Madison Simms.

Jennie gave birth to their first child, a daughter named Lula, two years into the Civil War. Ada followed on February 21, 1864, just as General George Armstrong Custer and one thousand Union soldiers descended upon Earlysville. By the time Minna was born, on July 13, 1866, the Simms family fortunes mirrored those of the South. The War Between the States had stripped Virginia of its antebellum grandeur and prosperity, revealing, historian Harold Woodward wrote, "a grim reality of poverty and decay. . . . Once-fertile fields were covered with scrub oaks and stunted pines, the landscape dotted with decayed fences, half-starved cattle, ramshackle houses and the remnants of crumbling mansions."

Minna and Ada's family headed back to their own tattered plantation in Greene County. The sisters' grandparents had died, forcing their father to stop practicing law and farm the land himself, hoping to salvage what was left of their crops. Minna and Ada welcomed two more sisters, Willie Florence and Flora, and two brothers, Warren and George, but these additions to the family presented challenges rather than causes for celebration. Agricultural prices were low, taxes and interest rates high, and income scarce. To make matters worse, Uncle Isaac, their father's older brother, filched the bulk of their grandparents' estate and ran off to Missouri.

When Minna was ten and Ada twelve, their mother and little sister Willie both died. Blame could fall on any number of persistent nineteenth-century maladies: influenza, pneumonia, typhus, scarlet fever, tuberculosis—the sisters would never say. Shortly thereafter, baby brother George was handed over to an aunt because the family was overwhelmed. He, too, was never mentioned again. The sisters both grieved and internalized these tragedies, tucked them into their developing sense of the world. People left too often and too soon, they realized, and detachment was as vital a commodity as compassion or love. In their later years, the sisters stopped mentioning their lost siblings altogether, and claimed to be from a family of five rather than seven.

The family moved to adjacent Madison County. Their neighbors included a former governor of Virginia and Confederate general and his five children, who lived in a mansion named Walnut Hills. Minna and Ada looked forward to their visits here, the hours spent among shiny, pretty things that distracted them from all they had lost. The sisters snacked at mahogany tables with bulbous clawed feet, let water from a bubbling lawn fountain tickle their fingers, sank into three-seater settees, velvet backs looming like the heads of Cerberus. It was a magical setting for Minna and Ada, and they realized how simple it could be to replace the realities they had for ones they wanted.

The sisters' most pervasive truth was that they strove not to have one. Minna in particular presented so many versions of herself, of her history, talents, and foibles, that the ever shifting composite sketch ultimately became her identity.

When Irving Wallace first contacted Minna, she claimed she was not the former madam he was seeking. In fact, Minna declared, she and Ada were merely socialites whose names the infamous Everleigh Club owners had co-opted. Therefore, she couldn't aid Irving in his quest to write a play featuring the brothel. Minna explained the convoluted situation in a May 1944 letter, her spidery handwriting and idiosyncratic punctuation spanning twenty pages:

> Dear Sgt Wallace,
> Aida and Minna Lester's past is not linked with the Everleigh Club on South Dearborn Street—Chicago—Illinois. . . . Aida Lester and I lived in Chicago during the first decade of the Twentieth Century— but in a fashion far remote from the famous sisters' exotic lives. . . . Suffice it to say that many times false rumors linked our puritan lives with the sensational career of the sisters referred to in your letter!! . . . Finally we took action—Aida Lester and I—we located the sisters of Dearborn Street—Chicago!!! They proved their innocence of linking their names with ours—I will not take time explaining—plotters of the South Side Levee—their enemies—had sought to cause them trouble—prompted by political Levee gangster feuds!!! These sisters reside in New York City!!! still fearing their foes they live isolated lives . . .
> After receipt of your letter yesterday I visited the sisters to whom you had addressed it. . . . I asked them if they would consider pecuniary considerations for such assistance as they might concede to you

for the setting and background of their Club on Dearborn Street—Chicago??— Their Answer was that they have an Album of photographs of the parlors and rooms of the Everleigh Club—They might part with those—but they must shun publicity. . . . I enclose clippings that suggest the past should be forgotten in this swift epoch!!

Minna enclosed eleven clippings in her letter to Wallace:

a suggestive advertisement for a lady's slip;

an advertisement for a new book about the marines;

an Associated Press story about a warrant officer in the South Pacific who wanted to hear the voice of his newborn son on a long-distance phone call, but heard nothing until he asked his wife to spank the infant;

a newspaper photograph from a Mickey Rooney film;

newspaper photographs of a radio actress and from the film *The Hitler Gang;*

a political cartoon of Adolf Hitler;

a newspaper clipping of the actor Jimmy Stewart, at the time a major in the U.S. Army, being decorated by a lieutenant colonel;

a picture from the *New York Times* drama section showing the sheet music and the casts of five Rodgers & Hammerstein musical comedies;

and three more cartoons depicting Himmler, Goebbels, and Hitler facing defeat.

She signed off:

Forget the Everleigh Club and the haunted past portrayed in the photographs of its vanished splendor shown in the album the sisters possess!!! Did not Byron declare "The past is nothing and at last—the future can but be the past"!! However if you still wish to have those Everleigh Club photographs—let me know!!!! Remember—the Everleigh Sisters names were Marie and Alice!!! The names Aida and Minna were borrowed from my name—and Aida Lesters when we were socialites in Chicago long ago!!!

Perhaps the former madam was suggesting, slyly, that recent world history was more valid than her own, but Wallace was prompted to question if Minna truly recognized where her creation ended and her reality began.

"I was strangely moved by this first letter from a sixty-six year old former madam of the world's most elegant house of rendezvous in recent times," he wrote, "moved by her elaborate and pathetically transparent story of having been a 'socialite' who had known the real Everleighs, and knew them still. . . . How much of what Minna had written me, I wondered, was conscious pretense based on elementary caution and how much was the sublimation of an old lady who had come to believe in a dream identity that she had invented for herself out of Wish?"

The first time Wallace spoke to Minna on the phone, she again used the third person when referring to the Everleigh sisters.

"The Catholics and Puritans in this country would be against such a play as you have in mind," she told him. "The Catholic Church is powerful, you know, and it's gaining strength. . . . It is against such women as the Everleighs, yet, Irving darling, when I lived in Chicago, some of the finest women I met socially were of the same class as the Everleighs. . . . All this condemnation of the Everleighs. They do not merit it. I *know*. The whole thing is like those Nazis on trial for their war crimes. Many of those Nazis followed orders. I don't mean that they're not guilty. They are guilty. But they followed orders, you understand. They had to do what they did. And the Everleigh sisters had to do what they did, too."

Minna asked Irving Wallace if he had ever seen a photograph of the Everleigh sisters, and he replied that he had not.

"One had warm brown hair," Minna continued, "and the other had natural golden hair, and it would be difficult to find anyone to portray them on the stage. They were very strange, not happy girls. There was so much tragedy in their lives."

In 1881, Minna and Ada's beloved older sister, Lula, became the third member of their family to die within four years.

"I had a sister, Lula, who played the violin," Minna told Irving Wallace. "Her arm became paralyzed at nineteen, and later she died. I was fifteen then. I wanted to kill myself, but Aida wouldn't let me."

After losing Lula, the sisters moved from Madison County, Virginia, to Warrensburg, a city in west-central Missouri. Several of their father's relatives still lived in the state, including conniving brother Isaac. Their new home must have been a culture shock, a place that straddled North and South, a former slaveholding state that never seceded from the Union. A downtown, with its modest skyline, replaced rambling plantations and the unbroken profile of the Blue Ridge Mountains. Construction continued on a railroad line throughout the Civil War, and now Warrensburg was a major depot, a straight shot to St. Louis.

If what Minna had said is true, she married a "wealthy devil of a man" here before she turned seventeen. But because she lied about her age to make herself twelve years younger, Minna's "seventeen" was actually twenty-nine. And if Ada married the brother of Minna's husband shortly thereafter, as legend holds it, she would have been thirty-one, not nineteen.

There are, in short, a dozen missing years in the sisters' lives.

Minna and Ada filled them in as best as they could, replacing tragedy with intrigue, parallel lives designed to fit over the ones they actually lived. They hailed not from the Blue Ridge Mountains, but from Bluegrass County down in Louisville, Kentucky. True, they said, their ancestors were a prominent Virginia family, but they were forced to flee Richmond when Benedict Arnold and his troops invaded in 1781. Minna, in fact, was even known as "Kentucky's most intelligent woman." (They also claimed to be from Evansville, Indiana, admitting their southern accent was part of the act. "The farm in Evansville—we couldn't stand it," Minna would add, laying it on thick. "This mortgage or that mortgage, the suffering, the hardships . . . we always liked nice things.")

Their father, they told friends and biographers, was a wealthy lawyer who spoke seven languages. Minna and Ada were his favorites, and he paid for their prestigious finishing school and elocution lessons—"born actresses," he always called them. Minna learned to read before she was five, and literature was in her blood. "Do you know I'm related to Edgar Allan Poe?" she asked Irving Wallace. "You'll laugh like hell, but it's true. On my mother's side we're the same breed as Poe's mother." A bevy of black servants plaited the sisters' hair when they were young and hemmed couture gowns after they became women and were careful to shield the girls from evidence that the world could be an ugly place. They were the only madams in history who had started out as debutantes instead of whores.

The sisters said they never chased boys—who needed them, really? They grew up believing Daddy was the only man who mattered; marriage was a trap silly girls fell into. Nevertheless, Minna claimed, she was only sixteen when a "southern gentleman" flattered her into dating him, then coaxed her into marriage. ("Lester" was his name, the story went, although she also alternately implied that was her maiden or middle name.) She demanded a grand ceremony at high noon, recalling her father's wry warning to be wary of men after dark.

Order whatever you please, her father said, and Minna—perhaps remembering the parties she had witnessed at the Walnut Hills mansion—later described a lavish reception that impressed society. She strove for simple elegance: glossy invitations, a modest spread of mushroom-and-clam bisque, boiled breast of bone chicken, hominy pyramids with cheese, rolls, olives, nuts, ice cream, and, of course, champagne. She and the bridesmaids carried bursting arrangements of lily of the valley. A rose motif latticed the damask tablecloth. Rose-petal candies, rose etchings on the crystal goblets.

The cake must be round, to assure eternal love. The mere mention of a rectangular confection shocked Minna into dismissing the caterer. The new chef draped her cake with blossoms to match her bouquet, and treasures lay hidden beneath the icing. She cut the first piece herself; then, in turn, each member of her party cut a slice, hoping to find a lucky trinket. There were sets of fortune's tokens: a ring to foretell the next to be married; a dime to indicate the wealthiest (a custom from which Minna suggested John D. Rockefeller Sr. got the idea for his "Rockefeller dimes"); a wishbone for the luckiest and a thimble to signify the old maid. The bridegroom had his own cake: dark chocolate, rich and laden with fruit. To close the festivities, servants tucked pieces in small white boxes and handed them out as souvenirs.

Minna devised a bleak ending for her fairy tale. Her husband proved to be a brute, she claimed, often closing his hands around her slender neck, fingers nearly meeting. He applied enough pressure to make his point, leaving red imprints on her skin. "No other man," he warned, "shall ever take my place."

She calmed her husband by agreeing with him but confided her misery to her sister. Ada wrote herself into Minna's story, adding an identical plot-line. She married another "Lester," the brother of Minna's husband, and he, too, had a penchant for strangulation.

Enough was enough.

Within the year, Minna packed her things, telling her sister that any fate was better than a silent windpipe, and took a train to Washington, D.C. Ada joined her a few days later. Good riddance to Louisville and Victorian marriage, to the horrors of a half-known life. They never went back, advising their beloved parents to forever extinguish the window lamps lit on their behalf.

"It is doubtful if Minna and Ada Everleigh ever forgave the brutal treatment they had received from their husbands," wrote Charles Washburn in 1936. "Theirs was a stored-up bitterness toward all males from which they could not escape. The way they studied men, their insight into the whims of men and their determination to make men pawns in their parlor were the antics of the spider and the fly."

Washburn was a friend and helped perpetuate the myths about their privileged Kentucky upbringing and cruel husbands. But his words were essentially true, reflecting the sisters' experiences—ones they never acknowledged or discussed—during all those missing years. Men in general, the sisters concluded, were gullible but not to be trusted; greedy but frivolous with money; predatory but easily trapped.

Naturally, Minna gave a different impression in her remarks to Irving Wallace.

"Irving," the former madam spider cooed, "I love men. I esteem your sex highly."

After fleeing their marriages, they joined a traveling stock company, saving money and meeting characters unlike anyone they'd known back in Kentucky. While on the road, the sisters said, they learned of a $35,000 inheritance (the equivalent of about $816,000 today). Their father died, according to one version (Montgomery Simms, of course, was still very much alive and well), while others made oblique reference to "estates in the South." By 1892, however, even Montgomery's scheming brother

Isaac had a run of bad luck, losing most of his wealth and land during the Cleveland administration, and it's unlikely that the sisters' newfound fortune was acquired through a family connection.

Their last show was in Omaha, Nebraska, where they found themselves stranded, unsure of what to do next. A casual remark from one of their cast mates sparked an idea they never would have had on their own.

"My mother would be angry if she knew I was on the stage," she joked. "She thinks I'm in a den of iniquity."

Now there's an idea, the sisters thought. What about a high-class resort? Men were brutes—let them pay to be made fools of. The sisters could enjoy revenge and comic relief at the same time.

There was another underlying motive. Minna and Ada noticed they were none too welcome among Omaha's women. Although "polite society" typically shunned show folk, the sisters were deemed sophisticated enough to attend several local parties. Yet there were never any second invitations. Pity we're too charming and worldly—and intimidating—for Omaha's housewives, they mused. As a test, Minna and Ada hosted a grand luncheon, but only a few townswomen graced the occasion with their presence.

The sisters were furious. So the women refused to visit, but their husbands surely would—especially if the invitations were to a brothel.

What a hilarious, delicious idea. It took one uproarious weekend to develop a plan, and the rest of their careers to weave these revenge tales into legend.

I n 1989, a Virginia woman named Evelyn Diment wrote to Irving Wallace, adding another possibility to the sisters' missing years:

> Dear Mr. Wallace:
>
> I have just received and started to read your book, THE GOLDEN DOOR [*sic*]. In your AUTHOR'S NOTE: How it Began, you write at some length about your meeting and friendship with the Everleigh née Lester sisters, Minna and Aida . . . almost all of what they related as their family history which they told you was a fabrication of the truth (a total lie), I know, because these two women were my Great-Aunts.

The real truth of their career beginnings were sordid and they were subjected to degradation, not even spoken about <u>ever</u> until the last several years.

I am sorry to have to say this, after your "long friendship" with Aunt Minna and Aunt Aida, but they hoodwinked you from start to finish about their family background and lives before they opened their, perhaps, never to be rivaled House of Pleasure. I suspect that they were trying to protect their real family from embarrassment, and managed to do so quite effectively.

My eldest brother, who is now sixty-six years old, was rushed to New York City after swallowing, as an infant, an open diaper pin which lodged in his throat. The family stayed with Aunt Minna and Aunt Aida while in New York during this family crisis.

I wish I could know with certainty where "your" truth and fiction overlap in your book, because in your first page, in which you have Aunt Minna recounting the story of their Kentucky background, lawyer Father, etc., to the young reporter—<u>there was not one word of truth in it.</u>

I wish I had known you around 1944, you could have gotten, at least, a portion of the unvarnished truth of their beginnings, et cetera. Not the concocted version Aunt Aida and Aunt Minna told you.

Most sincerely,
Evelyn E. Diment

Evelyn further claimed that the sisters "lied about their background. They were struggling because they were at the end of the Civil War and there were very few ways to make money. Their plantation was lost because they couldn't pay the taxes. They began as prostitutes and they became madams. Their father put them in the business, and then these women made a marvelous success out of it. . . . Southern families have a way of keeping things very quiet. And if anyone knew anything, they kept their mouth shut."

Whatever may have happened during the family's hardships, the sisters cared enough for their father to have his body relocated from Missouri to Virginia after his death in 1915. Today they are buried alongside him, their mother, and little sister Willie in St. Paul's Cemetery in Alexandria.

Minna and Ada rest side by side, together in death as they were in life. If they didn't marry men named Lester—if Lester is, in fact, a name they adopted, in the grand tradition of prostitutes, upon entering "the life"— then it is a secret the sisters took literally to the grave.

In bold lettering, their markers read:

MINNA LESTER SIMMS
1866–1948
AIDA LESTER SIMMS
1864–1960

I n Omaha by 1895, the sisters were ready to invest their $35,000 "inheritance." Most likely they convinced a powerful acquaintance—a cattle baron, maybe, or a railroad mogul—to back their burgeoning enterprise. "It is hardly conceivable," wrote *Real West* magazine, "that a couple of amateurs could break in without proper connections and set up an elaborate brothel in competition with existing houses at any time."

They found a run-down parlor house at 12th and Jackson streets, a shabby, fraying part of town, and began renovations. Ada sent notice to their old actress friends who sought work, promising good money and clean quarters. The sisters sat for painted portraits, Victorian-style glamour shots more suggestive of European royalty than the proprietors of a whorehouse. Ada donned a hat topped with a sprig of flowers and a lacy-sleeved, swollen gown so tightly corseted that her breasts seemed to beg for emancipation. Minna wore a bonnet and a dress layered with frothy ruffles. She reclined on a velvet chaise longue, one leg extended, a high-heeled foot pointed daintily.

Business was steady, but Omaha had seen better days. The financial panic of 1893 had ravaged the town, but its leaders—mindful of how expositions had benefited other cities like Louisville, Cincinnati, and, most notably, Chicago—had a solution. The town's Trans-Mississippi Exposition was to run for five months, from June 1 to November 1, 1898.

The sisters sensed an opportunity to corner the market on exposition visitors, and rented a building in the downtown business district at 14th and

Dodge streets. Such an optimum locale was bound to lure fairgoers who tired of the usual attractions and sought bawdy midnight indiscretions.

The exposition grounds were laid out in a fashion similar to those of the Mall in Washington, D.C., covering 108 city blocks. Myriad recent inventions were among the 4,062 exhibits—flushing toilets, faucets, X-ray machines, incandescent light bulbs, and an incubator for premature infants—all of which consistently drew large, drop-jawed crowds. Visitors tasted Jell-O and Boston baked beans for the first time. They saw Buffalo Bill Cody, by this time one of the most famous men in the world, and the same cast of scouts, cowboys, rough riders, and crack shots that had awed the crowds at the Chicago World's Fair.

More than 2.6 million people passed through Omaha during the exposition, and the sisters welcomed their share of the visitors. Though mentioned only in prudent, late night whispers, Minna and Ada made a lasting impression on the locals. A Mr. Tom Knapp, who grew up to be the Omaha city welfare director, delivered telegrams as a young boy to the Everleighs at their place of business.

"They were some punkins," he recalled seventy years later, in 1968. "They were some lookers."

By the time the exposition closed in the fall, the sisters had doubled their initial investment. What should they do with $70,000, and where could they go? The moneyed crowd fled as soon as the fair displays were hauled away, and Omaha's native population—a blue-collar mix of Germans, Swedes, and Danes—was not interested in champagne and $10 admission fees.

There was nothing left for them there.

While dives across the country specialized in the defloration of young virgins, beatings, bondage, and daisy chains—a continuous line of girls pleasuring one another with fingers and mouths—the Everleighs proved that madams could conduct business with decency and class. Some situations couldn't be helped. Many courtesans suffered from chronic pelvic congestion, a dull, persistent pain caused by continuous sex without orgasm. The latest medical books described a woman's most fertile period as during and after menstruation, but working girls knew better. Still, mistakes happened, and older women, usually retired madams, ran baby farms for prostitutes' children. Girls died from all manner of horrid abortion procedures, and syphilis was a dreadful hazard.

"It is claimed that this disease originates in the underworld," mused a madam named Josie Washburn, who worked in Omaha shortly before the sisters, "which is not wholly true, as it can be found scattered among all classes. The underworld is obliged to be on its guard all the time to elude it."

There were precautions one could take, sheaths made of animal skin, but clients often balked—"wet, flabby sheep's gut," as one man put it. Leave it to the French to improve upon the idea, offering products supposedly pleasing to both parties, with fanciful names like "le Conquérant" and "le Porc-epic." But even when harlots were appropriately vigilant, they often emphasized efficiency instead of fantasy—the "anti-Balzacs," as the Everleighs might say.

One laborer's experience in a modest brothel in New Orleans's Storyville was typical:

"You wouldn't believe how fast those girls could get their clothes off. Usually they'd leave on their stockings and earrings, things like that. A man usually took off his trousers and shoes. New girls didn't give you a second to catch your breath before they'd be all over you trying to get you to heat up and go off as soon as possible. . . . When it came to the actual act, though, the routine was standard. . . . I think the girls could diagnose clap better than the doctors at that time. She'd have a way of squeezing it that, if there was anything in there, she'd find it. Then she'd wash it off with a clean washcloth. She'd lay on her back and get you on top of her so fast, you wouldn't even know you'd come up there on your own power. . . . I'd say that the whole thing, from the time you got in the room until the time you came, didn't take three minutes. . . . Most all the married women you run across are just a different kind of whore. But a man keeps looking for somebody he can just feel—well, like he isn't always alone."

The sisters packed their finest dresses, lists of influential clients, and collections of butterfly pins and set off, two country girls eager to return Chicago's thrilling embrace. On the way, sitting face-to-face in their

Pullman Palace car, they determined to enforce the same standards that elevated their Omaha resort—no wringing a client's body as if it were a piece of wet laundry. Courtesans would be encouraged to perform orally as often as possible; there was less risk and more money involved. A man who came to their house would see everything he wanted to and nothing he didn't, and he would never feel rushed or cheated, disillusioned or alone.

The sisters also edited the story of how they became madams and planned to redefine what it meant to be one. A rejection of their impeccable standards would mean nothing less than war—against both prostitution as it should be and the invented histories they longed to have.

"THE LOVE GAME."

A pander working "the love game," assumes the role of a banker's son seeking rest and fresh air. He hoodwinks the girls by stories of great wealth and position, the upper part of the picture shows the gay times promised.

*All civilization has from time to time become a thin
crust over a volcano of revolution.*

—HAVELOCK ELLIS

As the century drew to a close, white slavery narratives began spreading beyond midwestern lumber camps. The sheer volume of stories bolstered the notion of a "traffic in girls"—especially in bustling urban centers like Chicago.

"Never before in civilization," wrote Hull House founder Jane Addams, "have such numbers of young girls been suddenly released from the protection of the home and permitted to walk unattended upon the city streets and to work under alien roofs." The city's status as a major rail center made it an ideal location for unscrupulous madams and procurers. How easy it was to feign a welcoming presence at the train stations, to talk of opportunities behind counters or desks, of stardom on stages. The girls came by the hour, bodies tilting from the weight of their bags, stepping from the platform into a world of unrelenting clamor and smoke and sin, knowing they'd just left a place they might never see again. Under the headline MISSING GIRLS, the *Chicago Inter Ocean* explored the mysterious disappearances of young women in the city and suggested an "agony column" listing all their names.

Reform organizations reflected this progress. The New York Committee for the Prevention of the State Regulation of Vice went national, reinventing itself as the American Purity Alliance. They planned for their first National Purity Congress, to be held in Baltimore in October 1895.

Two hundred delegates attended, representing philanthropic organizations from across the country. In subsequent months, Philadelphia, Boston, and New York hosted additional conferences. Subscription rolls for *The Philanthropist*, now the official journal of the American Purity Alliance, doubled in size by January 1896. One year later, they had circulated more than a million pages of literature—including a 472-page monograph of speeches from the inaugural Baltimore Purity Congress. One address, penned by a former journalist and WCTU missionary named Charlton Edholm, was titled "The Traffic in Girls."

In her first version of this address, Edholm spoke of "an organized, systematized traffic in girls," basing her case solely on evidence proffered by Englishman William T. Stead. But in 1899 she issued a revised edition—one that revolutionized the white slavery debate in America just as the Everleigh sisters arrived in Chicago, preparing a revolution of their own.

Edholm hails Stead in her prelude as "the deliverer and protector of little girls from human gorillas," but this time the substance of the report is based on investigations in America. "We have used facts which have come under our own observation," Edholm stresses. "There is a slave trade in this country, and it is not black folks this time, but little white girls—thirteen, fourteen, fifteen, sixteen and seventeen years of age—and they are snatched out of our arms, and from our Sabbath schools and from our communion tables."

She describes the "false employment snare," in which rural girls are tricked by want ads in big-city newspapers. Once trapped in a "haunt of vice," victims are held in debt slavery; the madam confiscates their clothes and charges an outlandish price for the scanty uniform of the brothel.

Beware, also, the missionary warns, of the snare of mock marriage and seduction:

"There are men," she writes, "who in their clubs bet on the virtue of a girl as men would bet on the speed of a horse, and some villain deliberately wagers that in a given time he will have accomplished her ruin and then at the expiration of the months or weeks he returns to his club in high glee, and tells 'the fellows' all about it—the drugs used, the liquors employed, the vows of marriage sacredly promised, the blackest of lies told, the tenderest kisses and caresses bestowed and—at last, the girl basely deserted or turned over to the keeper of a house of shame for twenty-five dollars, there to undergo such atrocities as would make even devils weep."

And the snare of drugs:

"When I was a bartender," one "converted" man confessed to Edholm, "those procurers used to come there, and often I've seen one of these men bring a beautiful girl to the ladies' entrance. . . . I would drop a little drug into whatever that girl had to eat or drink, and in a few moments she would be unconscious and that fellow would have a carriage drive to the door, that girl would be placed in it and driven right straight to a haunt of shame."

Procurers are nefarious, mostly foreign men, Edholm concludes, who scour dance halls for victims, stash chloroform-soaked rags in their pockets, pay slave wages, and prey on virgins as young as ten years old. She advocates temperance, women's suffrage, censorship, passing anti-vice laws, and eliminating the double standard of morality—meaning, of course, that boys should aspire to the moral purity of girls. (What a disgraceful irony, from the reformers' point of view, that women eventually adopted freedoms once reserved exclusively for men.)

With this updated "The Traffic in Girls," the American white slavery crusade finally and fully branched off from its British roots and came into its own. Reformers across the country repeated and embellished Edholm's narratives, panders used them as handy instruction manuals, and harlots memorized all the ways they might be tricked or trapped.

No one learned Edholm's stories better than a girl named Mona Marshall, who in 1907 would emerge from a brothel in Chicago's Levee district to change American history.

LORDS AND LADIES
OF THE LEVEE

Hinky Dink Kenna
(left) and Bathhouse
John Coughlin.

> *Laws should be like clothes. They should fit the people*
> *they are meant to serve.*
> —CLARENCE DARROW

After the Club's first night passed, and weeks tumbled into months, the Everleighs did not so much settle into a routine as construct one, carefully: how to discipline courtesans who stepped out of line, how much (or little) to interact with neighbors, which guests to admit, which to refuse, which to entertain gratis, and which to accommodate, no matter how bizarre or outlandish the request. They adopted madam personas that both reflected and exaggerated who they were. Ada was the executive, more adept at balancing books than making small talk; Minna was the mixer and mingler, who underscored each movement and italicized every word. Their moral code had all the stringency of a preacher's but none of the hypocrisy, and they understood, from experience, that some threats intensified only when acknowledged, while others carried a force all their own.

The Levee had its own list of commandments, long established but mutable, that kept the district functioning as efficiently as the Union Stock Yards. There was, it seemed, always a grand jury investigating something or other, always a crackdown or a raid in the works, always a reform group shouting from the sidelines about liquor licenses and closing laws. Yet such distractions remained peripheral as long as you knew where the boundaries were drawn and, more important, who ensured they stayed in place.

Ike Bloom, the Levee leader who had stopped by on the Club's opening night, kept his promise and visited again. His real name was Isaac Gitelson, and along with his brother-in-law Solly Friedman, he operated a dance hall called Freiberg's on 22nd Street. It was a famous resort, but typical of its kind—a bar in the front and a long dance room in the back, with tables scattered along the walls, an orchestra in the balcony, and platforms upon which prostitutes gyrated and beckoned to every man who entered. An office occupied a small room upstairs, where once a week Bloom sat behind his desk and waited for the delivery of hundreds of envelopes fat with cash.

In an attempt to keep the reformers at bay, he advertised his dive as a "dance academy."

Bloom had rules for his place, too, ethically flexible though they were: After 1:00 a.m., the official closing hour, a label marked "HONEY" was slapped across beer bottles, and seasoned patrons ordered whiskey by requesting "seltzer water." His girls were required to report in by 9:00 p.m. every night and coax men into spending at least 40 cents for every round of drinks. When they asked the bartender for "B" ginger ale highballs, the glasses were filled with colored water. It was an ingenious ploy: The girls made their quota, while Bloom saved money on booze. Long before customers caught on, the girls lured them away to the nearby Marlborough Hotel, where the price of a room was $5—most of which, naturally, was kicked back to Bloom.

Slowly but surely, Minna heard, Ike Bloom was nudging meeker men aside and assuming power throughout the district. Every time a new police captain rose through the ranks or was ushered in with a new mayoral administration, Bloom called him to "make arrangements" for protection payments, a request invariably taken in stride. So integral was Bloom to the web of Levee graft that his portrait, handsomely framed, hung in a prominent place of honor in the squad room of the 22nd Street police station. Together, Bloom and the cops determined the scale of prices:

Massage parlors and assignation houses, $25 weekly

Larger houses of ill fame, $50 to $100 weekly, with $25 additional each week if drinks are sold

Saloons allowed to stay open after hours, $50 per month

Sale of liquor in apartment houses without licenses, $15 per month

Poker and craps, $25 per week for each table

Bloom sent George Little, a Levee ruler he'd usurped and displaced, to make collections. The sisters agreed to the protection rates for a house of their caliber, amounting to about $10,000 annually, but were coy on the subject of buying their wine from Solly Friedman, or their provisions from four certain grocery stores in which Bloom and two powerful aldermen had part interest.

"Positively," Minna said, "the dive-keepers feared Ike Bloom more than the 22nd Street police captain or any inspector ever placed in charge of the district."

But the sisters, just as often, found Bloom unintentionally hilarious, a character whose vicious streak was well concealed by bumbling antics and awkward mannerisms. He always got Minna's name wrong, calling her "Minnie." He dispensed $2.50 gold pieces to his friends and cronies, and when his circle of devotees grew, he cut costs by switching to silver dollars. Those who knew him recognized the gesture as heartfelt. He wasn't buying friendship, but commemorating it. He relished publicity, bad or good or even deadly. A stabbing or shooting or overdose at his hall would only attract more customers.

One day, Bloom burst through the Everleigh Club doors, waving a paper and tearing at the few remaining hairs that sprouted from his scalp. "Now see what they done to me," he yelled. "They've changed my name. It says here in the paper that I am Ike Blossom—what's that, a rosey-posey?"

Minna bit her cheeks and felt the tip of Ada's boot kicking her shin under the table. Ike *Blossom*—good God, if someone had paid the papers to make such a mistake, it couldn't have been any better. Imagine, Ike Bloom, big, bad Levee leader—a *queer*.

"And why?" Ike raged. "I'll tell you. Last night a dame from one of Monkey Face Charlie Genker's Morgan Street joints drove a hat pin into a gent's stomach. He ain't going to die or nothing, but he has some kind of a pull. Look, here it is in the paper."

He threw it down on the table with a splat and watched the sisters read the headline:

FREIBERG'S CLAIMS ANOTHER RICH VICTIM

GIRL STABS WEALTHY MAN

Ike Blossom, as Usual, Maintains Silence
in Latest Underworld Affray

Minna could barely contain herself.

"Don't think I didn't bawl out the editor," Bloom ranted. "I gave him a piece of my mind. And what do you think he told me?"

Minna shrugged, afraid to open her mouth. If she began laughing at him, she might never stop. Ada tsk-tsked and shot Bloom a practiced look of consolation.

"He said they didn't want a libel suit," he said. "Who would I sue? I never sued anybody yet. My name is Ike Bloom, and the next time anybody turns it into Blossom I'll smack a house down—it's defamation of character. Have I got a claim, or haven't I? I wish I knew an honest lawyer."

Catching his breath, he reached into a pocket and pulled out two silver dollars, tossing one to each sister.

"Now you know where you stand with me," he said, smiling, and Minna at last freed her face and did the same. "Any time you want anything come over to Ike Bloom."

And he showed himself out.

"Big Jim" Colosimo, whose power in the district nearly equaled Ike Bloom's, didn't need the quotes around his name. He shared one fashion preference with Minna: Every finger bore a diamond ring, his cuff links were diamond studs, and an enormous diamond horseshoe accented his vest. He bought loose diamonds from thieves and won them from gamblers. When bored or distracted, he'd play with the jewels, pouring them from one palm to the other. He wore "paper suits," as he called them, made of slight seersucker material—so thin that you could see through it in the summertime—complemented by a matching derby with a black satin rim and a white bow tie, over which his ample chin dropped in a waterfall of flesh. He was enormous, with hulking shoulders and a deliberate, lumbering gait. His mustache, besides drawing attention upward and away from his chin, was thick and bristled enough to conceal his expressions. His was a natural poker face, but always betrayed by his cyclonic personality: He was the kind of man you sensed before you saw.

He visited the Everleigh Club occasionally, either when the sisters inquired about protection payments or of his own accord, boxes of spaghetti tucked under his arm and a jar of his special sauce—"red ink," he'd say with a wink—pinned beneath his chin. A bag of grated Parmesan cheese peeked from his pocket. He headed straight for the kitchen, and Minna and Ada knew to wait for him there.

"Draw up a couple of chairs," he said, motioning to both sisters. "Where's them big boilers?" He poked his head in a cabinet, crashing pots and pans. "Never mind, here's one."

Within minutes, Big Jim had wrapped an apron around his white suit and fragrant bursts of steam clouded the air. "What's up? Ike Bloom been bothering you again?" he'd ask rhetorically. "What's eating Ike, anyway? I always said he goes too far."

Minna despised spaghetti. Slimy noodles slathered in boring red sauce—what was the appeal? Forcing herself to clean her plate, she ignored the way her guest slurped his sauce and gnawed his bread, the crumbs that burrowed stubbornly in his mustache. It wouldn't do to offend Big Jim.

His stories, however, were fascinating. He described his early childhood in Italy and the boat ride to America when he was just ten years old. His father found work in Chicago, and Big Jim spent his first days in the city learning the Levee streets and how they worked: the pickpocket's quick dip and flick of the wrist; the pimp's bowlegged saunter; the unseeing stare of the addicts and freaks. He needed to help his family, he told the sisters, so he sold newspapers at first and then became a bootblack. He couldn't forget the scent of the polish on his fingers, etched in the ridges of his skin and beneath his nails. He smelled common. When he had money, and he was sure he would, his fingers would instead be covered in diamonds. Minna could relate.

By eighteen, he said, he picked pockets better than anyone he'd ever seen and had forayed into pimping. Six girls depended on him for protection and praise. On the side he was a Black Hand collector, extorting money from established Italian businessmen (and his eventual success came with an unfortunate bit of irony: Black Hand blackmailers now targeted him for payments). He went straight for a while, heading up a team of street cleaners that evolved into a labor union of sorts—a potential voting bloc that caught the notice of the city's Democratic machine. Big Jim was appointed a precinct captain, which marked the end of his time as a law-abiding citizen.

With his madam wife, Victoria, he operated two dives, the Victoria and the Saratoga, neither far from the Everleigh Club. He talked of his soft spot for harlots—more than once he roamed the Levee streets after a teary outburst, mascara stains blotting his lapel—but this image as a benevolent overlord was marred somewhat by his latest, and most lucrative, source of revenue.

Big Jim, the sisters heard, ran a white slavery ring.

His reputed partner was a wily Frenchman, Maurice Van Bever. A preening dandy who rode through the Levee streets every afternoon, driven by a coachman clad in a high silk hat and jacket trimmed with solid gold buttons, Van Bever also operated two saloons, the Paris and the White City. He and Big Jim, according to the rumors, organized a ring with inter-city connections, working with similar outfits in New York, St. Louis, and Milwaukee. Just like their Levee forebear, Madam Mary Hastings, they imported girls to Chicago with promises of good jobs and secure homes and sold them to brothel keepers—or forced them into their own houses—once they arrived.

A shameful arrangement, one the sisters could never understand or condone, but they decided there was no reason to broach the subject of Maurice Van Bever or white slavery. Their relationship with Big Jim required knowing what to discuss and what to keep private. Minna and Ada agreed: Some things were better left unconsidered.

But the true leaders of the Levee district, the sisters quickly learned, were aldermen Michael "Hinky Dink" Kenna and "Bathhouse John" Coughlin. Ike Bloom and Big Jim might have operated the assembly line, but Hinky Dink and Bathhouse John owned the factory. Their bailiwick, the First Ward, one of thirty-five in the city, encompassed the heart of Chicago, including the Loop—with its City Hall, office buildings, swanky department stores, hotels, restaurants, and theaters—and stretched south to 29th Street, claiming, too, all the Levee whorehouses, dives, and gambling dens.

The latter racket proved especially lucrative; many bordellos and saloons reserved a room for poker tables and roulette wheels and a wall to hurl dice against. The Everleigh sisters decided that gambling sessions in the Club should not exceed a half hour. "I have watched men, embraced in the arms of the most bewitching sirens in our Club, dump their feminine flesh from their laps for a roll of the dice," Minna said. "It always amused me to see potential Don Juans, who had deliberately visited our Club for biographical expression, becoming inarticulate except for such phrases as 'Come seven, baby needs a new pair of shoes' . . . if it wasn't unmanly to admit it, they'd rather most of the time gamble than screw."

Hinky Dink and Bathhouse John took a portion of every dollar generated in the red-light district, through gambling or otherwise, and counted Mayor Carter Harrison II as a personal friend and political sponsor.

"Everywhere the names of the sisters Everleigh and the names of Bathhouse John and Hinky Dink, their reputed protectors, were intertwined," wrote the aldermen's biographers. "You no sooner said, 'Yes, I'm from Chicago,' than your companions wanted a full description of the fabulous Everleigh club, the remarkable sisters, and the even more remarkable aldermen."

Minna found Michael Kenna smart but aloof. He owned a Clark Street saloon, the Workingman's Exchange, where he served lunch for free to any bum, tramp, hobo, and downtrodden potential voter who stumbled inside, and offered a mug of beer, "the largest and coolest in the city," for a nickel.

She pieced together bits of Kenna's history through conversations with Big Jim and Ike: He was born in the First Ward, quit school at ten, got a job as a newsboy. Rumor had it that an esteemed *Tribune* editor, Joseph Medill, dubbed him "Hinky Dink" because of his diminutive stature: He stood five feet one and weighed about as much as Minna. For this reason, he was also called "Little Fellow." He didn't care much for socializing and considered small talk a tedious waste of time. Kenna looked the same now as he had as a kid, with the body of a child and the face of an old man.

Hinky Dink came to power when he was elected to the Chicago City Council a few years earlier, in 1897. It was his idea to establish a standard rate of 50 cents per vote. He also launched the First Ward Democratic Club, of which every registered voter was automatically a member and encouraged to carry an identification card. Through this organization, which numbered forty thousand, he and Bathhouse John controlled both the wealthiest and most depraved sections of Chicago.

Bathhouse John was as gregarious and daft as Kenna was distant and deft. His open, approachable face capped an enormous frame; Hinky Dink reached only as high as his armpits. Throughout his life, Bathhouse, a married man, insisted he had never stepped foot inside the Everleigh Club (a claim his fellow aldermen scoffed at within City Hall corridors), but he took a liking to the sisters, Minna in particular, perhaps because she, too, was the "speaking partner" of a formidable duo.

"Whatever difficulties arose, we were told to see Mr. Coughlin," Minna explained. "He was the final word."

At her prompting, he told Minna he'd gotten his nickname as a teenager. Working as a "rubber" in Turkish bathhouses, first on Clark Street and then at the posh Palmer House, he learned about politics and those who contorted its rules. He was fascinated by these men, with their silk suits and overflowing wallets, their glib talk and intricate plots of election day high jinks, their practiced jokes and slap-shoulder bonhomie. He met congressmen and senators, moguls and millionaires—Marshall Field even came, on occasion, for a plunge.

"I formed my philosophy," Bathhouse said, "while watching and studying the types of people who patronized the bathhouses. Priests, ministers, brokers, politicians, and gamblers visited there. I watched, and learned never to quarrel, never to feud. I had the best schooling a young feller could have. I met 'em all, big and little, from LaSalle Street to Armour Avenue. You could learn from anyone. Ain't much difference between the big man and the little man. One's lucky, that's all."

He was the city's poet laureate, he claimed—"lariat," in his lingo. She'd heard of his composition titled "Dear Midnight of Love," hadn't she? It premiered at the Chicago Opera House right before she and Ada came to town. Newspapers all across the country called to interview him—it was a sensation. Minna read the papers, right? Good. Well, every Monday morning, the *Record Herald* printed a new melody of his. There was a ditty titled "Why Did They Build Lake Michigan So Wide?" But one of his best was "An Ode to a Bath-tub," which went, in part, like this:

> *I care not for ball games, nor fishing, or money unless to buy grub*
> *But I'd walk forty miles before breakfast to roll in the porcelain tub.*

Several of the Club's journalist patrons confided to Minna that John Kelley, a Chicago society writer, was the creative force behind the alderman's oeuvre—with the lone exception of "Dear Midnight of Love." But she didn't let on to the Bath—why blow his cover? Instead, Minna instructed her orchestra to play "Dear Midnight of Love" at least once every night in the alderman's honor.

The Everleighs knew instinctively to defer to Bathhouse John, and he returned the favor, recognizing how they would benefit the Levee. Shortly after the Club's debut, the sisters were invited to an annual party called the First Ward Ball, where Levee denizens celebrated their debauchery with impunity. At the stroke of midnight, the Bath, decked out in a green coat, lavender trousers, and silk pink gloves, rose and approached the sisters. He bowed, took each on an arm, and led them around the floor of the First Regiment Armory, with every lesser madam, pimp, cadet, harlot, and hanger-on trailing behind. Thus commenced his famous Grand March, and without saying a word, he had named these newcomers, Minna and Ada Everleigh, the queens not only of the Ball, but of the entire Levee.

The Everleighs didn't need anyone to confirm their vaulted status, but they appreciated the gesture nonetheless—as well as Bathhouse's vow to protect them from enemies, both inside the Levee and beyond.

There were some, of course, who didn't share Bathhouse John's ardor for the sisters, who wished the Everleighs would return to Kentucky or Virginia or wherever they came from. Each afternoon, Minna and Ada took a ride to the Loop in their elegant hansom, drawn by a team of sleek black horses and driven by a crisply suited coachman. Their choicest girl, bedecked in a frilly confection of silk and glittering jewelry, perched high in the back. While the sisters sashayed into their bank to deposit the previous night's earnings, the girl remained on display in the coach, preening and patting her hair, lifting a leg to tug at a high-buttoned shoe, letting her dress rise in the process, a curtain ascending. Afterward, the sisters rode through Chicago's streets long enough to give passersby a good look at what they had for sale at the Club, an advertising technique that both enticed clients and made fellow madams wonder who in the hell these two uppity Everleigh sisters thought they were, anyway.

The proprietors of the Levee's finer establishments were shaken when the Everleighs—novices who knew nothing about Chicago before setting up shop here—quickly surpassed them all, in terms of both volume and reputation. One brothel owner, Ed Weiss, used sheer cunning to combat the decline in business. Minna knew that Ed, who ran the resort next door, had put most of the Levee's cabdrivers on his payroll. When a drunken reveler stumbled into a hansom and asked for the Everleigh Club, he more often than not ended up at Ed Weiss's door—and rarely knew the difference.

Minna, in spite of herself, had to admire the old shyster.

But a circle of well-regarded madams lacked the innovation for such subterfuge, and hence spent most of their time stewing and sending subtle jabs the sisters' way. They did not, for one thing, invite the Everleighs to join the Friendly Friends (the Levee ladies' answer to the pimps' group, the Cadets' Protective Association), which served as a sort of labor union for madams, whose members gathered regularly for such genteel activities as knitting and tea sipping.

Clearly, Minna and Ada were unbothered by their exclusion from this society—a nonchalance that enraged Madam Vic Shaw, whose lavish house on Dearborn Street seemed emptier each night. Didn't the Everleighs realize every step they took within the Levee was on ground that she'd trod first? Those sisters purposely withheld deference and respect, even refusing to follow the aldermen's rules about where to buy food and wine. Vic Shaw would never forget the last Washington Park Derby, an event Levee madams attended alongside Prairie Avenue matrons. That afternoon, as she was getting dressed, one of her harlots called out, "Come look out the window, quick."

"There," Vic Shaw later recalled, "going down the street right in front of my house, were the Everleigh sisters and their girls in a tallyho! Of all things, a tallyho! With four horses, red tassels draped over their ears, and a boy on the front seat tooting a silver horn. Did my blood pressure go up!

"Well, I marched right over to Payne's livery and I said, 'I want you to get me a tallyho, only I don't want four horses, I want six.' I draped red tassels all over them. I sent my riders uptown to be fitted for custom-made boots and cream-colored pants. I got little yeoman hats and tailored riding coats for my girls. Then I ordered a silver horn twice as long as the one the Everleighs had and we set out for the derby. . . . On the way, we drove around the block past the Everleigh Club four times, and I kept that poor sucker tootin' that horn all the way. I'll be truthful. It never dawned on me to have a tallyho. But when I got the idea, you can't say I didn't do it up better than the Everleighs."

Their whole history was nauseating, all that talk about southern roots and debutante balls and their smashing success in Omaha and being related to that spooky "Raven" poet and some such nonsense. Well, Vic Shaw got where she was without the benefit of any pedigreed background—one of ten children, the daughter of an iron mine worker in Londonderry, Nova Scotia. She ran away from home at thirteen, still named Emma Elizabeth Fitzgerald but already an "apt pupil" who "knew the answers." First she joined a troupe in Boston and then Sam T. Jack's burlesque show on West Madison Street in Chicago. She'd come into some money, too, not through a fortuitous inheritance from a wealthy lawyer father like *certain* madams claimed, but by eloping with the son of a millionaire banker. When his family discovered he'd married a minor, they arranged a quick and discreet divorce. She kept her ex-husband's nickname for her, "Vickie," his surname, Shaw, and half of his fortune, and opened her brothel on South Dearborn Street.

So what if the finer points and prissy etiquette of the trade eluded her at first? Could one blame her for being beautiful and "more interested in men than in business"? One of her early clients, a wealthy Chicago businessman, told her bluntly, "You'll have to hire better girls if you want to stay in business." Soon after, a railroad magnate lodged the same complaint, then pressed $1,000 into her hand with the suggestion that she go to New Orleans and bring back some "thorobreds." Madam Shaw did just that. "And by 1900," wrote the *Tribune*, "the year the Everleigh Sisters moved in, she was established as queen bee of the brothels."

Vic Shaw might not have that title anymore; certain overrated, insufferable madams might have sauntered in on their red-tasseled tallyho and snatched it from her as if it were their preordained right. But Vic Shaw had recourse, little hidden pockets of savvy. She was *still* beautiful, her bosom ornamenting her figure like the prow of a stately ship; no one noticed the years she discarded when she claimed to be twenty-two. She had Roy Jones, a Levee vice king, whom she planned to marry. She had a good rapport with Bathhouse John and Hinky Dink. She had "strip-whip" matches, during which whores stepped inside a makeshift ring, wearing corsets and boots or nothing at all, and lashed each other's backs bloody; the Prairie Avenue set paid good money for these circuses.

She had stunning inmates, especially Gladys Martin, who even sat for promotional photos, her blond head budding from a white fur cape. She had an enforcer named Lillie Kowalski—"Lill the Whipper"—who dressed like a missionary but brawled like a longshoreman, beating up, over the years, more than a thousand harlots. She had an open invitation to all Everleigh courtesans should they ever desire to quit the Club and work for Vic Shaw's, the original.

Most important, she knew how to deliver a threat.

"Queer ducks, our neighbors," Madam Shaw told a cop on the beat whom she knew had a taste for gossip and trouble and no qualms about spreading either around. There—those Everleigh snobs would get the message. "They've a pull somewhere," she added, "but it won't last."

GREAT IN RELIGION, GREAT IN SIN

Members of the Purity Congress.

We discovered that the scrupulously strict were correspondently keen to discern suggestions of sex where nobody else would think of looking for them.

—MINNA EVERLEIGH

Chicago's turn to host the National Purity Congress came in the fall of 1901. That its red-light district had long been the wickedest in the country—a distinction recently underscored by the opening of a certain Dearborn Street brothel said to eclipse anything in Paris—only made it a more fitting locale for the reformers' convention. The city's myriad woes were finally matched by forces eager to solve them: the Moody Bible Institute; the Cook County Juvenile Court, the nation's first; Jane Addams's Hull House; the Anti-Saloon League; Graham Taylor's Chicago Commons; and the Pacific Garden Mission, responsible for the very public salvation of Chicago White Stockings player Billy Sunday, who was one night so captivated by a sermon preached from the roving "Gospel Wagon" that he accepted Christ as his savior, declined a lucrative contract, and launched a new career as the "baseball evangelist," traveling the world to preach God's word.

On October 8, a crisp Tuesday evening, delegates from across the country and from numerous foreign countries, including England, Holland, France, Canada, and India, filed into the First Methodist Church at Clark and Washington streets. The Reverend John P. Brushingham gave the opening address. England and America, he declared, are "one in language, one in God, but also one in sin, one in drunkenness, and one in the social evil." He welcomed the visitors to "Chicago, great in population, great in commerce, great in religion, and great in sin."

For the next three days, the church would be filled to capacity to hear ministers and missionaries, doctors and housewives, professors and white slave crusaders all lecture on every facet of vice. A purity worker named William P. F. Ferguson kicked things off with a speech titled "Police Headquarters and the City Hall in Their Relation to Vice."

"Precisely the same conditions which exist in Manila may be found in the large cities," he argued. "By a careful and exact system of fines and licenses and hush money the keepers of disorderly places hang the receipts for the payment of such exactions on the same hooks with their receipted grocery bills." Dr. Mary Wood-Allen of Ann Arbor, Michigan, followed with a condemnation of the press—especially the comics—for "lowering the tone of the human race by ridiculing the sacred process of wooing."

Other addresses included:

"The Cure of the Social Evil"
"How to Elevate the Home Life"
"A Strange Silence; Its Cause and Cure" (a rumination on the double standard)
"The Influence of Diet upon Character"
"The Solidarity of Vice and Vicious Methods"
"Divorce Not a Matter of Choice"
and
"The Relation Between Modern Social Vice and Ancient Sex Worship"

Closing the conference on Thursday, October 10, 1901, the attendees deemed the event a great success, marred only by one unfortunate incident. While the final speakers advocated for "purity in thought, word, and deed," Mrs. B. S. Steadwell, wife of the president of the Northwestern Purity Association, was approached by two well-dressed men. Might they, the men asked, see some of the literature she had for sale? Mrs. Steadwell became so engrossed in the discussion, and in the prospect of selling a few pamphlets, that she laid her purse on the table. After she'd sold 40 cents' worth of literature, the men abruptly ran off, taking the purse with them.

Despite this "active experience with vice," which left Mrs. Steadwell $3 poorer, the delegates were so taken with Chicago, in all its stunning achievement and shameless decadence, that they decided to reconvene there in 1906, five years hence.

KNOWING
YOUR BALZAC

The Japanese Throne Room at the Everleigh Club.

*If it weren't for the married men we couldn't have
carried on at all, and if it weren't for the cheating
married women we would have earned another million.*
—THE EVERLEIGH SISTERS

Pulled or prompted, men came to the Everleigh Club. They came to see the Room of 1,000 Mirrors, inspired by Madam Babe Connors's place in St. Louis, with a floor made entirely of reflective glass. In Minna's eyes, this parlor paid bawdy tribute to Honoré de Balzac's *The Magic Skin*—a mirror with numerous facets, each depicting a world.

They came to hear the Club's string orchestras—the only bordello in the Levee featuring three—and its professor, Vanderpool Vanderpool, whose repertoire included a chipper rendition of "Stay in Your Own Back Yard," one of the most popular tunes of the era:

> *Now honey, yo' stay in yo' own back yard,*
> *Doan min' what dem white chiles do;*
> *What show yo' sup-pose dey's a gwine to gib*
> *A black lit-tle coon like yo'?*

They came to see the thirty boudoirs, each with a mirrored ceiling and marble inlaid brass bed, a private bathroom with a tub laced in gold detailing, imported oil paintings, and hidden buttons that rang for champagne. They came to eat in the glorious Pullman Buffet, gorging on southern cuisine and the creations of the Club's nationally renowned head chef. On any given night, the menu's specials might offer

ENTREES

supreme of guinea-fowl

pheasant

capon

broiled squab

roasted turkey, duck and goose

SIDES
au gratin cauliflower

spinach cups with creamed peas

parmesan potato cubes

pear salad with sweet dressing

stuffed cucumber salad

carrots (candied or plain)

browned sweet potatoes

Minna's favorite boys dined again after midnight on a feast of fried oysters, Welsh rarebit, deviled crabs, lobster, caviar—unadorned save for a dash of lemon juice—and scrambled eggs with bacon. For special occasions—a courtesan's engagement, a birthday, the reappearance of a long-lost Everleigh Club client—Minna ordered the team of chefs to double the usual menu. The madam believed any event that diverted the course of a normal day was a valid excuse to host an epicurean free-for-all.

They came to see the library, filled floor to ceiling with classics in literature and poetry and philosophy, and the art room, housing a few bona fide masterworks and a reproduction of Bernini's famous *Apollo and Daphne,* which the sisters had failed to find in America. After learning that the original statue was at the Villa Borghese in Rome, Minna sent an artist to capture its image. She was haunted by how the exquisite nymph's hands flowered into the branches of a laurel tree just as the god of light reaches for her. A gorgeous piece, but she admired the statue mostly for the questions it posed about clients: Why did men who had everything worth having patronize the Everleigh Club? And what if the thing they desired most in this world simply vanished?

They came to see the ballroom, with its towering water fountain, parquet floor arranged in intricate mosaic patterns, and ceiling that dripped crystal chandeliers. They came to see the little oddities that made the Club like no place else in the world: gilded fishbowls, eighteen-karat-gold spittoons that cost $650 each, and the Everleighs' signature trinket—a fountain that, at regular intervals, fired a jet of perfume into the thickly incensed air.

"By comparison," wrote Herbert Asbury, "the celebrated Mahogany Hall of Washington, the famous Clark Street house of Carrie Watson, and the finest brothels in New York, San Francisco, and New Orleans were squalid hovels fit only for the amorous frolics of chimpanzees."

They came to see the soundproof reception parlors, twelve in all. The Copper Room featured walls paneled with hammered brass; the Silver Room gleamed sterling; the Blue Room offered cerulean leather pillows stamped with images of Gibson girls; the furniture in the Gold Room was encrusted with gilt. And a visitor mustn't forget the Red Room and Rose Room and Green Room, all done in monochromatic splendor.

They came to see the Moorish Room, featuring the obligatory Turkish corner, complete with overstuffed couches and rich, sweeping draperies; and the Japanese Parlor, with its ornately carved teakwood chair resting upon a dais, a gold silk canopy hovering above. (The *Tribune* noted that the Japanese Parlor was "a harlot's dream of what a Japanese palace might look like inside.") In the Egyptian Room, a full-size effigy of Cleopatra kept a solemn eye on the proceedings. The Chinese Room, entirely different from the ambiguously named Oriental Room, offered packages of tiny firecrackers and a huge brass beaker in which to shoot them—where else but at the Everleigh Club could a man indulge his adult *and* childish impulses?

"Next week," Minna often joked, "we are contemplating putting in a box of sand for the kiddies."

Ada, especially, grew obsessed with the Club's maintenance. On the rare occasions when she joined Minna in the parlors, she spent half her time wiping smudges from the mirrors, straightening the oil paintings, checking the gold piano for unsightly water marks. "It was a happy day," she said, "when we conceived the idea of using rubber washers from Mason jars on the bottoms of the glasses."

The gold piano, Ada hinted, had become the love of her life—even when one client vied valiantly for the title. A man, whose name Ada never revealed (sex, both sisters agreed, was a subject best confined to business), visited often and confessed he was wild about the elder Everleigh. Ada's admirer brought her flowers—a gesture, wrote Charles Washburn, akin to "bringing a glass of water to a lake"—and presented her with a three-carat diamond ring, which she accepted gratefully, though her jewelry collection included, among other pricey baubles, a necklace worth more than $100,000. He sent her candy, composed love notes, watched her as if she might vanish should he even briefly avert his eyes.

But her paramour's business called for him to relocate to New York. He wrote to Ada, inviting her to join him, promising marriage. Ada was tempted—it sounded like quite the adventure. She replied to his letter, but kept postponing the trip. The man wrote again and again, pleading his case, and finally involved a newspaper reporter who happened to be a mutual friend. Ada's lover sent the journalist a copy of her letter and asked what he could do to win her over. The reporter rushed to the Club to put in a word for his friend.

"Your letter to him plainly indicates how you feel," he said. "I never read such a charming note. It's literature; it's sentimental—it's everything. What's the matter with you?"

Still, Ada couldn't bring herself to go. Minna had her theories as to why: Perhaps, after the antics and glamour of the Club, her sister would be bored to pieces stuck in a marriage?

That wasn't it, Ada said.

The reporter ventured an opinion. "Maybe you didn't care to leave your sister?"

Ada turned to Minna, and the sisters shared a wordless exchange. The reporter had come too close to the truth, an unacceptable prospect to two women who believed facts could be rewritten and improved upon. Ada's tone lightened, and she gave an answer that sounded like something the very sister in question might say.

"I don't think it was entirely that," she quipped. "My sweetheart took a terrible dislike to our gold piano. He said it was feverish and unbecoming. I couldn't forgive him for that. I would have sacrificed my diamonds, anything, but not the gold piano."

To keep the piano shining, the mirrored walls intact, the rugs clean, and the perfume jets shooting, the sisters allotted $18,000 per year in renovations. It would be worth it, they reasoned, when patrons returned as eager to see the updated décor as the new selection of girls. It was time for the Gold Room, Minna's and Ada's favorite, to be entirely redone in gold leaf. A team of laborers replaced the gilt on everything from the goldfish bowls to the spittoons. It looked stunning, Minna thought, the whole room glittering from corner to corner, but that night a guest accidentally smeared a panel. The metal was still soft, and the man left a clear imprint. This wouldn't do, and Minna couldn't wait until next year's renovation to have it fixed. She called in a dauber right away.

"Come, I'll show you where a man put his hand last night," she said, leading the handyman upstairs.

He hesitated and seemed nervous. It occurred to Minna what he was thinking, but she didn't rush to clarify. Why ruin what was sure to be a perfectly good punch line?

"If it's all the same to you," he replied after a moment, "I'd rather have a glass of beer."

Literary sensations like Ring Lardner, George Ade, Percy Hammond, Edgar Lee Masters, and Theodore Dreiser came and listened to stunning creatures recite poetry classics. "Until at last, serene and proud, in all the splendour of her light," the Everleigh butterflies murmured in between sips of champagne, "she walks the terraces of cloud, supreme as Empress of the Night."

The Club entertained sports icons like James J. Corbett and Stanley Ketchel and, on one fateful night, Jack Johnson; theater celebrities like John Barrymore; a circus star named the Great Fearlesso; and gambling virtuosos, most notably "Bet a Million" Gates, who enjoyed good luck among the harlots even as he ridiculed their attempts at sophisticated discourse. "That," he joked to the sisters, "is educating the wrong end of a whore."

Pioneers of the automobile industry came. The production of "horseless carriages" had evolved considerably since two models—the prototype Morrison electric and a gasoline-powered car from Germany—were exhibited, with little fanfare, at the World's Columbian Exposition. In 1895, the *Chicago Times-Herald* sponsored a round-trip race from Chicago to Evanston, and two cars finished despite the foot of snow that buried the metropolitan area. No mere publicity stunt, the race launched Chicago's auto-manufacturing industry.

Within five years, 22 local companies began building and selling horse-less carriages, and by the century's turn, 377 of them vied for space on the city's clogged streets. The ensuing chaos—collisions with wagons, lax enforcement, arbitrary traffic signals and laws—failed to dampen the public's enthusiasm for cars, in Chicago or elsewhere. Crowds cheered as New York drivers raced thirty miles through the streets from Kingsbridge to Irvington-on-Hudson, north of the city; and in Detroit, a man named Ransom E. Olds invented an assembly line to churn out hundreds of his Curved Dash Oldsmobiles, sold to eager consumers for $650 each. Bicycles were passé, but cars signified money, modernity, and romance. Every man sang the new hit song "Come Away with Me, Lucille, in My Merry Oldsmobile" even if he couldn't afford to own one.

Chicago hosted its first major auto show in July 1900, five months after the Club's grand opening. After the presentations at the official Coliseum headquarters, the men retired en masse to the Everleigh Club. They were welcome anytime—manufacturers were known to spare no expense when wooing important dealers—but Minna and Ada, for the next eleven years, always designated one "Automobile Night" during the week of the show. Companies were welcome to set up corporate and expense accounts at the brothel for their employees. A man gained admittance only by flashing an official exhibitor's badge and was treated to a lavish feast at the Pullman Buffet, a bottle of wine, and a trip up the mahogany staircase.

Wealthy ranchers came to the Club from the Southwest; bankers and Broadway troupes sojourned from the East Coast; congressional committees indulged during breaks from the capital; and on March 3, 1902, royalty visited from overseas.

Prince Henry of Prussia had arrived in New York harbor in the dwindling days of February to accept a yacht built for his brother Kaiser Wilhelm II, emperor of Germany, and to present the United States with his own gift, a statue of Frederick the Great. Prominent Americans viewed the prince's trip as an opportunity to showcase the country's brightest thinkers and shrewdest capitalists, and to flex its developing imperial muscle. The United States now claimed Hawaii and Puerto Rico as territories and prepared to trade with a newly autonomous Cuba. With the eyes of the world poised to judge Prince Henry's reception, America would spare no expense.

"England's only chance to get even," joked the *Chicago Daily News*, "is to send us over a live prince as soon as we have recovered from Prince Henry."

The prince spent a few days in New York. He attended a fête in his honor at the Waldorf-Astoria and lunched at Sherry's with J. P. Morgan, Adolphus Busch, Charles Schwab, Alexander Graham Bell, and Thomas Edison.

Debate raged in the Second City, meanwhile, over an appropriate itinerary for Prince Henry. Chicago's twenty-thousand-plus German immigrants planned to line a brilliantly lit Michigan Avenue and roar as the prince traveled past, on his way to an elaborate banquet at the Auditorium Hotel. There he would dine with 165 "representative men" of Chicago, including J. Ogden Armour, Potter Palmer, Oscar Mayer, Marshall Field Jr., and Mayor Carter Harrison II. The planning committees also approved a choral festival at the First Regiment Armory, a tour of Marshall Field's department store, a trip to Lincoln's grave, another stop at the Auditorium Hotel for a grand ball, and a lunch and reception at the Germania Club. The visit, all told, would cost the city $75,000.

But the committee nixed a tour of the gory Union Stock Yards ("Prince Henry probably will brush the committee aside and visit the Stock Yards anyhow," the *Daily News* sniffed. "He will want to learn how Europe feeds its armies and navies") and remained ambivalent on whether visiting royalty should enjoy the "old feudal privilege" of kissing Chicago's debutantes. "It won't hurt the prince," one committeeman argued, "to get a taste of real American hero worship."

If Prince Henry did kiss the debutantes, he never told.

The sight Prince Henry most desired to see, however, was neither discussed by the planning committee nor detailed in the press. Such discretion benefited the Everleigh sisters, who in anticipation of the prince's arrival at the Club on midnight, March 3, were in the midst of frenzied planning. None of the Everleigh butterflies had heard of Prince Henry of Prussia before he announced his intention to visit, so the sisters prepared lessons—not about the German royal family (who cared?), but about how to entertain them properly.

Minna stood in front of her thirty courtesans, arms waving, a conductor nearing crescendo, and told them how it would be done. Prince Henry, she announced, was the sort of man who knew exactly what he wanted. So as Everleigh girls their job was to give him something he'd never even considered.

They would enact a mythological celebration centered around Dionysus, the Greek god of wine, agriculture, and fertility of nature and—closest to Minna's heart—the patron god of the Greek stage. She'd contacted an old friend from her theater days and ordered real fawnskin outfits for them to wear, with nothing—that's right, nothing—underneath. No petticoats, no stockings, no corsets. Not even shoes—at least not right away. Come now, they had to begin practicing. The ritual was complex, commemorating the dismemberment of Zeus's infant son at the hands of the Titans. There would be a cloth bull and some raw meat involved.

Around midnight on March 3, Prince Henry and his party rang the Club's bell. A tall man, the prince had an unruly sprig of a beard and skin like a cracked egg. High, shiny black boots hugged his legs, making his pants bunch out in tufts over his knees. The members of his entourage wore sweeping capes and frowns that stretched to their necks. Expressions improved markedly once Minna greeted her boys and escorted them to the Pullman Buffet for dinner.

At 1:30 a.m., Minna came to round everyone up, telling the girls the show was about to start—touch up their makeup one last time and don't forget they weren't to wear shoes. The harlots yanked pins from their hair and shook it out, slicing strands with their fingers, the messier the better. They rushed down the spiral staircase and into the parlor, where they found Prince Henry and his entourage at a long table. The girls whooped and swirled in circles, kicking, backs arching like drawn bows. The decisive clang of cymbals punctuated every move. One girl thrashed her way across the room, heading directly for Prince Henry, and just as she reached him she leapt, turned a half circle in midair, and landed on his lap, latching on to his neck. The others followed suit, and soon every man at the table was grappling with an Everleigh butterfly.

Minna dimmed the lights, the signal for the second act of the show. In rehearsals she'd used real torches but found that they'd "smoked up the room," so she'd decided to improvise during the real event.

A servant wheeled a bull made entirely of cloth into the room. The girls raced toward the structure, punching its head and biting its hide, spitting white flurries of cotton. Minna watched, nodding with approval. It was perfect, she thought. This was exactly how the infant Dionysus-Zagreus had been killed. For sound effects, a male butler bellowed each time a mouth clamped down on the bull. Then Minna pointed a finger, and servants fetched platters piled with uncooked sirloin. For ten minutes, the harlots tore into the raw strips, ripping the meat with feral bites, their faces stained with pink slashes of animal blood. The Germans loved it.

When the platters were empty, Minna threw on the lights. She would now take their visitors for a grand tour of the Club. The harlots trooped back upstairs, changed from their fawnskins into evening gowns, pinned up their hair, wiped the blood from their cheeks. A few girls brought dignitaries to their boudoirs, eager to display other talents besides playacting Greek mythology, and hurried downstairs to join the champagne toast when their guests were satisfied.

Minna instructed everyone to raise their glasses, toasting the kaiser in absentia and the prince in the flesh (although the kaiser, after learning of his brother's visit to the Club, cast a mild insult by asking the vintage of the wine served). She was delighted when the prince returned the favor, comparing Chicago with Berlin, pointing out the American city's ever growing German population. He called his new friends, Minna and Ada Everleigh, "fräuleins." Ada, who never drank beer, showed her respect by gulping down a tall mug of pilsner.

Minna then ordered the table cleared. She had one more surprise.

Two butlers helped Vidette, the best dancer among the Everleigh butterflies, up to the mahogany surface. The orchestra struck up "The Blue Danube," and the harlot kicked again and again, her feet flying higher each time, legs meeting and parting like a pair of scissors possessed. In the middle of her routine, one high-heeled silver slipper launched from her foot, sailed across the room, and collided with a glass of champagne. Some of the liquid spilled into the shoe, and a nearby man named Adolph scooped it up.

"Boot liquor," he called, raising the slipper high. "The darling mustn't get her feet wet."

Without further comment, he tilted back his head, drained the champagne from the shoe, and tossed it back to its owner.

"On with the dance!" someone yelled.

"Nix," said another guest. "Off with a slipper." He lifted a harlot's leg, resting it against his waist, and removed her shoe. "Why should Adolph have all the fun?" he added. "This is everybody's party."

Prince Henry's entire entourage rose, yanked a slipper from the nearest girl, and held it aloft. Waiters scuttled about, hurriedly filling each shoe with champagne.

"To the prince."

"To the kaiser."

"To beautiful women the world over."

Prince Henry of Prussia departed Chicago by 2:00 p.m. the following afternoon, but his slipper sipping began a trend that long outlasted his visit. "In New York millionaires were soon doing it publicly," wrote Charles Washburn. "At home parties husbands were doing it, in back rooms, grocery clerks were doing it—in fact, everybody was doing it . . . it made a more lasting impression on a girl than carrying her picture in a watch."

While the Everleighs made special accommodations for European royalty, they also welcomed those from the opposite end of the social scale. Madams couldn't be part of the underworld and entirely exclude the underworld—thieves, kidnappers, burglars, safecrackers. The sisters knew, from their own history, that those who subverted the official rules often created better ones, that the right sorts of lies could become the bones of truth.

They believed there were two types of men, "depraved blue nosers and regular fellows." If a member of the former group lodged a complaint, Ada was summoned to smooth things over. "*There, there,*" she soothed, blaming the trouble on the heat, on an inferior grade of champagne, on a girl's lack of refinement—never on the client himself. Minna handled the bruisers, the visitors who would sooner throw a punch than notice the label on a bottle of wine. "What kind of a man are you?" she'd chide. "Brace up, pardner, you're not that sort, and we are sure you can lick any man in the house." Then she would convince him, discreetly but firmly, that he didn't want to. Minna's men, just like most of her butterflies, were products of the lower classes and also considered on a case-by-case basis.

Clarence Clay was one hoodlum who made the cut. A thief with impeccable manners, Clarence would dart down to the Cort Theater near Randolph Street, crack open a safe, pillage the contents, and return to the Everleigh Club as if he'd slipped away to use the bathroom. Minna always knew what Clarence was up to but never betrayed him. He was amiable, never hurt anyone, and spent plenty of money.

The Everleighs had to be mindful, too, of criminals among the ranks of their courtesans—some of whom weren't as harmless as Clarence. "Honesty is its own reward," Minna told her girls, and in her own interpretation of the concept, she meant her words sincerely. "Never have any black marks on your record. What would your future husband say if he suspected you had mistreated a man? Keep on being good girls, even if it hurts." The sporting life wasn't shameful, Minna emphasized, but some of the people attached to the business were. Vic Shaw, for one—no doubt livid that Prince Henry steered clear of *her* house during his tour—interfered with Everleigh courtesans at every opportunity, encouraging them into "vicious pathways."

A harlot named Daisy took such a detour, sneaking a notorious bank robber—one who had not been approved by Minna—through the Club's doors. He carried two fat satchels and checked them with a servant. Daisy escorted the robber upstairs to her boudoir and commented, casually, that she had never seen a thousand-dollar note before.

"Send for either one of the two satchels checked downstairs and I'll show you," said the thief, perched halfway up on his elbows. "They're filled with big bills."

Daisy pushed the intercom button in her room and asked a servant to fetch the bags. The servant surmised what was happening and decided this was a situation that called for Miss Minna. Together they climbed the stairs to Daisy's room.

Minna flung open the door and saw the thief prone on the bed. Daisy was removing a container of powder from her dresser. "Excuse Daisy for a few minutes, please," Minna said, sighing.

Daisy stepped out into the hallway.

"No knockout powders in this house, you know that," Minna whispered in the harlot's ear. "And I'll give you ten minutes to get your friend off the premises. We do not cater to his kind. He's nervous and suspicious. He'll go quietly. Tell him anything."

The thief took his satchels of cash and left. Daisy disappeared. She didn't report for work that week, or take dinner in the Pullman Buffet, or tell the servants which gowns to clean. Minna and Ada wondered, between themselves, if the girl had met a bad end with her bad man. They never heard from her again, but they did get news about the bank robber. He was found in a Levee alley, not far from the Everleigh Club, his skull lopsided, his forehead frayed open like the petals of a flower. A few hard blows from a hammer.

No one paid much attention to the murder, but the cops came to the Club and sat in the parlor. Could the sisters offer any insights into the case?

Minna shrugged. "I do not know," she said, "of any hardware dealers among our patrons."

The Everleighs were relieved that whatever transpired between Daisy and her robber had done so outside of the Club. No gossip for the sisters' enemies to gather and collect, or false footnotes to ink beside their venerable name. But two madams couldn't guard all four corners of every parlor, and Daisy wasn't the only harlot tempted by vicious pathways. Some butterflies were limited simply by their inferior bloodlines and coarse histories; Longfellow's poetry would never mean more than a stream of memorized words.

Myrtle, from Iowa, whose rear end was "of the slapping kind," as one man put it, was common in every way but her looks. She loved to show off her gun collection. Any john who was lucky enough to climb the stairs with her heard about which trinket she'd bought in which pawnshop, how much it had cost, how pretty she looked cocking it.

"I think I'd be the happiest girl in town if I could find a diamond-studded revolver," she told one wealthy customer, and he promptly had one made for her.

One night, Myrtle decided to have a showdown among her most devoted admirers. She ordered them to choose a gun from a secret drawer in her boudoir and then meet her downstairs, in the Gold Room.

Myrtle shook her bottom one last time, for emphasis, before lounging on a chaise.

"Fight over me, boys," she teased. "I love it."

Growls and threats and curses gathered in an angry chorus and filtered down the hallway, attracting Minna's attention. The men were a fumbling knot of gray silk and derby hats. Something gleamed silver, quick flashes that played hide-and-seek amid the vortex of bodies. Minna had to look twice to be sure. Revolvers—two, three, four, five of them.

Her body tightened; a muffled pounding filled her ears. She flung a hand and found the light switch and made the room black.

"Gentlemen," she cried into the dark, "you are in the most notorious whorehouse in America." This was no time to measure words. "How would it look to your relatives and friends to see your names splashed across the front pages tomorrow morning?"

After turning up the lights, she gathered Myrtle's guns one by one. The men bade one another a good evening and left, properly, through the front door.

A fter Myrtle's antics in the Gold Room, the sisters, understandably, became wary of guns. When trouble came, as the sisters feared it would, it didn't knock at the mahogany doors. Instead it waited, lying dormant inside heads and silent inside mouths until it passed, undetected, into the Club. And then it was too late.

On May 25, 1903, a balmy spring night, a woman named Helen Hahn went out driving with Larry Curtis, a bookmaker and investor. Earlier that day, Curtis had a streak of luck at the racetrack, winning $4,500, and Helen was helping him celebrate. A stenographer at the Chicago Opera House, she lived in a modest home on the northwest side, and was curious about the way life moved outside of her own.

"As we were returning toward town," Helen said, "I spoke of the fascination slumming had for me."

Curtis asked her if she might like to see some of the parlor houses along the Levee, perhaps a certain place in particular—"one of the most gorgeous establishments that ever prospered in a red-light district."

Within minutes they arrived at the Everleigh Club, and navigated clusters of laughing couples until they reached the Japanese Parlor. Corks popped in quick succession, a muted series of fireworks. Roving plumes of incense smelled by turns musky and sweet.

"I found myself in a close little room, luxuriously furnished," Helen later said, "with colored servants going softly to and fro. There was music coming through the palms which hid what I afterward learned was the ballroom, and everything was much different than I expected. . . . Suddenly the sliding door between the two rooms was thrown open and a man in evening dress entered."

Later, on the police record and in newspaper reports, the man's name would be given as William H. Robinson. Levee gossips whispered that he was from Chicago and the son of a well-known millionaire—so well-known that during his foray into the Levee district, he announced he was "traveling incognito" under a pseudonym.

Whatever his real name—and the Everleigh sisters, of course, would never say—Robinson had started the evening accompanied by a friend and two showgirls. After dinner, the foursome ventured to the Everleigh Club.

The sisters were busier than ever. Six months earlier, final renovations within the "New Annex" at 2133 were completed. The additional parlors, boudoirs, alcoves, music and dining rooms generated more traffic, but with it came a greater potential for trouble. Neither Minna nor Ada was near the Japanese Parlor when Robinson pulled open the sliding door. No one to suggest to Robinson that he shoot off firecrackers instead of his mouth, no one to remind Curtis that he wasn't the sort to respond.

"I was sitting at the piano," Helen said, "but just drumming with the soft pedal on, and not playing so it could be heard out of the room," when Robinson lurched in and said something "ugly" about her, so ugly that she turned her head and pretended not to hear.

"[Curtis] sprang up as the man entered," Helen continued, "but he was so startled by the man's remarks that he did not say a word for half a minute. The intruder started for me and I turned around. The first thing I saw was a revolver and an instant later it went off." Curtis looked at the gun in his hand as if he'd never seen it before, a strange and sudden appendage, smoke curling up from the barrel.

Elsewhere in the Everleigh Club, its proprietors froze in midstep and quieted in midsentence, and then rushed toward the aftermath of a sound they never wanted to hear.

Robinson lay on the floor of the Japanese Parlor, unconscious. A ring of blood bloomed above his heart. A young woman sat at the piano nearby, weeping meekly into her palms. The sisters arranged for Robinson's transportation to People's Hospital on Archer Avenue and told a group of courtesans to summon the 22nd Street police. Two detectives stopped Curtis from making a getaway in a closed carriage.

Robinson's heart was spared, but the bullet embedded between his ribs, possibly puncturing a lung. He was revived and his wounds dressed. The following morning, he told police he was "too weak" to proceed with prosecution.

It was a lucky break for the sisters, and not the only one. Scandal, especially one involving gunshots and a millionaire's son, could dull the shine of a high-class resort, dilute all their talk of decency and uplift. Their journalist friends reported the story—they had to—but kept the coverage shallow and benign. Salacious mentions of "wild midnight orgies" in a "resort of considerable notoriety" didn't hurt the situation, and the Everleighs were not asked to comment at all. Hinky Dink Kenna was a doll, furnishing $1,200 for Curtis's bond. The two showgirls who had accompanied Robinson were fired, and his friend vanished altogether. Helen Hahn threatened to kill herself until learning that Robinson survived, then returned to her quiet life as a stenographer. Her urge to go slumming was sated for good.

Robinson became incognito once again. "The police," the *Daily News* pointed out, "show little interest in the case."

But one person in particular was *very* interested. Ten houses north on Dearborn Street, Vic Shaw asked discreet questions and took careful notes, built a cache of possibility in her mind. She wouldn't confront the Everleighs directly—"Silence," she often said, "is louder than a brass band"—and she hoped her quiet skulked behind those sisters all day long, seeped into their dreams. Next time a millionaire playboy met with trouble in the Levee, Vic Shaw would collect all the words she had stored up, and set them into motion.

INVOCATION

Member of the Midnight Mission (left) and harlots.

When I see a reformer, I put a hand on my watch.
—Bathhouse John Coughlin

Late on a Friday afternoon in August 1904, the Reverend Ernest Albert Bell kissed his wife, Mary, and their seven children—his little "lambs"—good-bye, paid 5 cents, boarded the Oak Park elevated train near their home in Austin, a neighborhood on Chicago's western border, and settled in for the ride downtown. The car thundered and swayed, and the city seemed to dart away beneath him. Factories spat wisps of gauzy smoke, church steeples pierced clouds, tenements stretched and leaned. Past Halsted Street, which cut a thirty-mile swath from the north end of the city to the south, the skyscrapers began their steady forward march. At the Chicago River, the El sputtered and clanked to a stop as the bridge yawned open to let a ship pass.

Bell clutched his Bible, written in Greek, and checked his pocket for his leather diary. He carried it with him always. Its pages were crammed with daily itineraries, lists of expenses, and impromptu petitions: "Deal bountifully with thy servant, that I may live and keep thy word," read one entry. Another pleaded simply, "Lord, help me." Beside him on the seat rested his black case of stereoscopic views, the culmination of hours of research in the still quiet of the Crerar Library. The salary was $50 to $75 a month, barely enough to feed his family of nine, but tonight he would begin a new line of work. Tonight he would kneel in prayer with others who feared the dark parts of Chicago were conquering the light.

He was thirty-eight years old and in a place he never thought he'd be. It was prideful to think so, but he was meant to do great things. That much was clear at birth, when his mother named him after the British prince who became George V, and again at age ten, when he passed the entrance exam for Collingwood High School in Ontario, and even more so six years later, when his father, dying from tuberculosis, laid his frail hands on Bell and whispered, "My son, I am building mountains on your head."

That mountain, Bell believed, was to establish an Oxford in India—a university as great as the one in England. After moving to the United States at age sixteen and graduating from Allegheny College in Pennsylvania, he studied there himself, poring over John Henry Newman's *Apologia pro Vita Sua* and mastering Sanskrit and Tamil. At night, in their sparse room in a boardinghouse on St. Mary's Road, Bell confided his dream to his new bride, Mary Greer. "I believe," he wrote, "that no greater work can be done in India at the present time than the founding of a distinctly Christian university in the heart of this Empire."

The dream burrowed deeper in 1891, when he, Mary, and their infant daughter set sail from London on the steamship *Mombassa*. It stayed with him during three long years as he ministered to lepers and cripples, first in Jaffna, on the northernmost tip of Sri Lanka, and then in Jubbulpore in central India. When he returned to America and settled in Chicago, he received cables from fellow missionaries, still in Asia, about the terrible famine. He became secretary of the Chicago India Famine Relief Fund but believed money without education was a shortsighted approach.

He wrote letters to men like Andrew Carnegie and Stanley McCormick, sharing his vision, lamenting that "no rich American has yet made the sacrificial offering of himself for the work of God in foreign lands." But his efforts were met with indifference. Bell was distraught. He had alienated his old colleagues by switching denominations too many times and had no one to turn to. Was he really as willful and obstinate as they believed? Was God punishing him? He underlined his Bible until his fingers cramped. He barely lifted his pen from his diary:

"If it be thy will to build the University by my ministry, *Empower me*, if not deliver me," he wrote. "This day is the tenth anniversary of Thy commission to me, as I have believed, to build the Christian University of India. . . . O Lord, will India ever be more heathenish or more ignorant, or in more desperate need of being taught? . . . When will India more urgently need the University than now? What is gained by delay? Defer not for thine own sake. O my God."

He looked for omens in the most common gestures. He tithed. He literally beat his breasts. A chance encounter in 1897 opened a new direction. One night, as Bell left the Chicago Theological Seminary, a young woman approached. At first, he didn't understand her. Did she need change?

Something to eat? A simple prayer? She spoke again, brushed his arm, lowered her eyes in an unmistakable way. He stepped back, ran home to Mary and the children. An Oxford in India remained his obsession, but he couldn't drive the encounter entirely from his mind.

"It startled him," his oldest daughter, Olive Bell Daniels, later wrote. "That sin had never confronted him personally before. Now in the very shadow of the seminary buildings a harlot had tempted him."

It occurred to Bell, too, that he was a prophet, not a preacher. He could not say many things to the same audience, but the same thing to many. He contemplated holding nightly air sermons in the vice districts, but his duties as pastor of the Neighborhood Church in Maywood, a western suburb, sapped his energy. A few years later, in 1902, he left the congregation and preached occasionally before the brothels of Custom House Place. He learned the stories of those who had come before him—the great William T. Stead, Josephine Butler, Charlton Edholm—but only recently felt called to fight prostitution full-time. The Victorian policy of segregated vice districts should be revealed for the folly it was. "Good women are a thousand times safer where no such hells exist to manufacture degenerates," Bell said. "Men who consort with vile women lose their respect for all women."

Certainly he would have greater success drawing attention to Chicago's own third world streets—for now, at least—than those in faraway India. He would craft his message and repeat it night after night, until the city had little choice but to notice him and listen.

Bell exited the elevated platform and lost himself in the throngs of people ending their workday. The fading sun ducked behind skyscrapers, as if afraid of the city it shined upon. Vendors called out, advertising bags of peanuts for 5 cents, their salty warmth mingling with the stench of burning coal. After turning onto South Clark Street, he looked for number 441—the same building where, for thirty years, Madam Carrie Watson offered sin for sale.

After the madam retired, Bell's friends, a married couple, bought the bordello. In a delightful bit of irony, they transformed it into Beulah Home, a rescue mission for white slaves (Carrie Watson, who in her prime had donated liberally to churches and synagogues, might have enjoyed a good laugh herself). As soon as every brothel door in Custom House Place was padlocked and every fallen woman saved, Bell planned to move his base of operations southward, to the newer Levee district, where a house of ill but very great fame held shameful court on Dearborn Street.

B ell's "saints," as he called them, were already assembled, sitting in tidy rows of wooden chairs. Deaconesses Manley and Lucy Hall, white bonnets tied crisply under chins, bent over Bibles. There were the Reverend Melbourne Boynton and anticigarette crusader Lucy Page Gaston—an odd creature, birdlike and shifty, all angles and sharp contours. A young theological student presided over the wheezy piano. The rest sifted through hymnals and let their voices wander up and down the scales, preparing for the long night ahead.

At 10:00 p.m., after hours of prayers and hymn singing, Bell exited Beulah Home, his saints following in a somber queue behind him. Flies swarmed in the unstirred August heat, mosquitoes pricked their necks. Behind them, a line of darkened warehouses stretched the length of the street; before them, brash lights blazed over brothel doors. Bell nodded at Boynton, silently asking him to begin.

"The wages of sin is death," Boynton said, speaking over the jumble of electric pianos. "We earn wages. We sin and we earn death. But life is a gift. Eternal life is the free gift of God if we leave our sin and come to Him."

They joined hands, kneeling in the horse litter and gutter dirt of Custom House Place, and Bell's Midnight Mission at last came alive, took shape and drew breath.

MILLIONAIRE
PLAYBOY SHOT—
ACCIDENT OR MURDER?

A young Madam Vic Shaw.

The Everleighs, as always, were in the middle.
All blind alleys in a Levee mystery led to their door.

—CHARLES WASHBURN

On November 27, 1905, five days after he'd been shot, Chicago heard and spread the tragic news that thirty-seven-year-old Marshall Field Jr. had died. The cause given was paralysis of the bowels.

Coroner Peter M. Hoffman vowed that he would conduct an inquest and get to the bottom of the matter once and for all. On December 1, he addressed the jury. "I desire to make a statement for the protection of my office and for the sake of the family and friends of Mr. Field," he intoned. "Because of his position, his wealth, and his prominence many superfluous rumors have been circulated as to how this shooting occurred. I say superfluous, because, although they came from many sources, I have been unable to find any foundation for them. Since the day of the shooting I have spent days and nights hunting down the rumors and have found that there was no cause for their circulation."

The jury, immediately and unanimously, found that the shooting was indeed accidental. But by then a rush of questions and theories had tainted that conclusion, and would continue to do so even long after the war against the Levee. "When young Marshall Field was shot in a Chicago resort," wrote a former police reporter, "I was one of the coterie who wrote that artless story of how he came to his death while cleaning a revolver in the privacy of his own room. You see, the young man died, and some sort of explanation was necessary. . . . And so long as the Marshall Field interests continue to advertise extensively, no newspaper will publish the story."

In 1924, nineteen years after Marshall Field Jr.'s death, a former Chicago resident named Vera Scott was arrested in Los Angeles in connection with a series of frauds. A onetime chorus girl who had danced in productions of *Hanky Panky* and *Hoity Toity*, Scott told police she shot Marshall Junior by accident during a wild party at the Everleigh Club. The heir, she said, was bloodied and weak but coherent, and he insisted on going home alone in a taxi. Afterward, the elder Marshall Field paid her $20,000 to leave Chicago and never mention the incident again. A spokesman for Marshall Field & Company dismissed Scott's story as "the ravings of a drug-mad unfortunate."

A year later, a New York millionaire named W. E. D. Stokes took the stand in his high-profile divorce trial and testified at length about his efforts to prove that his estranged wife had once been an Everleigh Club girl. During an extensive tour of the old Levee district, he stopped by the Everleigh Club, still cared for by the sisters' longtime housekeeper, Etta Wright. After he showed his identification and offered proof that he'd spoken with Minna, Etta ushered him past the Club's darkened entrance and led him to the first parlor on the right. The maid pointed to a mantel upon which rested a delicate, ornate vase.

"If that vase could speak," she said, "it could tell who murdered Marshall Field Jr. It was in this room that he was murdered."

Stokes, still seeking information about his wife, next tracked down Monsieur Emond, the Everleighs' French dressmaker. Emond first told his visitor, "If you've come to inquire about that Marshall Field murder, I won't tell you," but later he showed Stokes photographs of two Everleigh harlots. One, a Spanish girl, was Camille, and the other had the last name of Hughes—he couldn't recall her first. Emond told Stokes that "those two girls were mixed up in the murder of Marshall Field" and then added, "If I had not been a fool then, I could have got $50,000 for opening my mouth."

Arthur Meeker, who was a young boy in 1905 and a neighbor of the Field family, was playing with his sister on Prairie Avenue that fateful day. Marshall Jr., he later wrote, "stopped to speak to our nurse before going off to get himself shot at the Everleigh Club—if it was the Everleigh Club." He added, "It's impossible to say now what happened. All we can be sure of is that the version the family gave out and forced the papers to print—that the accident occurred while he was cleaning a gun at home in preparation for a hunting trip—had no truth to it. That, again, is something that couldn't be put over today; the power of the press would prevent it." (A reporter for the *Tribune*, John Kelley, would conclude the opposite: "There was no foundation for such a malicious story, but it spread to all parts of the city, and even to distant states. If such a thing had occurred in the Everleigh bagnio all the millions which the young man's father possessed could not have kept the 'boarders' from blabbing.")

Chicago magazine revisited the controversy decades later. In a 1984 piece titled "Good Rumors Never Die," a Highland Park resident claims his grandfather Henry Korr was a partner in a real estate and tax management firm. One of Korr's clients was the estate of E. J. Lehmann, a Chicago merchant who had opened his department store, the Fair, on State Street in 1871. As managers of this estate, Korr doled out a staggering allowance of $1,000 a week to Lehmann's son, Ernest, a playboy who reportedly enjoyed slumming in the Levee district with fellow department store scion Marshall Field Jr.

On that night in November 1905, according to Korr family legend, Henry Korr's phone rang. It was Ernest Lehmann, calling from the Everleigh Club. "I'm in trouble," he said. "There's been a shooting." Korr was frantic, thinking that Ernest himself had been shot, and he raced to the brothel—only to find, upon his arrival, that the victim was actually Marshall Field Jr., whom they rushed to Mercy Hospital.

If Marshall Field Jr. did indeed go carousing in the Levee, his logical destination would have been the Everleigh Club. As Field family scholar John Tebbel noted, "It is not unlikely that Field Jr. was an occasional visitor at the Everleigh, where liquor, women and roulette wheels were equally obtainable. If so, he would have been in good company, with the respected sons of Chicago's most respectable families."

Minna and Ada, for their part, insisted thirty-one years after the shooting that the young heir had never been a guest of the Club, and said they'd hired a private investigator of their own to look into the tragedy (he ultimately espoused the same explanation offered by the Field family). Given their adherence to discretion, their steadfast refusal to comment one way or another on matters either sensitive or personal, it is curious that the sisters said anything at all.

But at the time, in 1905, they were relieved to hear the coroner's public dismissal of "superfluous rumors." Unlike the unfortunate incident in the Japanese Parlor two years earlier, this shooting was attached to a Chicago name so prominent that there was no chance of it fading away quietly on its own. Hopefully, all that talk about blood in their parlor—blood on their hands— would finally cease. The papers let the rumor go, even if gossipmongers across the country hadn't, and they believed the matter to be put to rest. But the incident caused the first true fracture in the sisters' empire—one that, as the voices around them amplified, would continue to separate and spread.

Pony Moore, owner of two Levee dives, the Turf Exchange Saloon and the Hotel De Moore resort, started life as a black man—or, as he'd grown accustomed to being called, a "coon"—but he believed he could alter his destiny. To that end, during the early 1890s, he sought the help of specialists, who slathered his face with lotions and creams, took his money, and advised him to keep coming back. He did go back, and also took the added step of dousing himself with bleach, again and again, until eventually there was a Rorschach test where his face used to be, splotches of brown skin lingering like stains on a favorite shirt.

Moore, who called himself "the Mayor of the Tenderloin," was a familiar character in the Levee, albeit one with less muscle than he projected. He had some influence over the black vote, and hoped his clout would increase as more of his people came to the city. And they *were* coming: Chicago's black population grew from 6,480 in 1880 to more than 50,000 in 1905, most of them migrating from the South in search of jobs in the new industrial economy. The *Chicago Defender,* a newspaper that railed against prejudice, published its first issue in May 1905 and quickly attained national prominence, portraying Chicago as a progressive city that welcomed its burgeoning black population. The new Chicagoans settled mostly in the South Side, where rents were cheapest, near railroad terminals and the Levee district. They found work in steel mills and factories but also learned to operate a much more important machine—the one that governed Chicago politics.

Pony Moore wasn't the first black vice lord. That honor belonged to John "Mushmouth" Johnson, who, after working as a waiter in the Palmer House, opened his own saloon and gambling house on State Street in the heart of Whiskey Row. Calling himself "the Negro Gambling King of Chicago," Mushmouth Johnson cultivated the usual arrangement with Bathhouse John and Hinky Dink, delivering votes and protection payments in exchange for legal immunity and the title "Negro political boss" in their First Ward. While not worthy of such a grand official designation, Pony Moore was a lieutenant of sorts, and even scored a measure of respectability by joining the National Negro Business League.

Because the Bath and Hinky Dink knew who he was and appreciated his efforts to rally the black vote, Moore kept his gambling saloon and resort operating despite flagrant violations of the law. But throughout 1905, the city administration, under increasing pressure from religious leaders and civic reformers, revoked the licenses of a number of disreputable establishments.

It started in January, when a twenty-two-year-old named Mabel Wright, pretty and middle-class, swallowed a mug of chloroform and died on the floor of the American Dance Hall. "Dance halls killed my child," Mabel's mother wept. "The dissipation and false glamour had warped her perspective of life."

The American was shuttered, but it wasn't enough. Ministers excoriated Mayor Carter Harrison II and his successor, Edward Dunne, for allowing saloons to remain open on the Sabbath day, and declared the Levee should be eliminated altogether. Dunne demurred—"When vice is segregated," he reasoned, "nobody need find it who does not go hunt for it"—but in September he did close Freiberg's Dance Hall, an edict that lasted only a month. And Pony Moore was the latest reform victim: Police Chief John Collins, citing a complaint from a "fine colored lady" and "honest Christian" whose husband bedded a "low white female strum" and bought home a "nameless disease," snatched the Turf Exchange Saloon's license in early November.

The Mayor of the Tenderloin was dejected. He craved social standing; he needed to be needed. Pony spent weeks drinking until the world seemed to operate in triplicate, admiring the framed news clips hanging behind his bar (including one that described the enormous diamond stud he wore secured to his collar with a silver bolt and small padlock) and various other collected artifacts that brought to mind a more auspicious time in his life.

And one night, shortly after Marshall Field Jr.'s death—when he was sure he'd been forgotten altogether—the phone rang.

It was Madam Vic Shaw. She cooed her words, calling him "chicken," and asked if they could schedule a meeting. She needed to see Pony Moore as soon as possible.

Pony Moore sat, at the madam's behest, in the parlor of her resort. The piano professor was on duty, playing Scott Joplin's "The Ragtime Dance" and lustily crooning the words:

I attended a ball last Thursday night, given by the dark town swells . . .
Ev'ry coon came out in full dress alright, and the girls were society belles . . .
The hall was illuminated by electric lights, it certainly was a sight to see;
So many colored folks there without a razor fight . . .
'Twas a great surprise to me.

Madam Shaw was a large woman, with a swelling, tidal-wave bosom that looked ready to break over her corset. Her head bore an elaborate hat impaled with a wayward gathering of feathers. She wagged her finger at Moore, and his head pulled forward as if attached to an invisible string.

Here's the plan, she said. He'd get $40,000 if he could somehow frame Minna Everleigh for the death of Marshall Field Jr.

Moore let the idea spin in his mind, and then he saw how it could be done. Easy. All he needed was an accomplice, and half the population of Chicago, given the right circumstances, would delight in assuming that role. Besides, one didn't get to be the Mayor without learning how to cut a deal.

O n Christmas Eve, Minna indulged in her afternoon routine, gathering an armful of newspapers and lounging in the Gold Room. Scanning the headlines, she was struck by an article in the early edition of the *Chicago American*. Headlined POLICE DOOM VICE CENTER OF CHICAGO, the report claimed that Mayor Dunne and Chief of Police Collins finally would shut every resort in Custom House Place by May 1, 1906—no exceptions. Collins estimated that the district's "undesirable population" was as high as one thousand and that every brothel held "unfortunate women" in captivity.

"It is the plague spot of Chicago," Collins said. "Hundreds of girls have been brought there under the pretense of giving them employment. Girls have been lured from as far as Paris under promise of work in millinery shops. In three months we have rescued eight girls from the place."

There was that white slavery chatter again. But Minna was sure of one thing: She and Ada could expect new neighbors in the Levee district. The more industrious Custom House Place madams and pimps and saloon keepers would rather move their dives than quit altogether.

Minna folded the paper, nervously fingering her butterfly pin. It would be a hectic day. They had errands to run, banknotes to deposit, and holiday festivities to plan. She started up the stairs to find Ada but stopped midway. Vanderpool Vanderpool was warming up already, hard at work at the golden piano, and the cheery strains of "I'm a Jonah Man" took over her thoughts. She knew that was Van's sly signal to the girls to watch their step around a certain trick:

My hard luck started when I was born, so the old folks say,
Dat same hard luck been my best friend up to dis ver-y day
When I was young my mamma's friends, to find a name they tried
They named me after my Papa, and the same day Papa died.

The phone rang meekly beneath the music. Once, twice . . . There was silence, and then a butler called out for a courtesan named Nellie.

Minna, still stalled on the middle of the stairs, listened for the sound of the harlot's footsteps. The last few times Nellie had hung up the phone, she'd slunk away stealthily, as if the words she'd said over the line were following her. Minna crept up the remaining steps and closed the door of her own suite. She lifted her receiver—all of the lines in the house were connected—so she could hear who Nellie's caller was and what he wanted.

A male voice was on the line, strange and muffled. He identified himself as Pony Moore and told Nellie she knew the deal. After she and another harlot named Phyllis made it to his place, and after they'd enjoyed a little party with him and his friend, they'd go to the police station and Nellie would tell the sergeant that she saw Minna Everleigh shoot Marshall Field Jr. And she thought making money on her back was easy. . . .

"Come right over," Pony Moore slurred. "Bring along Phyllis and the $20,000 is yours."

Minna listened to the pair exchange vulgar good-byes and hang up. Her mind was a tangle and she worked to unknot it, thought by thought. Within minutes Nellie and Phyllis approached, asking to be excused for an hour.

Minna pushed her lips into a smile. Sure, she said. Take the time out. The butler swung open one side of the double doors, letting in the wind's mournful whine, and the girls were gone.

Alone, panic conquered composure. Minna scrambled, as fast as heels would allow, to the phone and dialed Bryant, a sergeant and friend at the

22nd Street police station. Vic Shaw was behind this, she just knew it. The officer came on the line. Minna's words shot out in a dry rasp: Meet her on the corner of Dearborn. . . . Yes, now. Hurry—she was about to be framed for murder.

Dollops of icy slush covered the street. Cold seeped through her shoes, bit her toes, and the wind shoved her to one side. She skidded, catching herself. Bryant's arm slung around her, and for once in her life she let herself be led.

The officer opened the Turf Exchange's door for Minna, and she was greeted by a belch of stale air. Bottle shards covered the floor, broken chairs tilted against walls. Positively horrid. They made their way to a closed room at the back of the bar. Bryant gave no warning—just raised his boot, launched his leg, and kicked open the door.

Four of them—Pony, a strange black man, Nellie, and Phyllis—sprawled across a worn sofa. Nellie straddled Pony and Phyllis his friend, gowns and petticoats bunched at their waists, the men sorting through layers of ruffles and fluff.

Pony finally noticed Minna and stared, but his eyes couldn't seem to focus. She recognized him, that sadly comic face that looked like a mushroom gone half-rotten, and he stood up, pushing Nellie aside and yanking at his pants.

"What do you want, you murderer?" he asked Minna.

His wagging, bejeweled finger caught a shaft of sunlight.

Minna would not dignify Pony with a response, and she held out a hand—*Don't you dare*—when Nellie tried to force an embrace. The courtesan caught the madam's furious gaze and couldn't look again. When she spoke she addressed the floor.

"We didn't do anything, Miss Minna," she said. "Honestly, we didn't do anything. Pony said he would give us $20,000 if we said you did it."

Minna didn't respond, and Nellie couldn't lift her face. The madam could see the harlot rummaging through her junk drawer of a mind, discarding this excuse and considering that.

"I owe you some money," Nellie said finally, "and I thought this would be the easiest way to get it. I'm sorry, Miss Minna. I'm sorry. Take us home, please take us home."

Phyllis and Nellie were both forgiven and welcomed back into the

Club. The Everleighs had always believed in second chances, having benefited from a few themselves. Besides, a madam had to expect a whore to be seasoned with a dash of liar and a sprinkle of thief; the job, after all, required flattering a man until his money became hers. If they took a hard line on all Club rules all the time, the Everleigh butterfly would be an endangered species.

Vic Shaw was another matter, however. The sisters knew she had concocted the scheme with Pony Moore; the Levee was already electric with talk of consequences. Again, Minna and Ada let their silence suffice. It occurred to them that Shaw's rancor was provoked not only by the ways the sisters catered to their boys, but by how they pampered their girls.

A prostitute in other houses, including Vic Shaw's, never entertained celebrities and princes, but wrestled in the nude and was disciplined by a whipper. A girl at Madam Shaw's did not always get an honest examination from an honest doctor, and could never forget that the body that earned her a living might one day cause her death. She did not get to move with grace and dignity from parlor to parlor, talking and flattering as if those were her sole obligations, but instead was ordered into line, told to stand straight and look pretty while the men sifted through them all, one by one, like secondhand suits on a rack.

And Vic Shaw realized that no matter how fine her girls' faces or trim their figures, how elaborate their gowns or skilled their technique, the harlots in her house would never have or be the best. Madam Shaw's girls considered a slot on the Everleigh Club's waiting list a superior position to the one they currently held, and right now, for Minna and Ada, that was revenge enough.

The Custom House Place vice lords did not surrender their space quietly. Debts were forgiven, insults retracted, drinks poured on the house in every saloon. The Cadets' Protective Association met with the Friendly Friends. The procurers sat down with thieves. Crooked real estate agents lunched with unscrupulous lawyers. Dive keepers chatted from their doorways with the gaming room bosses. Pickpockets sifted through their loot to see what they might contribute. During the daytime hours there was a terrifying calm.

With $50,000 in hand, the vice lords approached Mayor Dunne and asked to stay in Custom House Place until September 1906, four months past the official deadline. Chief Collins unequivocally declined, and the strongest resorts of that district settled along the blocks around the Everleigh Club.

These red-light refugees weren't the only—or most troubling—new arrivals. Every night but Monday, a group marched slowly, deliberately, through the Levee, as if it could be uprooted, an inch at a time, by the movement of their feet. The sisters recognized the leader as the Reverend Ernest Albert Bell. They'd heard he cost madams in Custom House Place $250 per night, telling passersby that Chicago, with each passing day, exchanged a pint of morality for a quart of wicked.

There he was now, Minna saw, making his way down Dearborn Street, his followers streaming behind him. She pressed her face against the parlor window to get a better look.

Bell sliced the air with a hand, and the group halted as one in front of the Everleigh Club.

His alpaca coat was a bit tattered at the hem, but his wide mustache was neatly groomed, its upturned ends like quotation marks framing his lips. He began waving his arms, as if he could gather and hold the air, and his mouth moved, wrapped itself around silent words.

Minna wanted—needed—to know what they were.

She opened one door just enough to let in a sliver of the night. Behind her the parlor was alive with the rush of bodies and music and innuendo, but she focused her ear toward the street and let the message come to her.

"Throw out the lifeline to danger-fraught men," Bell called, shouting above the clamor, "sinking in anguish where you've never been."

His voice circled and cornered. Men scattered or dropped to their knees, hiding behind splayed hands.

After a long moment, Minna turned to greet another customer, another of her boys. Bell and his Bible brothers might have pressured the mayor and the police chief to close Custom House Place, but the Levee would never surrender and fall. Hinky Dink and Bathhouse John had too much invested in the district—especially in the Everleigh Club, now as famous as Chicago itself.

PART TWO

Flesh
and Bone,
Body and Soul

1906–1909

MIDNIGHT
TOIL AND PERIL

Ernest Bell, preaching in the Levee.

*The ministers thundered at them. Those Scarlet Sisters
got more mention than the other 4,998 women of
ill fame in the whole city.*

—RETIRED CHICAGO POLICE CAPTAIN, 1936

The demise of the historic Custom House Place district seemed
quick and decisive, a simple matter of God lowering a finger and
extinguishing the district with one touch. But Ernest Bell knew
that impression was a trick of time; since the Midnight Mission's inception,
they'd spent nearly every night kneeling before Custom House Place
brothels, praying for darkest Chicago.

Bell knew politics, too, had played a part in the fall of Custom House
Place. Mayor Edward Dunne was well aware that his predecessor, fellow
Democrat Carter Harrison II, had faltered during the 1905 election over al-
legations of bribes and graft. Chicagoans were still fuming over the deadly
Iroquois Theater fire of December 30, 1903, caused by unenforced codes.
Harrison appointed a special graft committee in an attempt to salvage his
reputation, but when reports surfaced that the mayor had ordered the com-
mittee to whitewash the investigation, he was forced, after eight years in
City Hall, to step aside for Dunne.

Dunne, eager to avoid the same fate so early in his own administration,
told his men to decline the brothel owners' offer of $50,000 cash for per-
mission to operate past May 1906.

"Mr. Bell," Chief Collins said later, looping a pale forearm around the
reverend's neck, "I told them, 'If you had Marshall Field's money you *cannot*
stay here after the first of May, as I am Chief of Police, so help me God!' "

If the Midnight Mission's next goal was the destruction of the South
Side Levee, it made sense to focus on its world-famous icon. Bell had heard
plenty about the Everleigh Club's bacchanalian parlors and perfumed
fountains, its bitter, spinster-sister madams. Behind those grand mahogany
doors women lost their husbands, mothers lost their sons, girls lost their in-

nocence and freedom—and men lost their lives. Those rumors that spread across Chicago and beyond had passed, too, through Bell's ears: Marshall Field Jr., the son of the city's merchant prince, a family man and father of three, was shot dead there. A personal tragedy, an international disgrace. Bell could harness and diffuse that attention so that Chicago, the second largest city in America, no longer made room for the sinners who were destroying it.

He himself had yet to step inside the Everleigh Club. But he knew for certain that his prayer vigils were not going unnoticed, that every night but Monday, Madam Minna broke away from her clientele long enough to peel back a heavy swag and stare directly at him, her lips pursed in a beguiling half smile that seemed at once a dare and a tacit suggestion that they were in on the same joke.

Early one morning, on the train ride home, Bell fished his little leather diary from his pocket. At the top of page thirty-eight, in between scrawled addresses and entreaties to the Lord, he printed two words: "ADA, MINNA."

Donations were increasing. Victor Lawson, publisher of the *Chicago Daily News* and a godly man, gave $50 to the Midnight Mission, and Bell promptly sent a note. "Many thanks," he wrote. "Nothing I saw in India so nauseated me as the abominations of that street. A repentant man told me that he had seen enough there to make the stones vomit." Lawson contributed another $400.

After their usual warm-up, reciting prayers and reading scripture, Bell and his saints gathered their Bibles and pamphlets. One, titled "Sin Gone to Seed," featured a photograph of a man suffering from advanced syphilitic infection. His head—hairless, bearing footprint-shaped holes that sank deep into his skull—looked like a well-traveled patch of wet sand. Such a jarring image might succeed where words and prayers failed. The study of social hygiene was advancing rapidly; recently, a German scientist had developed a test to detect *Treponema pallidum,* the bacterium that caused syphilis. Bell believed it was every reformer's job to push beyond foolish Victorian conventions, to make sexual diseases an acceptable topic for polite society. Men must understand that harlots were responsible for more than 25 percent of surgical operations on good women, for the blindness of hundreds of babies.

They set out for the walk, a mile and a half south, stepping around manure and vomit and urine and puddles of beer, singing hymns along the way. Bell listened for the cries of prostitutes, some of them younger than his own daughters, being whipped behind barred windows and doors.

"Imagine yourself," Bell wrote, "in this awful district with Satan and all his cohorts let loose, seemingly. The cursing of men and the screeching of dope-filled and half drunken women; the banging of electrical pianos; the honking of autos; the throngs of young men going like mad into these houses of horror, where the air is reeking with the fumes of dope and tobacco and millions of germs; where women are in their scanty attire with painted faces and colored and false hair, with their honeyed words and foolish prattling, calling and alluring men into their fearful clutches and then to awful sin and death perhaps!"

When they arrived on South Dearborn Street, the Everleigh Club before them, he halted and thrust out his arm. The hot August wind kicked up scraps of trash. Music spilled from open windows. Swarms of men ducked behind the brims of their derbies, skittered into side alleys. Dozens more stopped and turned to Bell, faces open and curious.

Bell placed his wooden box six feet from the curb and mounted it. Now he stood a foot taller than the mob. Reverend Boynton herded several saints closer to the resort's front doors. A few feet away, Lucy Page Gaston lifted her arms skyward, the long full sleeves of her blouse drooping like wings.

Bell cleared his throat. He was on.

"Young men, where are your heads?" he bellowed. He touched his own head for emphasis.

A laugh bubbled up in the crowd. Bell pressed on.

"One night I dreamed that I saw a young man stepping carelessly on and off a railway track, near a curve around which the express would come thundering and screaming at any moment. Whether on the track or off it, the young man was indifferent to danger and wanton in his movements. But as I looked I saw in my dream that there was nothing whatever above his coat collar—he had no head."

Again laughter, longer this time. Bell paused, rolled the end of his mustache between two fingers, and took a breath. A difficult group, but he'd had them before.

"That explained his recklessness," he called. "He was void of understanding."

No laughs this time, but a low, gathering murmur. Bell raised his Bible, the pages facing the crowd.

"The word of God which says, 'Void of understanding they gather by troops at the harlots' houses not knowing that the dead are there and her guests are in the depths of hell.' "

There—there she was. A velvet curtain swept across a wide window and the Everleigh madam's face appeared, tentative at first, feature by feature, forehead then nose and then that mouth, again pursed in an expression at once impish and imperious. The streetlights picked up glints from the knot of diamonds at her throat. Shadows and shapes moved behind her, bodies twirling in dance, glasses rising.

And there he was again. Minna had grown used to the "visiting firemen," as she called them privately to Ada. They'd been out there nearly every night since the Marshall Field debacle in November 1905, almost a year now, and she'd stopped telling herself their antics had nothing to do with the Club. But she and Ada didn't understand the scrutiny—why single out the only madams on the line who wanted to make the profession as honorable as it could be?

"Truthfully," she said, "we were open to offers. We believed we could have adjusted an age-old problem if given half the chance to supervise its operation. We weren't consulted. In fact, we were never consulted about anything constructive. It was a personal crusade against us. We were touted as the forces of evil invading a God-fearing community to lure the innocent to perdition. Give the weeds a chance and destroy the flowers seemed to be the hymn—hallelujah!"

Still, no harm done—none yet, anyway. Persistence didn't necessarily evolve into success, and who knew, they might soon tire of their hellfire hollering and go somewhere else. Everleigh Club customers politely ignored the entreaties, discarded those grotesque pamphlets. Sometimes, if the mob grew too thick and unruly, clients were ushered in, discreetly, through a back door. No complaints about slower traffic here, that night included.

Behind her now, talking her ear off in between indulgent swallows of champagne, was one Vernon Shaw Kennedy, director of the Hammond, Whiting & East Chicago Electric Company and the South Chicago City Railway Company, and formerly "interested" in the Kennedy Biscuit Company. He enjoyed spending time in his office suite at the First National Bank Building or at the prestigious Chicago Athletic Club or playing in golf tournaments or trolling around California or vacationing in Africa (he just returned from a thirteen-month safari, in fact, had the madam ever been?)—anywhere, it seemed, but with his wife of seventeen years, Grace Cummings Shaw Kennedy, a "large holder" of First National Bank stock and proud owner of "one of the finest collections of gems in the city" (but surely not as fine as the madam's, he must say).

His wife would be filing for divorce soon, he was sure of it, and he felt bad about the four children. But really, they'd been "practically separated" for the past nine years and had always strained to be pleasant in front of the children and the servants, so it should be painless. Certainly Grace was aware of his, shall he say, *indiscretions;* a number of her friends even told her they no longer wanted to visit at the house because he'd made a few "improper proposals" to them. Tearfully at first, then matter-of-factly, she'd confronted him. In one case, deciding it was time, he'd admitted to an affair. Liberating. And when his wife invited a young woman to board at their Michigan Avenue mansion for a few weeks (perhaps as bait?), he seduced her—loudly—at 3:00 a.m., behind a tapestry hanging near the stairway. His wife, perched on the middle steps, listened the entire time. . . .

And so on and so forth. Edmund, would you be a dear and get Mr. Kennedy another champagne?

It appeared Mr. Kennedy was right about one thing—his wife would likely be filing for divorce. The Reverend Bell wasn't the only one peering into the Everleigh Club windows that night. After six years, a madam gets to know all her city's detectives, even the private kind, and one, a Mr. J. G. Gunderloch, had been stationed outside the Club since at least 8:00 p.m. He might as well lie down and take a nap on Dearborn Street—at the rate Mr. Kennedy was going, he'd be at the Club until sunrise, at least. She had to laugh: Those visiting firemen might have stamina, but they never outlasted the customers.

Bell kept the Bible aloft and reached with his right hand into the pocket of his trousers, fishing out a silver dollar.

"You bring your money with the burning name of God upon it"—here Bell raised the coin—"to buy the abominations of Sodom."

He stood with each arm lifted and taut, like Christ nailed to the cross, and fell silent. Let his words sink in. He heard harsh whispering around him, voices that seemed to scratch the air. To one side, through a sliver of vision—he did not want to disturb his stance by turning his head—he saw a small commotion, a burst of energy, and then an arm pulling back like the band of a slingshot. A small object whizzed and spun, hurtling toward him, and made solid contact with the side of his head.

An egg.

The yolk and muck settled into his hair and trickled down. Streaks traced the curves of his ear, wet the stiff strands of his mustache. From behind, another egg slapped his neck, dripped inside his collar, sluiced through the hollow of his back.

He thought of Mary, staring out their front window, exhausted but sleepless, waiting for the sound of his steps, the shadow of his waving hand.

Reciting any passage that came to him, out of order and unrelated, he crafted a patchwork sermon:

"Thus saith the Lord, 'I have no pleasure in the death of the wicked, but let the wicked turn from his evil way and live;

" 'From all your filthiness I will cleanse you';

"All we like sheep have gone astray; we have turned everyone his own way; and the Lord hath laid on him the iniquity of us all."

Without warning, his sight went hazy. Bell stepped from his box, and the crowd divided to form a slim passageway. Entering the alley between Ed Weiss's and the Everleigh Club, the reverend fell to his knees and let his face rest in his palms. He needed to pause a moment, to "tap the resources of God."

Rested, he pulled himself up and wiped the streaks of egg from his face. Hours of work still stretched before him—he had to pace himself to last until 3:00 a.m. He glanced back at 2131–2133 Dearborn Street, into the windows arched like half-moons, and this time they were empty.

ULTRA DÉCOLLETÉ
AND OTHER EVILS

Ike Bloom.

In Chicago our God lurks everywhere.
In the elevated train's husky roar . . . in the
humid mists of summer by the lake.
—Father Andrew Greeley

The new Abraham Lincoln Center, designed by Frank Lloyd Wright for his uncle, a reverend, was a brown rectangle of a building on Oakwood Boulevard, boxy windows dotting its façade like rows of gritted teeth. Early in the afternoon on October 9, 1906, more than 150 purity workers from all over the country—Philadelphia and New York, St. Louis and California—streamed into the auditorium. Bell and his saints had been waiting for this, the National Purity Congress, for months, especially since Chicago was once again playing host. They wandered through the crowd, connecting names with faces, learning about the red-light districts in other cities and the work being done to stop them. In turn, the visitors asked about Chicago—they'd heard so much about the Levee—and observed that the Lincoln Center was the ideal venue for a discussion about white slavery.

Mayor Dunne gave a welcoming address, and delegates debated resolutions against numerous "evils," including "any form of state, local, or police regulation of vice which may be in any way regarded as a permit" and "ultra décolleté." There was a scheduled debate between renowned anti-vice crusader Anthony Comstock and his archnemesis, Theodore Schroeder of the Free Speech League of New York, but the former fell ill and never showed. Schroeder took full advantage of the empty podium beside him, ridiculing Comstock's "hobbies" and arguing that "what is deemed objectionable is always a personal matter."

The Reverend John Halcom Shaw, pastor of the Second Presbyterian Church, illuminated the troubling conditions in Chicago.

"If there is one person to be pitied more than another in this great city," Shaw thundered, "it is the boarding house young woman. She comes from

Dakota or Oklahoma to make her living. If she is fortunate she gets into a big shop at $8 or $9 a week. If less fortunate, she gets less."

Shaw paused, wiped his brow. Bell leaned forward. The auditorium was silent as the reverend closed in on a dreadful truth.

"No young woman," Shaw continued, "can live in this city as she ought on that amount of money. She takes a hall bedroom in an inferior house and eats at cheap cafes. Instantly she is assaulted by fierce temptations—one financial and the other social. She must have the money and she craves the society of the other sex to which she is justly entitled. Many times she is doomed."

But the most powerful speaker, in Bell's opinion, was the Reverend Sidney C. Kendall, who was terminally ill and would die within the year.

"[Kendall's] whole soul was torn and bleeding over the shame of making commerce of women," Bell wrote. "He told us of the crimes of the French traders. . . . Some of his spirit remained with a few of us in Chicago and we could not rest until some effort was made here to rid us of the shame of slavery in the twentieth century under the flag of the free."

B. S. Steadwell, whose wife had been mugged in Chicago five years earlier, agreed. Kendall, he wrote, "so aroused the friends of the Federation in Chicago that they immediately organized for active warfare against the traffic, and since that time the real activities against the White Slave Trade in America have centered in Chicago."

After the third and final day of the conference, Bell, Sidney Kendall, and about two dozen fellow delegates journeyed to the Levee district, stopping at the 22nd Street station to persuade two officers to accompany them. The entire group wandered into a dive on Armour Avenue, coughing in the smoky-dank air.

A group of Japanese courtesans lounged at a table in the front room, bare legs tucked into high heels, dainty fingers curled around glasses of beer. The missionary women huddled behind their hoods, clutching Bibles and prayer tracts to their chests.

For a long, clear moment, the two groups of women exchanged stares.

One missionary stepped forward and tapped a harlot's shoulder. "Are you a Christian?" she asked.

Behind her, another purity worker swayed, her face pale, eyes roving and unfocused.

The harlot turned, confused. "Why—er—wot you want to know?" she stuttered.

"I mean, do you know God?" the missionary persisted.

The harlot's face crumpled. "O, you mean that," she spat. "How'd you get in here?"

The missionary was poised to answer when there was a loud *thunk* from behind.

Her colleague, poor thing, had fainted.

One of the cops suggested they venture around the corner to an adjacent, cramped room awash in a sickly bright light. A professor slapped piano keys. The air strummed and vibrated, glasses hopped on tables. A madam appeared at the doorway, skirt skimming the tops of her thighs.

"Come on in, boys," she called, and the purity workers crept forward.

A harlot appeared and leaned against the wall, rolling a cigarette between two fingers.

Bell watched as the Reverend S. H. Flower approached the girl with tiptoed caution, as if trying to coax a cornered animal. He offered a flyer emblazoned with biblical quotations and facts about venereal disease.

"Don't you think," he said, not unkindly, "that you could do better than this?"

Fixing her eyes on the reverend, the harlot dipped a hand into the short, frilly sleeve of her dress and produced a match. She lit her cigarette and sucked on the end for three exaggerated breaths, lips clenching and releasing. Leaning forward, she blew a fragrant cloud of smoke directly into the reverend's face.

The revelers howled.

One reverend hurried over to the piano professor.

"Would there be any objection," he shouted over the music, "to our conducting a meeting in here?"

The professor lifted his face but kept playing. "I don't own the ranch," he said, not missing a note, "but I'm afraid it might hurt business. You see, they like ragtime and light talk better here."

He turned back to his piano and struck up "Her Locks Were Like the Raven's." Retreating out the door, the missionaries began a warbled rendition of "At the Cross." One tune overtook the other, a discordant tumble of notes and words trailing them down the street.

They ended up at Freiberg's Dance Hall at 22nd and Wabash, run by that Levee leader Bell had heard so much about, Ike Bloom. The visiting reverend, eager to save face, stepped forward and rang the bell. Flower would handle this Bloom.

Bloom himself appeared, resplendent in a bright suit, wispy scraps of hair sprouting from his damp forehead. It was twenty-seven degrees outside, accented by a stubborn wind, but blistering inside the resort. He kept a hand stuffed deep in his pocket, jiggling what sounded like coins.

Reverend Flower begged entry several times and Bloom finally relented, swinging open the door and laughing, to himself, at their wide eyes and funereal dress. Thirty couples sat at wood tables, guzzling mugs of beer. The orchestra, gathered to the side of the bar, played a deafening waltz. Bell and his group pushed forward, stepping over outstretched legs. A hush spread slowly, snuffing one voice at a time, until the room was utterly silent.

The missionaries dispersed, dropping leaflets on tables and reciting statistics about dance halls. Didn't they hear about Mabel Wright, who had died in a place like this? About countless girls who sipped drugged champagne and woke up not knowing who they were?

The orchestra jumped to life again, cymbals smashing, trumpets belching. Reverend Flower found Ike Bloom. When the orchestra finished this tune, he asked, might his party sing a hymn, just one brief paean to the Lord?

The Levee leader shrugged. "Go ahead," he said. "Do what you like, but don't sing more than one."

Reverend Flower nodded. When the room quieted again, he began to sing "Washed in the Blood of the Lamb":

Are you washed in the blood?
In the soul-cleansing blood of the lamb?
Are your garments spotless? Are they white as snow?
Are you washed in the blood of the lamb?

The orchestra immediately offered a musical retort:

When you hear that the preachin' does begin
Bend down low for to drive away your sin
And when you get religion, you want to shout and sing
There'll be a hot time in the old town tonight, my baby. . . .

Bloom held up a hand. "None of that," he said. "Play the hymn for them!"

The musicians obeyed, dragging reluctant fingers across instruments, and the tune hovered over the crowd, quieting it down. Bell took the temperature of the moment, felt its power hot inside him, and believed that at least one person would walk out of Freiberg's anew with the spirit of the Lord.

He overheard E. M. Whittemore of the Door of Hope mission in New York call for Bloom's attention.

"Thank you, sir," she said, clasping her hands. "I wish you had more of this."

Bloom smiled, patted her on the shoulder. "My good woman," he said, "we don't agree in some things, but you do lots of good, sure."

He paused, and the workers leaned in to listen.

"You could," he added, "do a whole lot more somewhere else, though."

With a violent jangle of his pocket change, Bloom showed his visitors out.

A t last, just as Bell trusted he would, God sent him a sign that the Christian University in India remained darkened and locked inside him for good reason—the tragedy of a girl named Agnes. As Bell would later recount, Agnes's story found him on the morning of January 30, 1907, when he was visiting Mr. Richards, head of Beulah Home.

"We have an interesting case," Richards said. "I had to get the police to rescue a girl from a resort because the madam refused to surrender the girl to her own mother and stepfather. The madam said the girl owed twenty dollars for clothes."

"To whom did she say that?" Bell asked.

"To all of us, the mother and father and to me."

Bell spoke slowly, ironing the excitement from his voice—this might turn out to be nothing. "Did the girl want to leave?"

Richards nodded. "She had tried every way to escape and finally got a letter out to her parents. They went for her and were refused. They came for me. We finally had to get the police."

"Richards," Bell said, jumping up from his seat, "that's a case we can take into court with three good witnesses if the parents will testify. Where are they?"

The following afternoon, at the Harrison Street court of Judge John Newcomer, Bell watched Agnes tell her story and name her white slavers. The prosecutor was brilliant, cornering witnesses with his questions, laying them down one at a time, like slabs of stone, higher and thicker until there was no room to move.

Madam Panzy Williams was convicted, her picture taken and measurements recorded. Bell visited her in her cell.

"God loves your soul," he said, "but hates your devilish business."

He hung a portrait of Abraham Lincoln in his Midnight Mission office. Like the great president, Bell could be an emancipator, saving white slaves in both body and soul. All madams in the Levee, he decided, should hear the message he spoke to Panzy Williams. Next week, he and Boynton and Lucy Hall would knock on the door of every brothel, including the Everleigh Club.

THE
BRILLIANT ENTRANCE
TO HELL ITSELF

Hallway to the entrance of 2133, the Everleigh Club.

*The next worst thing to being a fanatic is
to be afraid of being one.*
—Reverend Ernest Albert Bell

Minna was not at all surprised when, during the first week of February 1907, the Reverend Ernest Bell, another preacher, a deaconess, and a detective from the 22nd Street station appeared on the doorstep of the Everleigh Club. Scornful talk about the pious convoy (the captain notwithstanding) had swirled through the Levee district, how they came armed with pamphlets and gory statistics about babies born blind from syphilis and innocent wives rotting away from within. Many of the madams and dive keepers humored the missionaries, some shut the door in their faces, others shooed them away. Minna tried a different approach—why not take a page from the book they claimed to live by? Do unto others and all that. Perhaps they might purge their brains of the Sodom and Gomorrah platitudes long enough to see that the sisters, too, stood for decency and uplift.

So she was polite and gracious, inviting them in as if they were long-lost friends or paying customers, looking past the slush and muck that seeped from their shoes into the Oriental rug. Up close, the Reverend Bell was all twitching nerves, his hand fluttering as he introduced the group and stated their purpose. The policeman stood behind, winking and shrugging at Minna in silent empathy, as if to apologize that his job required him to lock arms, even loosely, with the law.

It was late in the afternoon, the sun just beginning its descent, and the girls were in various stages of preparation. Some lingered upstairs, fastening clasps on chokers, applying Newbro's Herpicide to bring out the gloss in their hair. The rest, dressed and ready, mingled in the front parlor. Curious, they crowded closer to get a look at these somber men in frosted wool, this woman with her face tucked, like the center of a daisy, deep inside a flared bonnet.

Minna didn't mind letting them listen in. See if they could be persuaded to give up their $100-plus weekly earnings and gourmet meals in exchange for the glory of Jesus. "These [mission workers] were permitted to visit the brothel in the afternoon," Herbert Asbury wrote, "distribute their tracts, pray for the souls of the harlots, and endeavor to reform them. There is no record that any ever succeeded."

The visitors distributed leaflets to Minna and each courtesan. There was silence as they read:

IT IS A PENITENTIARY OFFENSE
TO DETAIN ANY WOMAN IN A HOUSE OF PROSTITUTION
AGAINST HER WILL
No "white slave" need remain in slavery in this State of Abraham Lincoln who
made the black slaves free. "For freedom did Christ set us free. Be not entangled
again with the yoke of bondage," which is the yoke of sin and evil habit.

Minna scanned the page and waited for the girls' reactions.

"Theologians in the inspiration of religious zeal appeared at the Ever-leigh Club there to kneel before the satin gowned inmates, and beg them in the name of the Saviour to abandon a life of shame," wrote Edgar Lee Masters. "The girls laughed in their faces; or else stared at them if they chanced to have some comprehension of the vast hypocrisy that reigned in Chicago. For nearly everything was a lie in the life of the city."

Now, at the first hiccup of laughter Minna turned, beamed a look. She would have none of that—not this first time, anyway. She explained gra-ciously, patiently, that the Everleigh Club was free from disease, that Dr. Maurice Rosenberg examined the girls regularly, that neither she nor Ada would tolerate anything approaching violence, that drugs were forbidden and drunks tossed out, that guests were never robbed nor rolled, and that there was actually a waiting list of girls, spanning the continental United States, eager to join their house. No captives here, Reverends. Sure, they were permitted to come back anytime; she and Ada would be happy to talk further, even give them a grand tour.

"The girls may have been vulgar," Minna allowed, "but they weren't hypocrites. They knew what kind of lives they were leading. The visiting firemen never got our slant."

She bade the crusaders good night, wondered if they would rearrange her words to create a story she'd never told.

B ell told the story often: The white slavery problem wasn't limited to the slums and dives and Bed Bug Row. No, it existed even in the Everleigh Club, the place that brought the Levee international fame, run by those "two sisters from Virginia, hard as steel," who "had suffered at the hands of the world and vowed to get from the world all it would pay." One night in February, right after Madam Panzy Williams was convicted of enslaving a girl named Agnes, he, Reverend Boynton, Deaconess Lucy Hall, and a detective visited the Club. There, finally, the madam of the house he'd preached in front of nearly every night for the past three years stood before him, with that unsettling smile that implied she knew Bell's next thought before he even formed it. She and several of her white slaves accepted copies of the Criminal Code of Illinois, and Bell waited, nervous, as they read.

"It was in this canvass that we visited the most infamous and notorious house in the West," Boynton wrote. "The madam of this particular house told us, in the presence of the policeman, that she had paid $160.00 each for two girls that had been sent her from the South. She also explained how safe her house was from violence and how free from disease, and yet, before our conversation ceased she admitted that she had placed 105 girls in a neighboring Christian hospital for treatment."

Bell echoed Boynton's version. "A Virginia woman," he wrote, "keeper of a notorious resort, patronized by millionaires, told Pastor Boynton, Deaconess Hall and myself that she had bought two women from a woman in New Orleans for $160 each. She told this in ordinary conversation and spoke of the transaction as lightly as a man would speak of buying horses or cows."

Bell's tales about the Levee canvassing awakened a few of the sleeping. The nightly open-air sermons got a bit more crowded. Some saints brought their children, girls barely thirteen years old, little palms lifted skyward as they marched past cackling madams and leering pimps. "There's enough of them little ones already on the road," one madam protested, "without bringing them good girls into this hole."

The British evangelist Gypsy Smith, who arrived in Chicago during the Panzy Williams trial, issued a final plea at February's close to 1,200 Christians. Each one of them, Smith challenged, should "draw a chalk line about himself and have a revival inside the circle" and work to quell the city's "immoral atmosphere that is growing into a whirlwind."

"Yes, yes," the crowd cried back, and Gypsy Smith vowed to return to Chicago in two years.

But these fitful bursts of progress weren't enough. The First Ward, the heart of Chicago's culture and commerce, was still run by the most crooked aldermen. The police department still favored segregating the Levee district rather than wiping it out altogether.

"As long as this evil must of necessity exist in every large city," Police Inspector John Wheeler had said recently, much to Bell's dismay, "I see no way to put a stop to it here except to get all of the women together in some large inclosure and apply the sulphur method of extermination, such as is adopted to destroy unclaimed and worthless dogs at the pound."

And every day, more of America's daughters were being tricked out of their own lives and lured into ruin. Bell found the numbers terrifying. In 1880, only 3,800 women found themselves adrift in Chicago, seeking work during the day and danger at night; now, there were nearly 31,500 collecting paychecks in the city—a growth rate more than three times that of the national average. Nothing was safe here for a girl on her own. Not the train stations or streetcars, the chop suey houses or ice-cream parlors, the dance halls or saloons or the streets that angled past them, the 10-cent vaudeville houses or late night boat rides on Lake Michigan, the department stores or wine rooms or penny arcades, the theatrical or employment agencies, the nickel theaters or amusement parks or automobile rides with a boy she thinks she knows.

Bell knew the battle needed to accelerate, to gain the urgency of an onrushing train, to overcome anyone who refused to climb on.

He thought often of Agnes's rescue and the conviction of Madam Panzy Williams. Lord, he prayed, send another thunderbolt to alarm the people of Chicago.

The Lord would soon hear Bell and answer him, sending a thunderbolt in the shape of a lawyer.

THE TRAGEDY
OF MONA MARSHALL

Mona Marshall, 1907.

There is not a life that this social evil does not menace.
There is not a daughter, or a sister,
who may not be in danger.

—CLIFFORD ROE

On the evening of May 25, 1907, Clifford Griffith Roe sat alone in his office on the second floor of the Criminal Court Building, a steady drizzle pattering a Morse code against the windows behind him. The view overlooked the jail where, in 1887, two hundred spectators watched as four men were hanged in the aftermath of the Haymarket anarchists trial. Roe was twelve years old at the time, an obstreperous presence in his Chicago public school classroom, and had already determined that he would be either a preacher or a lawyer. Now, weeks shy of his thirty-second birthday, he was about to blend the two professions more successfully and sensationally than even his boundless imagination could have dreamed.

That it was a Saturday night did not distract him from the work at hand, scouring law books and scribbling notations of upcoming cases. A Cook County assistant state's attorney for just five months, he was eager to impress his bosses. Let other young men of his age flit about town, escorting dates to the Chicago Opera House and showing off new $2,000 Cadillac Model G's in the dense State Street traffic. "Mr. Roe," noted one reporter, "takes life far too seriously to be a shirker."

His telephone rang, breaking into his thoughts. (Later, in a customary flourish of language, he would recall it ringing "imperatively.") He hurried to the receiver and said his name. A familiar voice barked over the line.

"This is Captain McCann," it said. "There is a girl down here who claims she has been sold as a white slave."

Edward McCann had Roe's rapt attention. The prosecutor had scored a conviction against Madam Panzy Williams—the pandering case brought to court by the Reverend Ernest Bell—but there hadn't been a single mention of that victory in the newspapers.

The captain, Roe knew, had just been named to his post. A graft investigation in April revealed that police, after taking out hundreds of warrants against brothel keepers, never made any arrests or returned the warrants to court. In reaction, reform-minded Chicagoans voted Mayor Edward Dunne out of office and elected Republican Fred Busse, who cleared out the police department as a show of good faith. Mayor Busse's new police captain vowed to keep a hard eye on the Levee.

"Can you come down the first thing in the morning and investigate?" McCann asked.

"I shall be there."

Chicago's youngest assistant state's attorney replaced the receiver, pulled on his black cutaway frock coat, and headed to the Drexel Avenue home he shared with Henrietta, his mother.

Henrietta and Roe's father, George, were natives of Indiana and of mixed Scottish, English, Welsh, and Irish descent, a lineage Roe would boast of throughout his life. The family moved to Chicago when he was three, where George, a "useful and upright citizen," dealt in real estate, joined the Disciples of Christ Church and the Republican Party, and instilled within his only son the idea that the world would one day need him. Roe grew up believing it, and as soon as he was able to talk he realized talking was his gift. Words were the only things he trusted; their logic was his currency.

"The day of Mr. Roe's birth he made a speech on the wrongs of infants," the *Tribune* wrote, "and he has continued talking on the rights or wrongs of some one or other ever since. He has ideas of his own and he has made up his mind that he is going to let the world know about them . . . he had one great ally—he was always sure of himself."

After earning undergraduate and law degrees at the University of Michigan, Roe returned to Chicago in 1902, shortly after the death of his father. He made partner in a major law firm before he turned thirty. Arguing against the best trial lawyers in the city, Roe caught the attention of the head state's attorney, who offered him a job in December 1906 and assigned him to the Harrison Street station.

"Not a marrying man," Roe immersed himself in his new position. His few indulgences included the occasional baseball game—all of Chicago was baseball crazy these days, since the White Sox and Cubs faced off in the 1906 World Series—and creative writing. He would, in fact, soon begin work on a play titled *The Prosecutor*.

The star of the play—the prosecutor—was named Clinton Randolph, and he was a "tall, broad-shouldered, powerful-looking man, clean-shaven, with a strong jaw, and dark hair slightly sprinkled with gray on the temples . . . not too young, and yet not even middle-aged, but with a face that shows experience and ripe judgment and great strength of character."

Clinton Randolph, just like his real-life doppelgänger, always got his man.

On Monday morning, May 27, the prosecutor boarded a streetcar near his office and settled in for the ride, about a mile south, to the Harrison Street police station. Blocking out the rush-hour chaos—the grumpy putt-putting of automobiles, the refrains of the street peddlers, the ceaseless clopping of hooves—he replayed yesterday's interview with Mona Marshall, the white slave who would make his career.

Mona told Roe she worked behind the ribbon counter at Marshall Field's department store. One day in March, a tall young blond man approached her. He touched Mona's hand, regarded her with a direct blue gaze, asked her if she would accompany him to a play. His name was Harry Balding, and he seemed, Mona said, the "best and dearest fellow in the world." Until the following night, that is, when he took her to the Prima Dance Hall. Her wine tasted bitter, but she sipped it anyway. Her speech slurred, the room spun, her eyes lost hold of the light.

Mona awakened in the Follansbee flats on Wabash Avenue, surrounded by Harry and several strange men. She knew, from the way they looked at her, that nothing was what it had been before.

How could she return home after being away all night, her honor ruined? She began to cry, but Harry promised to marry her straightaway. Yet instead of taking her to church, he drove her in a closed carriage to the Levee district, dropping her off at a brothel called the Casino. There the owner, Roy Jones, ordered her to remove her clothes. He tossed her a flimsy gown and told her she had to pay him for it. Harry collected every dime of the $30 per week she made whoring. He said he'd kill her if she tried to run away.

One night in late May, feeling brave, she scrawled, "I am a white slave," on a scrap of paper and tossed it from her window. A kind passerby brought it to the police. Captain McCann arrested Harry, six other men, and one woman, charging them with disorderly conduct and keeping a disorderly house. Then he called Roe.

It was clear to Roe that this problem with Chicago's Levee district—with its entire unholy underworld—was bigger than Mona Marshall, and he wasn't the only one who thought so. His job required a bit of socializing, usually down at the City Club or Henrici's or Vogelsang's. Beneath swirls of cigar smoke and the soft din of silver scraping china, he found Chicago's leading citizens ruminating on the scourge that was afflicting their beloved city.

What could be done about the plethora of nickel theaters showing lurid films like *The Thaw-White Case* and *A Husband Murdering His Wife*? There were children congregating at these places! No wonder Chicago was in the throes of an unprecedented crime wave. The newspapers printed scoreboards that tabulated murders and muggings, as if such crimes were scheduled like baseball games and horse races: a burglary every three hours, a holdup every six hours, and a suicide and murder every day. Women bashed on the head with pieces of gas pipe, coils of copper strung around their necks, a cloth wet with chloroform swathed over their nostrils. Easier prey than kicking a stray dog or beating a heaving horse.

"Chicago," the *Tribune* opined, "has come to be known over the country as a bad town for men of good character and a good town for men of bad character."

Last month's *McClure's Magazine,* the April 1907 issue, was even more troubling. Its lead story, "The City of Chicago," investigated the city's prostitution trade, and the results were spread out over eighteen sickening pages for all the country to see. Twenty million dollars' worth of business done per year, at least ten thousand professional harlots, countless criminal hotels, dives, saloons, and dance halls where women are snared and forced into the trade. The writer, George Kibbe Turner, discovered that "a company of men, largely composed of Russian Jews," operates between Chicago and New York and Boston and New Orleans and other cities, unloading each girl for $50 and then charging her with the debt—the victim, in effect, pays for her own sale. She's plied with alcohol and cocaine until her age trumps her market value and then drugged out of existence. As in the stockyards, not one shred of flesh is wasted.

"The effect of this single article was indescribable," wrote Louis Filler in his history of the muckrakers. "Coming as it did four years after [Lincoln] Steffens began his investigations into municipal crime, it found a national audience ready and able to appreciate it and apply its lessons at home."

Roe heard all of this chatter, filed it neatly in his mind. In the winter, immediately following the Panzy Williams case, he had approached these same men, told them stories of girls who came to Chicago from Peoria and Sioux City and Springfield, never to be heard from again.

"Instead of receiving their support," Roe said, "I generally received rebuffs and jests at the expense of my attitude toward the white slave traffickers."

He would go back to them when the time came—and the time *would* come. Now that this talk had started, he knew—this being Chicago—that it would only continue to bubble and froth, like so much waste in the river. If they were upon some strange and dire era, he would beckon it forward and give it a name.

As far as Roe was concerned, Chicago was lucky it had him.

R oe opened the door to the courtroom, housed inside the same building as the Harrison Street police station. He despised the place as much as he loved the work he did there.

"The walls of this musty old room," he wrote, "if they could speak, would tell many stories of how for years more criminals have been tried there than perhaps in any other place in the United States. It is the most dismal place imaginable, with scarcely any light except the artificial light, and teeming with more odours than could possibly be concocted by the ingenuity of man.

"Each day it is filled with the garlic and tube-rose of the Italians; the mysterious opium scent of the Chinaman; the highly perfumed sport is there, and the lodging-house bum, reeking with tobacco and whiskey; all this is mixed with the gases from the open sewage in the underground cells, which are worse than any of those of the dark ages. Then there are the fumes from the stables next door and adjacent, and stifling smoke from the ever-present puffing engines across the narrow street which separates it from the LaSalle Street Station. To top it all off comes the steam from the corned beef and cabbage and the frying of the odoriferous onion, which the cook in the cellar below is going to dish up to the prisoners for their noonday meal."

Roe breathed through his mouth and strode over to the section reserved for witnesses. He greeted Mona, who was accompanied by her mother. The poor woman had been bereft during the time her daughter was missing, believing she had eloped—and here the reality was so much worse. The defendants—Harry Balding chief among them—sat off to one side, wearing suits and ties and stoic expressions. Roe was gratified to see that reporters from every Chicago newspaper filled the spectator benches. Reverend Bell sat in the front row, visibly nervous, threading and unthreading his fingers.

Mona took the stand first, and Roe approached. He had the effortlessly assured manner of someone used to being watched, and in a loud, calm voice, he asked his witness to begin.

"I was working in a downtown department store when Harry B. Balding first made himself known to me," Mona said. "I was attracted by him. He is handsome and well dressed. I learned to trust him, he treated me so nice. I went around with him a bit, and he always was talking of automobiles and fine clothes. Finally he declared he loved me and wanted me to become his wife. I believed he was honest, and I thought I loved him. After a time he took me to the Casino at 2101 Dearborn Street. That was in February. Then, March 1, he took me out to get chop suey. On March 2 he took me to the Prima Dance Hall, Thirty-fifth Street and Indiana Avenue. There I met some other men."

Mona paused, and for a moment Roe's focus slackened, his brain stuck a few beats behind. Balding took the girl to the Casino in February? And then she went out with him again? This wasn't what she'd said during their interview at the police station. He cleared his throat and pressed on.

"Then what happened to you?"

Roe fixed his eyes on his witness, willed her answer to be familiar.

"Harry then took me to that flat at Twenty-third Street and Wabash Avenue. He got me there through his smooth talk. There were several men there. That was on a Saturday night. That night Harry coaxed me into going to the Grand Eastern Hotel. He made me stay there a week. I was ashamed to go home. Then he took me to the resort at 2101 Dearborn Street, where Roy Jones is proprietor."

The girl had said nothing, either, of any week spent at the Grand Eastern Hotel. And why had she skimped on the details about the Prima? The drugged wine, the spinning room, the waking up in a "clearinghouse" facing the men who'd raped her? Roe stole a look at Judge Newcomer. He was a good man, sympathetic to the cause. From his expression, it seemed Mona's succumbing to "smooth talk" and her sense of shame were enough. Fine, then, he'd just pick up where the girl left off.

"What happened to you there?" Roe asked.

"I was held there," Mona said. Her hat sat askew, shadowing half of her face. "They took my jewelry from me and refused to let me out without Harry's permission."

Good, back on track.

"Did Harry come to see you?"

"Yes, once in a while." Her voice sounded small, far away. "He used to come when they paid me. I got from twenty-five to forty dollars sometimes, but either they gave it to Harry or he took it from me. If I resisted, he knocked me down and took it."

Roe let his eyes shift again toward Judge Newcomer, who looked ready to leap over his desk and pummel Balding with his gavel.

"How long were you in that place?" Roe asked.

"I was there from March 10 until last Friday. Harry kept telling me he would take me out and we would go to St. Louis and be married. He didn't do it, however, and kept taking my money from me. I had no street clothes and could not get out. . . . They told me I was in debt to them and would have to stay unless Harry said otherwise."

Roe softened his voice, looked at Mona as if he knew her personally. "Did they keep you in the house all the time from March 20 to May 25?" he asked.

"No, they took me out one night and took me to the flat on Wabash Avenue near Twenty-third Street again. This is Willie McNamara's place, where they take all the girls."

"Did you know any of the other girls there?"

"Not well," Mona said. "There was one named Gilette, who was later sold to a place. Another, named Burns, was sold to the same place I was in, for twenty-five dollars, and she is there now. There was another one, Hazel Daily, whose husband put her in this house also. Then there is another little girl, named Gladys, out there still."

Roe paused and let those statements settle in the room. Mona or Burns or Gilette or Hazel or Gladys—and who knew how many other girls—could be their daughter. Their sister or niece or neighbor. Behind him, the crowd rustled and whispered.

He turned and called one of Harry's co-defendants, William McNamara, to the stand.

McNamara was broad and burly, a former boxing champion and reputed ringleader among the procurers. The sleeves of his suit coat stretched taut around his biceps. Roe launched a "severe cross-fire of questions," plucking confessions from the boy as if it were as easy as uprooting a bed of weeds.

McNamara admitted that he and his "associates in the procuring business," as Roe put it, lured girls and raped them, often several times, before selling them to brothels.

"I do not know why I did it," the boy said, speaking into his collar.

Judge Newcomer's voice came hurtling from the bench.

"Don't you think you ought to be taken out and shot dead for this?"

Roe fought a smile. He couldn't have written a better line himself.

The prizewinning pugilist slunk lower in his chair.

"Yes, sir," he said. "Since the reverend gentleman"—he pointed to Ernest Bell, who bolted upright in his seat—"talked to me of my sins last evening, I feel that I should be punished."

Bodies swiveled in Bell's direction. Roe paused his questioning, let the reverend have his moment.

Clifford Roe.

Upon what meat did the crusaders feed that they
could call us insurgents and witches?

—MINNA EVERLEIGH

Ernest Bell could feel a tangible shift in the city's mood. The battle against the Levee was a ball of kinetic energy that had been waiting for a push. This Mona Marshall case was it; she could do for the Levee district what *The Jungle* had done for the Union Stock Yards.

Judge Newcomer found every single one of those degenerate panders guilty, with Harry Balding receiving the stiffest sentence, $100 and a year in the Chicago House of Correction. Police Chief George Shippy closed that white slave hunting ground, the Prima Dance Hall. Captain McCann announced that every person connected with the downfall of innocent girls would be photographed and measured by the Bertillon system, and declared a crackdown on Levee interlopers.

"Half the disorder that is seen on the street at night is due to slumming parties," McCann said. "Young men and girls of highly respectable families come into this district to see the sights, and while here they do many things that hardened denizens of the Levee district would never do in public."

Newspapers, from the venerable *Tribune* to William Randolph Hearst's sensationalistic *Chicago American*, devoted about half a million pages, in Bell's estimation, to the war on white slavery after Mona Marshall told her story. Suddenly there were hundreds just like her, girls who turned victim as soon as they wandered past the sanctioned boundaries of their lives.

Adeline MacDonald, twenty, was snared by mock marriage and seduction. The daughter of a wealthy contractor, she moved to the city from the small town of Davis, Illinois, because some snake had tricked her, written letters declaring, "I have learned to love you as I never loved a girl before and probably never will again" and "I am willing to take you to Chicago, support you, and if you desire, secure employment for you at Marshall Field & Co.'s, besides taking you to dances, theaters, automobiling and yachting." He induced her to drink and escorted her to a brothel at 2106 Armour Avenue.

Ethel Rurey fell victim to the false employment snare. Sixteen years old, she was sweet-talked right out of her Wentworth Avenue home by a black man named H. J. Mitchell. He sold her to the owner of the New Paris at 2118 Dearborn Street for $10. Her father accompanied detectives during an all-night canvassing of the Levee and found Ethel in a second-floor bedroom, cowering inside a closet, peeking between a row of dress hems. "Don't speak to me," her father said. "Officers, lock her up."

"My mother ran away from home one year ago with a minister and went to New York City to live," Ethel sobbed inside her cell. "My father . . . was away from home most of the time, and I got lonesome. Then I met the colored man. He promised to get me a place where I could make some money, and I went with him."

Country girls Hazel Williams and Catherine Craig, both seventeen and pretty, were ensnared by the city itself. Working, respectively, as a domestic and a clerk, the girls met Madam Pauline Greenman. Showing off her collection of silk gowns and jewels, the madam regaled them with stories of the "happy, care-free life of the Levee"—which they immediately felt compelled to experience for themselves.

Accompanying editorials likened these cautionary tales of coercion and deceit to America's shameful recent past.

"There is undoubtedly more actual physical restraint imposed on these modern slaves of our cities," opined the *Chicago Record Herald*, "than was ordinarily imposed on the black slaves of the old plantations."

The Levee leaders rebelled against the increased scrutiny, as Bell knew they would. He suffered the usual assaults—pelted with eggs, bombarded by melons—but they grew more inventive, more vicious. Someone paid a cabdriver to plow his vehicle through their meeting at high speed, sending deaconesses diving to the curb. A French slave trader threatened to break Bell "into pieces" and "send him to the hospital." Someone hurled a rock at his head with such force it would have killed him had the Lord not guided it toward the brim of his hat. Mary lay awake all night, ghastly images galloping through her mind, listening for the door to creak open at 4:00 a.m., wondering if the night would come when she never heard it at all.

And on June 16, 1907, a Sunday, the manager of the Casino sent word through the Levee that a pack of "toughs" would drive Ernest Bell and the Midnight Mission from the Levee for good.

The only way to answer such a threat was to lay it in the path of his faith, and Bell did, two days later. In the midst of a heat wave so brutal that it took the lives of five men, the Midnight Missionaries bypassed the Everleigh Club for the first time to assemble before the Casino. Red lights bloomed over the group. Bell lifted his arms, giving the signal, and scores of voices fused as one, louder than the harlots' laughter drifting out from open doors in calculated bursts, louder than the blare of a hundred pianos:

Throw out the life-line to danger-fraught men
Sinking in anguish where you've never been.

The voices dropped off, then, one by one, thinning, cinching into knots. Choking, wheezing, gasping—and then it hit Bell, too, a wraith of fog that smelled "just like rotten eggs."

Sulphuretted hydrogen. Someone was gassing them.

He closed his eyes, the insides of his lids spackled with red pinpricks of light, and willed his voice to stay with him, pulled it up from his throat. He began preaching, braiding scripture with hymns and prayers, anything to prevent the Levee's sounds from overpowering his own. His saints rallied, too, putting one word in front of the other until their song regained its shape.

A man stepped forward through the mist, his body blurry around the edges. His mouth began moving, and Bell quieted long enough to hear what it said. The man was calling him names—"vile names" that were not repeatable—and Bell walked forward, too, meeting the man halfway. The gas wafted and lingered. He could taste it on his breath.

"Are you one of them?" Bell shouted, meaning the sort who lived off the women in the resorts. But there was no response.

The man was at the curb now, a foot away, his form and features finally clear. He lunged, closing the distance, and his knuckles, lined in a tight, taut row, connected with Bell's face.

There was a quavering aftershock, like a bell tolling between his eyes, and everything in his line of vision vibrated and dimmed. Voices lapped at him. Hands cupped under his arms, lifting him. A sprinkle of someone's sweat. Breath on his face, asking if he was all right, Reverend Bell, say something, anything.

The picture seemed to steady itself then, shook out the wrinkles and creases. He saw that a police officer was dragging the Levee thug to the 22nd Street police station.

Bell followed them there.

As he stood in the dank station, filing a complaint, his assailant, still restrained, glowered at him.

"I wish I had you in a closet," he said, "where I could murder you."

If Minna were a lesser madam, she might murder Nellie, or at least whip the harlot senseless. The girl stood before her, fists screwed into hips, chin thrust forward, rosebud mouth pinched tight. Minna sighed. She should have released the girl back when she'd conspired with that pitiful mottle-faced dive keeper, Pony Moore, to blame her and Ada for the death of Marshall Field Jr. But no—she'd been too soft, taking the harlot's teary apologies as genuine, settling the situation with a stern warning.

So how did Nellie thank her? The little vixen nosed her way into Ada's bookkeeping system, mucked with the numbers so that the inmates were getting paid more than they'd actually earned. This time when they caught her, Nellie was more defiant than sorry. Look at that expression—nearly daring Minna to dismiss her.

The last time Minna had been this angry with a harlot was when Phyllis betrayed two of the Club's sacred rules: No pimps and no drugs. This Phyllis—a different girl from the one who'd plotted with Nellie during the Marshall Field Jr. debacle—had come to the Club from Kansas City. Minna opened the door to find a petite blonde, nearly in tears. She leaned in to hear what the poor girl was saying.

"I hope you like me," Phyllis whispered. "The man to whom I was engaged died suddenly of heart failure—I just had to get away from unpleasant surroundings. I have no parents and here I am. It's a strange adventure for me, but I am sure I could learn."

By this point, Minna was sold—whoever this creature was, she was flawless—but she let the girl continue.

"My betrothed betrayed me," Phyllis went on, voice trembling, "which brings no regrets. From what I heard on the train, a life of shame in this adorable house must be the most glorious existence imaginable. May I stay?"

She stayed.

Within a week, the Everleighs' wealthiest clients were battling for her attentions. The sisters were stunned: This virginal nymph had instincts about the business that were lacking in some of their most seasoned courtesans. For one thing, the girl sure knew her Balzac. She blindfolded every man who had the good sense to choose her, leading him up to a boudoir laden with her personal flourishes—a genuine Turkish mattress covered with white cashmere; dimmed lights looming from the ceiling like dying stars; fresh-cut roses spilling from vases, petals scattered about the floor. The men knew such attention to detail wouldn't be lost when the focus turned to the business at hand.

But when the harlot ventured out one afternoon and didn't report back come nightfall, the madams suspected a serious problem. Another day passed with no sign of Phyllis, and then three more. The sisters' fears were confirmed through the Levee grapevine: One of their star girls was sacked out in an opium den on Bed Bug Row, high out of her tiny mind, cavorting with some Chinese pimp.

"When Phyllis finally showed up on the fifth day," recalled a fellow harlot, "looking like she had been drawn through a knothole, Minna told her to pack up and get the hell out and never show her face around there again. It wasn't the opium alone. That Chinese lover-boy also complicated things. Minna and Ada didn't want any pimps lousing up the telephone lines."

Even Vic Shaw wouldn't take this castoff, so Phyllis ventured first to Big Jim's place, the Saratoga, and then to the $1 door at the House of All Nations, where a harlot at the $5 door snidely inquired about her "toboggan slide" since she'd left the Everleigh Club. The ensuing catfight was heard throughout the block. With three front teeth missing and no money for dental work, Phyllis returned permanently to Bed Bug Row, making 22 cents per trick. A sad case, but allowing girls to mix with pimps would prompt accusations that the Everleigh Club dealt in white slavery—the sort of stain that could never be masked or erased.

Nellie's transgression wasn't as public or potentially dangerous, but a second offense could not go unpunished.

"What are you going to do to me?" the harlot asked.

Minna was silent for a moment, considering her words.

"Nothing," she answered, and sighed again. "If you had done to a church or to a bank what you've done to me they'd have you locked up—a horrible example. One of our girls had a father in St. Louis who went to jail for helping himself to a collection box in a church. They called it embezzlement and it was a terrible disgrace. And you, Nellie, have brought disgrace upon this house, but we won't go into legal bosh. Please leave as quietly as possible."

Nellie left, and her cohorts in the fraudulent entries were forgiven— this time. Still, Minna had a feeling they hadn't heard the last of the girl. Most likely she'd end up going to Vic Shaw, who always held the door open for Everleigh Club expats.

At least the latest Levee scandal touched the rival madam, for once, instead of the sisters. As owner of the Casino, Vic Shaw's husband, Roy Jones, had been entangled in the Mona Marshall spectacle, though his troubles likely would prove ephemeral. The price for stopping an indictment on a charge of pandering was $1,000, and twice that amount quashed a complaint of harboring a girl. Roy Jones could pay the graft fees and carry on as usual, no matter how aggressively Clifford Roe pursued him. The prosecutor was in over his head, battling a system they hadn't taught him in law school.

Minna waited a few moments by the front door, anticipating Nellie's return, a timid tap or a furious hailstorm of fists or an insistent pressing of the bell. And . . . nothing. Just spurts of muted music, the distant rattle of trains. She moved a foot to her left, pulled back the curtain, peered around the endless procession of carriages and grubby errand boys darting from house to house. No Nellie loitering on Dearborn Street, as far as Minna could see. In fact, no one of much interest at all, though surely the visiting firemen would resume their usual post in just a few hours.

She'd heard what Bell and his lemmings said after their Levee canvassing. She and Ada, apparently, not only paid top dollar for their girls and lined them up at the disease doctor's door, but were foolish enough to admit such things before the very people endeavoring to shut them down. What nonsense—and not even inventive nonsense at that.

Well, she had an alternate story of her own. And because she was not only the best madam on the line, but a lady, she upheld the Club's rules of unyielding discretion whenever she repeated it.

And she did repeat it.

A prominent reformer visited again, Minna said, this time by himself. No, she wouldn't divulge his name, but here's one hint—it was always in the newspapers, and everyone knew his face. One night, in order to experience the very conditions he devoted his life to destroying, the man came into the parlor, farther than he'd ever ventured before. He gave a pseudonym that fooled no one and said he was looking for some special attention.

"How much for a little party?" he whispered.

One of the harlots leaned in close.

"Special price of $25," she breathed, tickling his reddening neck, "for you."

With shaking fingers, the man pulled $50 from his wallet. The girl accepted the money, told him to follow her upstairs—she'd give him change and plenty else. When they reached her room, the man told her he'd decided against a party after all. Would it be all right if they just sat and talked?

"In that case," said the Everleigh butterfly, "you don't get any change."

Everyone who heard the story applied a layer before passing it on. Later, this mysterious visitor would be described as a "crusader . . . noted for his good works among the denizens of the Levee" and a "well-publicized muck-raker." Edgar Lee Masters spoke of "flexible moralists" who found the Club's back doors useful for "furtive exits." Some intimated he was a lawyer; others, a preacher. The sisters never revealed the visitor's identity or profession, but they did add a punch line: It was a lucky thing they didn't change their ways, or the poor fellow would be out of a job.

B ell's encounter with the thug on Armour Avenue earned him both a black eye and considerable notoriety. The *Daily News* called him the "star actor" in "one of the worst riots in the history of the 22nd Street red-light district." If the Levee thugs didn't know his name before, they did now, and now his character, too, was battered and bruised.

At the end of June, a group of Levee leaders accused both the Midnight Mission and reformers "who do not hide their motives under the cloak of piety" of blackmailing madams and dive keepers. After procuring a girl, they delivered her to any resort where her face and history were unknown. A week later, she was "discovered" by the same reformers who had placed her there. If the madam wanted to stop prosecution, she had to pay a hefty sum. If she refused, the reformers sent an anonymous note to the police.

"Would it surprise you much to learn," said one madam, "that so-called reformers placed girls in houses and then had the houses raided and 'white slave' cases fixed up?"

The attorney for another madam joined in. "Of all the evil characters in the world," he fumed, "a lying preacher is the worst . . . there are men parading the streets of Chicago at night in the garb of clergymen, and their hearts beneath are slimy."

Bell dignified the charge with four words: "It is a lie."

Even worse, they attacked the work he began long ago, before he'd even come to Chicago or heard of the Levee. Some scheming madam or pander circulated a rumor that the government was investigating Bell for fraud. The superintendent of the Midnight Mission accepted between $7,000 and $8,000 from people who believed they were donating to "vague" causes in India, and kept it for himself instead.

Because Bell was off working in the Levee, Mary had to defend him.

The allegations, she said, were the "work of enemies" and "without foundation."

The Lord blessed the persecuted, he reminded himself, and his thoughts were validated by a letter from his boyhood pastor back in Canada:

> We were glad to receive your letter, and to be assured that the heathen in Chicago have not yet made away with you. I expect to hear of your translation by the thug route, some of these days, if you still keep up the struggle against vice as you have done and are doing. You are braver than anybody ever thought you were. God must be holding you for a special work, in Babylon there.

It was easy to tuck those words in a place where Bell could always reach them, easy to coat his own words with similar courage and bluster. "The market for white slaves, the illegal red-light district, must be abolished," he wrote in the fall. "In Chicago, the Levee must go. *Delenda est Carthago!*"

But when the manager of the Casino—the very scum who sent Levee thugs to kill him—approached and said he would "gladly quit the brothel business" if he could "sell out," could one blame Bell for being wary?

When Big Jim Colosimo lumbered over, trapped Bell's shoulder between thick fingers, and claimed he'd once been an "honest man," wasn't it only natural to take a step back?

C lifford Roe tallied his successes: an average of one conviction per week as the summer of 1907 gave way to fall. When fall came, he again approached those leading Chicago citizens at the City Club and Henrici's and Vogelsang's. He sat down inside the ghostly haze of cigar smoke, spoke to them as they cut their steaks and sipped their wine. With the country in financial panic and banks closing every day, the streets filled with unemployed men from Chicago and elsewhere; surely they had noticed that certain sections of the city were even more bedraggled than usual. Ben Reitman, the "clap doctor" who treated prostitutes and eventually became Emma Goldman's lover, opened a "Brotherhood Welfare association" on State Street, outside of which congregated hundreds of hoboes, tramps, bums, drug fiends, and drunks, half of them stumbling about barefoot.

Roe reminded them of Mona Marshall, the girl who had awakened Chicago to the scourge of white slavery—and who could do the same for America. He explained that the state's attorney's office had a slapdash detective force, comprising four borrowed and constantly harried officers from the Chicago Police Department. He asked if they, as prominent men who cared how Chicago looked to the rest of the world, would fund his fight against white slavers, those "arch-enemies to society, the lowest of the lowly creatures on this earth" who "stifle truth and trample upon innocence."

This time, the men knew who Roe was before he told them. This time, no one laughed at him.

A nother force was converging, too, yet unbeknownst to the prosecutor or Levee leaders. In November 1907, the United States government, concerned about immigration in general and its relationship to prostitution in particular, formed a commission to study how people came to America and what happened to them once they arrived. Federal agents infiltrated aid societies, bunked in steerage levels on ships. They visited the schools of immigrant children to measure the size and shape of their skulls.

The government also dispatched a special team of inspectors to red-light districts across the country. Men posed as pimps and panders and common salesmen. Female "inspectresses"—a revolutionary notion in a time when municipal police departments still practiced exclusion— adopted the tawdry costumes and crude demeanor of inferior madams. Agents boarded trains for New York, San Francisco, Seattle, Portland, Salt Lake City, Ogden, Butte, Denver, Buffalo, Boston, New Orleans, and Chicago, determined to drag the darkest parts of the underworld into plain sight.

"THE DRUMMER, OR TRAVELING MAN WAY."

When a pander strikes a rural community he must work very smoothly, for every one knows that he is a stranger. He poses as a drummer or traveling man, and seeks the girls in this way, promising a fine time at balls, parties, etc. Once in his power she is lost.

Pray, forgive me, Sir, for the seemingly out of place story I relate here, but it is so very characteristic that I cannot abstain from telling it here. I met a man at Seattle, I was told he had grown rich as a leading importer of "human flesh" and has now given up his vocation as a pimp. I entered into a conversation with him. I was, to him, a drummer for a neckwear house.

"Yes, business is bad," I said to him in the course of conversation. With flippant cynicism or cynical flippancy he said to me,

"Why don't you get a few battleships to work for you?"

"Battleships? What is that?" I asked.

"Why, girls, of course, girls," he answered.

"And why do you call them battleships?" I inquired, to which he answered, "Because they have port-holes."

—SPECIAL IMMIGRATION INSPECTOR MARCUS BRAUN

MORE IMMORAL
THAN HEATHEN CHINA

The Oriental Music Room at the Everleigh Club.

The Shanghai is nothing like this.
Oh, how I'm going to love it here.

—Suzy Poon Tang

There was that old biddy again, her spindly legs scampering across Dearborn Street, looking like a fledgling about to take off for the first time. Minna squinted through a slit in the front door and then quickly pulled it shut. Yes, it was definitely her. Lucy Page Gaston. Peripheral ally of the visiting firemen and, most vehemently, head crusader of the Anti-Cigarette League. "The weed," as she called it, made one insane. *It was ruining the city's youth! Its smoke was akin to the devil's breath!* Gaston visited the Everleigh Club often to explain, ever so helpfully, why its inhabitants were doomed in the hereafter.

While Ernest Bell and his blatant lies were irritating, Minna and Ada found Gaston both hilarious and pitiful, and they ordered their harlots not to embarrass the crusader. Under no circumstances, for example, were the girls to smoke in Gaston's presence, tempting though the thought might be. And Ethel, an Everleigh butterfly who had a fondness for chewing tobacco—and spitting old plugs onto the Club's Oriental carpeting—wasn't permitted anywhere near the reformer.

But today's visit was bad timing. Minna was just about to step out for an appointment with Madam Julie at the Shanghai, a pleasure house that specialized in "sloe-eyed Oriental beauties," and now she'd be late. Gaston came bounding up the eleven steps that led to the 2131 side landing. Minna quickly ushered her inside—no need to waste the heat. Gaston's cheeks were slapped pink by the February wind, her eyes sunken and red rimmed. Up close, she looked less like an awkward hatchling than some mythological creature—maybe a Greek harpy, with the head and torso of a homely old woman flanked by wings and prehensile talons, a screeching beast that hauled victims off to the underworld for endless bouts of torture.

The harpy was in Minna's underworld now. The madam gave a polite hello, said it was a pleasure to see her again, and what might she do for Miss Gaston on this fine day?

"There is something you must do," Gaston shouted. Her words were stark, displaced chirps in the narrow space of the vestibule. "You alone can stop your girls from going straight to the devil."

"What is it?" Minna said, keeping her tone patient and sweet.

"Make them stop smoking cigarettes."

Minna promised Gaston she'd do her best, thanked her, and showed her out.

If she hurried, she could make her appointment with Madam Julie. Normally, Minna wouldn't have fretted about being tardy with a madam of such dubious standards, but Madam Julie happened to have something the sisters, and the Everleigh Club, needed.

For months now, one of their choicest clients—a multimillionaire businessman who spent a fortune in the Club each year, including a $5,000 Christmas bonus for both sisters—had been filling their ears with talk about a courtesan called Suzy Poon Tang. If the rumors were to be believed, she was, quite literally, a work of art.

Suzy Poon Tang, the story went, began her courtesan career in Shanghai, China, by propositioning from doorways. She did well without the services of a pimp and traveled to Singapore and then Hong Kong, where she became known for finishing a dance by licking her partner's cheek. One partner, dapper and fluent in English, enticed her to join his combination opium den/brothel in Macao. She'd be paid extra for learning how to prepare a customer's pipe.

Suzy did learn, and she learned well. Lay your man down and line up his utensils nearby: a bamboo pipe, a pot stuffed with opium, steel needles used to roast the drug over a lamp's flame. Prepare him for what was to come. "We've just received a brand-new stock of dreams," she'd whisper. "I hope, lover, some of them will please you." Take the opium, now heated and waxy, and roll it slowly between thumb and forefinger until it was as swollen and round as a golf ball. Place it on the bowl of the bamboo pipe, hand it to "lover," and encourage him as he inhaled.

But—and this was most important—satisfy him before he succumbed completely to the drug.

When Suzy heard a group of Asian girls were planning to sail to America, she decided to join them. A city called Chicago had a red-light district, including a brothel named the Shanghai, that rivaled anything in the Orient. They'd travel halfway around the world to work at a place designed to feel like home.

Before setting sail, Suzy Poon Tang journeyed to Tokyo and commissioned a tattoo artist to ink, just below her navel, a bouquet of roses so artfully authentic that one might be tempted to pluck it from her flesh. The artist suggested he might also decorate each cheek of her buttocks with a butterfly, but Suzy demurred, wanting just the elegant simplicity of the flowers. She told her customers at the Shanghai that renowned Hong Kong art critics paid handsome sums for the privilege of evaluating this masterpiece. For an extra $5, she would recline on a pillow, legs akimbo, offer a magnifying glass, and let them judge it for themselves. "It's better than looking at the original of *Mona Lisa* in the Louvre, isn't it, lover?" she'd coo, and count the minutes until the trick lifted his head.

The only problem was that the Shanghai was too undignified for the likes of the sisters' millionaire client. He implored Minna and Ada to hire the courtesan so he could sample her pleasures at the Everleigh Club.

It was a tedious ordeal—Minna had a host of errands to attend to, including planning Ada's upcoming "thirty-second" birthday celebration—but she took a cue from Marshall Field: Give the man what he wants, simple as that.

Just before 10:00 a.m. on Monday, February 10, 1908, Clifford Roe strolled south on LaSalle Street, the air dense with the promise of snow. Inside the Central YMCA building, he made his way to the auditorium, where he was scheduled to give a speech titled "The White Slaves and the Law" before five hundred prominent city ministers.

Since November, after convincing those Chicago businessmen to fund his white slave investigations, he'd lectured representatives from, among others, the Cook County Woman's Christian Temperance Union, the Social Settlement League, the Cook County Federation of Women's Clubs, the Chicago Purity League, the National Purity Association, and the Illinois Training School for Girls. He fed on the crowds, the way they latched on to his words, as if each successive syllable hoisted them higher above the city's maelstroms of vice.

Now he stood at the podium, waiting for the last rustle of movement to settle, the last throat to clear.

"A great many persons are yet skeptical of the existence of an organized traffic in girls," he began. "They seem to think that those advocating the abolition of this trade are either fanatics or notoriety seekers."

Always shoot with your critics' weapons, a tactic used by every good lawyer.

"They doubt the truth of the impossibility of escape, and content themselves with the thought that girls use the plea of slavery to right themselves with their parents and friends when their cases are made public."

That was for anyone—and he was certain they were out there—who still doubted Mona Marshall's story.

"However, if these same people could have been in the courts of Chicago during the past year"—as *he* was, remember—"their minds would be disabused of the idea that slavery does not exist in Chicago. The startling disclosures made in nearly a hundred cases ought to arouse not only the citizens of Chicago, but the whole country to the highest pitch of indignation."

On a roll now, Roe recounted the confession of Harry Balding, the main defendant in the Mona Marshall case. "All of the fellows around there—meaning the red-light district—were doing that," Roe said, reading from notes he took during his interview with the pander. "We did nothing else but go out and look around town and see if we could take a girl and bring her out there. Whenever we got a girl out there, they would give us so much money and tell us that if we got arrested that they would get us out . . . we would go around to penny arcades and nickel theaters and if we saw a couple of girls, we could always tell what they were by looking at them."

What Roe didn't mention, either in the aftermath of the case or now, standing before the ministers, were the niggling inconsistencies about Mona's story. A report that she fled from the flat where she'd allegedly been gang-raped and decided, without explanation, to return. The allegation by Captain McCann that Mona Marshall's own stepfather was a white slaver and may have had a hand in the girl's downfall. A contradictory version of Mona's escape—one that had her running, clad in a slinky gown, to the police station instead of scribbling a plea for help and dropping it from the brothel's window.

"There is a remedy, and it is this," the prosecutor concluded. "Demand

that the legislature of the state of Illinois change the laws to meet the requirements of modern times. . . . Up to the present time in most instances
only the small fry have been arrested. To bring to bay the leaders, those
who send these agents out, should be the next step toward eradicating this
evil."

Five hundred chairs scraped backward, a thousand hands clapped.
When the applause subsided, Roe and several clergymen, including Ernest
Bell and Melbourne Boynton, cut away for a secret meeting in one of the
YMCA's private conference rooms. By day's end, they formed a new
group named the Illinois Vigilance Association, an offshoot of the National Vigilance Committee. Reverend Boynton was named president, Bell
was secretary, and Roe would oversee legislative activity.

The following day's *Tribune* lauded the new group and its mission to
destroy the Levee, calling the district "more openly vicious than any part
of Paris and more immoral than heathen China."

Reverend Boynton issued the official statement.

"We have come to the conclusion that the only way to stamp out the
white slave traffic in Chicago is to wipe out the red-light district where it
breeds," he said. "We believe this can be done, and we mean to do it."

Boynton and Bell met on Tuesday, February 11, again, as it happened,
at the Central YMCA. The Midnight Mission often discussed business over lunch in the building's restaurant, and on this occasion seven
other active members joined them.

They bowed heads and prayed over their plates, then quickly sifted
through their business. Rufus Simmons reported that he had sent letters requesting donations to pay off $600 worth of bills and outstanding debts.
Deaconess Lucy Hall suggested that different churches send a band of
workers to the Levee one night a month.

Arthur Burrage Farwell, president of the Chicago Law and Order
League, spoke last. It was imperative, he argued, that they send a letter to
the mayor asking him to suppress the illegal sale of liquor in houses of ill
fame.

"Three times, committees have asked Mayor Busse to enforce the law in
this respect," he said, "but nothing has been done. Liquor alone is bad

enough. A disorderly house is bad enough. But when the two are in conjunction, conditions much worse obtain."

Farwell didn't say so directly, but he knew, in particular, of two prominent madams who had been operating for years without the proper license, who were so well protected by the police that they never even bothered to apply for one.

The Shanghai was on Armour Avenue near 21st Street, next to a Japanese brothel and two doors down from Big Jim Colosimo's Victoria. Certainly not on a par with the Everleigh Club, the Shanghai nevertheless was far superior to the $3 joints two blocks north on Bed Bug Row, charging a $1 entry fee and $10 for a girl's services (though Madam Julie allowed tipping for extra "Chinese tricks").

A wide flight of stairs jutted from the plain three-story brownstone. On the second floor, Minna opened an unlocked door and pressed a button shaped like a miniature Buddha. She heard the faint hum of a buzzer. A portal inside the vestibule gave way, revealing another flight of stairs carpeted in bright, heavy fabric, twisting upward and ending at a glass door.

Minna knew she was being watched. The door was actually a two-way mirror, forty-eight inches high and eighteen inches wide, and Madam Julie stood on the other side. A moment passed, and then the mirror erupted into a brilliant blaze of lights, fading into a pictorial of a Shanghai street at festival time. Images, projected through the other side, flickered across the glass: dragon heads bobbing in a lazy parade, gaudy banners slung across storefronts, dancers jumping and wheeling. If Minna were a customer, this would signal that Madam Julie had approved entry and was ready to collect her dollar.

The festival slide show dimmed and the mirrored door slid open. Madam Julie waved Minna forward, inviting her to enter the main parlor. She was American but had spent a number of years in the Far East, cultivating supply lines to whores in Hong Kong, Saigon, and Singapore. She spoke Chinese fluently. Straight black hair swept the middle of her back, and a perfect dimple, like a thumbprint, sank into one cheek. In her early forties, Minna guessed, but respectably preserved.

If Minna were a customer, Madam Julie would now clap her hands twice. A girl would sashay in carrying a tray piled with tiny boxes, each holding a sprinkling of tea leaves, with "COMPLIMENTS OF THE SHANGHAI" printed across the lids. Each customer received one in his outstretched hand—Madam Julie's idea of advertising. Then the harlot would soften the lights and roll up the Oriental rug, revealing a clear glass floor. Madam Julie would rear back and strike a gong, and her troupe of courtesans would march out, kimonos slit high on their thighs. One more strike on the gong and a spray of lights would illuminate the floor from below. The girls would commence a repertoire of poses, their skin catching the glint of the lights, waiting to be chosen.

This time, though, Madam Julie left the Oriental rug unrolled and the gong unbanged, and she and Minna sat together in her parlor. Madam Julie was hesitant at first—Suzy Poon Tang brought in more than her share of $10 tricks. But later that afternoon, they struck a deal: Suzy Poon Tang would relocate temporarily to the Everleigh Club, and Minna would pay the Shanghai's madam more than enough to cover the loss.

Suzy Poon Tang would need a tutor, and neither Minna nor Ada had the time to teach the girl. The sisters decided that Doll could do it. Doll was a green-eyed redhead who eagerly offered her vitals: five feet five, 118 pounds, 36-24-35. "I've always found it fun being a redhead," she said, "although I know that gentlemen usually prefer blondes because blondes know what gentlemen prefer." Plus, she was honest, and not as catty as the rest.

Also, the seasoned harlot wouldn't begrudge Suzy Poon Tang's earning potential, since she enjoyed her own loyal—and singularly kinky—clientele. One john, the Ladder Man, always requested that an eight-foot ladder be waiting for him in Doll's boudoir. "What a beautiful ladder in a perfumed heaven," he whispered, Doll's cue to start running around the room. The Ladder Man chased her. After a few laps she climbed the ladder, just a few rungs, so he could grab and pull her down, and then they played again. Minna and Ada didn't mind his fetish, but they made certain heavy cloth padding covered the ladder's top and sides. The mirrored walls in Doll's room mustn't be damaged or smudged.

Doll also entertained the Swinger (who liked the harlot to swing, trapeze style, from his extended, muscled arm). But her most lucrative—and strangest—client was the Gold Coin Kid.

The Gold Coin Kid was a bachelor, about thirty years old. His late father had been president of two Chicago manufacturing companies, and he flung money around like confetti. The Everleigh butterflies looked past the fact that the man still lived with his mother.

The Gold Coin Kid earned his nickname one night after several quiet, uneventful visits to the Club. Minna escorted him inside and inquired about her boy. He handed Ada a large black bag and asked if she would please check it for him.

"What've you got in there?" Ada teased. "Rocks?"

She showed him into the conversation parlors, where he mingled with the girls. He settled on Doll, she of the crimson hair and impressive measurements.

The Gold Coin Kid and Doll enjoyed dinner and champagne in the Pullman Buffet, during which Doll uncharacteristically ignored Club rules and drank until the alcohol took over her head. But as the evening progressed, she recalled later, it was clear that she had "deviated with a deviate."

Precisely at midnight, the Gold Coin Kid sent word asking if Ada might retrieve his bag. The madam did, and he tucked it under his arm as he followed Doll up the stairs. She locked the door behind them and he took her by the wrist.

"I've got a feeling I'm in love with you," he said.

She kissed him "real good" and answered, "Just you don't lose that feeling, sweetie."

He tightened his grip, the points of his fingers making a bracelet around her wrist.

"Every time I've been here before," he said, "I've seen you occupied with others downstairs, and whenever I inquired about you I was politely told you weren't available. So tonight I brought along my magic bag to guarantee an evening with you."

He released her and placed his black bag, slowly, ceremoniously, on the dresser and pulled open its latch. The bag was crammed with a jumble of $5 coins made of solid gold.

Doll, who thought she had seen everything, could only say, "Holy cow!" The Gold Coin Kid waited for her to recover, and after a moment she remembered where she was and what she was there for. She lifted her arms, shrugged her shoulders, and her gown fell. Her corset gave way with a few twists and tugs. Everleigh girls made undressing seem like a Houdini trick.

The Gold Coin Kid shrugged off his suit and shirt and tie, everything except a pair of multicolored briefs, and Doll shot him a look that said *Finish*. He was sorry, he said, but he wanted to leave that last bit of clothing on for now. He dipped his hand into his bag and lifted a heap of gold coins, letting them fall in a slow stream from one palm to the other.

"I know you'll find this game extremely interesting," he said, "and I'm sure I wouldn't care to play it with any girl but you."

Get on the bed, he said. He remained six feet away, by the dresser, and confided that as a young man, his favorite game was pitching pennies, and now he had an inexplicable desire to resume this childhood pastime. He would pitch the coins, if it was all right with Doll, at the "most erogenic area" of her body. She could keep each piece that hit the bull's-eye.

It was, naturally, all right with Doll.

Doll assumed a pose on the bed that provided the Kid with a can't-miss target, "leaning back with a graceful swanlike arrangement of my hands while keeping my knees apart." She called out her approval for each shot, counting score. He was such a darling, insisting on pitching until every coin hit its mark.

After that night, Doll amassed quite a collection of gold coins.

Minna ascended the stairs to Doll's bedroom and knocked. The girl opened the door, a translucent swirl of incense climbing the air behind her.

Minna explained the Suzy Poon Tang situation and wrapped her arm around Doll. Rubbing the girl's back, she said, "If I pay you well, much more than you could make in several days, would you permit the Chinese girl to spend tomorrow evening in your room while you brief her on our routine? That would enable her to start working the parlors on the following day, and I'd feel much more confident about her performance."

Of course, Doll answered.

Minna, still smoothing the harlot's back, asked another favor. "And, of course, you'll allow Suzy to sleep with you for the night?"

Yes, Doll answered.

Minna kissed her cheek. "Good girl. I feel you've solved my big problem."

Tomorrow, she would fetch Suzy Poon Tang, and Ada would help smuggle her upstairs. They'd have time later to explain to the rest of the harlots, to reassure them their own earnings wouldn't suffer. She'd leave a menu in Doll's room, tell her to order a feast for the Chinese girl. It was clear that Doll loved women, though Minna didn't care to know the details, as long as the Asian girl was soon fluent in Balzac.

On May 4, Roe and five colleagues with the Illinois Vigilance Association boarded the Chicago & Alton, heading two hundred miles southwest toward the state capital. The train rumbled through Joliet, Mazonia, Dwight, Bloomington, dozens of far-flung towns removed from the mayhem of the city. Roe gazed out the window, taking in a leisurely slide show of looming silos and waving spikes of prairie grass.

His mind was on his career. Numerous successful prosecutions aside, he was frustrated by the "archaic" and "moss-covered" Illinois statutes that were "full of loopholes through which the slave traders crawled." He had to prove each victim was unmarried, had been procured through deception, and was of previous "chaste life." That last stipulation was most troubling. If the rape gangs attacked a girl right away, thereby robbing her of her chastity, the case was as good as lost.

Most of his convictions were under the Disorderly Conduct Act, which carried only a $200 fine, but Roe hoped he could lobby the Illinois State Legislature to augment the white slavery laws. If his proposed bill passed, it would be the nation's first law aimed at panders and a major professional coup.

Beside him sat Adolph Kraus, president of the Chicago-based International Order of B'nai B'rith. Kraus was equally reflective, though his concerns were more global than personal. It was a year since the muckraker George Kibbe Turner alleged that most of Chicago's white slavers were Russian Jews, and the sting was still sharp. Kraus, during the furor that followed, toured the West Side Levee and determined that his people constituted 20 percent of the traffickers. That figure would grow, he feared, along with the Jewish population. Between 1880 and 1900 alone, some two hundred thousand Jewish immigrants settled in Chicago, many of them refugees who fled Russia after the horrific pogroms and settled in the slums along 16th Street near Halsted. Even the *American Hebrew* was casting blame, noting it was "possible" that Jews had imported white slavery to America.

"If Jews are the chief sinners," the newspaper reasoned, "it is appropriate that Jews should be the chief avengers."

The social worker Frances Kellor had spoken the truth when she studied Jewish participation in vice the previous year. "The Jew," she wrote, "has been taught early in life the value of morality and decency, and does not take up this business unless he is thoroughly vicious and bad"—unlike, say, the French, who did not, on the whole, find running a brothel an immoral or shameful practice, who considered it akin to operating a restaurant or department store. It was up to Kraus and every upstanding Jewish citizen to shape the perception of their people, before it was done for them.

The House passed the white slave bill 102–0, and the unanimous vote carried an emergency clause. The Illinois Senate immediately sent it to Governor Charles Deneen to sign. The law decreed that anyone convicted of recruiting for disorderly houses would spend six months to one year in prison and pay a fine between $300 and $1,000. Also, a pander could no longer wed his victim and use the marriage as a defense. Roe was "elated" that Illinois became the "pioneer state to pass a pandering law, directed at the slave traffic in girls and women." This battle, *his* battle, was at last stretching far beyond Chicago, and he couldn't stop it now, even if he wanted to.

"FRIENDS" MEETING EMIGRANT GIRL AT THE DOCK
"The girl was met at New York by two 'friends' who took her in charge. These 'friends' were two of the most brutal of all the white slave traders who are in the traffic."
—U. S. Dist. Attorney Edwin W. Sims
Foreign girls are more helplessly at the mercy of white slave hunters than girls at home. Every year thousands of girls arriving in America from Italy, Sweden. Germany, etc.. are never heard of again.

*I know it is repugnant to our system of government
to have any kind of espionage over our citizenship, but I
would keep such people under a certain surveillance.*

—SPECIAL IMMIGRATION INSPECTOR MARCUS BRAUN

I t was time, Roe decided, to call a friend in the federal government, Edwin Sims. His fellow University of Michigan alumnus was admired for his ambition, encyclopedic memory, and pedantic attention to detail. Sims, he knew, would already be aware that foreign girls, with the complicity of Chicago's police, were being sold into city brothels. What was considered typical Levee business was now a federal felony. The federal Immigration Act of 1907, set into effect shortly before undercover agents began infiltrating red-light districts, forbade importing women into the country for the purposes of prostitution, and mandated the deportation of any woman or girl found prostituting herself within three years of her arrival in America.

To friends, Sims was "Ed," but to the rest of the country he was a legal wunderkind, who at thirty-four served as assistant secretary at the 1904 Republican National Convention; who a year later was appointed solicitor for the Department of Commerce and Labor by President Roosevelt; and who, a year after that, became the United States district attorney in Chicago, charged with preparing the government's antitrust case against John D. Rockefeller's Standard Oil Company.

"Curiously enough," wrote the *Tribune*, "the reason of the success of Mr. Sims was identically the same as the reason for the success of John D. Rockefeller. It is expressed in just one word, 'organize.' There were 1,903 charges against the oil company and every one of these charges had to be verified by documentary and oral evidence. . . . It was a titanic task, but Mr. Sims set about it in his own way. . . . He had his facts marshaled in due order of their importance, each with its little budget of evidence ready to step out of the ranks at the precise moment when they should be needed. His opponents . . . did not know their man."

Sims, married and the father of four, vowed to work with Roe and his Illinois Vigilance Association to rid the city of these criminals.

"I am determined to break up this traffic in foreign women," he declared. "It is my sworn duty, and it should be done to protect the people of the country from contamination."

The announcement was a welcome one to most native-born Chicagoans. Their city was turning on itself, relinquishing its identity street by street; there were whole blocks drenched in odd smells, conversations built with peculiar words, hymns sung to false gods. "I am one of those who believe not only that our public schools should have moral and religious training in them, but that this training should be Christian," a Presbyterian minister wrote to one of Clifford Roe's supporters. "This land is a Christian land. The United States Supreme Court and many of our state supreme courts have unequivocally decided that it is. . . . I do not believe that we need to truckle or surrender our inheritance to infidels or Jews from Europe."

They were everywhere, these so-called new immigrants, arriving daily from Eastern and Southern Europe, most of them "undesirable" Italians, Poles, and Russians. Catholics were just as "unassimilable" as the Jews, what with their pagan customs and thirst for liquor, feeding their babies beer if the milk was delivered spoiled. Chicago's Italian population was approaching forty-five thousand—almost three times what it was in 1900. They were overrunning Halsted and Taylor streets with their "Little Italy," devising rackets for the gambling halls, killing in the name of the Black Hand.

Mongrels, all of them, pulling America's identity in dangerous directions, leaving her misshapen and newly strange.

"We no longer draw from Northern Europe," wrote one native-born observer in 1908. "This enormous influx hails from Russia, Austria, Hungary, Italy, and the southern countries about the eastern end of the Mediterranean—men of alien races, mixed in blood and of many tongues and often the last results of effete and decaying civilizations. . . . We no longer receive accessions from the best peoples but from the mediocre and the worst."

Sims sent for Secret Service agents from Washington and twenty-five deputy United States marshals and unleashed them into the Levee. They discovered, in mid-June, a "syndicate of Frenchmen" operating from the Dearborn Street resort of Emma "French Em" Duval and her husband,

August. The French had introduced unthinkable perversions into American culture; even the word *French* was now slang for oral sex. The Duvals kept their girls in a barred breaking-in facility called the Retreat located in Blue Island, a small town sixteen miles south of the Loop, and worked in concert with another French couple, Alphonse and Eva Dufour, who ran a brothel at 2021 Armour Avenue, not far from the Shanghai.

On a Tuesday night, June 23, a squad of marshals swarmed Madam Eva's resort. For a moment, a swath of the Levee paused, craning to see the commotion. At the nearby Paris, whose proprietor, Maurice Van Bever, was the most powerful Frenchman in the district, harlots and johns sprang from beds to peer out the windows. Three young French girls were dragged from Madam Eva's, a weeping triumvirate in gauzy robes and tattered tights, and locked in cells at the 22nd Street station. Sims questioned them, deciphered their broken English.

"They show that they have been drilled remarkably well," he said. "When I asked them separately how long they had been in the country, each said five years. Asked how they got here and into disorderly houses, they told stories of similar character. One said she came over to work in a corset factory in New York and was unable to get any more work. Another said she came over with a French family six years ago, and after the family went back to Paris she stayed in New York. The step from the Tenderloin to the Armour Avenue house in Chicago was easy."

Federal agents seized Eva Dufour's books and gathered enough evidence to arrest two thousand additional Frenchwomen in Minneapolis, St. Louis, New York City, New Orleans, and Kansas City, all of whom had been sold into brothels via the Chicago headquarters. Sims—who before entering college worked briefly as a newspaper reporter—was adept at disclosing just enough information to maintain interest in his crusade without jeopardizing its progress. Further raids were in the works, he allowed, but he couldn't elaborate owing to the possible presence of Levee spies in his office, eager to tip off his plans.

It was positively surreal. Only three months earlier, Roe had traveled to Springfield to speak at the Capitol, and now that majestic domed structure was overrun with militia, encampments arranged in precise rows across the lawn. The city where Lincoln made his home had erupted in race riots on Friday, August 14, 1908, after a twenty-one-year-old white woman allegedly was snatched from her bed and assaulted by a Negro. In the days since, a mob of white residents, wielding guns and ropes, torched black-owned businesses and homes. William Donegan, an elderly Negro who had been a close friend of Lincoln's, was strung up on a tree near his home and hanged to death. After an overwhelmed Mayor Roy Reece was forced into hiding, Governor Deneen called in 4,500 National Guardsmen, and finally, on August 17, Springfield was easing into a tentative peace.

Roe, on the first day of a rare vacation, devoured the newspaper reports, paging through the late editions as he headed from Chicago to Elgin, a northwestern suburb. His sixty-nine-year-old mother, Henrietta, sat next to him, her body swaying with the motion of the train, suitcase bumping against her knees. She planned to spend the next two months with her daughter—Roe's sister—who lived in Elgin with her husband, editor of the *Elgin Daily News*. She worried about leaving Roe home alone, but he told his mother not to worry, he'd be fine. He promised her that he would come out to Elgin every night to visit, even if just for an hour or two.

After pulling into the station, Roe helped his mother onto the platform and down the stairs. He carried her luggage in one hand and held her steady with the other. It was unbearably hot, and if her palms were sweaty she could lose her grip on the railing and fall. His sister's house was within walking distance, and at the corner of Chicago Avenue and State Street they paused for breath. After a moment, Henrietta stepped from the curb just as Roe turned to pick up her suitcase.

Before he saw the automobile he heard its sounds, the grumble of motor vying with the shriek of brakes—uglier, almost, than the sight they accompanied, all four wheels passing over his mother's body, legs and torso and arms and head, missing nothing. Roe ran to where she lay, flat and flattened halfway between the curb and the middle of the street. Henrietta's left elbow was posed unnaturally, her eyes flipped back, unseeing pearls. Blood leaked from her ears. Off to the side a strange woman, the driver of the automobile, was screaming—high and low, closer and removed, the erratic cadence of church bells.

An ambulance sped Roe's mother to nearby Sherman Hospital. Henrietta didn't regain consciousness during the ride, but her pulse still twitched under the thin skin of her neck, beneath her bony wrists. The doctors circled and rolled her away. Roe called his sister, who arrived within moments, and they sat together in the waiting room. The screaming woman appeared, too, accompanied by husband and friends. Roe comforted her, said the accident was "unavoidable."

Doctors doubted his mother would survive. A blood vessel inside her head had ruptured, and she had suffered severe internal injuries. No sign of Henrietta's brain rousing itself by 2:00 a.m., no improvement at all. When the end came at 6:00 p.m. on August 20, Roe was by her side. For an entire month he didn't pursue one court case or save one girl.

He began work again in mid-September, timing his return with a lengthy feature in the *Tribune* that praised his war against the white slave traffic. Roe told the reporter that he enjoyed creative writing, loved his work, and still lived with his mother.

Madam Eva Dufour and her husband posted $25,000 bail in October and escaped to France, a disappointing finale to Edwin Sims's raids throughout the summer. But he had made considerable progress in spreading the word about white slavery, and in establishing himself as an authority on the subject. At Ernest Bell's urging, Sims submitted an article to *Woman's World*, a general interest magazine delivered to more than 2 million homes throughout rural America.

Sims described his work in the Levee and concluded:

It is only necessary to say that the legal evidence thus far collected establishes with complete moral certainty these awful facts: That the white slave traffic is a system operated by a syndicate which has its ramifications from the Atlantic seaboard to the Pacific ocean, with "clearing houses" or "distributing centers" in nearly all of the larger cities; that in this ghastly traffic the buying price of a young girl is from $15 up and that the selling price is from $200 to $600—if the girl is especially attractive the white slave dealer may be able to sell her for as much as $800 or $1,000; that it is a definite organization sending its hunters regularly to scour France, Germany, Hungary, Italy and Canada for victims; that the man at the head of this unthinkable enterprise is known among his hunters as "The Big Chief."

The magazine arrived at homes in Peoria and Lincoln and Macon, Georgia. Housewives browsing for tips on needlework and recipes instead read Sims's words by the flicker of gaslight, and passed on his warning to everyone they knew.

Suzy Poon Tang lasted only one night at the Everleigh Club. The sisters' millionaire client was so taken with "the roses he found blooming at the gateway to ecstasy," as her courtesan tutor, Doll, later put it, that he whisked her away to his North Side mansion and married her within the week. The rest of the Everleigh butterflies, relieved to be rid of the competition, cornered Minna and Ada and assaulted them with kisses, thanking the madams for releasing her.

And a harlot they'd lost in unhappier circumstances was found again. Nellie, plotting, plundering Nellie, turned up in the river, her skin blanched and limbs ballooned, bumping up against the moorings along a stretch of water where the crew teams raced on Saturday afternoons. The police recovered her purse, too, inside which she had tucked a note:

"I've made mistakes all my life, and the only persons to forgive me were two sisters in a sporting house. Kindly tell, for me, all the psalm-singers to go to hell and stick the clergymen in an ash-can. That goes double for all the parasites who talk a lot but don't do a damn thing to help a girl in trouble. Call Calumet 412. I'm sure of a decent burial if you do."

Minna and Ada obliged, selecting for their fallen courtesan a gleaming, silk-lined casket and dozens of vivid bouquets, and took turns consoling all the girls who had known poor Nellie. Along with liars and thieves, madams inevitably hired harlots with the saddest tendencies of all.

IT DON'T NEVER GET GOOD UNTIL THREE IN THE MORNING

The annex of the Coliseum, on the eve of
the 1908 First Ward Ball.

The Tribune *has come out against syphilis.*
Bet you 8–5 *syphilis'll win.*

—ANONYMOUS

A s usual, Ada was ready first, her dark honey hair rolled and pinned, her quiet gray gown ribbed with jewels, her lips coated in a soft pink gloss. Reclining on a silk settee in her sister's boudoir, she watched Minna pace across the length of the floor, ornamenting herself, one at a time, with rings and bracelets and necklaces and pins and brooches until her every inch shone and blinked. At last, fastening around her waist a thick stomacher of diamonds, emeralds, and rubies, Minna was satisfied.

Midnight approached, and the First Ward Ball could not properly start without them—Bathhouse John Coughlin called them the perennial queens of the event. The Everleigh butterflies were already milling about the downstairs parlors, just the right touch of daring with their mousseline waists, slouching plateau hats, and long strands of pearls dipping behind corsets. Katie, Ethel, Lillian St. Clair, "Jew Bertha" Morrison (not to be confused with "Diamond Bertha"), Virginia Bond, Bessie Wallace, Rose Harris, Belle Schreiber, Grace Monroe, and the rest all looked impossibly refreshed despite the recent visit from a client named Uncle Ned. Once a year, around the holidays, Uncle Ned took over the Music Room, thrust his bare feet into buckets of ice, downed a tall glass of sarsaparilla, and ordered the girls to circle him and sing "Jingle Bells." Shaking a tambourine, Uncle Ned shouted again and again, "Let's all go for an old-fashioned sleigh ride . . . *wheee!*"

The harlots insisted they didn't mind Uncle Ned, but Minna knew his antics grew tedious. "Entertaining most men at dinner or in any one of our parlors," she pointed out to Ada, "is more tiring than what the girls lose their social standing over."

Stunners, all of them, but Minna chose only one, the current pick of the house, to ride beside her and Ada in the leading brougham, drawn by three pairs of matched bays, red tassels swishing by their ears (take *that*, Vic Shaw). The rest of the girls would follow in comparatively plain hansoms and hacks, and hurt feelings would be forgotten as soon as they pulled up to the Coliseum. They should be thankful, really, that the Levee's annual fête was happening at all.

Before it was called the First Ward Ball—or "the Derby," in Bathhouse John's terminology—the affair was known simply as "the party for Lame Jimmy," the crippled pianist and fiddler hired by Madam Carrie Watson in the early 1880s. Officially, the event was a benefit to raise funds for the professor's medical care; unofficially, it was an excuse for Chicago's underworld to, as Madam Watson put it, "reign unrefined." Held at Freiberg's "Opera House" (Ike Bloom's attempt, at the time, to cultivate a bit of class and confuse the reformers), it enabled police captains and patrolmen to mingle peacefully with dope fiends and pimps and cadets and thugs, who, bowing to Levee decorum, checked their brass knuckles and blackjacks at the door.

More than three hundred revelers encircled Lame Jimmy, who sat stoically, fiddle poised beneath his chin, and played his repertoire of maudlin ballads, culminating in a discordant rendition of "Auld Lang Syne." Saloon keepers recited rambling toasts to the professor, swaying with glasses hoisted in the air, spilling as much champagne as they drank. Madams wiped away tears with gloved hands; it was the one night of the year when public displays of sentimentality were as chic as Gibson girls.

Lame Jimmy's party carried on happily and without incident until 1894. On January 31, at 6:00 a.m., a Harrison Street policeman named Charles Arado challenged his brother, Louis, also a cop, to shoot down a ceiling chandelier. Louis, drunk out of his mind, obliged, whipping out his pistol and sending crystals crashing to the floor. The shots attracted the attention of another cop, Officer John Bacon, as he patrolled 22nd Street. Bacon ran into Freiberg's and saw the smoke rising from Louis's gun.

Bacon approached his fellow officer. "Give it to me," he said, holding out his hand.

Louis laughed and shoved the gun back into his pocket. Brother Charles appeared beside him. "You're looking for trouble," Louis said. "I could lick a dozen like you."

He swung and connected hard with Bacon's chin. Charles followed with a punch on the shoulder.

Bacon stumbled out onto 22nd Street and wobbled toward the patrol box on Wabash Avenue. The footsteps of the Arado brothers grew louder behind him. "There he is," Charles yelled, and fired his own gun. The bullet whizzed past Bacon, and he returned fire. Three, eight, ten shots launched across Wabash, and one of them found Charles Arado.

"He has killed me, Louis," Charles said, and his body folded slowly, knees first, chest following, head coming to rest on the tracks.

The resulting civic protest was strident, and not even the intervention of Bathhouse John, a frequent presence at the festivities, could salvage the tradition.

Early the following winter, Bathhouse John was sitting in Hinky Dink's saloon, the Workingman's Exchange, lamenting the paucity of funds for the spring elections. The dependable gush of First Ward graft had abated, since gamblers were, at that moment, the main target of reformers' wrath. The den owners paid reduced protection rates or shooed the Coughlin-Kenna collectors off their properties altogether. The conversation then drifted to talk of Lame Jimmy—a shame, wasn't it, that the winter would have to pass without his party?

Then the idea struck Bathhouse John Coughlin. What if they sponsored a *real* ball, an opulent, fantastic, important ball, in a venue that could hold thousands?

"We take it over, Mike, we take it over!" he yelled, shaking Hinky Dink's slight frame, the bar stool wobbling beneath him. "Why, done right, there's thousands in it, tens of thousands!"

First Ward saloon keepers could be persuaded to donate booze, madams would come to show off their newest strumpets. Everyone was invited, from the classiest parlor houses to the lowest nickel cribs. Not merely invited, but expected.

The inaugural First Ward Ball took place at the First Regiment Armory, on Michigan Avenue and 16th Street, from 8:00 p.m. until the attendees were too drunk to tell time. Clergymen called it "a Saturnalian orgy," a "vile, dissolute affair," a "bawdy Dionysian festival," a "black stain on the name of Chicago." But Bathhouse John called it a success: $25,000 for the aldermen's coffers and a new Levee tradition—one that must surpass itself, in both profits and depravity, with each successive year.

And so it did, through the turn of the century and beyond. At the 1900 event, Bathhouse John, with great aplomb, welcomed the Levee's newest and already foremost madams, the Everleigh sisters, and Hinky Dink confided to the *Tribune* that it "don't never get good until about 3 in the morning." Two years later, the aldermen were informed that hard liquor could no longer be served in the Armory, so they rented the Coliseum instead, promising the Ball would be a "screecher." It was: Bathhouse John, clad in a "dream" of a vest, welcomed judges and congressmen and fifteen thousand First Ward constituents. "It is the best we have ever had," Coughlin insisted. Hinky Dink waxed practical, itemizing the distribution of the Ball's profits: "charity, education" (which consisted of hiring "good speakers to teach the people of the First Ward to vote the straight Democratic ticket"), and "burying the dead."

Reform groups had kept quiet tabs on the Ball over the years, but none cataloged its offenses as thoroughly as Arthur Burrage Farwell. The "dean" of Chicago reformers, as the *Tribune* called him, became serious about his mission work in 1888, when he returned home from a business trip to find his young son ill. That night, the boy died in a convulsion. Farwell's wife had taught their son the bedtime prayer Now I Lay Me Down to Sleep, to which the child added a line of his own: "God bless all the little boys, and all the little girls, and all the ladies."

Grief stricken, Farwell began devoting so much of his time to fighting the social evil and liquor—especially liquor—that his livelihood suffered. In June 1907, he finally quit his job as a shoe salesman to work full-time for the Law and Order League.

"Mr. Farwell," the *Tribune* reported, "is the generally recognized type of the modern Chicago reformer. He is a convincing, forcible talker—a short gray haired man whose eyes grow misty as he speaks of others' troubles."

Bathhouse John and Hinky Dink scornfully called him "Arthur *Garbage* Farwell" but didn't object when he purchased a ticket for the 1907 First Ward Ball. Let him come, get his kicks. Farwell took indignant note of the twenty thousand guests (a conservative estimate) guzzling ten thousand quarts of champagne and thirty thousand quarts of beer, the unconscious bodies piled like matchsticks in the aisles, a madam named French Annie stabbing her beau with a hat pin, a stampeding mob of men trampling one another to witness a circus act, and a thirty-five-foot bar collapsing to the floor during one of hundreds of fistfights. All but two aldermen, sick at home, were present.

"It's a little of the bunk," said Bathhouse, who found himself $40,000 richer the next morning. "You know."

Farwell wasn't so understanding. "The annual orgy forms a terrible commentary on the rule of the people of Chicago," he argued. "Can anything be more terrible than this?"

It was terrible enough, he concluded, to warrant a trip to the mayor's office as the 1908 gala approached. With less than two weeks to go, Farwell, Dean Sumner of Saints Peter and Paul, and several other reformers paid a visit to Mayor Fred Busse in City Hall.

"A real description of the 1907 ball is simply unprintable," Farwell began. "You must stop them from putting another on this year. You must stop this disgrace to Chicago. You must stop it in the name of the young men who will be ruined there."

The mayor squirmed in his chair, let his hands fall limply to his lap. "What do you want me to do, gentlemen?" he asked finally.

"You can refuse a liquor license. That will stop them."

Mayor Busse blinked. Farwell tried a different approach, planted his hands on the desk, and leaned in.

"Mr. Busse, you cannot in good conscience issue the liquor license for this affair. Suppose you had a young friend whose character and life you prized highly. How would you like to have such scenes of debauchery as are allowed at this ball to bring degradation and perhaps destruction to your friend? Prevent a repetition of this vile orgy!"

Farwell, perhaps, was unaware of Busse's own fondness for drinking and debauchery, of how he'd once boasted to reporters, "They don't need anyone sleuthing around after me. They can always get me any evening at J. C. Murphy's saloon, Clark Street and North Avenue." Perhaps he was unaware, too, of Madam Vic Shaw's special offer during the previous year's mayoral election—coupons featuring Busse's picture and these words stenciled beneath:

OUR PAL
IF HE WINS AND YOU
FIND THIS CARD IN
THE PARLOUR ~ BRING
IT TO MADAME
YOU GET $5.00 IN TRADE
~ FREE ~
ELECTION NIGHT
~~~ ONLY ~~~

And perhaps Farwell didn't know what Busse knew about the First Ward's voting power, which included even enfranchised Republicans. Besides, Busse figured, Farwell and his ilk had to be exaggerating the depravity of the Ball. Chicago had never cared much for the fainthearted or prudish; it was a city that kept one eye closed in a perpetual wink while the other looked away.

Sorry, Mayor Busse told his visitors, but a liquor license had already been issued.

The Bath and Hinky Dink continued preparations, and even encouraged Levee revelers to disregard any notion of a dress code (not that they needed any such prompting, but why pass up a chance to make a point?).

"The gents with whiskers is going to holler anyway," Bathhouse said. "If our ladies wore fur overcoats and black veils, somebody would roar, so let 'em go as far as they like. That's me."

But the aldermen's bravado was fleeting. On December 7, 1908, the *Tribune* published a warning in bold print:

The Tribune desires to announce that it will print a list of the names of the "respectable" persons who attend the First Ward Ball next Monday night. Every effort will be made to make the "among those present were" as complete as possible.

Now this, the First Ward leaders acknowledged, was a problem. True, Chicago's rank-and-file press corps spent more time at the Everleigh Club than in their offices. Minna always recalled the morning a fire erupted in a warehouse near the Levee. Flames spread, trapping several inside. An alarm shrieked through the streets.

An editor at the *Tribune* called for reporters. No one responded. Sighing, he picked up the phone and dialed the Everleigh Club's phone number: Calumet 412.

"There's a 4-11 fire over at Wabash Avenue near Eighteenth Street," he said. "Any *Tribune* men there?"

"The house is overrun with 'em," a maid replied. "Wait a minute, I'll put one on."

But newspaper publishers and owners weren't at liberty to indulge in such behavior. Any newspaper that profited from writing about the Levee had an obligation, at the same time, to editorialize against the district. The *Tribune*, as Chicago's paper of record, had taken the lead on both fronts.

Hinky Dink, now worried about sagging sales, assumed charge of the tickets himself and recruited Ike Bloom to help. First Ward henchmen again made the rounds, carrying rolls of tickets and lists, deciding who could be hit up and how hard:

"Mercy, a hundred tickets!" moaned a madam on the list. "Why, it was only seventy-five last year—and my girls don't go anymore, it is getting that common!"

"You've got two more girls here than you had last winter, ain't you," the collector pointed out. "Well, then."

And the madam found a hundred tickets clenched in her fist.

"Seventy-five tickets?" asked a businessman, sitting in his Loop office. "Your ball is getting pretty rough, and the newspapers—"

"You got a permit for a sign last year," the collector interrupted. "Didn't you? Huh?"

He did indeed, so seventy-five tickets now cluttered his desk.

Ladies of the Levee, at the behest of Hinky Dink, circulated the Union Stock Yards, flashing legs and waving reams of tickets at meatpackers. One hundred more reported for "nightly duty" in the back room of a saloon owned by Jim O'Leary (son of Mrs. O'Leary of Great Fire fame) on South Halsted Street, advising cattlemen in town for the stock show that they really must stay just a bit longer, check out the fabulous Derby at the Coliseum on the fourteenth. Bundles of tickets were shipped to red-light districts across the country, where sympathetic madams doled them out to harlots and loyal clientele.

And someone harassed the reverend of Garfield Boulevard Presbyterian Church, the latest reformer to join Farwell's anti-Ball efforts, leaving two menacing telephone messages and mailing eight letters, each written in the same firm, bold hand:

> If you dare to go to the First Ward ball
> Or write a single lying word about it this year
> A bomb will be put under your house and you
> and your family will be blown up.
> Mark what we say; this means business.
>
> —Pro Bono Publico

Five days later, on December 13, after Farwell failed to get a last minute court injunction, and after newly elected state's attorney John Wayman pleaded with Bathhouse John to compromise with the reformers ("We won't let parents bring their children," was the alderman's response. "Yah, even preachers can come—if they behave themselves and promise to stick by the rules"), a bomb did go off, not beneath the home of any clergyman, but at the building where every Chicago madam, whore, pimp, and degenerate would gather the following evening.

A t 8:20 on the evening of December 13, a dreadful boom rattled the Coliseum. The building's night custodian and his crew of thirty men were cleaning up debris from the international dairy show, and several of them went hurtling to the floor. The custodian and a dozen others who were still standing ran from the Coliseum into its annex. No windows remained along the front wall, just jaws of glass gaping open inside the frames. The storeroom was a confusion of worthless scraps. Entire sheets of roofing steel were shorn off and tossed fifty feet.

The men navigated the rubble and found that an adjacent junk shop was also demolished. The bomb had been planted in a narrow passageway separating the two structures, one hundred feet from where the cleaning crew, just a moment earlier, had been pushing mops and brooms. The explosion rocked the Oregon apartments and the Midland Hotel on Michigan Avenue, shattering every window in the rear of both buildings, as well as homes and storefronts along Wabash Avenue two hundred feet away. Pictures dropped from walls, vases slid from mantels. A man was catapulted from his kitchen chair. A ramshackle boardinghouse, across from the junk shop, rattled loose from its posts and now listed to one side.

Suspicions first fell upon the city's gambling factions. But a police inspector, after arriving on the scene, offered another scenario.

"You can draw your own conclusions," he said, "as to who might have had a hand in the work. Reformers of a certain type have turned heaven and earth in their efforts to prevent the ball from being held."

Bathhouse John and Hinky Dink remained undeterred, calling for a late afternoon rally at their State Street headquarters. The Ball had to have "tone," as First Ward forces called it, which meant meticulous preparations and careful selections. Round up the burliest collectors and station them by the doors. Detail the Levee pickpockets to posts outdoors—they'll be banished from Chicago for good if there are any complaints against them. Loyal precinct captains and First Ward employees, including "First Search" Hansen (so-called because, as coroner's deputy, he was the first to loot a corpse's possessions), were appointed cloakroom custodians and given blue ribbons to pin to their lapels. The men, already feeling the spirit of the Ball, looped arms around shoulders and swayed, singing, "Mariutch, she danca da houtch ma coutch, down at Coney Isle!"

Bathhouse left the meeting satisfied and rushed off to a last minute fitting for his specially designed costume—plain and drab this time, just to throw everyone off. On his way, he chatted briefly with reporters.

"Seems to me," he said, "that it would be better for the preachers to put in their time trying to get men into the church in the same proportion as women. They would be in better business than attacking our dance."

The preachers, meanwhile, gathered at the Church of the Covenant at Belden Avenue and Halsted Street. They held hands and swayed and lifted their faces, offering furious denunciations of the Ball. U.S. District Attorney Edwin Sims, still riding his popularity from the summertime Levee raids, spoke on the evils of white slavery. The discussion was more

relevant than ever, he argued, with the Derby taking place that evening—
that wretched, sinful gathering that recruits its "feminine element" largely
from the resorts of the 22nd Street district.

U nbelievable, this traffic. Trolleys stalled all along Wabash and State,
automobiles and cabs parked askew, carriages lined in an endless
chain. Fifteen thousand men, women, and children darting through the
frigid December night, curious for a glimpse of this strange procession, the
painted ladies in their furs and extravagant hats, wide brims circling their
heads like miniature rings of Saturn. Lifted above the mass, moving slowly
toward the Coliseum, the Everleigh sisters heard the cries "They're here!"
and watched the crowd part, as if by Moses's hand, for their brougham. Behind them, and behind their thirty butterflies, followed the lesser Levee attractions.

And they were all out tonight: Frankie Wright, madam of the Library,
so-called in ironic homage to six unread books she'd stacked on a shelf. Big
Jim Colosimo's white slavery partner, Maurice Van Bever, and his wife,
Julia. Big Jim himself and his wife, Victoria. "Terrible" Johnny Torrio, Big
Jim's new bodyguard, just imported from the Five Points neighborhood of
New York City. Years later, Torrio, too, would import another Five Points
gangster: a young comer named Alphonse Capone, whose first job entailed
buzzing madams to warn them of imminent raids. Capone, like every good
First Ward thug, would enroll in Hinky Dink Kenna's Democratic Club,
but he had more than voter drives in mind. Capone wrested all control of
the ward from the longtime alderman, who became, as the *Tribune* put it,
"too old and feeble to defend his empire."

Ed and Louis Weiss, the Everleighs' crafty next-door neighbors, were
in line, and there was Vic Shaw, her white slaver husband, Roy Jones,
squeezed by her side. Policemen encircled the sisters and their girls, protecting them from groping hands as they entered the Coliseum, a sprawling urban castle with spires and turrets—Chicago's answer to Madison
Square Garden.

Inside felt like a racing heart, thrumming and pulsing to its own erratic
beat. "So close was the press," the *Record Herald* noted, "that even those already drunk were forced to stand erect." Thirty thousand people in a
venue meant for half that number, lunging and thrashing, bodies colliding.

Mouths screamed through nickel-store masks. Women wilted and collapsed to the floor—"Gangway, dame fainted!" was a frequent cry—and then were lifted and passed from hand to hand, crowd surf style, to a growing pile of weary bodies in a tucked-away corner.

The air was damp with breath and sweat, the floor slick with spilled beer, ankle deep. Men dressed like women, women dressed like men, androgynous revelers dressed like jockeys, clowns, Indians, Gypsies, and page boys, madams with fur capes slung over bare shoulders, harlots in slit skirts, peekaboo waists, bloomers, and even bathing suits ("mighty little suit of any kind," quipped the *Tribune*), one notorious magdalen dressed like a nun.

Minna knew what came next: The band struck up the Everleigh Club's theme song, "Stay in Your Own Back Yard," in honor of the sisters' arrival. This was the one night of the year when the parameters of their own backyard shifted and stretched, when they took to the same dance floor as the pimps and white slavers and cretins who would never be permitted past the Club's doors, when any ignorant observer who knew nothing of Levee hierarchy might fail to distinguish them from the rest. It was a reminder, panting quietly in her ear, of how low they once were, all those indignities that had to be wrapped in lie after lovely lie—wrapping too thick, now, to ever tear open.

Every eye beamed on them, and Minna and Ada pushed through the writhing crowd with leisurely grace, heading for their private box on the north side of the room. Reserved for Levee leaders and rich slummers, the boxes ran all the way around the dance floor and a step above it, similar to those at a horse show. Hundreds of men crowded the Everleigh box, waiting for the sisters and their butterflies.

Here came Bathhouse John Coughlin, not looking at all like himself, dressed in a funereal black suit and shoes, the only dash of color his vivid lavender cravat and a red sash laced around his bosom emblazoned with the words GRAND MARSHAL. Where was his usual costume—the violet trousers, the spit-shined yellow pumps, the white waistcoat brocaded with red rosebuds and carnations, the pink gloves, the silk top hat, the swallowtail coat forked in back like a shark's fins, deep green and large enough to cover a billiards table? Surely he had his reasons for the subdued attire, but this was not the appropriate moment to ask what they were.

It was midnight, time for the Grand March.

Bathhouse arched his back and held his arms aloft, looking like a 250-pound capital Y, and then folded, as deeply as his girth would allow, into a deep bow. Minna and Ada rose and stood on either side of him, snaked their arms through his. Vic Shaw fumed from her box and would later claim she was the madam queen of the Ball—co-queen, at the least—and that she took turns with the Everleighs in leading the march.

"It was usually me," she insisted, "though I never went much for those purple pants the Bath wore. Hink had better taste. He always wore a tux."

But Vic Shaw was lying—she hadn't been queen of the ball since the Everleighs came to town.

Bandmaster Erlinger cued the musicians and flourished his wand. Minna, Ada, and the Bath skipped to the south end of the hall, and anyone still capable of standing, or at least leaning on a nearby body, lined up behind them. Tens, dozens, hundreds, thousands, following the alderman and the sisters in a wobbly procession, singing the First Ward Ball anthem until their throats were raw:

Hail, hail, the gang's all here—
What the hell do we care; what the hell do we care—

"I intend to stay until it's over," Dean Sumner fumed to a reporter. "Six o'clock in the morning, if necessary. I want to know what goes on here."

As the dean spoke, a harlot stumbled over to him. She winked and beckoned, curling one finger down at a time, a slow-motion invitation. The dean's jaw took a slow stroll southward.

Bathhouse John pranced and twirled an Everleigh sister beneath each arm.

Hail, hail, the gang's all right—
What the hell do we care now?

"Why," Hinky Dink exclaimed to a reporter, his normally paper white skin flushed pink from champagne, "it's great! It's a lallapalooza! There are more here than ever before. Those reformers tried to blow up th' place, an' look what they got for it. The *Tribune* thought people was gonna stay away. Well, look at it! All th' business houses are here, all th' big people. All my friends are out. Chicago ain't no sissy town!"

The parade was as thick now as it was long, at least twenty thousand strong and still growing, picking up stragglers as it turned the corners of the Coliseum. Thousands more outside, lacking tickets and clout, beat on the doors. The tuba stuttered, the trumpet wailed. Bathhouse signaled one more lap.

"The Hon. Bathhouse Coughlin and the Hon. Hinky Dink Kenna," the *Tribune* would write the next morning, "gave the social event of their lives last night—and the event was the crowning disgrace of Chicago. They packed the Coliseum so full of gentlewomen of no virtue and gentlemen attached to the aforesaid gentlewomen that if a great disaster, thorough in its work, had befallen the festive gathering there would not have been a second story worker, a 'dip,' thug, plug ugly, porch climber, dope fiend, or scarlet woman remaining in Chicago."

The last marchers stumbled off the dance floor, and the wine merchants set to work, stacking champagne bottles in tall pyramids on tables. College boys elbowed for room next to street bums, shaking cups in the air, heckling for free drinks. A woman draped herself over a box, her body limp as laundry on a line, and gave an order:

"Pour champagne, cul, pour champagne into me mout'."

A cop hauled her away. Another woman, dressed as a five-year-old boy, wielded a sand shovel and guzzled champagne from a tin pail. Courtesans lay facedown on the floor amid broken glass. Men tore at gowns and got stabbed with hat pins. A harlot swung a whip across the exposed buttocks of five drunks lined against the wall.

Back at their box, Minna and Ada welcomed the young rakes who crowded around them. Could they have a sip of champagne from an Everleigh girl's slipper, just as Prince Henry of Prussia did during his visit all those years ago? The madams obliged, refilling glass after glass, spending at the rate of $50 an hour, faster than anyone else. Empty wine bottles piled high on their table and spread throughout their box. One of Farwell's men from the Law and Order League stood nearby, struggling to hold his pen steady.

"We saw as many as thirty fights in the course of an hour," he wrote, "and there were always six or seven going at once at any time. This was particularly true of one corner of the hall, where the proprietors of a notorious house in Dearborn Street had a box, over the railing of which they were handing out free wine and champagne. The crowd fought around the box like wild beasts to get the liquor, the women swearing as loudly as the men."

Ike Bloom, too, noticed the fury of business at the Everleigh box, the glasses touching in spirited toasts, the slippers lifting to eager mouths.

"Keep it up, Minnie!" he yelled to Minna, tipping his derby. "You're the only live ones here!"

She waved back, but the thought, temporarily dormant, roused itself and fluttered inside her mind: There was no way to tell how long being live ones would last.

DISPATCH
FROM THE U.S.
IMMIGRATION COMMISSION

DANGEROUS AMUSEMENTS—THE BRILLIANT ENTRANCE TO HELL ITSELF

Young girls who have danced at home a little are attracted by the blazing lights, gaiety and apparent happiness of the "dance halls," which in many instances lead to their downfall.

Correspondence captured in raids instituted by agents of the commission shows some of these methods of recruiting. These letters are extremely valuable "human documents" relating to persons of the class in question. The men seem to feel affection for their children; they talk tenderly with reference to the fortunes or misfortunes of their mothers or relatives; they send polite greetings to one another and to their friends. At the same time they discuss the characteristics of the women in question with the same coolness that they would name the good points of a horse or a blooded dog which they have for sale.

DEAR FRIEND:

I can assure you that I have found a woman the like of whom you can never find; young, beautiful, and who fully decided to leave. . . . I could send her by the first mail steamer, so as soon as you get this letter send me the ticket or the money. . . . I will send you her photograph. Her beautiful teeth alone are worth a million.

MY DEAR MRS. —

I have just been to see the cigars; they are fine, young and good-looking; she has four of them, but it seems that they are in debt here to the extent of $300 each: that is for their fare and other expenses for bringing them from Japan . . . now, if you feel like advancing them $300 each, they are ready to go at once . . . this money you will get back as soon as the cigars earn it.

FRIEND ARTHUR:

. . . For your friend who was just arrested I am very sorry. Well, this will cost him a lot of money. It is very dangerous, this kind of business. A person has to be mighty careful. I have seen it coming. Here in Chicago the trouble is not over yet.

Belle Schreiber, Everleigh Club butterfly
and Jack Johnson's paramour.

*I am not a reformer. I am trying to make
reform unnecessary.*
—ARTHUR BURRAGE FARWELL

On Saturday, March 13, 1909, Minna, accompanied by her two maids, climbed into the Everleigh Club's automobile. Painted a cheerful yellow, with a boulder-size arrangement of artificial flowers affixed to the hood, the machine had replaced their carriage as her chosen mode of transportation for jaunts downtown. But instead of directing her driver to the First Dearborn Bank for the usual daily deposit, Minna requested the Municipal Court Building. The car headed north to the Loop, cold needles of rain rapping the windows, as she prepared for her date in the courtroom of one Judge Cottrell.

The charge: selling liquor without a license.

Arthur Burrage Farwell had been exceptionally busy lately, gathering evidence about licenses (or the lack thereof), sending undercover Law and Order League detectives into dives—even on New Year's Eve—to see what transpired after the 1:00 a.m. closing law. He also convinced fifty ministers to coordinate a day of sermons against the "trade in rum," a ploy that guaranteed headlines. The whole city had gone mad lately; the health commissioner was arresting people for spitting, of all things, and proposed an ordinance against smoking on elevated trains and streetcars as a way to combat the "spitting evil."

Minna remembered the advice an Illinois congressman once imparted to Bathhouse John: Stick to the "small stuff" and let the "big stuff" alone. The approach worked quite well for the alderman, politically as well as financially, and its reversal was equally successful for the Everleigh sisters. Since their graft fees and friendly relations with the police allowed the Club to remain open, why demand protection against the reformers' pettier attacks? This court date was bothersome, sure, but inconsequential in the scheme of things, and the jury proved as much with their verdict: a fine of $25.

F or all the agitation over the First Ward Ball, the bomb throwing and threat slinging and churlish back-and-forth, the Levee showed no signs of submission. Business had been brisk despite the visiting firemen's nightly vigils outside their doors. The most recent damage, in fact, had been wrought not by the Bible brothers but by the Weiss brothers, Ed and Louis.

The Weisses' old ploy of paying cabdrivers to drop off drunken revelers at their resorts instead of the Club was more lucrative than ever, owing to the advent of the automobile. Even worse, Ed married a former Everleigh Club girl, Aimee Leslie, who helped him run his place, using her impressive bordello pedigree to lure potential clients too foolish to distinguish an imitation from the original.

"They have us in the middle," Minna joked to Ada. "But they've yet to get us in a corner."

One night in April, a few weeks after Minna's court date, two men appeared at the Club's door knowing exactly where they were and what they wanted. For once, the madam yearned to escort clients—and wealthy clients at that—to the Weiss brothels herself.

Jack Johnson and his manager, George Little.

As his name implied, Little was short and squat, with a face that invariably looked as if it had just been slapped, flushed and tinged with shock. Once the stable manager at the Palmer House, Little had worked his way up, making the right connections and a few real estate acquisitions in the Levee. He now owned his own saloon, the Here It Is, on the West Side, and ran a combination bar and brothel called the Imperial on Armour Avenue, next to one of Maurice Van Bever's dives.

Most important, Little was the "Levee czar"—the man sent personally by Ike Bloom to collect protection payments for Bathhouse John and Hinky Dink. Minna and Ada gave Little nearly $800 a month, the most of any house on the line, which didn't include occasional emergency contributions to thwart harmful legislation in Springfield.

But that night, George Little wasn't there to collect. By his side stood a man, six feet two and two hundred pounds, his frame overwhelming the doorway. A $1,500 diamond ring, a gift from Little, gleamed atop the knuckle of one long finger. He was a boxer—the new heavyweight champion of the world, no less—and he was famous not principally for his skill inside the ring but for the color of his skin.

His name was Jack Johnson, and he wanted in.

The sisters didn't consider themselves prejudiced. Minna, after all, never forgot why she lost her religion—the day a Negro burned to death in her Virginia hometown and she watched, sickened, as white children lined the pews of the church to snicker at the sight of his charred bones.

"Even if I am a Virginian," Minna later explained, "I am not intolerant. But I do know that every colored woman hates every white woman. . . . I know colored women, and they would kill white women who took their men. . . . In his heart, every colored man hates white men. That's a reality. I don't believe in illusions. . . . And as for Desdemona kissing Paul Robeson in *Othello*, that I don't wish to see."

But the sisters knew they had to be careful; any misstep or lapse in judgment could impugn their house. Inviting Scott Joplin to play ragtime for an evening alongside Vanderpool Vanderpool was one thing; inviting Joplin to climb the stairs with the choicest girls in Chicago was quite another. The Club's clients appeared to agree. When they spotted Johnson in the doorway, the men's raucous laughter diminished into a scuttle of whispers, and then a taut silence.

Minna looked at Ada, noted the same understanding in her return gaze. She slipped through the crowd—*Excuse me darling, pardon, I'll be right back*—and pulled George Little aside. With all due respect, Minna said, she couldn't allow his friend into the Everleigh Club.

George Little replied that, with all due respect, he was in charge of doling out protection.

A look passed between them, each tracking the course of the other's brain, a carousel of cause and effect. There was a slim, subtle difference between a request and a threat, and Minna, familiar with the nuances of each, nodded at George Little and let them both pass.

What Minna didn't know, what she couldn't have known, was how charming the Everleigh girls would find the boxer. They marveled at his physique, the camel hump of his biceps. They giggled at his jokes, slipped their dainty hands in his. When Jack Johnson invited five of them—Belle Schreiber, Lillian St. Clair, Bessie Wallace, Virginia Bond, and "Jew Bertha" Morrison—to take a ride in his big shiny touring car, they pulled on their fur capes and piled in.

The sisters were thankful the incident had passed, but the following afternoon, word spread through the Club that Jack Johnson would come by again to pick up the girls. He wanted one harlot in particular, Belle Schreiber, a twenty-three-year-old brunette who had joined the Club the previous year.

Minna cautioned all five butterflies, one at a time, to refuse Johnson's offer. If they were found in the company of the boxer, in direct violation of her and Ada's wishes, they would lose the best job they ever had. A loyal lieutenant trailed the girls, spotted them cruising around town in Johnson's car, and reported the bad news to the madam. Minna held firm—five of her best courtesans banished in one shot.

But the waiting list for the Club, if unfurled, would reach clear across Dearborn Street. They would find new girls, *good* girls, ones who obeyed rules—or at least sought redemption if they happened to break them.

Clifford Roe's life seemed stark and empty with his mother no longer in it. He crammed work into every moment. There were so many cases streaming into the courts, so many laws to push and speeches to give, that deciding what to pursue took nearly as much time as the pursuits themselves. He traveled to Iowa to advise a Council Bluffs congressman who was sponsoring an antipandering law. The Pennsylvania State Legislature began planning one of its own. Presuming other states would follow suit, Roe, along with Ernest Bell, Arthur Burrage Farwell, and Harry Parkin, an assistant U.S. district attorney under Edwin Sims, expedited the process by appealing directly to every governor in the country.

"That there is a systematic traffic in girls of American homes—a hunt, sale and ruin of our girls—has been established by federal prosecutors in enforcing federal laws which apply to alien girls, by state prosecutors and rescue workers," they wrote. "It is beyond question a fact—a menace to all American homes, for the traffic is ruthless, insidious and national—even international. Approximately 100,000 girls per year are recruited, more from rural than urban homes. . . . Is there adequate law or punishment in your state? . . . Delays cost 180 daughters per day. Please telegraph your reply—at our expense."

Even if the states complied, and quickly, young girls would be at risk as long as the federal government remained uninvolved. In order to spur those politicians into action, Roe needed a sensational case, one that proved an underground network among states, one worthy of national headlines, with a victim more sympathetic—and credible—than Mona Marshall.

At first, Ella Gingles appeared to fit those requirements nicely. Early on the morning of February 19, 1909, the janitor at Chicago's Wellington Hotel unlocked the fifth-floor bathroom to uncover a ghastly sight. Gingles, eighteen, lay bloody and semiconscious on the floor, her arms tied over her head, her legs bound at the ankles. She was blindfolded and gagged with a towel. Patches of her hair had been ripped out. Next to her body lay a bottle of wine and a vial of laudanum, both half-empty. She was sprawled on her side, wearing only a thin nightgown with the name "A. Barrette" stitched on the collar. Thirty slash wounds crisscrossed her face, torso, arms, and legs.

When Gingles came to, she said she was an Irish immigrant who worked in a lace shop in the lobby of the Wellington Hotel. Agnes Barrette, who owned the lace shop, had tried to send Gingles to French Lick Springs, Indiana, to become a white slave. Gingles refused, and Barrette retaliated by breaking into her room and stealing some of her lace and jewelry. Then Barrette forced her to sign a confession claiming that she, Gingles, was the thief, and that the shop owner was merely recovering her rightful possessions. Shortly thereafter, Gingles was walking to her home on LaSalle Avenue when Barrette threw pepper in her eyes and bashed her on the forehead. The next thing she knew, the janitor at the Wellington was trying to rouse her as she lay battered and raped on the bathroom floor.

The girl's lawyer, naturally, hoped that Roe would take the case and nail Barrette with a pandering charge. But Barrette, a thirty-one-year-old respected businesswoman, had a solid alibi. The girl's gaping wounds turned out to be minor scratches; the blood on her gown was red wine. The alienists were called in. While some continued to believe she was the victim of a white slavery plot, the press, in Chicago and across the country, ran wild with speculation that Gingles was an autohypnotist, a monomaniac (in which case she would have no memory of cutting herself and truly believed her story), or in a state of hysterical insanity. Roe examined the scene at the Wellington Hotel, visited Agnes Barrette's lace shop, and concluded that "the whole thing looks queer."

He advocated publicity as a means of stopping the white slave traffic, but that approach clearly carried some unintended consequences. Gingles's story, though strikingly detailed, sounded like an osmotic recitation of every white slave case he'd ever tried. As his reputation and clout spread—he was known now as the William Lloyd Garrison of the white slavery movement—he had to exercise caution, be precise in his judgments. *The New York Times* covered Ella Gingles daily, but Roe would have to find another girl—one who would make the case for a comprehensive federal law, to protect all of America.

HAVE YOU A GIRL
TO SPARE?

The Paris, white slave headquarters for Maurice Van Bever.

*It is a conceded fact that woman has been reared as a
sex commodity, and yet she is kept in absolute ignorance
of the meaning and importance of sex.*

—EMMA GOLDMAN

Roe didn't yet know it, but his girl—his most important white slave case yet—was about to find him.

While the Everleigh sisters dealt with the aftermath of the Jack Johnson incident, interviewing and tutoring their five new harlots, a girl named Mollie Hart boarded the Nickel Plate Road in St. Louis, heading for Chicago. A man calling himself Bill accompanied her. Mollie's husband, Mike, planned to join her within a few days. He scraped by doing carpenter work in Missouri, and heard there was better money to be made waiting tables and bartending in such a big city.

Mollie, for her part, planned to "keep books."

She and Bill arrived at the LaSalle Street station in Chicago. They lingered over breakfast, celebrated their arrival with several glasses of wine, watched the city blur past them. In the early evening, Bill took her to the Paris, 2101 Armour Avenue, and Mollie insisted she didn't "know what kind of a place it was."

She slipped from room to room, still tipsy. There was a piano and a settee on the first floor and a wide space where a door should have been, leading to an adjacent saloon. The lady of the house, Julia Van Bever—who preferred to be called "Madam Maurice"—found her and pointed in the direction of the dining room. Mollie was to go back there, where three other girls were waiting.

With her husband standing nearby, Madam Maurice issued instructions. When the police come, the girls should say that they knew they were in a "bad place," and that they'd been in such places before. She asked each girl her age.

"Nineteen," Mollie answered.

The couple corrected her—better to say "twenty." And from now on, her name was Fern.

Mollie stood quietly and listened, not knowing what else to do. She realized, finally, that she was "supposed to be sporting," and decided it was best to pretend she knew all along.

The girls were fed supper and ushered upstairs. Maurice Van Bever came to visit Mollie by himself. He promised again that he would give her husband work as a bartender, better pay than anywhere else, $18 a week. She could even go to St. Louis and ride back to Chicago with him.

"Now, when you go to St. Louis, get some girls and bring them back with you," he said. "I will give you fifty dollars."

The day's instructions and preparations finished, Minna took her stack of newspapers into the Gold Room to relax before clients arrived. She picked up the *Chicago Daily Socialist* and spotted an article about Ella Gingles, that strange Irish girl who had turned the nation's eye toward Chicago with her salacious tale of white slavery.

"It was discovered," the article read, "that one of the protecting influences which was keeping the arm of the law off this white slave gang was Mayor Fred A. Busse, who is a habitué of the Everleigh Club, the notorious south side resort to which the Barrette woman who tortured the Gingles girl sells innocent and good looking girls for a price which varies from $50 to $200."

Minna's lips parted, her blood surged. She read the sentence again, and then the next.

"Both Busse and the Barrette woman are close friends of the Everleigh sisters who run the notorious resort. There is at this time in that resort a little Jewish girl less than 17 years of age who was sold to the Everleigh sisters by the Barrette woman for the sum of $200. There are now on the outside of the resort two other girls who declare that the Barrette woman tried to induce them to go to the Everleigh Club. . . . If further proof were needed of the connection of the Barrette woman with the Everleigh sisters the court room scene at the late trial of Minnie Everleigh"—if only her name were the only error in this piece—"for overstepping the bounds a bit, furnishes all that is desired. Agnes May Barrette came into court with Minnie Everleigh and sat by her side during the trial as a friend."

Before she could find Ada, the telephone rang. It was a *Tribune* reporter, a friend. He asked if Minna had seen the *Socialist,* and would she care to comment on the allegations?

This was one time when she damn well would.

"The story printed about Miss Barrette in the *Socialist* in this matter is a lie from beginning to end," she said. "I do not know Miss Barrette and she never accompanied me to court in the trial of any case against me. I was in court alone with my two colored maids, and Miss Barrette was never with me. No girl ever came here on the direction of Miss Barrette as far as I know. And the statement that we have a 17-year-old girl here is a lie."

She hung up the phone, clutching the newspaper in her hand, and called for Ada. Obviously, the *Socialist*'s editors resented the Club because neither they nor their audience could afford to step through its doors.

Ada appeared, her face tight with worry. She knew Minna's voice, the subtle shifts and tone and tenor, the arbitrary nature of her reactions. Her anger could hide beneath a forced gaiety or, like now, demand to be recognized for what it was.

Minna rattled the article in her sister's face, suggested they leave town. Just for a few months, until the fall. They'd go to Europe, travel around the world. They had surrounded themselves with good people, not this Miss Barrette, whoever she was, and the Club would run smoothly in their absence.

Ada agreed, and they set off in the yellow convertible, heading north on Dearborn Street to the Federal Building. United States Commissioner Mark A. Foote agreed to see them right away. The sisters, if they so desired, could leave the country immediately; he would expedite the process and just forward their passports along. They thanked Commissioner Foote and went home to pack.

The sisters bade farewell to the girls, instructed the staff to mind them carefully, and took a cab to the LaSalle Street station. The 20th Century Limited would whisk them to New York, where a luxury liner awaited. It had been ten years since they'd arrived in Chicago—time to escape its smoke and noise, its unrelenting spotlight. They'd see the *Apollo and Daphne* in Rome, slip into the anonymity of London fog.

Sarah Joseph worked as a "servant girl" in a house on Geyer Avenue in St. Louis. She'd met Mollie Hart a year prior, in the summer of 1908, in a downtown department store. They became fast friends, getting together after work at chop suey restaurants and dance halls, and then Mollie moved to Chicago. During a weekend visit to St. Louis, she insisted Sarah meet with her. She had something very pressing to discuss.

Sarah just *had* to move to Chicago, Mollie urged. The lights, the theater, the White City amusement park with its electric tower and water chutes and dance performances featuring, if Sarah could imagine, a fifteen-foot snake—there was nothing else quite like it. Sarah finally agreed; the big city wouldn't be so overwhelming with a close friend by her side.

As Mollie had promised, Sarah's ticket was waiting for her, already paid in full. She boarded the train, coming over the Wabash line. In Chicago, Mollie greeted her at Union Station. The two friends clasped arms and kissed cheeks, and Mollie waved over a hansom. They traveled south for eighteen blocks, and Mollie asked to stop at 21st Street and Armour Avenue.

Sarah had taken care that morning, selected a fine hat and dress, and now she stood on this horrid corner, breathing in the putrid perfume of varnish from a nearby factory, the faint scent of unwashed skin. A large brown building squatted before them, brick along the bottom half and clapboard along the top, with jutting awnings and curtains pulled tight across windows. Several men loitered by the curb, hands thrust inside pockets. It was 8:30 in the morning, and the metal doorknob was still cool inside her palm.

A man sat on a settee in the front room. He was elegant, dressed in a suit and silk top hat. He seemed to be waiting for them.

"I realized that Van Bever's place was a house of prostitution after I got there," Sarah said, "but I did not come to Chicago for that purpose. . . . I had never been in a sporting house before."

Van Bever had told Mollie what to say in her telegram to Sarah and escorted her down to the Negro housekeeper to make sure it was mailed. He had instructed Mollie's husband, Mike, to make sure they got "that Jew girl, Sarah Joseph, and bring her back."

Now, Mollie introduced her friend to her boss.

"You're a good-looking girl," Van Bever said to Sarah, "and ought to make a good living."

"I want to go home," Sarah said. She begged him for a train ticket.

"You'll like it," Van Bever answered, "when you get used to it."

In the midst of giving speeches, trying cases, and lobbying governors, Roe found his office thrown into turmoil. His boss, State's Attorney John Wayman, indicted Edward McCann, the respected police captain who had called in the Mona Marshall case. McCann was accused of accepting graft in the West Side Levee, ruled by the Frank brothers, Julius and Louis. Several reformers sided with McCann, including Jane Addams.

"I believe Inspector McCann is one of the most honest and efficient police officials that has ever had charge of this district," she said. "It hardly seems probable to me that a man who has done so much in the fight against the white slave traffic should be guilty of accepting money from these same people."

All told, Wayman's graft investigation, from McCann to rank-and-file officers to underworld cretins, had resulted in 105 indictments involving more than three hundred people—the greatest mass of indictments ever returned in one day in Cook County. It was a mess, but at least it was timely.

Roe was getting out.

His friend Adolph Kraus of B'nai B'rith and the Commercial Club of Chicago had contacted him and requested a meeting. Would he, they asked, consider resigning so he could prosecute panders full-time? The former group was more troubled than ever about Jewish involvement in white slavery, especially with the Frank brothers further shaming their race in the McCann debacle. To add one more stab of insult, both men were members of Kalverier synagogue, a prominent congregation in Chicago. "The revelations made at the McCann trial gave the world the wrong impression of the Jews and their morality as a race," said one of Kraus's associates. "The world is apt to believe that the Jews condone such things."

The Commercial Club, for its part, had just commissioned Daniel Burnham's "Plan of Chicago," a visionary ideal of the architect's City Beautiful movement: a permanent ribbon of green space around the city perimeter; a neoclassical museum for the center of Grant Park; a chain of Venetian-style canals and lagoons linking to the site of his 1893 World's Fair. Chicago should be known for its ambition and indefatigable civic spirit, not as the national hub for the trade in white girls.

Roe tendered his resignation letter to State's Attorney Wayman on August 21, 1909, and spoke with the press eleven days later, lying about both his reasons for quitting and his future plans.

"There is nothing political or personal about my resignation," he said. "I simply believe I have served the public long enough, and as I can return to private practice and make a great deal more money, I believe I should do so. . . . In addition to this, I have recently been selected as dean of the Chicago Business Law School, and that will take some of my time lecturing at night."

That fib would have to suffice during the final preparations. Roe had an initial pledge of $50,000, a sizable portion of which came from the *Tribune*, to fund his organization. He decided on a slogan: "Protect the Girl!" He hired a private secretary to work with him at home—he could not bring himself to leave the one he'd shared with his mother—and assembled a personal staff of detectives to concentrate exclusively on white slavery.

The detectives soon happened upon their first major break. One of them intercepted a letter written by a girl named Mollie Hart, intended for her husband, Mike, warning him to change his plans because he was being watched:

> Well, dear . . . if you get any girls coming up here you had better leave and send them a few days later or either get off at Hinsdale and put them in a hotel for a few days, or else don't bother with the girls. Mr. M. Van Bever said so you had better do something and don't fool too long and get the boss sore at you. . . .
>
> Burn every letter and telegram you receive from here. Leave the girls behind. . . . The girls will have to wait a few days but you come back at once alone.

Roe's detectives knew that Mike Hart would never read this warning, and the boy's capture would expose Van Bever's extensive white slavery ring. If girls were being sold and shipped across state lines, then President Taft would want to take immediate action.

DISPATCH
FROM THE U.S.
IMMIGRATION COMMISSION

William Simes

Harry Frank
"Frank, you are an inhuman
wretch. I'll give you the limit
of the law." $1,000 fine and one
year in prison.

Richard Dorsey
$300 fine and 6 months in prison

Louis Fleming
$800 fine and 1 year in prison

Clarence Gentry

Frank Arnell
$300 fine and 6 months in prison

Thomas England, Jr.
$600 fine and 1 year in prison

Andrew Lietke, alias Andy Ryan
$300 fine and 6 months in prison

CRUEL AND INHUMAN WHITE SLAVE TRADERS

Roe's rogues' gallery of panders.

Doubtless the importers and pimps have a wide acquaintance among themselves, and doubtless in many instances they have rather close business relations with one another; and inasmuch as all are criminals anyone escaping arrest can naturally appeal to another anywhere in the country for protection. Even a pimp whom he has never seen will give him shelter if he comes with a proper introduction. There are two organizations of importance, one French, the other Jewish, although as organizations they do not import. Apparently they hate each other; but their members would naturally join forces against the common enemy.

SO MANY
NICE YOUNG MEN

Gypsy Smith's parade through the Levee.

We have struck a blow for Jesus.
—Evangelist Gypsy Smith

The summer of 1909 had been a mixed one for Bell. Edward Mc-Cann's arrest and trial was a devastating blow to the battle against white slavery. He and Dean Sumner had both testified on the police captain's behalf and were deeply saddened by his conviction. Perhaps Clifford Roe was right when he said that "it is not always the fault of the broom that it does not sweep clean, but sometimes the person who holds the broom is to blame." How could Captain McCann remain honest within such a broken system?

Mary had fallen ill, too, and was recuperating at Battle Creek Sanitarium in Michigan. He missed her desperately but insisted that she stay put until she was well enough to travel. Late at night and in between meetings, he scribbled letters to his wife, equal parts update and endearment. "Now rest as long as you choose," he wrote in his ornate, hurried script, "though we need your head here." He tried for levity, suggesting he might address his letters to "Bitter Creek."

His wife's absence became a roving presence in the other parts of his life, a persistent reminder of visions unfulfilled. He'd left India thirteen years ago, but the knowledge of what he couldn't accomplish there remained a bruise too fresh to touch. His sermons felt listless and rote, hazy around the edges, words without a message. "Gracious God," he scrawled on a Midnight Mission pamphlet, "Please put this work on its feet, or please lift me up out of it."

The one shining spot in his life, at the moment, was his book contract. Currier Publishing, the parent company of *Woman's World*, asked him to edit an anthology of essays to be titled *War on the White Slave Trade: Fighting the Traffic in Young Girls*. They promised him a $400 advance, part of which, he told Mary, could be set aside for college expenses for daughter Clare and son Rex. Several prominent reformers, including Roe and

Edwin Sims, agreed to contribute. Agents of the magazine planned to knock on doors all over the country and sell copies, one by one.

Bell toured the Levee during the day before his sermons, jotting down observations, listing the nationalities of the dive keepers. Two or three places owned by Italian men, most notably Big Jim Colosimo. A "score of resorts . . . all of them extremely flagrant," managed by Jews. The French were the worst offenders; no fewer than fourteen resorts had blinking signs with "Paris" or "Parisian" in their names.

In early October, just when Bell needed it most, the Lord sent news that made him forget about McCann and every empty sermon, the sinners who slipped past his reach. Gypsy Smith, the British evangelist, kept the vow he'd made two years earlier and was returning to Chicago. He planned a march through the Levee district that would make the First Ward Ball seem like a quiet, intimate gathering.

Detectives arrested Mollie Hart first, on October 8. The girl left the Paris without incident, her only defense an offense: It was all Maurice Van Bever's fault; he used her as his tool, and she had to obey him or else. Sarah Joseph, the Jewish white slave, was rescued and sent to the Florence Crittenden Home for protection.

Mike Hart was more elusive. He never received his wife's letter, but he heard of her arrest and avoided the traps detectives set for him. Roe's cadre of sleuths posed as underworld figures and kept on Hart's trail, finally spotting him on the corner of Wabash Avenue and Harrison Street.

Van Bever, however, was nowhere to be found.

"When Mollie and Mike were arrested," Roe wrote, "the word spread through the underworld of Chicago like wild fire."

And the underworld of Chicago spread their own word in return, releasing story after story, each one subsuming and erasing the last. Van Bever had fled to France. Van Bever had fled to Seattle. Van Bever was still in Chicago, hiding out in a downtown hotel.

This last lead was confirmed by Roe's best sleuth—a man called, simply, "the Kid"—who summoned two city policemen. Too late—Van Bever was again invisible. Roe's men were everywhere at once, watching all edges of the city, depots, streetcars, boats, carriages. There Van Bever was, climbing into a closed carriage on State Street, heading south. And there he went, disembarking from that carriage and jumping into another traveling north on Dearborn. His comrades were always prepared, closed carriages idling, ready to spirit him away at any hour. Detectives took a cue from this approach, paying off certain hansom drivers and express wagons to follow Van Bever and offer him rides, pretend they were on his side.

Still no luck.

On the afternoon of October 13, Roe was walking through the Loop, heading west on Washington Street. City Hall stood to his right and the Chamber of Commerce to his left, a magnificent building with an interior courtyard awash in natural light. There, parked nearby, was a closed carriage he'd seen before. Its coachman, also familiar, wore a high silk hat and maroon livery festooned with solid gold buttons.

Roe stepped into the shadow of the building. All around him the city roared. He hid inside its noise, waiting, heart pecking at his chest. Time lolled, lazy and oblivious, seconds into minutes, and then there he was, Maurice Van Bever, stepping out of the Chamber of Commerce. His coachman opened the carriage door.

Roe stepped forward, out of his chaotic cocoon, and touched the man once, softly, on the shoulder.

"Your name is Van Bever?" he asked.

"The man so bold as a slave owner turned deathly white," Roe later recalled. "There seemed to be not a drop of blood left in him."

Van Bever stuttered, then steadied his voice. "Yes," he said, and that was that.

Roe motioned for a nearby policeman to make the arrest. The pander was permitted, per his request, to travel to the Desplaines Street station in his own carriage. Once there, Van Bever insisted he didn't even know he was wanted. "If the Hart woman accused me of assisting her in any way in that work, it is not true," he added. "I have always lived up to the orders of the police department in having all the girls registered at the stations. I never was arrested before, and I do not care to say anything more until I consult my attorney."

Roe's men captured Julia Van Bever next and began searching for panders in St. Louis. The press seized news of the "underground railway" between the two cities. At last, because of the Van Bever case, federal legislation seemed imminent. Ernest Bell, Arthur Burrage Farwell, and Edwin Sims were planning to consult with Congressman James R. Mann of Hyde Park.

"Chicago at last has waked up to a realization of the fact that actual slavery that deals in human flesh and blood as a marketable commodity exists in terrible magnitude in the city today," Roe boasted. "It is slavery, real slavery, that we are fighting. . . . The white slave of Chicago is a slave as much as the Negro was before the civil war . . . as much as any people are slaves who are owned, flesh and bone, body and soul, by another person. . . . That is what slavery is, and that is the condition of hundreds, yes, thousands of girls in Chicago at present."

He hunkered down to prepare for his upcoming trials. Maurice Van Bever, if convicted, would be his most important success to date.

The Frenchman's longtime partner in the Levee, meanwhile, made some preparations of his own.

Bell was distraught. All that excitement, all those prayers of thanks, and now the Gypsy Smith march might never happen.

Chicago's chief of police, Leroy Steward, refused to grant a permit. Appointed by Mayor Busse during the McCann scandal, the new chief wanted to hone the department's image, even imbue it with an air of refinement. He spoke of his interest in theosophy and "primal topics." Delicate, wire-rimmed glasses sat low on a pointed nose, a pipe remained clenched perpetually between his lips. There would be no unseemly talk of graft payments during *his* tenure.

It wasn't proper, Steward argued, for an evangelist to bring undue attention to the Levee district by leading a parade through its streets. It was "inherently vicious," he added, "a huge slumming party" and "sensational advertising scheme." But Gypsy Smith persisted. Sin must be exposed before it could be destroyed.

On October 16, two days before the parade's scheduled date, Chief Steward finally relented. Prolonging the evangelist's campaign to secure a permit would only ensure a larger crowd than had been expected in the first place.

He ordered a cavalcade of mounted policemen to escort the marchers, hoping to prevent any rioting.

The department also dispensed a secret order to the Levee:

> If you show yourself tonight during the parade, if a light shows from your house or if there is any sign of life from it while the parade is passing, you might just as well go out of business.
>
> Keep off the streets, in the houses and away from the windows tonight.

Every resort must comply, including the Everleigh Club.

Minna and Ada had returned to Chicago in the fall, relaxed and refreshed, talk of Agnes Barrette and seventeen-year-old Jewish girls duly forgotten. The Levee was a bit jumpy, what with the McCann trial and a new police chief eager to "decentize" the city, as he put it, but Hinky Dink made the necessary assurances. "The women have to be somewhere," the alderman said, "and they might as well be where they bother the least people."

The sisters decided they would heed part of the police department's order. Vanderpool Vanderpool must sit on his hands, and no one could climb the stairs, but clients would be admitted and free to mingle, quietly, about the parlors. Minna unlocked her frustration, speaking words meant only for Ada's ears.

"A girl in our establishment is not a commodity with a market-price, like a pound of butter or a leg of lamb," she ranted, while her sister *mmm-hmm*ed in all the right places. "She is much more on the same level with people belonging to professional classes, who accept fees for services rendered; she charges in accordance with the client's means. She doesn't 'sell herself' as these egg-heads keep shouting. Such statements are unfair and unjust. . . . A saner and truer conception of womanhood and of the responsibilities of women is the only way I know of that we can expect to take the sting out of 'slipping.' "

Ada let her sister finish. Minna fretted and fumed when they were alone, but never in front of the girls, her boys, or the visiting firemen—*especially* the visiting firemen. In fact, just as the Gypsy Smith cavalcade passed by 2131–2133 South Dearborn Street, Minna planned to gather everyone together and propose a raucous toast.

There were thousands, Bell thought, seven, eight at least, packed inside the Seventh Regiment Armory, a sprawling brick structure with a tower on each end, raised up like the arms of Jesus. He was the warm-up act to Gypsy Smith's main event, having preached just moments before to his largest audience ever. And now the crowd belonged to the evangelist, this brilliant man who was born in a tent and never attended even one day of school. Smith stepped through the mass of bowed heads and clasped hands, waiting for a chorus of prayers to drift into a single "Amen." Silence, now. He was humble, simply dressed, with worn loafers that rasped across the floor as he paced.

"A man who visits the red-light district at night has no right to associate with decent people in daylight," he shouted, pointing. "No! Not even if he sits on the throne of a millionaire!"

Bodies turned toward the exit, and the rear of the crowd became its head. They spilled out onto 34th Street wordlessly, closed in on either side by a squad of mounted policemen. Lit torches lashed at the night sky. Three brass bands followed, quiet except for the drums, pounding a heartbeat rhythm that kept pace with footsteps. Children marched alongside parents, wearing long black gowns that rippled at their heels.

North on State, west on 22nd. Shouts from the sidelines seared the quiet. Bell watched as onlookers crowded the curbs, jeering and laughing, and good Lord, they were being followed now by thousands, *tens* of thousands, fringing out on all sides. On Dearborn Street, every window was shuttered, every curtain drawn, every door locked, every light darkened.

"To Evangelist Smith's young crusaders," wrote Charles Washburn, "it must have seemed that vice was a deadly dull trade."

The missionaries knelt as one before the Everleigh Club.

Gypsy Smith raised an arm. The brass bands sputtered into song:

Where is my wandering boy tonight?
The boy of my tenderest care

The boy that was once my joy and light
The child of my love and prayer
Where is my boy tonight?
Where is my boy tonight?

Minna's boys were being good sports about the diversion, packed together on the silk divans and lined along the hallways, Everleigh butterflies keeping them silent company. Even Colonel MacDuff, a prominent Chicago attorney who stayed at the Club for days at a time, played along. The colonel, weary from trying cases, usually stormed through the doors, slapped $500 in Minna's palm, picked three girls, and headed upstairs. He ordered fried chicken and wine to be served in the boudoir and grew furious when clients tracked him down. Shooing them away, using a chicken leg for emphasis, the colonel explained he must be "thoroughly rested" before resuming work. But tonight the lawyer heeded Minna's wishes, waiting downstairs, sans chicken leg, with everyone else.

Dim the lights, the madam reminded Edmund, and make sure champagne flutes are filled.

The hymns crept into the pristine quiet of the parlors, uninvited guests demanding attention. "Wandering Boy." The Twenty-third Psalm. The Lord's Prayer. "Nearer, My God, to Thee." And then finally, thankfully, the procession moved nearer to Thee their God all the way out of the Levee.

Within ten minutes, the district was again ablaze, one light setting off the next, a contagious constellation. String bands and professors were released from quarantine. Corks launched into ceilings, dice somersaulted across tables. High heels clicked up stairs in a muted symphony of expectation.

Minna raised an arm, and a hundred glasses kissed in sweet mock tribute.

Clifford Roe barely slept. The neat compartments of his life spilled into one another. White slave letters piled on his desk. "Dear Sir," read one, ". . . I have not been out of the house for three months. I have not got any clothes to wear on the street because I owe a debt. I wish you would come and see me and I can tell you everything. . . . I am a White Slave for sure. . . . Please see to this at once. —VIOLA, Armour Avenue."

He interviewed victims during the day and gave speeches for various clubs at night. Ernest Bell's book inspired him to begin work on his own, titled *Panders and Their White Slaves*, based solely on his experiences in court. There was always a case on the docket. Mike and Mollie Hart were both convicted at the end of October. He traveled to St. Louis to extradite more panders back to Chicago.

And the trials of Maurice and Julia Van Bever crept closer on the calendar.

Julia Van Bever, and madams in general, puzzled Roe. He sifted through the files on her background: twenty-eight years old, born in Luxembourg in 1881, high school education, immigrated in 1900 to New York City, where she worked as a dressmaker and then ran a boardinghouse on West 50th Street. Moved to Chicago in December 1907 and married Maurice Van Bever two months later.

"How a woman like Julia Van Bever can retain so much that is womanly in appearance and so little that is womanly in nature," he wrote, "is a mystery."

Maurice Van Bever's trial was first, on November 10, 1909. The defendant sat "sphinx like and brazen" as Roe delivered his closing argument.

"He kills his victims body and soul when he gets them into his dens," he said. "I cannot imagine a worse fiend than one who makes good girls bad and bad girls worse, and this man Van Bever is one of them." Roe knew the value of a dramatic pause. "I hesitate," he concluded, "to call him a man."

Roe expected Van Bever's attorney, Daniel Donahoe, to be relentless. The prosecutor sat at his table, bracing himself.

"Sarah came to Chicago of her own free will and accord," Donahoe said, one hand chopping the palm of the other for emphasis. "She came on the train alone. Mike Hart says that he met her at eleven o'clock in the street in St. Louis." He tweaked his delivery, then, invited the jury to marvel at the lunacy of it all. "Eleven o'clock at night on the street in St. Louis, this innocent little Jewish girl. God help us and God help the Jews. If they were all innocent as little Sarah, we would soon be able to pay off our mortgages."

He continued for a long time, citing legal precedents, quoting a member of the British Parliament, adding the occasional witty aside. Roe let his eyes scan the jury—trouble. "Van Bever's lawyer," he noted, "had made a deep impression." Roe would have to readdress. The prosecutor rose and strode toward the jury box.

"Gentlemen," he began, "when you come to defend a man when there is no evidence upon which you can predicate an argument, it is one of the—I won't say 'tricks of the trade' of the lawyers, but it is one of the ways of lawyers to try to make the prosecutor the defendant by trying to embarrass him."

And Roe, as usual, talked his opponent down.

At the November 27 sentencing, the judge gave Maurice and Julia Van Bever the highest sentence under Illinois law for the first offense: one year in the Chicago House of Correction and a $1,000 fine. But the pander vowed that neither he nor his wife would ever go to prison and immediately appealed his decision to the state's supreme court.

Van Bever had an impressive defense fund—"thousands of dollars," Roe wrote, "probably a large portion of it contributed by the ring of slave traders who wanted to see the Pandering Law smashed into pieces"—and was able to return to the Levee. There was nothing the prosecutor could do to stop him, at least for now.

His only recourse was to make Van Bever's freedom as unsettling as possible. Roe would circle around him, remind the pander that lawyers, too, had a wide web of associates and were skilled at setting traps. In fact, just as Van Bever's trial closed, Roe's detective scored a lead on the Frenchman's partner, Big Jim Colosimo.

"We have positive evidence that the agents who obtained women for the Colosimo resorts not only plied their trade in St. Louis, but conducted a traffic between New York and Chicago," Roe announced on November 28. "The details of this organization's methods and its treatment of the women victims have been found to contain all the repulsive features revealed in the evidence produced against the Van Bevers."

But Big Jim was even more elusive than Van Bever. They couldn't find him loitering at depots or slinking between carriages or in the back room of any Levee saloon. No one seemed to know his face or recognize his name. It was as if this obese man in a seersucker suit and boater hat had simply vanished into the murky Levee air.

Colosimo, the official report conceded, "could not be reached."

"Time will show that great good has been done," Gypsy Smith insisted after the march, and why not let him think so? The Levee leaders knew what they saw after the last torch was extinguished, the last prayer offered. They knew twenty-five thousand men had come and knocked on their doors, guzzled their wine, and groped their women—the busiest night in the history of the district. And they sang their own hymns of praise: "I haven't done as much business in a single night since I have been located in this district," said one madam. "We had to shut our doors because we didn't have room for any more patrons," said another. "Greatest business we ever had!" said a third. A Negro resort keeper fired three celebratory shots in the air. "You'da thought it was the militia coming back from the war," Vic Shaw added, "and that was the night that we all had the biggest business we'd had in years."

For once, Minna agreed with her nemesis. "We were certainly glad to get all this business," she said, "but I was sorry to see so many nice young men down here for the first time," her tone so sweet and unaffected it seemed possible she meant it.

IMMORAL PURPOSES, WHATEVER THOSE ARE

Edwin Sims.

*I deplore the Mann Act as lending itself to a dreadful
pun, the revenge that the Gods of Semantics take
against tight-zippered Philistines.*

—VLADIMIR NABOKOV, *Lolita*

arly in December 1909, Ernest Bell found himself in Mayor Busse's
office, standing between Arthur Burrage Farwell and Bathhouse
John Coughlin. Since the summer, in the midst of editing his anthology, Bell had assisted Farwell in his efforts to defeat the First Ward
Ball. After the 1908 fiasco, which reformers and First Warders alike agreed
was the most depraved—and the most successful—in history, Farwell had
begun his anti-Derby campaign early.

Unlike last year, when Busse insisted the aldermen had gotten a license
fair and square and sent Farwell on his way, the mayor now appeared re-
ceptive, weighing the political ramifications of both sides.

Bell turned to Bathhouse John.

"You," said the reverend, "are leading yourself and others to damna-
tion."

The alderman shrugged. "It's not worse than other balls."

"But you run it for your own profit."

Coughlin's lips twisted into a smirk. "Well, don't you make your living
off the people down there in the district?"

Bell was not privy to the later exchange between the mayor and the alderman, but the 1909 Ball, held on Monday, December 13, was nothing
more than a concert. A band played to empty rows of chairs, and the dance
floor was dry and deserted. Three thousand people did not a Grand March
make, especially with no Everleigh sisters in attendance.

Rather than credit the reformers, Bathhouse John blamed the Ball's "fiz-
zle" on the "hoodoo" of the number 13.

"If the day had been any other except the thirteenth," he argued, "the
ball would have been given, and it would have been a bigger success than
ever before."

Bathhouse John produced a list of combinations of words, all the letters adding up to thirteen, that had jinxed him:

> Leroy T. Steward
> Chief of Police
> Twelfth annual
> First Ward Ball
> At the Coliseum
> Monday evening
> Dec. Thirteen, '09
> The Grand March
> John J. Coughlin
> First Ward Bard
> Alderman Kenna
> Kenna-Coughlin
> Bathhouse John
> Reform Has Come

That same week, Senator William Dillingham, Republican of Vermont, submitted to Congress several partial reports regarding the Immigration Commission's investigations. Female agents discovered corrupt aid societies that knowingly sent immigrant girls to brothels. Anthropologist Franz Boas had posed the theory that immigrants experienced physical changes as they assimilated and concluded that "the head form, which has always been considered as one of the most stable and permanent characteristic of human races, undergoes far-reaching changes due to the transfer of the races of Europe to American soil. The East European Hebrew, who has a very round head, becomes more long headed; the South Italian, who in Italy has an exceedingly long head, becomes more short headed; so that both approach a uniform type in this country, so far as the roundness of the head is concerned."

The most important—and anticipated—report was titled *Importation and Harboring of Women for Immoral Purposes.* On a Saturday morning, people from Syracuse to Indianapolis to Oakland, California, sat down to breakfast and read the wire service dispatch from the nation's capital.

"In explanation of the act of laying bare to the public the horrible details of discoveries by its agents," it began, "the commission says that the 'white slave traffic' is the most pitiful and the most revolting phase of the immigration question. This business has assumed large proportions, and it has been exerting so evil an influence upon the country that the commission declares that it felt compelled to make it the subject of a thorough investigation."

Owing, in part, to the decorous tenor of the times, the article omitted talk of battleships and portholes, of cigar euphemisms and million-dollar teeth, and focused instead on what might be done to "blot out" the traffic. The federal government, it surmised, should forbid the transportation of persons from one state, territory, or district to another for the purpose of prostitution.

The government was already on the case. On December 6, Congressman James R. Mann of Chicago, motivated by the Maurice Van Bever case, introduced a bill titled the White Slave Traffic Act. Referred to the Interstate and Foreign Commerce Committee, of which Mann was chair, it quickly became known as the Mann Act. Within days, President Taft, in his annual message to Congress, expressed verbose approval.

"I greatly regret to have to say," he began, "that the investigations made in the Bureau of Immigration and other sources of information lead to the view that there is urgent necessity for additional legislation and greater executive activity to suppress the recruiting of the ranks of prostitutes from the streams of immigration into this country—an evil which, for want of a better name, has been called 'the white slave trade.'" Taft allocated $50,000 for the employment of special inspectors and declared Mann's bill "constitutional."

A new branch within the U.S. Department of Justice called the Bureau of Investigation—the "Federal" to be added later—would be charged with tracking down Mann Act violations. The Bureau, at this point, employed only twenty-three agents, but James Mann's law launched its transformation from a small office concerned with miscellaneous minor crimes to the government's most recognizable and powerful legal arm.

The congressman took all the credit for his eponymous act, but Edwin Sims, still the master organizer, was its true author. A longtime friend of Mann's, Sims drafted the bill in the fall, advising that persons found guilty of transporting in interstate or foreign commerce any woman or girl for the "purpose of prostitution or debauchery, or for any other immoral purpose" be fined a maximum of $5,000 and spend up to five years in prison.

Neither Sims nor Mann explained exactly what sort of behavior might constitute "any other immoral purpose."

On December 6, as the Mann Act was making its legislative debut, Sims contacted Ernest Bell:

"Personally I feel that, having drafted the bill, the matter of securing its passage devolves upon workers like yourself," Sims wrote. "I firmly believe that if the associations and individuals interested in the suppression of the White Slave Traffic organize some sort of effective campaign, they can speedily secure the passage of the proposed law."

Bell was delighted to receive the letter. When it was going well, this battle against the Levee moved like high tide, pushing in farther each day, eroding, claiming fresh ground before it crested back. The Gypsy Smith parade left a mark. The victory against the First Ward Ball surpassed it and left another. His book, on its way to selling seventy thousand copies in seven months, drew the boldest yet, and the Mann Act was right behind it, gathering force, waiting to advance.

And then the Lord called a troubled young man home one night, leaving a mark in the Levee of His own.

PART THREE

FIGHTING FOR THE PROTECTION OF OUR GIRLS

1910–1912

MILLIONAIRE
PLAYBOY DEAD—
MORPHINE OR MADAM?

Madam Vic Shaw, 1910.

*I was the pet of Chicago . . . now, if they'd
only bring back the good old days.*
—MADAM VIC SHAW

The young man listed through the Everleigh Club parlors, steadying only when his hand found the curve of a girl's shoulder, a boat tethered momentarily to its dock. Minna watched him, wondered how much champagne he'd drunk. There he went, unmoored again, sliding along the wall for support, raising his empty glass to signal for another. He was handsome, pretty almost, with fine, elegant features; only his ears, protruding like teacup handles, marred the symmetry of his face. The high collar of his white shirt grazed his chin, and a matching tie, cinched tight, disappeared down a black double-breasted sack coat. A gray bowler hat, the latest style, perched atop short blond curls.

He was Nathaniel Ford Moore, only son and heir of James Hobart Moore and a frequent guest of the Club. The elder Moore, a close friend to J. P. Morgan, was a capitalist with a controlling interest in National Biscuit (the forerunner to Nabisco), Continental Can, Diamond Match, and the Chicago, Rock Island & Pacific Railroad. The younger Moore inherited his father's money but not his ambition. Only at the age of twenty-six did Nat, as he was called, deign to consider working for a living.

"I know it will mean getting up pretty early in the morning and a lot of other inconvenient things," he'd said, "but I'm ready to stand for all of them. Loafing makes one very tired, you know."

But on this night, January 8, 1910, Nat Moore appeared to have dismissed his resolution. The boy was a drunk and an addict, known to inject morphine into his arm with a solid gold syringe, but his money and willingness to spend it compensated for such unseemly habits. On his twenty-first birthday in 1905, he came down to breakfast to find a check for $100,000 tucked under his plate. Two years later, he threw a legendary dinner at Rector's in New York for thirty couples. It was Nat's birthday again, but his friends opened the gifts—diamond sleeve buttons for the men and specially made pearl neck-laces for the ladies. For his next party, he instructed servants to spread a cache of $20 gold pieces across a bed of ice. One by one, Nat, a married man, stood behind the chair of each female guest, dangled a chilled coin before her face, and dropped it into her décolletage.

Watching him now, Minna wondered if he'd indulged in anything be-sides champagne. Earlier in the evening, a Levee morphine salesman had asked at the door for a courtesan named Katie. The harlot spoke with the visitor in the alcove for a few hushed minutes and then proceeded to tail Nat Moore around the Levee parlors, hoping to entice him upstairs. Katie, before becoming an Everleigh butterfly, had been a common pickpocket and thief, so adept at snatching watches and wallets that she could have done it full-time. But she was beautiful and stately, possessing an eloquent grace that belied her trashy mouth and scheming mind. The Club's clien-tele loved her.

Katie certainly wasn't above rolling the young scion, dropping some poison into his glass. And after the Diamond Bertha tragedy, the sisters wanted to be especially vigilant, with clients and courtesans alike.

The harlot named Diamond Bertha was equal parts lady and bruiser: She had no problem crashing a bottle of champagne over a man's head if that's what the moment called for. She draped diamonds on every available inch of her body, even outjeweling Minna. The sisters loved her dearly but had to let her go. They weren't bothered by her use of bubbly as a weapon, but her necklaces and bracelets and rings were attracting a bad element—violent robbers.

So Bertha packed up and set off not for Vic Shaw's dive, thankfully, but for New Orleans. Within six months of her arrival in the Storyville district, she was killed, found in an alleyway, her hands, adorned with every bracelet and ring she owned, sliced off at the wrists. The sisters were ques-tioned—the harlot had "Calumet 412" scribbled all over her notebook and calling cards—and they told the police the truth: They knew the thieves in Chicago, but not in the South. If only Bertha had called for help before whatever was threatening her touched down.

Just to be safe, Minna decided to cut him off. If Nat couldn't drink, he couldn't be drugged.

She gave word to Edmund: No more champagne for Nat Moore. Katie realized the edict had been issued as a preemptive measure on her behalf.

Cheeks pinking, mouth pursed into a button, the girl stomped around the dancing couples and bowing servants. She clasped Minna's arm, spinning the madam around.

"So damned suspicious," Katie spat. "You and your holy manners. Who the hell are you to tell any of us what is right and what is wrong?"

Minna kept her voice low, her words smooth. "I want no stains on this house."

"As though it hasn't got plenty already," Katie said, moving in closer. "To hell with you and your lily white bunk."

Minna returned the girl's stare, the two of them resolutely still inside the Saturday night chaos. Then Katie whirled on her heel and stormed out.

The girl walked north, shivering, mounds of blackening snow crunching beneath her heels. She knocked on the door of 2014 South Dearborn Street, Vic Shaw's place.

A half hour later, at 1:00 in the morning, Minna bade good night to her boy and made sure Nat Moore was escorted to a cab. But he did not go home.

V ic Shaw made it her business to know when any man of prominence stepped inside the Levee. Saloon keepers on her payroll called her with sightings, and drivers delivered them to her door. Nat Moore, as fallible as he was wealthy, always lurked on the periphery of her senses. She knew he was in the district ten days ago and nearly overdosed in a resort—whether it was hers, she'd never say—and that a team of doctors pounded his chest and drugged him back to life. She knew he was in the district four days before that, and collected from him a $1,500 check that he owed toward his account. And she knew he was in there tonight. Katie, the girl who'd stormed down from the Everleigh Club begging for a job, confirmed it.

A saloon keeper friend of Vic Shaw's found Nat Moore at a bar on Wabash Avenue and brought the playboy to her brothel at 1:30 a.m. Shaw's friend was wearing Nat Moore like a cape, the playboy's lifeless arms slung over his shoulders, hands clasped beneath his chin, the tips of his black loafers flung out behind him, grating along the ground. Vic Shaw welcomed them inside and took some of the burden from her friend, letting Nat Moore's face come to rest on her pillowy bosom.

Three of her best girls, including Pearl Dorset (yet another Everleigh

Club defector), swarmed around Nat Moore, jockeying for position, whispering in his ears. Their attention revived him a bit. He straightened up, snapped his fingers, and ordered a round of champagne. When the Shaw housekeeper, Hattie Harris, came across him, his eyes were weighted, his lips slack.

"Nat was the biggest baby who ever visited this place," she said later. "He seemed to care more about being petted and talked to than anything else."

"I'm tired," he told Hattie, "and I want to go to bed and rest."

He turned toward the three harlots. "Come, talk to me until I get to sleep."

The four of them climbed the stairs together and splayed out across a bed, limbs twining. Hours later, at 9:00 a.m., Hattie Harris walked by the room and still heard the murmur of disparate voices through the closed door. He called out for her, and she peeked in.

"Hattie," he said, "you're tired and need rest, but before you go to sleep please bring me a cold glass of beer."

Hattie did as he asked, and by the time she came back upstairs the four of them were asleep. She left the beer on the nightstand, and shut the door behind her.

At 3:00 in the afternoon, the velvet curtains backlit by a willful winter sun, Pearl Dorset stirred. The other two girls and Nat Moore were still. She leaned across the bed, fit her mouth by his ear, and asked the playboy if he wanted some coffee. No answer.

She laid her hand on his face; his skin felt thick and chilled beneath her fingers. She shook him, then shook him again. She moved his head from side to side, something he couldn't seem to do on his own, and spread open one empty eye.

Pearl's scream was louder than any ever induced by Vic Shaw's disciplinarian, Lill the Whipper.

One hour later, the phone rang inside the Everleigh Club. It took Minna a moment to distinguish the voice on the other end, words choppy with rage, each syllable an exclamation.

Katie.

"They're framing you," the harlot whisper-screamed. "They've got a dead body at Shaw's and they're going to plant it in your furnace. It's Nat

Moore. Yes, he's the one. They've got it all fixed. You must stop 'em. It's a dirty trick and I won't let 'em do that to you."

The line went dead.

Minna accessed that pocket of her brain where her thoughts were calculated and stripped of impulse, where she was most like Ada. This was Vic Shaw, she reminded herself—jealous, inept Vic Shaw, who had already tried to frame her for murder and failed. A pathetic, mediocre madam who couldn't influence the mayor, or turn Bathhouse John and Hinky Dink against her and Ada, or whip the entire country into such a religious frenzy that it lost all ability to reason. A madam doomed to remain relevant only to herself.

Minna would call a trusted lieutenant, walk down the street, and make sure Vic Shaw understood that this battle had been decided long ago, and it was the Everleighs who had won.

C hez Shaw was half the size of the Everleigh Club; a double-decker bay window dominated its left side. One plane of glass on the bottom was broken out. An ornate basket-weave molding curved over the front entrance, dropping down into two Corinthian-style columns that flanked a mahogany door. A rectangular window on the second floor was topped by a long, arched one on the third that curved like a fingertip; at a distance, it appeared Vic Shaw's brothel was flipping off Dearborn Street.

Minna and her friend climbed the seven steps to the front door and barreled in. Shards of glass glittered across the wood floor; the window had just been broken. The front parlor was a vortex of waving arms and screeching voices, Vic Shaw positioned at its eye.

"What's going on here?" the Everleigh lieutenant called.

Bodies unlocked, fists unclenched. A harlot released her grip on another's hair. Two plump arms, sheathed in black silk, pushed forward through the mob, separating it, and the madam of the house emerged. A black feathered hat sat cockeyed atop dark hair. Balled fists disappeared into the folds of her waist.

"None of your goddamn business," Vic Shaw said, taking her time with each word.

It had been a while since Minna had seen her rival up close. Vic Shaw had gained at least seventy pounds since the sisters came to town, the weight distributing itself cruelly around her midsection, its circumference now equaling that of her breasts. Three chins drooped over a neck as thick as a bear's. Heavy powder settled in the deep lines around her mouth, and her eyes were two dead things lost amid streaks of paint. She lied about her age, too, Minna knew, shaving off at least a decade, turning middle age into relative youth. But Shaw's body, having earned her a living for most of her life, had tired of the ruse. It was claiming its due now, with interest.

"Nix on that," Minna's friend said. "What's up? Who's the victim—murder, eh? I can see it written all over you."

The harlots, nervous and weeping, let the story come tumbling out. Vic Shaw announced that her place was closed for now. All the inmates should scram—"to China," she suggested. There was nothing left for the madam to do but call the police, so she did, glaring at Minna all the while.

Nat Moore's body was collected and dressed, at the request of his young widow, in a long purple robe, then laid out in a darkened room of their apartment on Lake Shore Drive. Officers from the 22nd Street station arrived around 5:00 p.m. to question Vic Shaw. The madam, hysterical, at first denied the whole incident, rambling one flailing excuse after another.

"I was at the Studebaker Theater last night," she insisted. "I arrived home at 3 o'clock this morning, and I have been here ever since. I know Mr. Moore well. He was a fine fellow. The last time I saw him was the other night at the College Inn. He had not been at my house for over a month.

"No body was taken from my house today or any other time. Nobody has died in my house." She was crying now. "I have been trying to get out of this business for a month. I want to lead a better life."

Roy Jones corroborated her story.

"I have been here since 4 o'clock this afternoon myself," he said. "The police must have some wrong information. My wife doesn't have to lie and I don't believe she has lied. We have been wanting to quit this business. There is nothing doing anyhow under this administration."

The inquest was held Monday, January 10. An autopsy determined that the official cause of death was acute dilation of the heart, endocarditis, persistent thymus, chronic interstitial nephritis, and chronic gastritis. No morphine was found in his system.

Vic Shaw also testified, speaking this time with more candor. "In the afternoon I was told Nat was dead," she said. "I consulted my husband, Mr. Jones, and he advised me to call the police." She didn't mention the Everleigh sisters at all but threw a tacit barb in their direction, suggesting that Nat Moore was "apparently under the influence of more than a spree" by the time he arrived at her door.

The papers kept the sisters' name from the reports, too. But as with Marshall Field, rumors about the death rippled through the Levee, and the city, and beyond. The sisters were staying one step ahead of trouble but never quite outrunning it—"bound to be blamed sooner or later," Charles Washburn wrote, "for almost anything."

GIRLS
GOING WRONG

THE SECOND MEETING—SHE KNOWS NOT THE DANGEROUS TRAP BEING SET FOR HER.

The smooth tongued villain tells of his affection and undying love for her. He paints a beautiful picture of how happy they will be. She is enraptured and promises to meet him and go to dinner with him.

Many a working girl at the end of the day
is so hysterical and overwrought that her
mental balance is plainly disturbed.

—JANE ADDAMS

On January 27, two weeks after Nathaniel Moore was buried, four hundred Chicago society women met at the corner of Monroe and LaSalle streets, ankle-deep in snowdrifts. Scarves looped over heads and beneath chins, holding hats in place. Mrs. Emily Hill, president of the Cook County chapter of the WCTU, reminded the ladies that they were to be quiet, not demonstrative, clapped her hands, and watched with approval as the crowd whittled into a long stream of pairs. Bookended by police officers, they marched along the sidewalk, stopping traffic at each corner, "determination," one witness noted, "in every face."

Reaching City Hall, the women filed inside the building, still holding their silence. Mayor Busse received them with a mixture of amusement and dread. For the past two weeks there had been a number of preliminary meetings, newspaper reports, and general blather about women's disgust with city officials and women taking charge of the anti-vice battle and how there would be no Levee district at all if only women could vote and be elected and so on and so forth.

Politically, Busse knew, it was risky to disparage or dismiss them outright. The suffrage movement was gaining traction not only in Chicago, but throughout the state and country. Segregation was the most practical approach to vice, but one had to be cautious these days about expressing that opinion. Women could take his plain common sense and twist it into an "open endorsement of immorality" or something equally incendiary, and his Republican Party, never a popular ticket locally, would suffer at the polls. At the same time, it was difficult to listen to their ridiculous pronouncements—"Let the men take the children and care for them," ranted one female, "and permit the women to go out and enforce the laws"— without wanting to, well, bolt to the nearest saloon for a stiff drink.

The ladies packed tight into Busse's office, breast to back, curving in crescents around his desk. The spillover had to wait in the hallways, where they clasped hands and prayed in fervent whispers.

Mrs. Emily Hill faced the mayor, cleared her throat, and read from a prepared statement for two calm minutes. But toward the end of the third, her eyes moistened, her cheeks flushed, the studied composure abandoned her voice. She dropped her palms on Busse's desk and leaned in, so close that he could feel the winter on her skin.

"Mr. Busse," she cried, "you are the mayor, and you must abide by the laws. There is a city law which forbids the operation of one of these—these houses of ill fame. Obey that law and carry it out! . . . Oh, Mr. Mayor, Mr. Mayor, pray for divine guidance and you will conquer all!"

Their police officer escorts stood off to the side, shaking in silent laughter.

"I may pray," Busse replied tartly, "but I'm not going to do it here . . . I'll consult my advisers," he added, waving them away, "and see what can be done."

Busse took slightly more than a month to "consult," but on March 5, 1910, the mayor held a press conference. Stressing that Chicago's "vice problem is exactly like that of any American city," he announced the formation of the Chicago Vice Commission. Thirty members—among them such prominent citizens as Julius Rosenwald, president of Sears, Roebuck & Co.; Alexander Robinson, vice president of the Continental National Bank; Edward Skinner of the Association of Commerce; and Louis Kohtz of the Aetna Fire Insurance Company—would explore every facet of the social evil in Chicago.

Bell and his inner circle didn't expect to be appointed; they were too controversial. Edwin Sims was a fine choice for secretary, but Graham Taylor's inclusion could be problematic; the head of the Chicago Commons adamantly endorsed segregation. Dean Sumner was elected chairman. With his cathedral near the West Side Levee and as a witness to past First Ward Balls, Sumner was well acquainted with the evils of vice. Still, he questioned the wisdom of ridding Chicago entirely of its districts.

At night, while Mary slept, Bell knelt on the floor, his face pressed against their bed.

"Now Lord," he prayed, "make that commission work. Fill Dean Sumner full of facts till he vomits!"

Clifford Roe was no longer "not a marrying man," as he'd once told the *Tribune*. On March 7, he would wed Miss Elsie Martha Hercock of Chicago at Christ Reformed Episcopal Church and then depart for New Orleans. Roe recognized his good fortune—what other woman would understand her husband's desire to tour the Storyville district and lecture on pandering during their honeymoon? They would return to the house that had been his mother's and make it their own.

The *Tribune* learned of Roe's wedding, but the loquacious reformer was uncharacteristically quiet about the details. He did not discuss how he met Elsie, the circumstances of their courtship, who would serve as witnesses. The society pages printed nothing about the length of the bride's train or the brilliance of her bouquet. It was as if the prosecutor who equated negotiating with failure had at last found a deal he was willing to make: He would keep life with Elsie private, and the world couldn't take her away.

In the weeks before the big event, Roe busied himself with work, finishing an article about white slavery for his college fraternity's magazine. An accompanying profile of Roe would mention the imminent publication of his first book, *Panders and Their White Slaves*. Hopefully, the advance notice would boost sales. So far, Roe knew, more than four hundred thousand people had bought Ernest Bell's anthology, earning the reverend a small fortune.

Most important, he needed to write to John D. Rockefeller Jr. The son of the Standard Oil baron was thrust into the white slavery debate last fall when George Kibbe Turner, the muckraking *McClure's* writer who first exposed conditions in Chicago, similarly scrutinized New York. On the eve of the 1909 elections, Turner accused Tammany Hall of running the city's prostitution business and exporting white slaves to urban centers across the country. City officials, pressured to act, convened a grand jury to investigate traffic in girls.

The judge appointed Rockefeller Jr. as foreman. But he'd never patronized the demimondes, Junior protested, and would be embarrassingly inept in the role. The judge was adamant. "You owe it as a duty to the city," he insisted, "to do your part in crushing out the vile practices that are said to exist."

The arrangement was a setup. Tammany Hall bosses knew Junior. For the first eight years of his life Rockefeller Sr. clothed his namesake in his sister's hand-me-down dresses, frilly confections with doily collars and silk sashes, a Little Lord Fauntleroy in drag. Junior was shy and nervous and prone to debilitating breakdowns that lasted for years. He was as repressed as his father was libertine. Clearly, Junior was his mother's son, and too squeamish to immerse himself in New York City's underworld. The grand jury would go through the motions for a month or so and issue some benign, inconsequential report.

Tammany was wrong. Once Junior accepted the post, it became his clearest path to autonomy—the one task he could conquer without the burden of his father's might. "I never worked harder in my life," he said later. "I was on the job morning, noon, and night." He declined to talk to the harlots himself, but spared no expense finding the best people to investigate for him.

So he called Clifford Roe.

Roe cut out several newspaper clippings about recent white slave trials and enclosed them with a letter to Rockefeller. He hoped the grand jury was making progress, he wrote, and that they might meet in New York in the very near future.

On Thursday night, March 7, immediately after exchanging vows, the new Mr. and Mrs. Roe boarded a train for New Orleans. Upon their arrival, they took a carriage (Roe refused to travel by automobile) to the exquisite Hotel Grunewald on Baronne Street. A marble staircase descended into a lobby cluttered with imported statues, and a parlor called the Gold Room hosted the most exclusive parties in town, just like its illicit counterpart nine hundred miles to the north, on South Dearborn Street.

And so, for Americans, after three years of hearing about the perils of cities, after being asked by ads in *The Washington Post* if they "admired the ostrich" or preferred frank, "anti-ostrich" articles about "girls going wrong," after witnessing Clifford Roe push successfully for new pandering laws in twenty-eight states and the District of Columbia, it all came down to the spring of 1910, when their fears were both officially validated and addressed.

Illinois congressman James Mann, wearing professorial wire glasses and a tidy white beard, stood before his colleagues and spoke about his bill. While the representative, admittedly, hadn't traveled the Middle Passage, he felt justified in making a ludicrous comparison. "The white slave traffic," he said, "while not so extensive, is much more horrible than any black-slave traffic ever was in the history of the world."

Representative William E. Cox of Indiana agreed, declaring white slavery "a thousand times worse and more degrading in its consequences." Virginia's representative Edward Saunders spoke of white slavery's "headquarters and distributing centers in New York, Chicago, San Francisco, Denver, and many other American cities." Thetus Sims of Tennessee admitted that whenever he thought of "a beautiful girl taken from one State to another . . . and drugged, debauched, and ruined . . . [sold] to any brute who will pay the price, I cannot bring myself to vote against this bill." And Gordon Russell of Texas counted among the bill's supporters "every pure woman in the land . . . every priest and minister of the Living God . . . [and] men who reverence womanhood and who set a priceless value upon female purity. Upon the other side you would find all the whoremongers and the pimps and the procurers and the keepers of bawdy houses. Upon that other side you would find all those who hate God and scoff at innocence and laugh at female virtue."

On June 25, 1910, the last day of the session, President William Howard Taft signed the White Slave Traffic Act into law. "Now let's hope," he told Congressman Mann, "they put some of the scoundrels in prison."

Bell was going on tour, a Progressive Era rock star who was no longer a mere opening act for Clifford Roe. The reverend's book had educated millions of parents about the white slave evil, set sons on a righteous path, saved daughters from certain ruin and death. He would leave Chicago on September 29 and return the last day of October, hitting twelve American cities and parts of Canada, seven thousand miles in all. Other prominent reformers would be along for the ride, but Bell was singled out by the newspapers as "a tower of strength."

On the eve of his departure, the Midnight Mission members threw a farewell party in the German Room of the Grand Pacific Hotel. Bell had confidence that work in the Levee would maintain momentum during his absence. Over the summer, they began printing pamphlets in thirty-four foreign languages and moved into new headquarters at 2136 Armour Avenue. Chronic plumbing problems aside, it was an ideal locale, with windows overlooking the hardest stretch of the Levee. His saints vowed to keep pressure on the Chicago Vice Commission, send a letter arguing that "segregation provides the best rendezvous for white slavers and other such criminals who are best maintained by a centralized and commercialized evil."

Still, Bell was uneasy as his train pulled out of Union Station that night, plumes of smoke ghosting across a slate sky. Dean Sumner, so far, had kept his thoughts about the commission's progress to himself, and Bell had to rely on newspaper reports and random scraps of gossip. He knew the Chicago City Council had officially recognized the commission and appropriated $5,000 for its investigative work—developments that, on the surface, should be construed as positive. But there was something that worried him even more than Sumner's ambiguity, something that lodged like a ten-pound rock inside his chest: City council passed the ordinance without a single dissenting voice; even Bathhouse John Coughlin and Hinky Dink Kenna voted with the ayes.

Hallway to the entrance of 2131, the Everleigh Club.

I do not mind mankind's crimes,
but I do mind its hypocrisy.

—MINNA EVERLEIGH

D on't worry, was the word from Bathhouse John and Hinky Dink. Mayor Busse was confident that the Vice Commission was going to recommend segregation as usual. Besides, what sort of investigation were these fools going to conduct with a paltry $5,000 budget? One single block on South Dearborn Street earned more than that over a weekend. Hell, the Everleigh Club alone could pocket that amount in a single night!

Most significant, the aldermen confided, it looked as though Carter Harrison II planned to run for a fifth term, and if anyone recognized the lunacy of wiping out the Levee, it was Harrison, son of Chicago's favorite son. The Busse administration had been tolerable, but a Democrat always set things working just right, made the machine hum and whir and click into place.

"A Republican is a man who wants you to go t'church every Sunday," Bathhouse John pointed out. "A Democrat says if a man wants to have a glass of beer, he can have it."

Minna had to admit that after a flurry of activity, the visiting firemen seemed a bit subdued—cowed, even. Reverend Bell, for one, took a leave of absence from his usual post outside their door. Roy Jones, Vic Shaw's repulsive husband, was back in business, operating a full-fledged casino on State Street that fronted as a cigar store. And Clifford Roe had tried to implicate the Everleigh Club in a white slave case, suggesting that one Mr. Charles Herrick had forced his estranged wife, Sophia, to work there—a ludicrous charge that withered after a day of honest scrutiny.

Investigators and Vice Commission members would soon be making the rounds, Bathhouse and Hinky Dink warned. Let them in, answer their questions, and see them on their way.

A sensible enough edict, the Everleighs agreed. The sisters' hope that reformers would consider their point of view endured, but such optimism was ailing and limp and scarcely worth the maintenance. Six years, now, of dispensing philosophy about uplift and decency the same way the visiting firemen did tracts about Jesus and disease, and still the lurid narrative about the "social evil" persisted without a postscript. Not even the occasional donation to the crusaders' cause inspired a footnote or thoughtful addendum.

The Levee and the Everleigh Club had its own narrative, longer and infinitely more spectacular, and Minna decided it deserved an update of its own. Since the Club had nothing to hide and plenty to advertise, including a delectable new courtesan nicknamed Brick Top, she planned to issue a promotional brochure. Nothing crude, of course, just lush sepia photographs showcasing each parlor and a mild introduction. The Club hardly needed the publicity, but the cause of segregation could surely use a hand. Besides, if the reformers couldn't be persuaded, let them at least be peeved.

Lord, the things they'd seen. Throughout the summer, fall, and now winter of 1910, Graham Taylor, Dean Sumner, and their Vice Commission colleagues had interviewed hundreds of cadets, madams, saloon keepers, shyster physicians, morphine dealers, pimps, and every category of courtesan—white slaves, streetwalkers, resort inmates, harlots who flitted from appointment to appointment like doctors making house calls. Girls could buy a wad of opium tucked inside a folded playing card as if the drug were an ordinary piece of chewing gum. A madam on the West Side estimated that she and her lone boarder received up to four hundred men per week. One brothel employed eighteen inmates, twelve of whom had syphilis and continued to entertain—if one could call it that—with the full knowledge of the madam. Necrosis had set in on one girl's hand, cells blackening beneath her palm, and still she put it to work. In one house, four harlots performed an exhibition with animals, a description of which was "too vile and disgusting to appear in print."

On this day, though, they were visiting the "highest-grade resort," the Everleigh Club. A raw wind sliced through South Dearborn Street, resisting them as they climbed the eleven steps to the landing. No electric signs blazed atop the door; the house was lighted only by the stark yellow spray of the arc lamps and the parlors within.

The head madam opened the door quickly, as if she'd been expecting them. Her silk gown was fitted, and a flock of butterflies made entirely of diamonds perched across its bodice. The other madam, her sister, lurked in the background. Two Negro maids scuttled about with dusters and rags. A Negro man dressed in bright silk livery stood guard nearby, arms clasped behind his back, face tilted toward an intricate tin ceiling. A fountain hissed in the corner, misting what smelled like liquid honeysuckle. From somewhere in the near distance a violin murmured Beethoven. Courtesans did not walk through the parlor so much as glide.

"I found the twenty or more inmates appearing so well in the early evening," Taylor noted, "that it would have been difficult to distinguish them from high-school graduates or college students. They produced the pennants of several colleges, as though they used them to attract or amuse their patrons. The two middle-aged sisters who had long kept the place were intelligent and well-mannered. They extenuated their nefarious trade by saying that it had to be, and that they, as well as others, might profit by conducting it as decently as it could be managed.

"When asked how they procured inmates, they replied that they always had a waiting list, but insisted upon each one of them answering for herself. Dean Sumner and I were permitted to interview them . . . few of these inmates failed to claim that they were only there temporarily and would leave the life they were leading when they had earned a competence. Their 'madame' somewhat boastfully bade us to persuade, if we could, any of them to leave forthwith. Before leaving the handsomely furnished clubhouse, bearing a name that ranked it as aristocratic, I inquired of the madame how she dared to deal so destructively with both the body and the very life of each inmate. Her hollow, hysterical laughter fittingly accompanied her flippant reply."

"I am writing," Minna said when she could speak again, "what I will call *The Biography of a Lost Soul.*"

The other madam, the quiet one, let the prim line of her lips soften into a smile.

T he call from one of Roe's private sleuths came on the evening of November 19. Maurice and Julia Van Bever, the detective said, were about to sell the Paris, the one on 2101 Armour Avenue, and flee to Paris— the one in France. If Roe hurried, he could stop them.

The prosecutor phoned the police, who raided the Paris, arrested both Van Bevers, and charged them with trafficking in women. The Frenchman and his madam were shipped off to the Bridewell for one year, their appeal from the state supreme court finally denied.

Van Bever's partner, Big Jim Colosimo, still could not be reached.

But the arrest at last cleared the part of Roe's brain where the case had lingered for a year, making room for tasks undone. There was his book promotion, for one thing. Presses across the country were churning out as many white slavery narratives as copies of the Bible. One, Reginald Wright Kauffman's *The House of Bondage,* would go through eleven printings in less than nine months. And here was Roe, with his superior legal credentials and impressive analysis of the white slave evil, selling a fraction of that amount. Most insulting, Kauffman's book was a *novel.*

When, shortly after the turn of the new year, Roe received a letter from John D. Rockefeller Jr., he hoped the New Yorker had changed his mind about issuing praise for *Panders and Their White Slaves.* "I am sorry not to comply with your request for a statement regarding the book which could be used publicly," Rockefeller had written previously. "I have been asked many times to make criticisms of books but have never done so except in the case of the book by Mr. Kauffman which deals with the problem of the social evil in New York."

Rockefeller's latest letter, however, didn't mention Roe's book. This time, in fact, it was the New Yorker who wanted something. "I propose," the missive read, "that you come to New York as soon as you can close up matters in Chicago and undertake here just such a campaign as you have carried on in Chicago." Rockefeller was offering $5,000 per year, and the public would be told that the prosecutor moved east to practice law, not to hunt white slavers. "The matter," Rockefeller promised, "will be kept entirely among ourselves in the little group at this end." If Roe agreed, he could start as soon as possible.

Minna hired a professional photographer to capture all fifty rooms of the Everleigh Club. No pictures of the girls, she reminded him. This was a *tasteful* brochure, nothing like the crass calling cards that littered the Levee streets. Following him from parlor to parlor, boudoir to boudoir, she determined which angles and corners would best capture the whole, her only source of passion and point of pride—her entire world— framed between her hands. Don't get just the beds and dressing areas, she ordered, but the alcoves, too, and several views of the ballroom, a close-up of the gilded throne in the Japanese Room, a shot of the Mosque Room leading into the Moorish Room, the puddle-deep rugs and gilded spittoons, the EVERLEIGH sign, each letter in exquisite scrolling cursive, suspended above the entry to the Pullman Buffet, the graceful turn of each hallway as it met the stairs.

Finished, he bound the best images between a rich leather cover. Minna called it "The Everleigh Club, Illustrated" and composed a simple intro- duction. "Fortunate indeed," she wrote, "with all the comforts of life sur- rounding them, are the members of the Everleigh Club. This little booklet will convey but a faint idea of the magnificence of the club and its appoint- ments."

She mailed nearly two hundred brochures to regular and prospective clients, and gave a few to her most trusted courtesans to distribute at their discretion. To the outside world, the gesture would be seen as a classy re- minder of a place that was already a household name. But in Chicago and throughout the Levee, the brochure was a deliberate challenge issued to those vying to shut the Everleigh Club down: Here it was, and here it would stay.

THE SOCIAL EVIL
IN CHICAGO

Mayor Carter Harrison II.

*Here's the difference between us and Dante: He wrote a
lot about Hell and never saw the place. We're writing
about Chicago after looking the town over.*

—CARL SANDBURG

Thehe First Ward aldermen were right. Like his father before him,
fifty-year-old Carter Harrison II was seeking a fifth term as
mayor of Chicago. The elder Harrison, assassinated by a mentally disturbed Irish immigrant at the close of the World's Fair, was a Yale
alumnus and Shakespearean scholar, but Chicago's working class adored
him nonetheless. "Our Carter" had been one of their own, at ease with any
crowd or conversation, a popularity that transferred to his son.

The son, too, was handsome and charismatic, his mass of untamed
black hair tempered by a dapper mustache. His campaign flyer for the 1911
election blared: THE STREETS OF CHICAGO BELONG TO THE PEOPLE * PER-
SONAL LIBERTY * EQUAL RIGHTS FOR ALL * SPECIAL PRIVILEGES TO NONE *
NO BLUE LAWS FOR CHICAGO—an egalitarian message embraced by the
city's immigrant beer drinkers and saloon keepers. His policy regarding
the Levee was similarly relaxed. "I have never been afflicted with Puritan
leanings," he wrote. "I have also recognized the apparent necessity of
prostitution in such social organizations as have been so far perfected in
this world of ours."

Bathhouse John and Hinky Dink were thrilled to have their old comrade in the race, especially with the whiff of reform fouling the air. For the
February 28 primary election, in which Harrison faced former Democratic
mayor Edward Dunne, the First Ward bards hauled men in from flop-
houses and the local insane asylum (prompting Hinky Dink to remark that
the mentally ill were more politically astute than even the most erudite Republican). Scores of black voters, who had migrated north to Chicago
pledging allegiance to the party of Lincoln, were rightfully converted by
complimentary food and beer at Kenna's saloon. When the machines were
closed and votes tallied, Harrison emerged as the Democratic nominee, his

margin of victory in the First Ward double that throughout the rest of the city.

The Republican opponent, Hyde Park reformer Charles Merriam, began lobbing personal insults against the aldermen. "Hinky Dink has put aside his mask of humility and buffoonery," Merriam said, "and has come out to name Chicago's mayor." Publicly, Hinky Dink feigned shock and hurt, but privately he accelerated his efforts, raising the price of votes and assembling a venerable First Ward army to strategize. Ike Bloom, Solly Friedman, and Levee collector George Little reported right away. Suddenly, Big Jim Colosimo could be reached.

The *Tribune* treated Harrison's victory with ho-hum indifference. CARTER HARRISON ELECTED, read the headline. SAME OLD FRAUD IN RIVER WARDS.

The mayor-elect prepared to move into the brand-new City Hall, a mammoth structure comprising one hundred thousand cubic feet of granite and 4 million bricks, its classical columns and soaring archways more suggestive of a Roman bath than municipal drudgery. But a pertinent issue would soon demand his attention: The Chicago Vice Commission was ready to submit its report.

On April 5, 1911, the day after the election, the thirty members of the commission gave a somber presentation to the city council and Mayor Fred Busse. *The Social Evil in Chicago* was a sociological marvel, a four-hundred-page tome that rivaled William Sanger's groundbreaking 1858 work, *The History of Prostitution*, in the scope of its investigation. (To Bathhouse John and Hinky Dink's dismay, the Vice Commission received another $5,000 to continue work in the first months of 1911.)

Divided into ten parts, with numerous subset categories and tangents, the report detailed every facet of prostitution in Chicago: cadets, the "fake marriage situation," and obscene shows; "kept" women and unseemly couplings in manicure parlors; problems with whiskey, morphine, cocaine, murder, and theft; whether or not brothels prevented the rape of innocent women; and the "question of defectives, especially degenerates and sexual perverts." Each finding was presented in the driest language possible, as if to emphasize that this was science, not porn for puritans.

All in all, the commission concluded, there were no fewer than 1,020 brothels in Chicago and five thousand full-time prostitutes—a "conservative but fair" estimate that didn't account for the thousands of streetwalkers, part-timers, or girls who hustled on the side. The Levee's annual profits from vice were calculated, "ultra" conservatively, at nearly $16 million per year ($328 million today). Harlots' and madams' names were changed, and an elaborate code replaced specific brothel addresses.

"The (X523), at (X524), (X524a) Dearborn Street," read one entry about the Everleigh Club. "This is probably the most famous and luxurious house of prostitution in the country. The list received from the General Superintendent of Police on August 16, 1910, did not give the address of this house . . . the gilded palaces of sin patronized by the wealthy are immune from punishment, even to the extent of being saved the humiliation of appearing upon a police list."

The report commented on "gregarious" men:

. . . there is a large number of men who are thoroughly gregarious in habit; who mostly affect the carriage, mannerisms, and speech of women . . . who are often people of a good deal of talent; who lean to the fantastic in dress. . . . In one of the large music halls recently, a much applauded act was that of a man who by facial expression and bodily contortion represented sex perversion, a most disgusting performance. It was evidently not at all understood by many of the audience. . . .

On harlots in the Everleigh Club and other respected houses:

These women are the heavy money earners of some of the "best" houses in Chicago. The majority of them are apparently in robust health . . . [they] hold the lead in professional prostitution and earn weekly from $50 to $400. This would seem to largely disprove . . . the solemn statement . . . that "in five years these girls will all be dead."

And on what Minna would call "wear and tear":

It is undoubtedly true that the women in houses are longer lived and better off than the street walker or possibly than the clandestine prostitute—with her, service is largely mechanical—not an act appealing to sentiment or affection—while with the latter type especially, the physical stress upon her body and nerves and strength caused by expression of "love" as they understand it, makes demands upon endurance that are unknown to the professional prostitute.

On causes, during one particular survey, for entering the life:

Nine were seduced; three could not earn enough to live on in any other way; two were enticed by other women into the life; two were too ignorant to do any ordinary work; two lost their husbands by death and two by desertion; two said they were naturally bad, one said she wanted to, was "born with the devil in her," the other that she "was bad with boys before she was 15"; two for dress; two ruined by drink and one each on account of trouble with family, poverty, money and because she was tired of drudgery (this girl said dance halls ruined her).

On the lower houses:

One madame testified before the Commission that in a 50-cent house on the West Side, she with one girl took in $175 to $200 per week. She also testified that she herself entertained 60 men in one night at 50 cents each. This madame is supporting members of her family, and has $7,000 in the bank.

And again on the Everleigh Club:

A Dearborn Street resort distributes a very elaborate booklet which describes in glowing terms the comforts to be found within the walls of that "sumptuous" house. In fact no one need "feel the chill of winter nor the heat of summer" in this place. . . .

Pervert methods are on the increase in the higher priced houses. The inmates who perform these services earn from two to three times as much money as the so-called "regular girls." In one notorious place known all over the country and which caters to a so-called high class trade, these methods are used almost exclusively. The inmates gave testimony before the Commission that they do this on the advice of their physician, who says it prevents disease and other troubles.

Chicago, the commission declared, should waste no time in establishing a morals court and appointing a morals commission.

But their final—and most shocking—recommendation called for the "absolute annihilation" of the Levee district.

Ernest Bell had awaited the Vice Commission's report as if for the birth of his own child, and the idea that the Levee might one day be darkened and desolate was every bit as miraculous. He gathered his saints around him in the Armour Avenue house, their tears vying with laughter. "Praise God," they sang, eyes shut, throats knotted, "from whom all blessings flow."

But a disconcerting story shadowed their celebration, stripped a layer of joy from their prayers. When Edwin Sims and Dean Sumner delivered the report to Mayor Harrison after his inauguration, he ceremoniously tossed it into the trash.

Clifford Roe left for New York on April 1, 1911, "enthusiastically looking forward with much hope" to fighting white slavery full-time in a new city. His best sleuth, the Kid, was accompanying him, and they would be aided by men from the New York District Attorney's Office. Rockefeller had warned Roe that things were done differently in New York, that hysteria and hyperbole had to make room for rational discourse. The oil scion was especially troubled by an upcoming East Coast tour planned by Ernest Bell. "If the methods employed in this tour," he wrote, "are to be the kind which I assume Doctor Bell usually employs, it seems to me that, particularly in the East, more harm may result than good."

Roe made it clear that he understood.

His benefactors in Chicago—Julius Rosenwald, Adolph Kraus, Harold Swift of the famous meatpacking family, and twelve others—incorporated as the Committee of Fifteen and promised to continue the battle against vice. They had an ingenious idea, printing out little square flyers, like base-ball cards, featuring the names, physical descriptions, and photographs of white slaves. One featured a young woman wearing a long, filmy white dress. She held an open parasol behind slim shoulders, as if drawing an arrow, and the text beneath her image read:

MISS GOLDIE MYERS

Believed to be held in some disorderly resort, Nineteen years old.
About five and a half feet tall, weighs one hundred and twenty-five
or thirty pounds. Very light complexion, light natural blonde,
wavy hair. Report to the Committee of Fifteen, 10 So. LaSalle St.

Roe rented an apartment on Broadway. Rockefeller's personal secretary, Charles Heydt, took Roe to select office furniture, sponsored his membership at New York's City Club, and provided a car for his investigators. "[Roe] himself does not care for automobiles," Heydt told Rockefeller, "and has an aversion to them on account of his mother's death in one."

Soon after he settled, Roe set out for the "dollar houses" on the East Side, one eye fixed on the virtue of innocent girls, the other on his legacy.

Ada preferred to bat away threats with humor, switching to denial when jokes began to sound emptier than silence. Denial triumphed in the weeks after the Vice Commission report; Ada limited her conversation to banal talk of business matters and the thickening July heat. She kept to routine, selecting a harlot to accompany her on afternoon errands to the Loop, calling for their elegant carriage instead of the automobile, a Luddite at heart. Each woman lifted a vivid parasol above her pale face. The courtesan's highlighted her figure, made it look like the curving stem of a flower. Ada, her true forty-seven years at last betraying her fabricated age, seemed to wilt, ever so slightly, beneath her own.

Minna, too, adhered to routine, working through her stack of newspapers every afternoon in the Gold Room. She read about the vice commission report, scoured for references to the Club. They mentioned their "perversions" and protection from the police. They estimated the Club's annual revenue to be $100,000, although $120,000 was more accurate. Good—they were appropriately perturbed by the advertising brochure. One investigator was gratuitously nasty. "They had little fountains squirting perfume in the various rooms," he sniffed, "but the aroma isn't sufficient to remove the moral stench from the nostrils of a law-abiding citizen."

She kept tabs on Carter Harrison. The mayor had posture like Big Jim Colosimo's pasta, bending just enough to placate the visiting firemen without breaking to their side. He insisted that "all of the rules issued under the last administration will be enforced"—no soliciting from doors or windows, no vulgar exhibitions, no swinging doors, no women in saloons without male escorts. His new police chief, John McWeeny, was doing what they all did immediately after being appointed, making a few splashy arrests, just to attract attention, before finalizing graft arrangements with Ike Bloom. After collaring five prostitutes on the West Side, McWeeny, with one cruel comment, illustrated exactly why the Everleigh Club was necessary.

"Those women have got to get off those streets," he said. "Let them jump in the lake if they want."

McWeeny would soon fall in line, but Minna didn't expect the visiting firemen to retreat. They'd been out there for six years now, as much a part of the Levee landscape as unconscious bodies and Negro professors and girls who would feel old far longer than they ever felt young. It was maddeningly predictable, the usual insults and allegations spouting from familiar mouths. Ada might force laughter or retreat into silence, but she, Minna, would step forward and beckon them even closer. She would once again take what they loathed most and highlight it, string it up for all the world to see. Time to update the brochure, she decided, and declare the two attractions a visitor to Chicago mustn't miss: the Union Stock Yards and the Everleigh Club. Beneath the reformers' stiff collars and pious expressions were *men*, Minna reminded herself—the flies to her spider.

PAINTED,
PEROXIDED, BEDIZENED

Police Chief John McWeeny, 1911.

Girls will be girls, but they should be restrained.

—LUCY PAGE GASTON

One afternoon in early October 1911, Mayor Carter Harrison II opened the door to Vogelsang's. The cursive *V* in the restaurant's sign resembled a seagull in distant flight, wingspan stretching along the odd side of West Madison Street. He headed for his table, shaking hands with men as he passed, cigar smoke burrowing in his throat. A waiter hovered, slid out his chair. Charlie Plamondon, hot dog king Oscar Mayer, and Murray Keller—the last a western representative of a prestigious French champagne house—had already arrived, and they raised wineglasses in greeting.

Courses were devoured and toasts proposed, glasses refilled for thirds and fourths, and the mayor felt a "sudden longing" for champagne. An idea struck him. German cities, he pointed out, had more than one mayor. Berlin alone had an *Ober-Bürgermeister* and at least two ordinary *Bürgermeisters*. Why not elevate Chicago to the same class? He issued a challenge to his friends: The first one to find a bottle of Pommery 1904 would be named to a special post, night mayor of Chicago, "with all attendant privileges, perquisites, and prerogatives."

Striking the air with a finger, Charlie Plamondon summoned the headwaiter and made the request. Yes, Vogelsang's had the brand and the year. They downed the first glass in honor of Plamondon, Chicago's newest official, who sniggered through his impromptu oath of office.

The following Monday, the night mayor and his wife set out in their electric brougham for a show and dinner at the Congress. On the way home, Plamondon suggested a detour through the Levee district—what better way to launch his duties than a quick investigation of the underworld? At the very least, the sojourn would make for interesting conversation at the next Vogelsang's luncheon. His wife, a good sport, played along.

After cruising down Dearborn and Armour, his wife's grip on his hand tightening with each passing block, Plamondon turned on 22nd, then swung north on Michigan Avenue. At 18th Street, an electric automobile puttered onto Michigan from the west. It was remarkably similar to his own, Plamondon noted, but "lit up like a prairie fire." The car cast a blinding haze, as if the sun were rising behind its dashboard, and a cascade of exotic flowers trailed across the hood. In the backseat, propped up on plump cushions, sat an even plumper woman, hair twisted and tucked beneath what looked like a dead peacock. Diamonds dripped from ears and winked from fingers. Her neckline descended to midtorso, revealing stupendous half-moons of breasts. Plamondon's wife squeezed harder. The automobile tripped over a sunken patch of street, tossing the woman so that one breast escaped from its thin silk confines. Laughing, shoulders shaking and head reared back, the woman took her time tucking the breast back where it belonged, waiting until every passenger and pedestrian on this elegant boulevard had gotten a good look.

Plamondon's wife was hyperventilating.

He noticed a policeman on the corner and pulled over. Who, he asked the cop, is that flashy individual?

The officer looked at the car, trailing a comet of light, and shrugged. "Vic Shaw," he said.

The next morning, Plamondon filed his night mayor report to the real mayor. Harrison surmised that the "notorious brothel keeper" left her resort on Dearborn, stopped by her husband's saloon at 18th and Wabash, and then headed home to her new Michigan Avenue apartment. Embarrassed that such a flagrant display was spotted outside the Levee parameters—and by a friend, no less—he thanked Plamondon and sent a sleuth to investigate.

The mayor recognized his tricky position, moderating a delicate tug-of-war between the First Ward aldermen, who backed him politically, and the reformers, who could no longer be dismissed as crackpots or prudes. The anti-vice crusade that had been launched to clear Chicago's reputation had itself wrought the most damage.

Once again, the nation was focused on the Levee district; even Theodore Roosevelt recognized *The Social Evil in Chicago* as a central document of the age, deserving of careful study and effusive praise. It did not "serve merely to gratify emotions that are foul and base," the former president reasoned, but was a "contribution to the cause of morality and decency." The young journalist Walter Lippmann, meanwhile, declared the investigators' approach flawed, their conclusions futile, and their views on sexuality puerile. The idea that "sex must be confined to procreation by a healthy, intelligent and strictly monogamous couple," Lippmann would soon write, summing up the commission's position, "forced the Commission to ignore the sexual impulse in discussing a sexual problem . . . yet who that has read the report itself and put himself in any imaginative understanding of conditions can escape seeing that prostitution today is organic to our industrial life, our marriage sanctions, and our social customs?" Plus Dean Sumner was at it again, trying to convince the U.S. postmaster general to permit 1,800 copies of *The Social Evil in Chicago* to pass through the mails so that other cities might again follow Chicago's example and appoint vice commissions of their own.

Call girls had always worked Michigan Avenue from 12th Street to 35th Street, taking clients to designated houses and disorderly hotels, but Harrison knew that this thoroughfare could not, under any circumstances, flower into another segregated district, a Little Levee. "It was far from my ideas," he wrote, "that the more notorious, the more luxurious of the houses should conduct branch institutions, succor sales, in decent neighborhoods."

So when his investigator discovered that a number of the older residences along Michigan Avenue had been purchased recently and converted into resorts, the mayor issued an order: Move all disreputable women from Michigan Avenue at once and close all disorderly flats. Brazen taunting of the respectable citizenry would not be tolerated, Harrison added, and solicitation by pimps must cease.

The Michigan Avenue offenders dutifully departed, and Harrison hoped the Levee madams would, from now on, stay in their own backyard.

Minna didn't recognize the policemen who appeared at her door on October 21. It wasn't Bryant, who helped her thwart the Marshall Field Jr. plot, or the trusted officer who accompanied her to Vic Shaw's during the Nathaniel Moore mess, or any of the number of rank-and-file cops she tipped now and again. A fist of panic curled inside her. Perhaps McWeeny had dispatched two new underlings to discuss graft payments? Or maybe another symbolic raid was planned, like the attack on Michigan Avenue, and these men had come to warn the sisters? Best to remain calm, avoid jumping to conclusions. Peculiar behavior only invited unwarranted suspicion.

She opened the door, welcoming inside the officers and the smoky breeze of Dearborn Street.

Without preamble, the men introduced themselves as detectives—no wonder they were unfamiliar—and explained the reason for their visit. Herbert Swift, son of the famous meatpacker and brother of Harold Swift (the latter a member of Clifford Roe's Committee of Fifteen), had died the previous evening on a Chicago & Northwestern train en route to Milwaukee. The cause was yet unknown, and they'd heard that an Everleigh Club girl had planned an out-of-town excursion—perhaps she accompanied the heir. Would Madam Minna know anything about this?

The panic rapped at her chest. A wealthy packer's son had been a frequent guest of the Club, memorable not only for the size of his tab, but for the inanity of his conversation. "Women have no minds," he'd said once, after alcohol had impaired his own. "All they can do is dance." Whether the imbecilic patron was the dead man or his reformer brother, Minna would never say. And one of the Everleigh butterflies *had* left Chicago for a "visit," as she called it, although no one outside of the Club knew of this sabbatical. Minna didn't believe her girl had anything to do with this unfortunate circumstance, but the last thing they needed was the ghost of another dead millionaire traipsing through the parlors.

Sorry, Minna said, but she knew nothing about this. It was both the proper—and truthful—response.

"Did one of your girls hit a guest with a champagne bottle?" the detective persisted. "Had a certain patron promised to take one of your inmates away with him? What's been going on here that we don't know about?"

Ada, summoned by a servant, now stood next to her.

"We do not know," Minna said, "what you are talking about."

His partner released a weary sigh. "Who were your prominent guests the last few nights?" he asked.

Minna's thoughts came in a rush, and she felt Ada next to her, rigid and cold. This was their last chance to just give up and talk, to tell the detectives everything they didn't know. But a simple admission of ignorance amounted to a betrayal of discretion, one that would count against the Club. And after eleven years, there would be no stains on this house.

"We do not know the names of our guests," Minna said finally.

A moment passed, bulging with unissued threats. The two visitors turned and let themselves out.

On Sunday night, October 22, Ernest Bell boarded a train for Columbus, Ohio, host city for this year's International Purity Congress. Already temperatures were plummeting, honeycombing the windows with frost. He was the lone delegate from the Midnight Mission, joining representatives from every temperance society, law and order league, and anti-vice group throughout the United States and Canada. Bell was slated to speak about the white slave traffic, as was his old comrade Clifford Roe. New York City's underworld would have a few days' respite from the prosecutor.

The most sensational topic was certain to be Iowa's recent legislation. The Hawkeye State had passed the Red Light Injunction and Abatement Law that so far disproved the arguments against ending segregation. A Des Moines reformer, slotted to address the purity congress, wrote an essay about the law for Roe's second book. Steep penalties against deed holders—even if they were merely renting property to madams—were vital, as was sending the message that the city was no longer complicit.

Bell had been arguing that same line of reasoning for years. Five years hence, most of the girls in Chicago brothels would be dead, and thousands more recruited to replace them. But if a law like Iowa's passed in Illinois, if the Levee were closed and kept closed, then entire generations of girls would be saved to respectable lives. Bell was certain that the first mayor who took such a definitive stance against city-sponsored vice would be applauded by 90 percent of the voting population of Chicago.

The train groaned into motion and pulled out of Union Station. Bell stared through the scrim of ice, watching his city's slow retreat.

Within twenty-four hours, another member of Chicago's finest rang the Everleigh Club's bell. The new police chief himself, John McWeeny, stood at their threshold, coarse ginger eyebrows arched into tepees. A thin film of frost covered his dark wool coat, and a pale, meaty hand emerged from its sleeve, coming to rest on the door frame.

Minna elbowed her sister. Finally—the chief had dispensed with the bravado and bluster and sat down with Ike Bloom. He was making the rounds, letting madams and dive keepers know of any changes in graft fees or payment schedules. He would set things right, and the thrum of panic that was quavering through the Levee air would at last subside.

Chief McWeeny cleared his throat. He had come to inquire, he said, about "an unpleasant happening," bloating those last three words in a way that told Minna this was not yet over, that he needed to fill his pockets with power for just a bit longer before turning them out to Ike Bloom. Her own panic returned, restless inside her, but a slow anger pooled around it.

Ada nudged her back, expressing agreement without saying a word, and then stepped forward.

"Mind your own business," she said, and Minna had to look, check if that arctic voice, that cocksure inflection, truly belonged to her sister.

It did. Ada's expression was at once wild and immobile.

Minna remembered what this heartless louse had said about the five prostitutes he'd arrested on the West Side.

"Jump into the river," she told McWeeny, and closed the door in his face.

The locks clicked into place. Minna turned to her sister, watched as Ada's anger gave way to humor. It was a palpable switch, a weak light thrown on just behind her eyes.

"Pretty flimsy threat, this one," Ada said lightly, making it sound like a question.

The whisper of the perfume fountain was deafening behind them. Minna knew it was up to her to voice the answer neither of them wanted to hear. She could craft the prettiest lies in the world, but never for Ada.

"I'm afraid," she said, "they mean business."

F or weeks, Mayor Harrison had been hearing about this brochure. When visiting associates asked about the city's greatest attractions, he mentioned the soaring mosaic Tiffany ceiling inside Marshall Field's, the virtuosic performances of the Chicago Grand Opera Company, the mercurial blues of Lake Michigan. But he was forgetting something, they said, laughing—what about the Everleigh Club?

Even when the mayor left town it followed him. At one recent banquet, a young man approached, pumped Harrison's hand, and observed, "Pretty snappy town yours, isn't it?," a hard wink in his voice. The mayor heard that thousands of brochures had been mailed far and wide to every state in the Union, an ironic postscript following the delivery of 1,800 vice commission reports. Chief McWeeny had called upon "the terrible pair of sisters" two days ago in a halfhearted attempt to back them down, only to retreat himself. Now, finally, Harrison's own copy of "The Everleigh Club, Illustrated" lay open on his desk.

He couldn't close the entire Levee district, despite the reformers' constant rallies and phone calls, but he could no longer let inaction serve as official policy. Harrison decided to buy some time, using the brochure on his desk as currency. He was the first native of Chicago to be elected mayor, and during this, his fifth term, he would defend his city. Those "painted, peroxided, bedizened" sisters, he would announce, would not be permitted to raise its skirts, shame it for prurient thrills.

Shortly before noon on October 24, 1911, Harrison took out a piece of paper and a pen. He wrote this "truly historic" order in longhand, unwilling to trust even his stenographer. After tucking it into an envelope, the mayor called for a special messenger, who carried it immediately to the armory station and delivered it into the police chief's hands.

"Close the Everleigh Club," the paper read. Effective immediately.

YOU GET EVERYTHING
IN A LIFETIME

The Everleigh Club, 2131–2133 South Dearborn Street.

How dear to my heart is the old-fashioned harlot,
When fond recollections present her to view;
The madam, the whore house, the beer by the car lot,
And e'en the delights of the old fashioned—
Here a rhyme is needed to rhyme with the word "view."

—EDGAR LEE MASTERS

Harrison's order shouted itself across Chicago. Hinky Dink Kenna burst in, face grave atop his pipe cleaner of a neck. Out of breath, slight shoulders heaving, he did not so much speak his words as exhale them.

"On the square, does this go? For keeps?"

"As long as I am mayor," Harrison said.

"Okay!"

And he rushed out.

Murray Keller, champagne salesman and Vogelsang's lunch companion, rang Harrison's phone. Won't the mayor reconsider? he asked. The Everleigh sisters were two of his best customers, and they would hold him in great favor if he convinced his friend in City Hall to change his mind.

Harrison demurred—politely, at first—and finally used "rather sharp language" to silence Keller's pleas.

The tornado of rumors began its inevitable twist. How could this happen to the Everleigh Club, pillar of vice, immune from the law? This was Vic Shaw's doing, no question; she had sent a copy of the Club's advertising brochure to the mayor. Perhaps an Everleigh girl did end Herbert Swift's life on a train outside of Milwaukee. Obviously, Marshall Field Jr. was still haunting South Dearborn Street. "The most persistent gossip," Harrison said, "associated it with the death by gunshot wound of the only son of a famous millionaire merchant prince." But the reason, the mayor insisted, was the Everleigh Club's "infamy, the audacious advertising of it"; "it was as well known as Chicago itself and therefore a disgrace to the city."

Now all Harrison had to do was wait.

Inside the Everleigh Club, the phones pulsed and trilled. Reporters, clients new and old, wine and food suppliers, former harlots, friendly politicians, and madam acquaintances throughout the country all checked in. Minna answered each ring. It was only lunchtime but she was in full dress, a tangle of necklaces overlapping butterfly pins, ten fingers stacked with rings. Journalist friends were beginning to arrive. She appeared "cool and comical," Charles Washburn noted, "though she must have been boiling over within." Her laughter rose and fell but never quite died; her face refused to let go of its smile.

"You mustn't believe all you read in the papers," Minna told each caller. The afternoon edition of the *American* had already printed news of the order. "Come on over tonight and see for yourself."

She slipped away to a back parlor, found a square of quiet. It was time to make a phone call of her own. If this were a tragic production, she would play the lead with dignity and aplomb. She connected with the 22nd Street police station and asked to speak with Captain P. J. Harding.

"Is the report that my place is to be closed correct?" she asked.

The command had not yet arrived from the chief of police, Harding told her, but he expected it "every minute."

Minna thanked him, ordered her lips back into a smile, and returned to the parlors.

But minutes passed, then hours, and still the command didn't come.

Ada rounded up the butterflies, told them to bathe and dress, to report to the parlors as soon as possible—no questions asked. Minna lit a gold-tipped cigarette—somewhere in Chicago, Lucy Page Gaston was sniffing suspiciously—and stood at the door, asking after her boys, waving them all inside. Yes, yes, of course they were open, don't mind those silly rumors—*no one* interfered with the Everleigh Club. Edmund brought her a glass of champagne; the buzz was even sweeter accompanied by day-light's fading glow.

Harlots crowded behind her. They wanted to stand at the door, mingle on the landing—it wasn't proper protocol, but did Madam Minna mind? For once, she didn't. Girls from the Weiss brothers' houses on either side joined them, and within moments, as if heeding a silent alarm, Dearborn Street was alive with courtesans, the fall wind slapping bare shoulders, tug-ging at tightly coiled hair. They did the chicken scratch and the bunny hug—what did the character of their dancing matter, since the reformers believed they were all ruined anyway?—and kept on long after the sun traded places with the moon.

If only Ernest Bell were at his usual post in front of the Everleigh Club, the "Gibraltar of the district," to witness all those lost souls fleeing to the streets—heading toward him, for once. Every white slave for blocks could have received a pamphlet, whispered a prayer, sung a hymn. Instead he was in his room at the Hotel Vendome in Columbus, writing a note to Mary, en-tirely unaware that the brothel he'd targeted for the past six years was at last being struck.

Journalist friends were begging Minna, the "speaking partner of the Everleigh sisters," as they called her, for comment. She glanced at Ada, who nodded, one curt dip of her head.

"I know the mayor's order is on the square," Minna began. "When my maid brought me the afternoon newspapers, I got Captain Harding of the Twenty-second Street station on the telephone . . . he said the order had not come to him from the chief of police, but he expected it every minute. Ordinarily, when orders affecting the Twenty-second Street district are is-sued from police headquarters in the afternoon they reach the Twenty-second Street station before 8 o'clock in the evening. It is after that hour now, so it may not come to me until morning."

The professors all started up again, sending torrents of music through the parlors and open doors. "They can play a bugle call like you never heard before," the crowd sang, "so natural that you want to go to war. . . ."

"I don't worry about anything," she continued, waving a hand "liter-ally coruscated with diamonds," as reporters would note. "You get everything in a lifetime. Of course, if the mayor says we must close, that settles it. What the mayor says goes, so far as I am concerned. I'm not going to be sore about it, either. I never was a knocker, and nothing the police of this town can do to me will change my disposition. I'll close up the shop and walk out of the place with a smile on my face. Nobody else around here is worrying, either. If the ship sinks we're going down with a cheer and a good drink under our belts, anyway."

A voice rose up from the crowd—how could the sisters leave Chicago when, as the mayor said, they were as well-known as the city itself?

"If they don't want me in Chicago," Minna responded, "there are other cities. But this is my home and I would rather continue to live here. Honestly, I hate to leave. But one must live."

She paused, considering her words, her face still held hostage by that smile.

"Well, boys, we've had good times, haven't we," she said. "You have all been darlings. You've played square. And we thank you sincerely. Just think—our last night."

No one spoke for a moment. The jaunty tumble of "Alexander's Ragtime Band" seemed rude and out of place. Minna let her eyes wander, admiring every gilded surface, breathing the mingled scents of roasted duck and sweet perfume, her paradise almost lost. She raised her flute of champagne.

A reporter kindly took the hint. "Happy days," he toasted.

"Happy nights," Ada added.

Glasses were drained, refilled, and drained again. A second wind gusted into the room. Crowds mothed around Ada's piano to toast Vanderpool Vanderpool. Men passed a statue of a golden nymph on their way up the stairs, slapping her naked bottom for good luck.

"It may be their last chance," Ada said. "Let 'em go as far as they like."

An hour later they were still going far, and Minna felt a timid nudge of hope. She followed an old reporter friend to the telephone. He'd call the mayor to see if this closing order had been rescinded. A maid answered and said Mayor Harrison was in his bedroom.

"It's only 10 o'clock," the reporter urged. "Perhaps the mayor has not gone to sleep yet."

She went to check. The moment stretched unnaturally, a chronological rubber band. Minna moved in closer, cupped her ear against the phone.

"Mayor Harrison is sound asleep," the maid said finally. "I don't want to take the responsibility for waking him up."

They tried John McWeeny next, and again at 11:00, and again at midnight. Still no word from the chief. But toward the end of the next hour, 1:00 a.m. on Wednesday morning, October 25, the chime of the doorbell intruded into the parlors. Minna made her way to the 2131 entrance, a roaring quiet in her ears, the journey seeming at once interminable and brief. With each step the parlor, receding behind her, leaked a bit of color and noise.

Four squads of police from the 22nd Street station stood on the other end of the threshold. The largest officer stepped forward; Minna recognized him. Obligatory sorrow tugged at his eyes and the corners of his lips, as if he had been sent to report a death. It was an appropriate expression, Minna thought; she knew the Everleigh Club longer than she had known her own mother.

"Sorry, girls," he said. "From downtown. Nothing we can do about it. . . . If it was us, you know how we'd be."

"We've been expecting it," Minna said. "What would you advise us to do?"

"Clear out the house. Get rid of all the guests."

Clients began their slow procession down the stairs and through the parlors. The piano chirped a final note. Pear salad was left to wilt on plates. Maids scrambled about, matching coats with their owners. A chorus of weeping rose from one corner, where harlots huddled together and clasped hands. Minna and Ada stood by the open door, proffering cheeks for chaste kisses.

"You'll be going strong within a week," each boy said, tipping a high silk hat.

Dearborn Street was a crush of elegant carriages and electric cabs, throngs of curious passersby filling the spaces between. They had read the newspapers, too, and came to protest the police order. One low, lusty boo emptied into another, like a sequence of lingering bass notes. Arc lamps dropped spotlights on a hundred private farewells.

When the last guest had exited, Ada minded the harlots while Minna rushed upstairs to her boudoir. Locking the door behind her, she willed her mind to stand still, the knot to dislodge from her throat. She picked up the phone, connected with Freiberg's Dance Hall, and asked for Ike Bloom. The music beamed through the receiver as loudly as if it were playing in her room. Bloom's usual barked hello was softened; he'd been expecting her call.

She and Ada would pay and pay well, Minna said, skipping pleasantries, if Bloom could offer sound proof that there was even a slim chance of continuing. Just say the word, and the Everleigh Club would wage a last stand.

"Go away for a few months," he said. "There's a nasty rap against the place and it may take months for the smoke to clear. Nobody else was closed, which is the tip-off—they were gunning for you and they've clipped you. Nothing we can do this morning. It's one of those things— what the hell. We stalled the order all day, didn't we? I did all I could. I'm licked on this one. Call me in the afternoon. But make up your mind it will cost you forty g's. Worth it, ain't it—what good are them oil paintings if the joint is shut? Hock one of 'em if you're short. Things aren't as simple as they used to be. Now go to bed and forget it."

Minna replaced the phone and crept back downstairs. Servants paced the length of the parlors, asking her, "What do you think?" For once in her life, she didn't know. She found Ada and ordered the courtesans to the Gold Room.

"We're going from bawd to worse—retirement," Ada joked, falling into a divan. "Let's go to Europe."

One harlot stomped her heel soundlessly into the lush carpet. Tears forked down her cheeks, sopping up powder and rouge.

"What about us?" she asked, sobbing. "Where can we go?"

"There are plenty of houses," Minna said.

"Not like this one."

The Everleigh butterflies clustered close together, dresses of scarlet and emerald and sapphire still vivid beneath the dimmed lights, a tangle of jewels in a chest. Six hundred of them had come and gone, and here was what might be the final group. It occurred to Minna that this conversation was the most intimate act the Club had witnessed in all its eleven years.

"I'm afraid there never will be one like the EC," she said slowly. "You all have a little money due you, enough to last a month or two. I would suggest that you clear out from the Levee entirely. It has nothing substantial to offer. . . . Find a job, a husband, anything, but don't depend upon this life for a career. It's washed up, as we used to say in the theater. It's done for, good and done for. . . . In this town, they have been known to rob a man of thousands of dollars, toss his body into the lake and forget it. We get into a little mess and they call out the cops. You figure it out."

She closed her eyes and sank deeper into the settee. Ada's cold hand found hers. The crying died out, a sniffle at a time. A moment passed, and then there was a small frenzy of energy, a sound like a nesting bird. Minna opened her eyes to see a harlot tearing her dress. A sleeve separated from its bodice, a triangle of bright silk swooning to the floor.

"Why not?" the girl said, crying again, and went after the other sleeve. "I won't need it anymore. A hell of a manicurist or a waitress I'd make in this getup."

Her hands matched the fury of her sobs, splitting the neckline to reveal her corset, rampaging the hem into long tatters. Bits of fabric flurried in the air. No one moved to stop her. The harlot thrust a finger first at Ada, then at Minna. "And neither of you did a damn thing to stop 'em!" she screamed. She leaned over to an end table, grabbed a champagne flute, and hurled it against the far wall.

The crash lured a policeman from his post at the front door. He stood by the parlor entrance, unnerved by the sight of thirty weeping women— one half-naked, clearly hysterical—and shattered glass.

"Want me to lock you all up?" he asked, a listless threat.

The half-naked harlot stumbled toward him, fists raised. "Brave, ain't you? Who do you think you're scaring, you big bum?" She picked up an abandoned champagne bottle from the floor and reared back. Minna jumped up and latched the harlot's arms from behind, fit her lips against her ear.

"Poor kid," she whispered. She gave the cop a look. "Leave her to me, please."

He nodded and left the parlor.

The girl twisted until they were facing each other. Her mouth opened in the dip between Minna's shoulder and neck. "I'm sorry," she said, crying again.

Minna traced a hand along her back. "We're all nervous and unstrung," she soothed. "I understand just how you feel. It's a terrible shock to all of us. And there is nothing any of us can do about it. I think we better all start packing."

She released the harlot, who held the remains of her dress together as she walked from the parlor. One by one, the other girls followed and trudged upstairs. The madams waited until the last bedroom door had slammed shut, then sneaked away to Ada's boudoir. They needed to discuss an attack.

Ike Bloom was stalling, the sisters agreed; at this point, he didn't know much more than they did. Mayor Harrison was another question mark. Someone or something had gotten to him. Was his attack on the Levee fleeting, or did he plan to run for higher office? Bathhouse John Coughlin always boasted that Our Carter's son would one day be president. If he were indeed dreaming of a career beyond Chicago, he'd need to pander to the city's upper tier. If not, this was all for show, and things would ease slowly back to normal.

Best to leave town for six months and wait things out. The sisters determined they had about $1 million in cash (nearly $20.5 million today), a stash of diamonds worth $200,000; $150,000 in oil paintings, antique tapestries and Oriental rugs; and client IOUs totaling $25,000. They'd start off in Rome, pay respects once again to *Apollo and Daphne*, and see what beckoned from there.

As the sun began its climb the sisters still lay across Ada's bed, sleep proving as fickle as everything else.

At 8:00 a.m., they rang for coffee and the morning editions. News of the Club's closing occupied every front page. Chief McWeeny telephoned the 22nd Street station from his home over the police wire at 12:45 a.m., a full twelve hours after Carter Harrison gave the order. The sisters' clout, it was implied, accounted for the delay. The mayor seemed to be playing both sides. "Vice in Chicago can exist only under the most stringent regulations," he said. "The Everleigh Club has been advertised far and wide." He balanced this sly endorsement of segregation by vowing to close "a score" of resorts in the South Side Levee. The *Chicago Daily Socialist*, strangely enough, appeared the most optimistic about the Club's chances, headlining their story EVERLEIGH CLUB CLOSED; WILL BE OPENED AGAIN.

Downstairs, trunks crowded the hallways and harlots bustled about, writing letters and sending telegrams. Every few moments, a Western Union messenger appeared at the door, delivering offers of employment from madams around the country. "Two French blondes," one wire requested. "Can use two all-around brunettes," read another. "Best five-dollar house in New Orleans with positive security and hundred dollars weekly for five girls under twenty-five—STOP—will advance railroad fare."

Offers also came, naturally, from Vic Shaw and her closest madam comrades. One of the Everleigh sisters' favorite courtesans, Grace Monroe, accepted a position at Madam Zoe Millard's place, 2034 South Dearborn Street. Madam Millard was a friend of Vic Shaw's, and loathsome even without that unseemly social connection.

"Until I get something better," Grace said, apologizing.

By 10:00 p.m., several cabs idled in front of 2131–2133 South Dearborn. Harlots were more resolute, now, than teary, lining up to kiss their madams good-bye. The sisters also maintained composure, emphasizing gratitude over regret, hinting that the Levee might not go without them for long.

After the exodus the Club seemed subdued and sickly, caught at an unflattering angle, and the sisters decided to let it rest. They would go see a matinee, step into another world for an afternoon. After calling for their automobile, they asked the servants to take down any important messages, and set out for the Loop.

That afternoon, Mayor Harrison strolled east on Monroe Street, breathing in deeply as he passed the Delft Candy Shop. He spotted an alderman, Joseph Kostner, walking toward him. The men shook hands and waited for the rattle of the elevated train to subside before attempting conversation. The mayor was about to discuss the Everleigh Club closing, at Kostner's prodding, when the alderman pointed a finger across the street.

"Don't you recognize your friends over the way?" Kostner asked, laughing.

Harrison squinted through the traffic and crowds.

"I looked across the street," he wrote later, "to see a pair of females rigged out as though for a fancy dress ball in the lightest, the brightest of garb with bright hued hosiery, dainty hats, low shoes, the flimsiest of flimsy gossamer gowns of delicate hues suitable for young girls in their teens. It was the notorious pair of sisters. They were headed west; I turned back, hustled to the corner, crossed to their side and sauntered slowly to get a good view.

"Whited sepulchres they were, or rather gaudily bedaubled sepulchres, moving mincingly along, proud of the attention they excited, for who could help but stare at these caricatures of human kind, with their absurd affectations, poor, wretched, doddering burlesques of femininity?"

Alderman Kostner followed the mayor across the street and appeared by his side, out of breath.

"Had the sisters recognized you," he said, "what they would have called you and done to you would not be fit for description!"

Two days later, Chicago awoke to find itself under a mantle of snow, the first fall of the season. Sweepers were affixed to streetcars to clear the tracks, and men got to work in the Loop, shoveling piles into horse-drawn carriages to be hauled away and dumped into empty lots. President Taft planned to arrive in Chicago that evening for a three-day visit, and City Hall didn't want any complications.

On South Dearborn Street, unimportant to such official business, rolling drifts were permitted to linger, a serene vision that belied its denizens' current mood. In the Club, Minna and Ada covered the last mahogany table, packed away the last crystal flutes, draped a sheet over the last statue. Everyone was gone now, even the servants and maids, though the sisters told Etta Wright, their longtime housekeeper, that they'd be in touch upon their return to Chicago.

Throughout the week, Levee lords and their emissaries had rung the Club's bell, trying to persuade the sisters to stay in the city, even if undercover, and answer the reformers' salvo. Ed Little, owner of ten resorts on Federal and Dearborn streets (and no known relation to George Little), came to pay his respects and told the sisters the Club could be reopened for $20,000, half the amount Ike Bloom had suggested. Minna was skeptical.

Could she have the personal promise of Bathhouse John and Hinky Dink? she asked.

Little didn't know. The aldermen were being cagey; maybe they, too, were trying to determine how far the mayor might go.

Big Jim Colosimo and Ike Bloom, those vicious sweethearts, were waiting for the Everleighs at the LaSalle Street station. Big Jim captured a sister in the crook of each arm and squeezed. They'd be "going strong" as soon as they returned, he promised. Bloom offered a bony hand and leaned in close. "You ain't got a thing to worry about," he said. "We'll have you back in no time. We'll get the Little Fellow and Johnny Coughlin to work on the mayor."

The 20th Century Limited lumbered forward on the tracks, and a smartly attired Negro porter hauled the sisters' luggage to their car. They waved from the observation platform as the train blasted out of Chicago, gusting great spires of smoke. They would leave the city just as they'd arrived back in the winter of 1899, dining at a table set with expensive English china, slipping between Marshall Field's silk bedsheets, dreaming— fitfully now—of the finest brothel in history.

"Do the best you can, boys," Minna called to her friends. "We wish you luck. We've had ours."

HAVE YOU A GIRL TO SPARE?

Sixty Thousand White Slaves die every year. The Vice Resorts cannot run without this number is replaced annually. Are you willing to give your daughter to keep up this terrible business?

*It is the code of honor among wolves that
no high-minded lamb will squeal.*

—HENRY DEMAREST LLOYD

The Everleigh sisters were fortunate to have made it out of Chicago at all. The Bureau of Investigation—which, thanks to the Mann Act, now employed agents in every state and large city—had enlisted the cooperation of major railroad companies. Executives at L&N, Illinois Central, the Southern, and Chicago & Northwestern, among others, distributed circulars ordering ticket agents to watch for women or girls "known to reside in the so-called segregated districts." Prepaid tickets, a favorite trick of panders, could not be delivered to female residents of red-light districts, nor could scarlet women place deposits on tickets for anyone else, even if the intended recipient lived nowhere near a whorehouse.

These early investigative efforts proved expensive, and Congress, still suspicious of this nascent Bureau of Investigation, played stingy with its budget. In October 1911, money for white slave investigations dried up entirely—a predicament that, in the parlance of the reformers, "aroused" them to send thousands of petitions, telegrams, and letters to every politician in Washington, D.C. Ernest Bell, returning home from yet another white slavery tour (this time through Europe, following right behind the Everleigh sisters), put the Midnight Mission on the case as well, asking his main lieutenant, Melbourne Boynton, to draft letters to Congressman Mann and President Taft.

"I note that special action by Congress is required to secure the necessary funds for enforcing the provision of the Mann White Slave Act," he wrote. "It should be generous enough to allow for a nation-wide, vigorous enforcement of the law against the unspeakable traffic." Their efforts soon paid off. The Bureau of Investigation launched a subagency called the Office of the Special Commissioner for the Suppression of the White Slave

Traffic. Mann Act violations were again a top priority, so much so that the Bureau's director resigned his post in order to become this "special commissioner."

Closer to home, Bell and his fellow reformers had another reason to celebrate. "Mayor Harrison deserves greatest credit for closing up the Everleigh Club," Dean Sumner crowed, "the most notorious dive in the United States if not in the whole world. What to do with the girls who have gone astray is yet an unsolved difficulty. Bad women are a dangerous element."

But Bell and his cohorts were concerned less with a solution to these "dangerous elements" than with destroying the one neighborhood that welcomed them.

"My dear Mr. Mayor," Boynton wrote to Carter Harrison, "there is no excuse for the continuing of such a lawless region. . . . It is particularly objectionable and dangerous in the presence of such a large population of foreigners. American ideals and institutions are trailed in the dust by such official recognition of vice."

Less than two weeks later, Boynton was at it again.

"Dear Sir," he wrote to Mayor Harrison, "even Salt Lake City has abolished its vice district. Ought not Chicago to do as well as Mormondom?"

Harrison received these missives, sighed, lowered his head to his hands, and decided to steal some more time. In March 1912, he ordered another probe of the Levee district, this time to be conducted by the Chicago Civil Service Commission. Maybe, if he were lucky, their investigators would contradict the vice commission report and recommend that the red-light district continue on as it had been—separate and, in its own complicated way, equal.

John D. Rockefeller Jr. decided against continuing Roe's work in New York City's vice districts, though he declined to cite any specific reason, and the prosecutor took slight umbrage at the fact that Junior had a colleague break the news. "I am instructed to advise you," the letter stated, "that the Committee feels it unwise to continue the experiment beyond the present fiscal year ending April 1, 1912."

Nevertheless, the termination was fine with Roe. He'd discovered a vast network of panders among New York City's cabdrivers and even beat them at their own game, paying $600 a month in protection fees to crooked policemen so he could operate a "pretended" disorderly house in the Tenderloin. (Big Jim Colosimo and Maurice Van Bever, eat your hearts out.) But owing to the undercover nature of the project, the press had gone an entire year without printing Roe's name. Other reformers and groups, in the meantime, had finagled their way into the spotlight. Katharine Houghton Hepburn, mother of the future actress, and other prominent suffragists even papered the streets of Hartford, Connecticut, with sensational handbills:

DANGER!

MOTHERS BEWARE!

60,000

INNOCENT GIRLS

WANTED

TO TAKE THE PLACE OF

60,000

WHITE SLAVES WHO DIE

THIS YEAR IN THE U.S.

The Cincinnati Vigilance Society (which organized in 1910, after Roe's visit to the city) claimed credit for numerous Mann Act arrests. And vice commissions modeled after Chicago's were convening even in such unlikely hotbeds of sin as Minneapolis and Lancaster, Pennsylvania. It seemed to the prosecutor that he silenced himself just when he was needed most. Besides, Elsie had just given birth to their daughter, Marjorie, and the mission to save young girls was suddenly, and fiercely, personal. Roe put aside his hard feelings (as well as any lingering reluctance to discuss his private life) to send a birth announcement to Rockefeller, who offered his "cordial congratulations."

So upon hearing Rockefeller's verdict, Roe embarked on two endeavors sure to renew his national reputation as the premier white slave crusader. He began another book, *The Girl Who Disappeared*, dedicating the work to "my devoted wife, who has inspired me to greater efforts in the campaign for better and purer manhood and womanhood." And he reached out secretly to reformers across the country with this proposition: Why not merge all of the principal organizations fighting the white slave traffic into one cohesive group? His plan was brilliant in its simplicity. Strategic head-quarters would be staffed with lawyers, detectives, and educators. When-ever a city—any city—wanted to start a crusade, this group would supply detectives to investigate conditions and lawyers to prepare evidence.

His old Chicago colleagues were on board. Reverends and even a cardi-nal signed on. Capitalists—"the wealthiest men in this country"—pledged support. The former president of Harvard University volunteered his ser-vices. They would call themselves the American Vigilance Association, and the prosecutor created two prestigious roles for himself, executive sec-retary and general counsel.

On April 3, 1912, shortly after the AVA announced its inception, Roe submitted a sixty-one-page final report to Rockefeller detailing his work in New York City. "Until the public conscience has been aroused," he con-cluded, "it is my opinion that it is quite impossible to obtain indictments or convictions of procurers of girls in New York City. The hypocrisy of the double standard of morals is also very evident here. The cases which have been set forth are such cases that would result in convictions in almost any other city in America."

And with that, Roe returned to his city, Chicago, just in time to shape the escalating war against the Levee.

Even Europe seemed to regard the sisters with dark and suspicious eyes. The priceless paintings were leeched of color; the Seine ap-peared dull and unmoving, an uninspired slab of sheet metal. Paris—where the *filles de joie* were rarely insulted with pamphlets and prayers, where bon vivants and libertines outnumbered puritans and prudes—was a rude reminder of what Chicago would never be again. In Rome, they stared for hours at the magnificent *Apollo and Daphne*. Minna described the piece in a letter to a friend. "The Greeks construed Apollo's loss of Daphne," she wrote, "as symbolizing that all mortals shall be denied the Heart's Desire, ever the unattainable." Bernini's masterpiece now evoked the sisters' own sad circumstances.

They returned to Chicago in mid-April 1912, just as William T. Stead, the savvy reformer who started this whole mess, died, along with 1,500 others, when the *Titanic* sank in the frigid waters of the Atlantic. Moving back into the Club right away was out of the question, although they did ask Etta Wright to resume her duties as caretaker. No need to let the place fall apart. The sisters scoped neighborhoods where they might live in the interim and decided the West Side suited them nicely. A practical but handsome Prairie-style house at 5536 W. Washington Boulevard was perfect, with its gently sloping roof and bracelet of stained-glass windows. No professor, no stringed orchestras, no expensive automobiles crowding the curb—but, this being Chicago, everyone on the street knew the true identity of those two faux spinster sisters. Minna and Ada were courteous and kept to themselves, hoping they could make a "final stab" at reopening on Dearborn Street before the West Side evicted them, too.

They made discreet inquiries, letting only a select few Levee leaders, including Ike Bloom, know they had returned. His Freiberg's Dance Hall was bombed in November. The explosion blew out the back door, and blame naturally fell on the reformers. Julia Van Bever had been released from prison and was once again gainfully employed as a Levee madam. Aside from that, the Chicago Civil Service Commission was poking around, but the investigators—at the moment, anyway—seemed concerned mostly with gambling among the Chinese factions. And another of those white slavery narratives was published, inventing some ridiculous "tragedy" at the Everleigh Club.

"This home of vice," began the story about the Club, "is located in a three-story stone mansion. Around it radiates the elite of the district. It is owned by two sisters, immensely wealthy, who have made their fortune through the barter of girls' souls." The lie about the Club involved a pregnant girl. An elderly woman on a train told her she'd receive good care at 2131 South Dearborn Street, Chicago. Once the girl arrived, a doctor drugged her and aborted her baby. When she awakened, two harlots held her down while a strange man raped her. Shamed and ruined, she accepted her fate as a white slave. You had to hand it to those reformers: They concocted better stories than the ones at the nickel theaters.

Bloom was glad to have them back—the place was a pit without the Everleigh Club. Once things settled a bit, and he'd had a chance to consult with Chief McWeeny, he would let the sisters know the plan for their grand reopening.

In the meantime Minna and Ada kept busy doing nothing much at all. Avoiding the curious eyes of the neighbors, they ventured down to the Loop and lost afternoons perusing the stacks at McClurg's bookstore (having a special affinity, naturally, for the "Saints and Sinners" corner) and slipped into theater balconies at night, clad in silk gloves and sedate strands of pearls, looking less like madams than the society ladies who disdained them. From the safety of a closed carriage, they toured the Levee, noting that the Club appeared to be in good shape—unmolested, windows intact, Etta razing the cobwebs inside, just waiting for its owners to bring it back to life.

But before that happened, before Ike Bloom or Big Jim or anyone talked them into unlocking the double mahogany doors, Minna wanted to replay the closing in her mind, to detect nuances that might have escaped her during that terrible, final week of October 1911.

There was a reason, she concluded, that she had not received the personal assurance of Bathhouse John and Hinky Dink about the Club's reopening. Suppose someone else in the Levee had influenced the aldermen, urged them not to expend themselves in efforts to save the Club? Suppose it was someone who had *always* undermined the Club? Not Vic Shaw, who was bumbling and obvious, but someone subtle and sly? Someone like Ed Weiss, owner of the brothel next door, husband of former Everleigh Club butterfly Aimee Leslie, close confidant of Bathhouse John and Hinky Dink. The men would stick together in the end, wouldn't they, despite the fact that the Club paid hefty protection and lured visitors to the Levee from around the world. Well, if Ed Weiss had acted preemptively and secured the aldermen's loyalty behind Minna's back, then she would take out an insurance policy of her own.

Over the following weeks, the madam who had been discreet for eleven long years loosened her grip on hallowed Levee secrets.

"In the days when the Everleigh Club was being openly conducted with huge profits," she began, growing more resolute with each word, "all orders came from Hinky Dink Kenna and Bathhouse John Coughlin through the persona of Sol Friedman, to whom the aldermen assigned the whisky, taxicab, groceries, and clothing privileges in the segregated district. Insurance had to be taken from Coughlin's company and a choice of four provision stores was in force. After the Club was closed Ed Little, owner of ten resorts on Federal and Dearborn Streets, came and told me it could be re-opened for $20,000. I refused to pay, and others visited me. I insisted I must have the personal promise of the aldermen, and this was refused."

Minna paused, took a sip of wine. She couldn't help fuming about the threat that was permitted to flourish next door to the Club, and the way the two most visible politicians in Chicago disappeared in the week after its fall.

"We were supposed to have real protection," she wrote, beyond caring if she sounded whiny or peevish, and then recalled the instance of two disorderly hotels. "When the Ridgeway and Devonshire Hotels opened on Prairie Avenue, outside the Levee, complaints were made by the Levee keepers to Alderman Coughlin. The hotels were closed." Ed Weiss, she added, violated the "Levee code" that no house should vie with the Club as long as she and Ada kept up with protection payments.

"Alderman Coughlin," she continued, "telephoned me personally one time for $3,000 to help stop legislation in Springfield."

The canceled check, she added, was still in her possession.

"I always entertained state legislators free in the Club," she admitted in another letter. "George Little made the collections in the Club and took the money to the office in Freiberg's Hall."

What the hell, she figured. For the rest of her life, she would scrupulously decline to reveal the names of patrons, but now she divulged every last confidence of the men who had squandered her money and her trust, in equal measure.

The price for stopping an indictment on a charge of pandering was $1,000, she wrote. On the complaint of harboring a girl, $2,000. And on a charge of grand larceny against a client of a panel house, $500. She estimated that $15 million in graft had been collected in the Levee over the past dozen years, and the Everleigh Club alone had kicked in more than $100,000 in cash.

Minna tucked the letters away, waiting to see what happened next; she wanted to react, for once, rather than act. What happened next was a visit from Ike Bloom in late August. Would the sisters, he asked, be willing to subscribe $40,000 toward a pool to not only relaunch the Club, but stall raids and crackdowns in general? He was in complete charge of all the details. In fact, if it made the sisters feel any better, he was "acting on orders from Chief of Police McWeeny."

The sisters told Bloom they would consider the offer and get back to him soon. They did not tell him, however, about Minna's letters, folded and bound together, bombs with fuses yet unlit.

Just as cops questioned accomplices separately, so, too, did the sisters, calling Big Jim Colosimo for a meeting at a time when they knew Ike Bloom was busy elsewhere. Sure, he could bring his spaghetti and all the red ink he wanted. The West Side house wasn't nearly as large or well appointed as the Everleigh Club, but it still had a kitchen. The big guy plodded in as he always did, whirling his arms around in the cabinets, making a horrific racket, emerging with two big boilers. Apron strings strained around his girth. Water boiled, sauce burbled, and Big Jim got down to business.

"What's up?" he asked, but he already knew. "McWeeny has got Ike bluffed. I'd like to see the gent who could bluff me." He paused, stirring intently. "I think you'll like this sauce—I dug up a guy to raise mushrooms for me. Can't beat 'em."

Minna had doubts about the sauce, but she needed to keep him focused.

"A $40,000 shake to keep open," she said, and tried her best to play dumb. She wanted to see what Colosimo knew and what he didn't, what he withheld and what he offered too readily. "I don't think Bloom has anything to do with it. We want your advice."

"That's what I'm here for," Big Jim said. "I'll tell you how to handle it. Tell the collectors that you'll give 'em the dough in monthly payments of $5,000 a month. Stall 'em. After all, Johnny Wayman will be the guy in the big cleanup of the Levee if there is one. The idea is to get a fat pool together to square the North Side. But why should you ladies be the goat for the big end? . . . That's a stiff touch—forty thousand. Them are numbers Bloom doesn't know, you can bet your bottom dollar on that . . . five thousand a month or nothing, that's the ulti, ultimat—"

"Ultimatum," Ada said sweetly.

Interesting, Minna thought. Johnny Wayman was the state's attorney and the "North Side" a reference to his office. Big Jim wanted their money as much as Ike Bloom did, though he was trying to soften the request. Still, he offered no promise that such a hefty contribution would placate Bathhouse John and Hinky Dink, that the Club could reopen and stay open.

And she had never known the state's attorney to be on the make—quite the opposite, in fact. He was the only honest one in the bunch.

"Take it or leave it, tell 'em," Big Jim said, setting down enormous, reeking bowls of what looked like bloodied worms. "Pitch in," he added, a faint warning now lacing his tone, and it was clear that he meant more than just the spaghetti.

The sisters choked down the pasta. Their guest filled the room with his hulking presence and cheery patter, but they felt very much alone.

Meanwhile, Roe's old Committee of Fifteen—the foremost Chicago group of the new American Vigilance Association—took a cue from Bell and the Midnight Mission and began haranguing Mayor Harrison. The committee's investigators discovered five girls "all under the age of eighteen, all of whom had homes in Chicago, and all of whom were being sought by their parents" trapped in the South Side Levee brothels of "Dago Frank" Lewis, Harry Cusick (manager, under Roy Jones, of the infamous Casino), and Louis Weiss, brother to the conniving Ed. On August 22, 1912, they sent a pointed letter to City Hall, asking the mayor when he might be available to discuss this travesty. To the committee's surprise, they received a response the following day:

"I beg to acknowledge the receipt of your letter," Mayor Harrison wrote. "I have revoked the saloon licenses of Harry J. Cusick. I have not yet located a license in name of Frank Lewis. I have given instructions to the Chief of Police to close, and to keep closed, until further notice from my office, the houses at 2033 Armour Ave., 2014 Armour Ave., 2117 Dearborn Street, 2127 Dearborn Street and 32 W. 20th Street."

Within the week, Dago Frank, Harry Cusick, and Louis Weiss were charged with harboring minor girls, and Committee of Fifteen investigators hinted that evidence was mounting against Big Jim Colosimo, Blubber Bob Gray, "Jew Kid" Grabner, and Ed Weiss.

The Everleigh sisters monitored the developments with mixed feelings. While increased activity didn't bode well for a grand reopening, it was delicious schadenfreude contemplating the demise of the Weiss brothers. But at 2034 South Dearborn Street, two houses down from Vic Shaw's, Madam Zoe Millard barreled out her front door and embarked on one of her infa-

mous, fearsome rages, pinwheeling her arms, pushing past bewildered errand boys.

"If there had been no Everleigh Club, there would have been none of
this," Madam Millard shouted. "The Everleighs were too damned exclusive even to be nice to the reformers."

One of her inmates, Grace Monroe, appeared at the door. The former
Everleigh Club butterfly called her new madam's name, halting Millard in
midrant.

"They are clean and good," the harlot said, loudly enough for the
neighbors to hear. She steeled herself for what she knew was coming next.

Millard turned, slowly, on the flat heel of a jeweled slipper and started
back toward her brothel. Another madam, who was never identified,
slipped in behind Millard and pulled the door closed.

Two of them were rampaging the poor girl, Minna heard, and she was
already in the yellow automobile, racing down to Dearborn. Not
even Ada could stop her. Eyes shrinking behind swelling skin, nose bloodied, teeth chipped, back crisscrossed with welts, wrists snapped like wish-
bones. Minna barely remembered the drive, or screeching to a crooked halt
outside number 2034, or pushing in the door to Zoe Millard's and seeing
Grace still cowering in the corner, the madam's fat white fist raised and
ready to fall again. She forgot her aristocratic airs. She forgot her disdain
for crude language. She forgot her skill for talking clients out of fighting.
She forgot her words, on the Club's last night, that she was not a knocker.
She forgot that in real birthday time, she had just turned forty-six, a butterfly approaching her final phase. All of that was replaced, in one spinning
second, with the memory of every filthy hand on her skin, the ugly tumble
of all those missing years. Minna stepped up to Madam Millard, curled her
fist, and swung.

JUST
HOW WICKED

Big Jim Colosimo (left) with his attorney.

"**W**e're getting nowhere," Ike Bloom fumed. "You have the knack for making everybody sore. I'm surprised somebody hasn't taken a shot at you."

Minna bit her lip. Let him holler. She'd gotten the best of Zoe Millard, blackened both her eyes, but the police inflicted the worst injury of all—shutting down the madam's brothel on September 5, 1912, the day after the brawl. The Friendly Friends—including Millard and Vic Shaw, but, naturally, no Everleighs—held an emergency meeting, but the largest kitty they could muster was a piddling $30,000. ("Pikers," Ada scoffed. "It'll take a million to grease the ring-leaders against vice.") Now, in mid-September, a grand jury prepared to convene, and Levee leaders were growing desperate. Minna called Bloom to check in and feel him out, and she'd expected a furious lecture. His spittle practically shot through the receiver.

"The Levee has it in their minds that your obstinacy is the reason for the cleanup," he continued. "Why don't you see Bathhouse John, make a deal, be a good fellow and play ball with the rest of us? We're all in the same boat. We've got to organize our forces. Supposing I call a meeting? You make a speech, say you're sorry—anything. They'll be tickled to death to find you a regular. C'mon, what do you say?"

Minna laughed. Her obstinacy was the issue? *She* should be sorry? While Big Jim served up threats with his pasta, and the aldermen forgot which brothel made the Levee the only respectable district in the world? She could listen to Bloom now, accept his reprimands and borrow his optimism, but Minna knew, better than anyone, that not all lies were created equal.

"I could throw a party for some of these law and order leagues," she offered. "But as for the Levee, I'll go my way and the rest can go hang."

Bloom was still muttering swear words when, gently, she lowered the phone. When she lifted it again, she dialed the numbers of several major Chicago newspapers and asked to speak to the city editors. It was time to take out her cache of weapons—all those letters composed by secret light, truth at long last dusted off and doled out.

She had prepared statements outlining every facet of vice in Chicago, Minna said, naming names and quoting prices and casting blame. Perhaps she might consider making them public, if the editors were interested.

On September 26, the Cook County grand jury held a private executive session. After an hour, during which reporters waited with ears pressed against the closed door, the foreman emerged and motioned for the deputy county sheriff. Another interminable wait. When the sheriff finally reappeared, he wiped his brow and exhaled a long hiss of breath.

"Wow!" he said. "They're going to rip off the lid."

"What lid?" asked a voice in the crowd.

"Graft, vice police, politics, white slaves." He swept the horizon with his hand. "They're going to tear the mask from the face of vice. If those fellows do what they say they're going to do, they'll make history . . . and they say we are about to be the busiest little office in Cook County if we get all the persons they are going to examine to find just how wicked a community this is . . . politicians, policemen, gamblers, resort keepers—all are fish for the grand jury net."

Before adjourning for the day, the grand jury issued subpoenas for a woman named Virginia Brooks, who had organized a hatchet brigade in West Hammond (a Cook County town just outside Chicago proper), threatening to pull a Carrie Nation; the mayor of West Hammond himself; Arthur Burrage Farwell, who was expected to provide information on dives that violated liquor laws; Clifford Roe, invaluable for his expertise on the white slave traffic; and the city editors of the *Tribune* and the *Daily News*.

State's Attorney John Wayman, Roe's old boss, was the lone member of Cook County's law enforcement body who seemed wary of the subpoenas. He was in an impossible position. When he ran for election at the end of 1908, he deftly played both sides, taking subtle aim at critics who denounced his ties to the United Societies—"The man who takes the holier-than-thou position and says he is going to keep clean of the whole nasty business," he said, "washes his hands with invisible soap in imperceptible water"—while also vowing to jail every criminal in the county. At the same time, his relationship with First Ward politicians was relatively cordial; Bathhouse John even declared the forty-year-old "the handsomest man in Chicago." Now, the state's attorney was unsure whether to placate the reformers, align himself with the segregationists, or teeter along a fine line in between.

"This grand jury did not consult with me," Wayman said, "and I know practically nothing of the proposed investigation." He didn't know, either, that it was only the beginning of his trouble.

The following afternoon, a Saturday, ten thousand men, women, and children gathered in the Loop, preparing for what one observer called "the most pretentious street parade of its kind." A storm skulked between flattened clouds, dropping just as the procession began. Mounted policemen flanked the crowd, directing traffic. Clergymen, including Bell and his Midnight Mission, sang "Onward, Christian Soldiers" in a tribute to the legendary Gypsy Smith march. Girl Scouts, Boy Scouts, students of the Moody Bible Institute, and members of every conceivable civic and religious group in Chicago fanned out in all directions, rippling and shifting, an entire Lake Michigan of reformers.

The stated purpose of the parade was to "protest against the lawless saloon, the red-light district, the debauched ballot, and a hundred other powers of darkness," but, as the *Record Herald* put it, "the aim of the crusaders seemed to be rather diffuse." Virginia Brooks, the West Hammond ingenue who recently exported her crusading efforts to Chicago, had planned to lead the throng mounted on a white stallion and dressed as Joan of Arc, but at the last minute she decided that such attire would make her a "subject of ridicule." Fifty floats advanced slowly amid the crowd, slathered with signs and strung with banners, a gaudy colony of mutant ants.

There was Lucy Page Gaston and her entire Anti-Cigarette League, waving through dense curtains of rain, declaring CUBS MUST CUT OUT CIG-ARETTES. The Anti-Saloon League wasn't far behind, boasting a similar sign: BOOZE BEAT THE CUBS. Another float, sponsored by the city's Norwegian churches, carried twelve young men cap-a-pie in armor and a thirteenth clad in bright pink tights and a bearskin coat, representing the god Thor. He sliced through the rain with a hammer and bore a placard around his neck: THE GREAT GOD THOR WITH HIS HAMMER, THE NORWEGIANS WILL HELP SMITE THE SALOONS.

Arthur Burrage Farwell and his Chicago Law and Order League lorded over a float designed to look like a "pure ballot." One Boy Scout wore a Satan costume and warned, I'LL GET YOU IF YOU DON'T SWEAR OFF—leaving exactly what one should swear off up to the imagination. Another company of Scouts dragged a small cannon through the slick streets, festooned with a banner declaring, WE'VE TURNED THE GUNS AGAINST THE SALOONS. The Washington Park Church outdid everyone, its members riding atop a mini–morality play. The first float depicted Uncle Sam handing a proud dive keeper a liquor license next to a man guzzling beer on a bar stool; the second represented the drunkard's squalid home, where his wife labored wearily at a washtub while he beat her about the head; and the lone, stark image for the final act was a vehicle dressed up to look like the county hearse.

John Wayman, Shakespearean scholar and fan of farce, would have appreciated the sprawling lunacy of this spectacle—if only its participants hadn't concluded the festivities with a postparade rally, where they violently assailed Chicago's officials in general, and its state's attorney in particular, for failing to close the Levee.

Minna's fingers shook as she lifted the receiver to call Chief Justice Harry Olson of the municipal court. Never in her life could she have imagined volunteering information about the Levee district to an authentic arm of the law—a member of the Chicago Vice Commission, no less—but that was before certain men appeared on her doorstep, their faces half-shrouded by bowler hats, giving her a look that spiked her heart and iced her blood. Big Jim Colosimo had always used violence and evil to navigate his world the way other men used a compass, but she never thought he would steer those urges in her direction.

The men identified themselves as representatives of the vice lord. They'd heard an unsettling rumor that Minna planned to release an "affidavit." If she did—if one word of the laws of the Levee turned up in print—then she and that sister of hers were as good as dead, did Minna understand?

Judge Olson was on the phone now, patiently deciphering her nervous jabber, assuring her he would accept Minna's letters and keep them safe. He understood that he could not release them, or even tell anyone they existed, until the city's foremost madams no longer called Chicago home.

During the final days of September, the grand jury proceedings devolved into their own chaotic parade. State's Attorney Wayman further enraged the reformers by throwing out several indictments, including one against a Democratic precinct captain and political henchman for Hinky Dink Kenna. Since they were based on evidence jurors heard outside of the courtroom, Wayman explained, "they aren't worth the paper they are written on . . . the cases would not stand in court a minute." Arthur Burrage Farwell called for Carter Harrison's impeachment. The mayor was already in a bitter mood, since the Chicago Civil Service Commission, which he'd hoped would argue in favor of the Levee, instead complained about a mile stretch of "half-naked sirens" dangling from windows. The last thing he needed was more grief from Farwell, so Chicago's chief executive retorted, "One might expect almost anything from a man of Mr. Farwell's type. Why should I waste time shouting at a sparrow?"

Roe's Committee of Fifteen received an anonymous letter:

The South Side Levee is rejoicing. The $50,000 fund which has been raised will soon be made back when the entire district will be wide open.

—One Who Knows

And on the last day of the month, Cook County sheriffs, with subpoenas in hand, began searching for Minna and Ada Everleigh.

The county authorities had one problem: Where, exactly, were those Everleigh sisters? Not in the Dearborn Street resort, obviously, and a maid who cared for the place from time to time professed ignorance. The sisters' friends in the press, too, were appropriately cagey, reporting that "it was not generally known that [the Everleigh Club's] former owners are in the city, but the grand jurors have been so informed. . . . As they are said to have retired altogether from the resort business some of the members of the grand jury, it is said, believe they will be willing to give some information to the body concerning Levee conditions, and especially the part played by politicians and police in the arrangement of protection for divekeepers."

On that Monday night, as the deputy sheriffs scuttled about, the sisters waited in their West Side home, aware they were being sought and that it wouldn't be too long before they were found. A municipal judge knew they were in the city, after all, not to mention Big Jim and Ike Bloom and any number of madams who would gladly piggyback the authorities to the Everleighs' front door. Minna and Ada agreed that they owed no one, now, except themselves, but they also couldn't forget the visit by Colosimo's thugs, and the fact that Big Jim did not believe in second warnings.

The bell rang late in the evening, long past their new neighborhood's bedtime. Ada nodded to Minna, who rose and walked her singular walk, that caterpillar bend and hump, and for once did not call the men who stood at the door her "boys" or profess how glad she was to see them. She and Ada were hereby served, and ordered to appear in the Criminal Court Building first thing in the morning.

I t was odd, being in the Loop for business again but without stopping at the First Dearborn Bank to deposit earnings, without a butterfly perched in the backseat, stretching out a leg, tugging at a boot, letting her hem glide up her thigh. The Criminal Court Building presided over Hubbard Street, all leaping columns and long windows, with a jail nestled at the rear. The sisters were escorted to the waiting area outside the grand jury room, and every eye turned on them, weighted stares that Minna acknowledged with her usual tight smile, and Ada with a haughty lift of her chin.

They saw familiar faces—police officer friends who were also subpoenaed to talk about protection payments. Clifford Roe was milling about, as was State's Attorney Wayman, who was being pummeled by the reformers—unfairly, the sisters knew, as he was one of the few who had never taken a cent of graft.

They waited and waited, but no one called them to the jury room. The afternoon edition of the *American* offered a bit of insight into the jockeying behind the scenes. "Minnie and Ada Everleigh," it reported, "were called to appear before the probe body as a result of evidence given by a witness that one of the women had told him of a collector of vice protection money. The woman was expected to divulge the name."

Minna didn't appreciate the pressure, of course, but in red-light districts elsewhere, circumstances were considerably more grim. As the sisters sat in court, the police chief of Atlanta, Georgia, announced that the city's brothels would all close within five days owing to the efforts of a group called Men and Religion Forward. The order left prominent Atlanta madam Nellie Bushee so bereft that she plunged a dagger, fatally, into her heart.

State's Attorney Wayman had had enough with the impromptu investigations and unorthodox handling of indictments and witnesses. Deriding the assemblage as a "runaway jury," he decided to call their bluff.

"Gentlemen," he began, pacing the length of the box, "I am through with this grandstand attitude. You tell me what you want to do and I will see that it is done. Do you want to drive all the resorts out of Chicago? If you do, adjourn until tomorrow noon and I will present sufficient evidence to indict and convict every resort keeper in Chicago."

He paused, looked directly at each juror.

"If that is what you want," he continued, "I am with you. You vote the indictments and I will make the prosecutions. Is that what you want?"

There was a clearing of throats and shifting in seats. One juror leaned forward. "No, not exactly that," he said. "We want to investigate conditions so that we can tell which are the bad places."

"What do you want to do then?" Wayman asked. "Indict the keepers of 'bad resorts'?"

"Yes," the juror said, and echoes of affirmation followed.

The state's attorney smiled. "Then this grand jury wants to go on record as censors of vicious resorts, does it? This body expects to indict and prosecute bad resort keepers and advertise those which it brands as good?"

The jurors turned, looked at one another, trapped themselves in silence. No one knew how to answer. Finally, the foreman stood. Would Mr. Wayman retire and give them until five o'clock to decide their attitude toward the entire investigation?

Sure, Wayman said.

At the appointed hour, they called the state's attorney back in and said that they were finished, leaving a roomful of uncalled witnesses, including the Everleigh sisters. The September grand jury adjourned officially, this time for good.

Two days later, on October 3, Wayman conferred privately with Chief Justice Harry Olson of the municipal court, the judge to whom Minna had entrusted her letters about the Levee. When the state's attorney reappeared, he was, witnesses said, in a state of "furious passion," clenching fistfuls of air, his lips collapsed in a stern line. A chorus of questions arose, and Wayman raised one lanky arm, the cuffs of his suit coat sliding to reveal a knobby wrist.

"There is an apparent effort to lay the blame for Chicago's vice at my door," he said. "Nobody is going to be able to say that I protected the social evil."

Without another word, the state's attorney obtained warrants for 135 Levee pimps, panders, brothel keepers, and madams, including Big Jim Colosimo, Ed Weiss, Roy Jones, and his wife, Vic Shaw.

The news moved, made itself known: "Wayman's out to pinch the whole district." It rattled across Chicago's skyline on the El, climbed into streetcars, alighted into carriages, folded into automobiles, buzzed over telephone wires, electrified Midnight Mission headquarters, and infested the Levee. It reached the West Side and rapped on the stained-glass windows of a charming Prairie house on Washington Boulevard, where two former madams, retired for almost a year, raised glasses and toasted, feeling, at last, vindicated rather than vilified.

"Looks like we saved $40,000," Minna said, sounding happier than she felt, but not by much.

FALLEN
IS BABYLON

State's Attorney John Wayman, with one
of his three children.

Have patience, my friend, for sooner or later you, too,
will get sore at everybody.
—STATE'S ATTORNEY JOHN WAYMAN

T he sun had long since made its own escape as patrol wagons scythed through the Levee streets. Halfway around the world, the first Balkan war was imminent, but the battle in Chicago seemed, at the moment, just as merciless and bloody, terrified harlots slinking through back doors, jumping through windows, everything they owned bundled in tablecloths and slung over shoulders, wondering where to run, knowing as much trouble awaited them outside the district as in.

"Another Johnstown flood, the approach of an invading army, or a plague," one witness noted, "might have caused a similar scene." Electric pianos stuttered to silence, abandoning songs in midverse. Thousands descended southward from the Loop, leaving steaks half-eaten and shows half-watched, such scripted entertainment bland in comparison. Pots boiled over on stoves, bottles of beer and whiskey toppled and slicked the floors, and men fled half-dressed through the streets—their trousers left, along with any dignity, beside a courtesan's strange bed.

Ernest Bell and his Midnight Mission members wandered out from their house on Armour Avenue and were joined by Salvation Army workers with blaring trumpets and throbbing drums. "Onward, Christian soldiers," they sang, "marching as to war . . . ," the lyrics sounding like an antidote to the fleeing girls' screams. A small dark man barreled forward, stopping when he saw the missionaries. Bell recognized him in turn: one of Big Jim Colosimo's thugs.

He braced himself—during the past month, his saints had been doused with valerianate of ammonia, asafoetida, and other drugs—but the "little swarthy" dive keeper flushed with excitement, not anger. "Brother Bell," he said, "your prayers are being answered," and the crowd propelled him on. The missionaries ventured into an abandoned brothel and prayed on the parlor floor, splinters of glass gnashing their knees. Gangs of looters interrupted the sermon, charging in and scurrying off, liquor bottles tucked inside jackets, cheap oil paintings balanced on heads.

A patrol wagon rambled to a stop at 2014 South Dearborn Street, Vic Shaw's brothel. Officers found twenty harlots and one man—but no madam—and piled them all into the back of the van, flailing and cursing. On to the resort of "Black Mag" Douglas, where the madam was arrested but permitted to drive in her own barge-size automobile to the police station, where she immediately posted bail. At the next dive, only a "Negress cook" was found inside, wiping dishes and humming as if it were any other night.

Madam Julia Van Bever, too, was carted away and let go, after Hinky Dink's bondsman paid her fine. At Annie DeMuncy's, 2004 South Dearborn Street, sixteen women were arrested—most of them teenagers—and twenty-five men; from Marie Blanchey's, twenty women and thirty men; from Phyllis Adams's, twenty-four women and twenty men; and from the brothel of Madam Aimee, otherwise known as "Mrs. Ed Weiss," ten harlots in various stages of packing and hysteria. Ed Weiss, Roy Jones, and Big Jim Colosimo played along, gallantly permitting the police to haul them away, and were released in less time than it took to arrest them in the first place. Back in the Levee, they called for an emergency meeting, to convene the following morning.

One by one, they arrived at Colosimo's Café, 2126 Wabash Avenue. Roy Jones, Blubber Bob Gray, Ed Weiss, and Ike Bloom found Big Jim waiting at a secluded table in the corner. Opened two years earlier, the nightclub had become one of the most popular in the Levee, luring Chicago's elite, on both sides of the law, to marvel at its gaudy splendor— the splashes of gilded paint, the mahogany-and-glass bar, the green velvet walls, and the ceiling, with its mural of a naked cherub frolicking amid woolly clouds.

"It is rather extraordinary," wrote one Chicago historian, "that a murderer, a white slaver, Black Hand blackmailer such as Jim Colosimo could attract the best people in Chicago, famous visitors to the city, to his Colosimo's Café. Not only the Potter Palmers, the Marshall Fields, but a late-supper group might have Al Jolson, John Barrymore, and Sophie Tucker."

That morning, though, the Levee leaders had the café to themselves as they sipped coffee and debated strategy. They needed $40,000 more for their coffers, they decided, to augment the $50,000 slush fund that "One Who Knows" had leaked to the Committee of Fifteen. With enough cash, they could tip some of the state legislators in their favor and secure passage of some decent laws at Springfield. It wouldn't be a bad idea, either, to get all of their respective whores in on this counterattack. Calling themselves the Committee of Fifteen in mock homage to Roe's group, the vice lords disbanded, ready to implement their plan.

After rounding up their harlots, the men issued the following orders:

Get on your loudest clothes and more paint than usual and parade.
Go to residence districts. Ring doorbells and apply for lodgings.
Get rooms only in respectable neighborhoods.
Don't accost men on the streets, but be out as much as possible.
Frequent respectable cafés and make a splash.

The invasion of the harlots began on October 5, 1912, at four in the afternoon. Two thousand of them formed a tawdry procession down Michigan Avenue, wearing high feathered hats and plummeting gowns, faces streaked in crimson rouge, bare legs goose-bumped in the cool fall air. They sidled up to society women and winked at their husbands, sweeping long painted nails along the blushing men's backs.

At 35th and Michigan, six prostitutes coordinated the lighting of cigarettes with theatrical aplomb, moving one terrified passerby to call the police. Hers wasn't the only complaint; scores of other respectable women reported being insulted by "undesirables." Refugees from the lower dives, who had not glimpsed sunlight in months, wore bedraggled kimonos that showcased the track marks vining up their arms. Knocking on doors, they explained they had been driven from their homes. Were there any rooms available?

Invariably, there weren't, so the Beulah Home, the Life Boat Home, the Florence Crittenden Home, and the American Vigilance Association all offered lodgings and help. "I'll take care of any of them who come to me," one missionary woman said, "or see that they are cared for in some way."

But not one harlot applied. They didn't want to go anywhere, except back to the Levee.

The ersatz Committee of Fifteen enjoyed unequivocal success. Mayor Harrison, who was still recommending segregation when anyone bothered to ask his opinion, distanced himself from Wayman's actions, opening a tense schism between state and municipal forces. As soon as Chicago's police drove prostitutes back into the Levee, the state's attorney ordered raids and sent apologetic officers to toss them out again. The harlots climbed into the backs of the patrol cars, waving handkerchiefs at the same crowds of men who would be waiting in the district, cheering, upon their return.

This chaotic whiplash continued for a day and a half until both sides were weary and exhausted, and the dive keepers decided they could better see where the standoff was heading if they dimmed their lights for a while. The harlots—quietly, this time—said farewell to the Levee. They found private flats or left Chicago altogether, planning to reinvent themselves in Bloomington or Springfield or Peoria, the same small, bored towns they'd fled long ago. On October 7, the Levee, for the first time since the Great Fire, hushed its music and froze every movement.

"Fallen is Babylon!" Ernest Bell wrote the following day. "Or at least the vice district at Twenty-second is greatly shattered. . . . Within a week Chicago has ceased, at least in a substantial degree, to be a vice-protecting city . . . we must look earnestly to God to make plain His will and His way to continue to uphold the Cross in the night life of our city."

Minna and Ada, too, monitored the Levee's final, exhausting week, its tossing and turning, like a fitful child, before finally drifting to sleep. The sisters wondered how many of their former butterflies were among the Michigan Avenue invaders—girls who had left the Club years ago and forgotten, sadly, that they once looked choicer than the society women they were ordered to intimidate, that they could have moved into those elite neighborhoods without anyone raising a question. They wondered if Grace Monroe had healed, if those wrists, delicate as a swan's neck, were now unbroken, if her back was free from scars. They wondered how the others, scattered across the country, were faring in their new lives, if they remembered Minna's advice and stayed respectable by all means.

They began preparing for their own next act, telling Etta Wright, momentarily displaced from 2131–2133 South Dearborn Street, not to worry, that they would reinstate her as caretaker before too long. They debated where to live, just as they had during that winter after leaving Omaha, and decided on New York, somewhere on the Upper West Side, maybe, near Central Park. And they vowed to return to the Levee only in their minds, where their boys were always satisfied and foes kept their distance, and where soft light kissed Minna's jewels each time she opened the mahogany door.

LITTLE
LOST SISTER

The Everleigh sisters at rest.

I suppose we all want to leave something behind.
—Minna Everleigh

ut the Levee soon awakened from its nap.

When November came, despite Clifford Roe's determination to "fight to the death against segregation" and the continuing agitation between State's Attorney Wayman and Mayor Harrison, Ike Bloom showed up at the sisters' West Side door. Luckily, he reminded the Everleighs, they had nothing to do with the current imbroglio—it was an ideal time for them to reenter the scene. C'mon, they could do it. Freiberg's was enjoying brisk business, and so were the dives of Big Jim, Roy Jones, and Ed Weiss.

"We'll make everything clean and respectable," Bloom insisted. "We'll give the whole line your treatment. How's that?"

He reminded them that one Chicago reverend, a Dr. Frederick Hopkins, had come out strong against the "scattering of evil" across the city.

"Who is that guy, O, yes, Dr. Hopkins, the preacher?" he continued. "He's on our side. We're a necessary evil. We'll line up a few more ministers. It's a cinch."

A thin sheen of sweat glossed Bloom's face; it seemed he was trying, equally, to convince himself. The sisters shrugged.

"It can't be done," Minna said.

"The hell it can't. We'll give generously to the churches. We'll make all the gals say their prayers and sit in them goddamn pews. Don't tell me it can't be done. Preachers got to be greased the same as bulls. What d'ya say? What the hell—you and I will go to church ourselves."

Minna couldn't help it—Bloom always made her laugh.

"Ike, you're getting hot, but not hot enough," she said. "To square the Bible brothers will take more cash than you'll ever be able to subscribe. The idea is gorgeous, but the cost is prohibitive."

Bloom sighed and turned to go. His gangly legs strode halfway across the lawn, then he turned around. It was worth one more shot.

"You sure you won't fight it out?" he called.

"I'm through," Minna hollered back, and Ada nodded. "I want trees in the backyard and sunshine—mostly sunshine. S'long, Ike."

It was the last time the sisters ever saw him.

They were wise, as it turned out, to ignore his pleas. The pressure became so unbearable that even Mayor Harrison relented, and on November 20, more than a month after Wayman's initial raids, he ordered his officers to cooperate with the state's attorney and close every resort, no exceptions.

"Five minutes of real police activity, which gives a rough idea of how such matters can be handled when they want them handled," the *Record Herald* reported, "wiped out the South Side Levee district in Chicago. It ceased to exist as if by magic, not because of the enforcement of the law, but because of the apprehension of it. A few minutes before six o'clock last evening policemen began nailing the doors of Tommy Owens' café at 2033–35 Armour Avenue. They were acting on the orders of Mayor Harrison, delivered at last in an unmistakable manner. Echoes of the blows of their hammers had hardly died away before the entire district was deserted. By six o'clock not a woman was to be found in it."

But the Levee limped on for two more years. Not until 1914 was Ike Bloom's picture finally removed from its position of honor, on the wall of the 22nd Street police station. That year, too, Chief Justice Harry Olson called a reporter for the *Chicago Examiner*. He had a series of letters, he said, written some time ago by Minna Everleigh, the "former queen of Chicago's underworld," and it was time to release them "in the interest of public policy."

Freiberg's Dance Hall celebrated its last night on August 24, 1914, and hundreds of devotees—including two women who said they'd spent every evening there for the past ten years—came to pay their respects. Late in 1915, after Carter Harrison's successor, "Big Bill" Thompson, declared that Chicago was once again a wide-open town, Bloom resumed his business, and the resort operated for several more years, calling itself the Midnight Frolics.

He fell from prominence during Prohibition and died on December 15, 1930, literally half the man he once was; diabetes had necessitated the amputation of both legs.

he Everleighs never again saw Big Jim Colosimo, either, but after leaving Chicago—moved either by forgiveness or a pragmatic appreciation for Levee etiquette—they once again considered him a friend. His power rose in proportion to Bloom's decline, and by 1915, he was the indisputable overlord of prostitution on the South Side. Five years later, he divorced his longtime wife, Victoria Moresco, and married a showgirl named Dale Winters. Meanwhile, his bodyguard since 1908, Terrible Johnny Torrio, had been imploring his boss to export dives and roadhouses to several suburban communities. Colosimo balked, distracted by his new love, and on May 11, 1920, after entering his famous café, he was shot, once, in the back of his head.

Ike Bloom gave a eulogy, and Bathhouse John Coughlin knelt by the big guy's casket and recited a series of Hail Marys. The murder officially went unsolved, although Torrio was suspected of ordering the hit, and after the funeral he took on a new partner, Al Capone. The sisters were questioned, but reminded the police they'd been out of Chicago for eight years and knew nothing. "It surely wasn't a disappointed spaghetti eater," Minna added.

tate's Attorney John Wayman never caught a break. In October 1912, even as he was ordering raid after raid on the Levee, ministers, including Ernest Bell, derided his actions as a "death bed confession" and passed a resolution declaring that he should receive no personal credit for closing the vice district. After a failed run for governor, he returned to private law practice. He slept little, retreated deep into his own mind, began muttering to himself. On April 18, 1913, with his wife downstairs and three young children playing in the front yard, he shot himself twice below the heart.

"I am sorry," he told his wife. "I hope I will live."

He died at 1:30 in the morning, after hours of consciousness.

"He was an outcast the same as the Everleighs were outcasts," Charles Washburn wrote. "The reformers knifed him; the police knifed him. He sat on a keg of dynamite."

After the Levee fell, Ernest Bell moved his Midnight Mission to the Loop, renaming it the Midnight Church and appointing himself pastor. He still took to the streets occasionally, holding open-air meetings and keeping tabs on brothels, and after the advent of radio he broadcast sermons from the Chicago Temple. The financial windfall from *War on the White Slave Trade* dwindled, and by 1916, he was forced to ask his brother, Chauncey, for help. "Dear Ernest," his brother responded, "I am sorry that the apples are not falling into your basket at the Midnight Mission. So far as I can help in agreed contributions to the education of your boy and girl I shall be pleased to do so . . . I hope the way will brighten up for you soon."

His one perceived failure stalked him for the rest of his life: As late as 1919, Bell was still despondent about the Oxford in India. In November of that year, he composed a handwritten letter to "Our Father Who Art in Heaven," confessing "how convinced I have been about it, as though a volcano were scorching my very soul; and how almost utterly thwarted I am and nearly in despair about it till I would rather die than live this baffled in an enterprise that seemed, by so many evidences, to be from God."

Eight years later, though there still was no Oxford in India, Bell at least received validation from an old colleague and advocate of segregation, Graham Taylor. "The song you sung at me eight years ago," Taylor wrote, "sings on still soaring overhead of all I was, am, or may be—except your fighting me hard & fighting me strong—when I was wrong—and that friendly criticism expresses the truest friendship."

Bell died the following year, on October 27, 1928, at Suburban West Hospital in Oak Park, of a brain tumor.

White slavery, and its various repercussions, far outlasted the Levee and the rest of America's red-light districts. Popular culture embraced the same lurid narratives that, ironically, were constructed to police it. Hollywood developed an entire new genre of films, the "white slave picture," churning out titles like *The House of Bondage* (based on the book Roe resented most), *The Inside of the White Slave Traffic*, *The Exposé of the White Slave Traffic*, and *A Victim of Sin*.

By far the most popular—and successful—white slave picture was Universal Studios' 1913 release, *The Traffic in Souls,* which earned a remarkable $450,000 and was based on John D. Rockefeller Jr.'s grand jury inquiry. The protagonist is the head of New York's "Citizens League," who happens to bear a striking resemblance to Junior. In a plot twist that pleased everyone but the reformers, the character turns out to be a white slaver himself. Theatrical productions flourished, too. The verbosely titled *The Black Traffic in White Girls and Why Girls Go Wrong* was a hit in Defiance, Ohio. *Little Lost Sister,* based on Chicago's Levee district, sold out the Lyceum Theater in Detroit, and five companies toured it during the 1913–1914 season. The success enabled one of its producers to purchase an exquisite home on Washington Boulevard, where the queens of the Levee once lived.

"A wave of sex hysteria and sex discussion seems to have invaded this country," one popular journal opined in 1913. "Our former reticence on matters of sex is giving way to a frankness that would even startle Paris."

The white slavery panic prompted one unequivocally positive result. In the spring of 1913, the Illinois State Legislature created a Senate Vice Committee to investigate the link between prostitution and wages. The presidents and proprietors of every major Chicago department store were subpoenaed and forced to submit to a rigorous interrogation: How many women did they employ? How much were they paid? What were the company profits? Would it be a hardship on the company to raise women's salaries? Would they support minimum wage legislation? For some, like Julius Rosenwald of Sears, Roebuck—one of Roe's staunchest supporters—the experience was acutely embarrassing. Although a minimum wage bill failed in Chicago, the actions of the Senate Vice Committee prompted the passage of eight other minimum wage bills, and the state legislatures of Minnesota, Michigan, California, Missouri, Iowa, and Pennsylvania launched inquiries modeled after the one in Illinois.

But America's long, strange moral panic also wrought shameful consequences. Federal authorities used the Mann Act to persecute black men who dared to consort with white women; boxer Jack Johnson, the only black patron ever permitted inside the Everleigh Club parlors, was arrested in the fall of 1912, as the battle against the Levee raged. Former Everleigh Club butterfly Belle Schreiber, Johnson's scorned lover, testified against the boxer, who ultimately served a year in prison. Blackmailing escapades were rampant, most notably in the divorce proceedings of Frank Lloyd Wright, whose estranged wife alerted FBI agents when the architect and his girlfriend left their home and crossed state lines to go into hiding together.

"We now went," Wright said bitterly, "before this august limb of the Federal law on the charge of having violated that malign instrument of revenge diverted from its original purpose to serve just such purposes as this: the Mann Act. Mr. Mann and his wife used to sit across the aisle from me at my uncle's church."

The Mann Act continued to shape many aspects of American life. It spurred the development of the FBI during Prohibition and beyond. In 1944, J. Edgar Hoover, disturbed by Charlie Chaplin's radical politics, began monitoring the actor's sex life and had him booked on a Mann Act violation (Chaplin was acquitted at his trial). The Mann Act remained a familiar pop culture reference throughout the 1960s, when Frank Sinatra made bawdy jokes about the law, and reinforced a national political ethos that, to this day, scares elected representatives from casting any vote that can be perceived as a strike against "values."

But as World War I drew near, white slavery suffered a backlash nearly as frenetic as its ascent. Reformers began shifting their focus from sexual slavery to social hygiene and, in the process, retooled the way they thought about prostitutes. They weren't victims, but feebleminded, maladjusted girls who threatened America's physical and moral health. Prominent newspapers and pundits scrambled to distance themselves from the very hysteria they nurtured.

"It owed its passage," *The New York Times* wrote of the Mann Act in 1916, "to a misapprehension or misrepresentation of its real language and inevitable result, and to a sort of moral panic in Congress, the reflection of the spasms of amateur sociologists and mythmakers of the magazines." A. W. Elliot, president of the Southern Rescue Mission, an organization that worked with prostitutes, declared that "there never was a joke of more huge proportions perpetuated upon the American public than this white slave joke." A former mayor of Toledo, Brand Whitlock, called white slavery and its ribald narratives "a sort of pornography to satisfy the American sense of news."

Sociologist Walter Reckless, in 1933, conducted a study of white slave cases prosecuted in Chicago from 1910 to 1913, all of them investigated by Roe's detectives. Out of seventy-seven cases, he found sixty-three instances of pandering, twenty prostitutes who were minors, three girls held prisoner, fifteen abused, and fourteen who decided to enter the life of their "own free wills," without prompting from any man at all. "Agnes," the first white slave Ernest Bell brought to Roe's attention, was not an innocent American girl drugged at a dance and whipped by a "Negress," as the prosecutor would later write, but a Swedish immigrant who slept with a black man for $5 and a place to stay for the night.

Even Roe, who devoted the "best years of his life" toward constructing the furor over prostitution, began sloughing off its layers and picking at its bones. He knew there was credible testimony from escaped prostitutes and white slavers. He knew that on Christmas Eve 1913, another young Chicago girl sat before a judge, her face a map of slash marks and scars, and testified that her pimp beat her and took everything she earned at a brothel on South Dearborn Street. He knew that Maurice Van Bever and Big Jim Colosimo lured girls with lies and kept them through means far more wicked. He knew there was a small truth tucked inside even his tallest tales, but also that it was no longer fashionable to tell them.

So in January 1914, the William Lloyd Garrison of the white slavery movement stood in front of a Salt Lake City audience and fit new logic over familiar old themes. "There has been too much hysteria over white slavery," he said. "Everything that pertains to the social evil has been classed as white slavery. The idea that women are forced against their will to become inmates of immoral houses after being drugged and by coercion is preposterous. The real white slaver is the man who profits through commercialized vice or the women who run the houses in which commercialized vice is permitted. . . . I have prosecuted and convicted over 500 white slavers, and I know what I am talking about."

Roe died of heart disease in Illinois Central Hospital on June 28, 1934, two days after his fifty-ninth birthday, with Elsie and Marjorie at his side. Obituaries—printed in *The New York Times* and picked up by all the wire services—read like a high school yearbook entry for "Most Likely to Succeed": assistant corporation counsel for the city of Chicago, 1915–1918; president of the American Bureau of Moral Education; three times delegate to the International Purity Congress; member of the Hamilton,

Quadrangle, University, South Shore Country, and City clubs of New York and Chicago.

Perhaps Roe would have been most pleased, though, by the fact that he made news on June 25, 1985, more than a half century after his death. Only one major newspaper, *The Boston Globe*, marked the seventy-fifth anniversary of the Mann Act, but at least it was thorough in its coverage, mentioning Mona Marshall's "I am a white slave" note, and the ambitious young prosecutor who knew precisely what to do with it.

As glad as Vic Shaw was that the Everleigh sisters fell first, she was happier they didn't linger in Chicago to witness her own long, hard fall. She changed along with the Levee, moving, after 1912, from her longtime house at 2014 South Dearborn to several flats and houses before finally settling at 2906 Prairie Avenue, a grand old mansion just beginning to tatter around its edges. That neighborhood was shifting, too, from the "street of the stately few" to one of the haggard multitudes, as Chicago society began migrating to the Gold Coast.

The years didn't so much slip by Vic Shaw as rear up and assault her. Roy Jones divorced her to marry one of her whores, and Vic Shaw had many more "chickens" but never another husband. She began using dope. Her eyes grew emptier; her body, fuller; her mind, smaller. She turned to bootlegging during Prohibition, still keeping in touch with old friends like Hinky Dink Kenna and Bathhouse John Coughlin, and making new ones, like Al Capone.

Vic Shaw stood trial for a drug charge and was sent to federal prison in Dallas, Texas. Paroled two years into her five-year sentence owing to a "bad heart"—the Everleigh sisters would have appreciated the poetic justice—Chicago's oldest and longest-working madam returned to her city claiming she'd found Jesus.

But true redemption remained elusive. Outside the Prairie Avenue mansion, she hung a temperamental electric sign that blinked TRANSIENT HOTEL. The men she now welcomed didn't notice the scrolling iron gate, the gently carved stairways, the sleek cherry paneling and mantels, but merely staggered in and reminded her of what she no longer was.

"I can't stand to see the people who come here now," she said in 1949, "after all the wonderful people this house once had."

She stopped bothering to dress in the morning and conducted her business while reclining on her bed, wearing a faded blue satin nightgown, barking orders to a black maid named Precious and two housemen, Montgomery and Will. One morning in 1949, when a journalist and photographer came for an interview, she jumped up, horrified.

"My God! A man!" she said. "Give me a few minutes, chicken."

"She waddled her 207 pounds over to the dressing table," the *Tribune* reported, "put on a 'new face' complete with pancake makeup, lipstick, eye shadow, and two pats of Chanel No. 5 behind her ears; stuck a jeweled comb in her white, upswept hair-do; rose theatrically to all of her fat 5 feet 2, and with dramatic gestures ordered 'Precious' to 'send the man in!' "

"Charmed, indeed," she cooed in greeting, and released a mournful sigh. "It's pitiful, in my line, to grow old, you know." She told the reporter that she was seventy.

When Vic Shaw died two years later, in November 1951, it became clear she had succeeded in outdoing the Everleigh sisters in at least one aspect of her life. Whereas Minna and Ada bumped back their ages by twelve years, Vic Shaw regressed nearly twenty. Born in 1862—two years before Ada—she was eighty-nine when she left the Prairie Avenue mansion for good.

Minna and Ada sold their West Side home in Chicago and moved to the Upper West Side in New York. On the morning of their arrival, a procession of vans lined up outside the elegant brownstone at 20 W. 71st Street, and neighbors peered from windows to watch the movers carrying piece by curious piece: statues of Greek gods, an entire library's worth of books, lush tapestries and silk curtains, wall-size oil paintings of Rubenesque models showing their naughty parts, two marble-inlaid brass beds, a golden piano that shined up everything in its path.

Who were these two refined old ladies, walking every morning together along Central Park, arm in arm, heads nearly touching, their whispered conversation broken occasionally by a shot of raucous laughter? The loud one said her name was Minna Lester; the quiet one, Ada Lester. They kept to themselves, but, if pressed, mentioned their "former plantation home in the South." Over time, after passing some unspoken test, a neighbor was invited for a visit. Another joined soon after, and another, and another.

Gloved servants presented steaming cups of fragrant tea and little cakes on silver platters. They read from Browning and Kipling, and called themselves the Lester Poetry Circle.

Soon, as the neighbors hoped they would, the mysterious Lester sisters opened up about their past. Oh, those nude paintings? The collection of racy books? Don't mind all of that—these were their beloved grandfather's things. He struck gold in California in 1849 and left them all of his valued possessions, including the risqué ones, and being two sentimental old saps, they just couldn't bear to let them go. Please, take no offense. . . .

Over the years, old friends stopped by, bringing pockets of Chicago along with them. On July 13, 1928, Charles Washburn rang the brownstone's bell; it was the first time he'd seen the sisters since they'd left the Levee. Minna answered the door, wearing $100,000 worth of jewelry and that inimitable smile. It was her sixty-second birthday, but she wouldn't admit to being a minute over fifty. She asked her boy—one of her all-time favorites—how he was.

"If you're all decked out to impress me," Washburn said, nodding at the diamonds, "you can take them off."

"I just want you to know I still have them," Minna replied.

She had dismissed the servants for the day, then called her poetry circle friends and asked them not to visit. Lighting a perfumed cigarette, she led Washburn through the house, asked him if anything looked familiar. It did. There was the statue of Apollo reaching for Daphne, the wood stairway that spiraled upward to the boudoirs, Ada's prized gold piano. Not the Everleigh Club, exactly, but a snapshot of its ghost.

"How come your poetry circle doesn't suspect?" Washburn asked. "All this gold leaf . . . those nudes on the walls. Don't they ask questions?"

"Can we help it if an ancestor was a gold miner and we inherited these priceless antiques?" Minna said. "What the hell, I don't smoke when the circle meets. They don't suspect a thing."

There were further deaths and disappointments: Their father passed in 1915; much of their fortune disappeared in the Crash of 1929; and in 1933, the Everleigh Club, no longer sumptuous within, was razed to a heap of bricks and plaster. It was depressing, enduring its destruction for a second time, but Washburn kept his promise, visiting every year on Minna's birthday, drinking champagne in their parlor, taking out all the pretty memories for just an hour or two.

In the early 1940s, Theodore Dreiser and Edgar Lee Masters called Endicott 2-9970 and picked up the sisters, and four American legends spent a night cruising around New York, remembering Colonel MacDuff waving his chicken leg, and the way the butterflies gathered around the fountain in the Turkish Room, struggling to learn the differences between Dowson and Longfellow. A nice young writer named Irving Wallace became a pen pal in 1946, and he would never know how much the sisters appreciated his calls and letters, the questions that prompted them to try on all their old skins, and marvel that they still fit.

But the end was coming, and Minna was too practical not to herald it. "Someday," she said during one of her conversations with Wallace, "if I no longer have any money, if I'm broke, rather than let them put us in some old ladies' home, I'll turn on the gas in this house."

She never had to do that, but on July 13, 1948—her eighty-second birthday in real years—Minna wasn't able to welcome Charles Washburn for his annual visit. He came, instead, to see her at Park West Hospital. "She seemed like my own grandmother," he noted, and leaned in close to hear her whisper. She told him she hoped she would meet some of her favorite actors in heaven, and then returned to Chicago one last time.

"We never hurt anybody, did we?" she asked again and again. "We never robbed widows, and we made no false representations, did we? Any crimes they attributed to us were the outcries of jealousy. We tried to get along honestly. Our business was unholy, but everybody accepted it. What of it?"

Minna died on September 16, 1948, in her hospital bed. No one witnessed that fierce spirit leave the little gray lady it lived inside. Ada was stuck home with a broken leg, and had to say her good-byes all alone.

The surviving sister organized an auction of the paintings and statues and priceless family "heirlooms." Charles Washburn bought the $15,000 golden piano for $90 but later discarded it, on the advice of his friends, because it seemed to bring bad luck. Ada followed Minna on January 6, 1960, dying at the home of a nephew in Charlottesville, Virginia, weeks short of her ninety-sixth birthday. Maybe those twelve long years without her little sister grew kinder over time; maybe the memory of Minna bloomed full and rich enough to fill some of that ugly, empty space, and do justice to the person she had been. But in December 1948, only three months after that dark day, Ada sat down and took out a stack of holiday greeting cards.

"Best Wishes for a Happy New Year," they read, the words scrolling around a cheery print of a bubbling champagne glass. She thought for a moment, and then signed: "New Years Eve 1948. We are wishing for you a Happy and Prosperous 1949. From our Family to yours—Cordially Aida and Minna Lester," deciding there was room in their lives for one more lie, and this one the loveliest of them all.

Ada Everleigh, circa 1905 (left) and Minna Everleigh, circa 1911.

POST SCRIPT

CLARA BOFFER, FRIEND AND CONFIDANTE TO THE EVERLEIGH SISTERS

In 1972, Pat Algiers took a high school graduation trip to Florida and stayed with her great-aunt, Clara Boffer. One afternoon, while sifting through Clara's collection of leather-bound books, she found a series of old, hand-tinted photographs tucked between the pages of a volume of Elizabeth Barrett Browning. In the photos young women, wearing gowns of crimson and violet and sapphire and gold, posed in rooms that seemed to belong in far-flung corners of the world. Moroccan tapestries covered the walls, a gilded piano gleamed from a corner, a mahogany staircase wound toward a tin ceiling. Pat asked her aunt who and where these pretty girls were.

"I didn't know those pictures were there," Clara said. "These books were from two nice old ladies." Clara told Pat about the women she knew as Minna and Aida Lester.

After leaving Chicago for New York's Upper West Side, Minna hired Clara, a typist with her own business, to transcribe her novel, *Poets. Prophets. Gods.* The leather books in her aunt's library, Pat learned, once lined the shelves of the Everleigh Club, a grand turn-of-the-century brothel owned by those two nice old ladies. Minna's ornate scribble filled the margins, instructing her courtesans—the pretty girls in the pictures—which passages to memorize and why.

The Everleigh sisters found a kindred spirit in Clara Boffer, who had, Pat recalls, "an uncanny eye for style, an insatiable need for adventure, and an inexhaustible passion for business." Born in 1901, Clara left her family farm at age fifteen and secured work as a domestic for a beer baron in Milwaukee. Clara realized she was both smarter and prettier than the baron's daughter when the heiress enrolled in a stenography course. Clara quit her job and attended Spencerian Business School, a six-month education that changed her life.

Clara ventured from Milwaukee to Chicago to San Francisco to Oklahoma to finally New York City, where she counted among her friends Henry James and Minna and Aida Lester. She exchanged confiding letters and photographs with the sisters, some of which Clara kept stashed away for safekeeping until her great-niece stumbled upon them during that summer of 1972. Below are four of those letters, written shortly before the Everleighs' deaths, and above are two rare pictures, taken back when they were most alive.

Thursday—April 20—1944 New York

Dear Clara Boffer

Greetings with fond remembrance . . . I think now that spring is here you should have a little diversion for instance a clever screen play—or maybe two—dear Clara!!! I suggest that "Lady in the Dark" with Ginger Rogers or "Cover Girl" with Rita Hayworth—or—"The Heavenly Body"—with William Powell might prove diverting. . . .

Sister Aida Lester joins me in fond best wishes—dear girl—for your health and happiness! Meantime I view with dreadful apprehension the planned invasion of Europe by British and American troops!!! More than words can express the prospect of this cataclysmic event appalls me!!! My book—"Poets. Prophets. Gods." awaits for its Epilogue theme, "The Handwriting on the Wall" of the civilization we have known—this holocaust of Death!!! I feel Rome will be demolished before this demonic war ends!!!

Not later than the Christmas season of 1944—this book's finale must be recorded!!! . . . May I be granted your aid, dear Clara, the inspiration that you alone can accord to me!!!

Five excerpts have been completed and typed—but two are to be written!! I could not carry on without you—I shall need you—dear comrade you are my beloved adopted sister!!!

Love to you,

From Aida and Minna Lester

Holiday Season 1944–1945 New York

Dear Clara Boffer

Christmas greetings and New Years best Wishes from sister Aida Lester and from me . . . May the Christmas season be for you and for your loved ones serene and happy and may the New Year be the best that you have known. . . .

Have you seen the screen play—"to have and have not" with Humphrey Bogart and Lauren Bacall??? A sensational photo film—see it when leisure permits. . . . We shall be with you in spirit. . . .

Love from Aida and Minna Lester

Monday, July 15 1946 New York

Dear Clara Boffer

Fondest Greetings . . . how adorable of you to send to me the gorgeous flowers in remembrance that July 13 is my birthday anniversary. . . . Flowers—never do that again—my dear, my dear!!! There are no more birthdays for us to keep as we older and wiser grow!!! Still, I shall ever cherish the collection—pinks-rose-lavender-violet-vivid crimson-haunting pale yellow color—blending so exquisitely. . . .

As a souvenir of My Book—"Poets. Prophets. Gods."—May I ask that you accept tiny memento enclosed?? See some screen play—if inclination prompts and leisure permits—your beautiful typing of my volume—the inspiration of your personality . . . meant more to me in the composition of my book than any one else on Earth could have contributed!!! My volume, while completed—will not be published in 1946. . . .

Let's hope dearest girl that fate will be kind to me—and grant me— the privilege of seeing you when "Poets. Prophets. Gods" is published!!!

Ever with fond remembrance with love—

Yours, Minna Lester

Sister Aida always asks to be remembered

dear girl to you. . . .

May 1956

My dear Clara,

I have not heard from you for a long time and wonder how you are? I slipped on the stairs here in my home and sprained my back. I have suffered a good deal with it. But today it seems better. But still it is difficult to write somehow.

I am wondering how you are and where you are? Have you forgotten your old friend? I would love to hear from you at your leisure dear friend. It is a lovely cool day here in Virginia and I'm so thankful for my many comforts, and Blessings. I have become a real Christian. May God bless you Clara.

From my heart, yours,
Aida Lester

All letters reprinted with the permission of Patricia S. Algiers.

ACKNOWLEDGMENTS

The publishing process is as terrifying as it is exhilarating, especially for a first-time author, and I am eternally grateful to my editor, Julia Cheiffetz, for accompanying me on the ride. Her keen critical eye improved every page, her jokes in the margins provided much-needed comic relief, and her commitment and support were unstinting. My deepest thanks to the entire team at Random House: Gina Centrello, Tom Perry, Jack Perry (who's gone above and beyond the call of duty so many times I've lost count), Dan Menaker, Jennifer Hershey, Sally Marvin, David Underwood, Jane von Mehren, Tom Nevins, Benjamin Dreyer, Steve Messina, publicity gurus Barbara Fillon, Megan Fishmann, and Amanda Ice, Lynn Buckley, Bridget Piekarz, and all of the reps who worked to get this book into readers' hands. My book couldn't have found a better home.

I'm fortunate to have the brilliant Simon Lipskar as my agent. We met late in the game, but he immediately earned my respect and my trust; every writer should have such a skilled and enthusiastic advocate.

Steven Wallace swooped into my life like a benevolent fairy godfather. I'm grateful for his tireless efforts on my behalf, and for his humor and friendship. Lunch is always on me.

Rick Kogan is my permanent Billy Goat escort and my very favorite thing about Chicago.

During the long process of researching this book I depended on the assistance, generosity, and kindness of numerous people. Debbie Vaughan, researcher extraordinaire at the Chicago History Museum, supported this project from the beginning and answered a million questions along the way. Rob Medina, also of the Chicago History Museum, patiently—and quickly—processed several requests for photographs. Gerald W. Fauth III, trustee of St. Paul's Episcopal Cemetery, where the Everleighs are buried, painstakingly helped me piece together the sisters' early years. William Diment and Evelyn Diment provided information about the Simms family lineage and spoke candidly about their famous ancestors. Amy Wallace and David Wallechinsky helped me track down their father's correspondence, and Hilary Masters shared his father's memories of the Everleigh sisters. Esteemed Chicago historian Ann Keating offered to fact-check a few crucial passages. David J. Langum sent me several obscure journals, offered sharp insights about the reformers and their motives, and hooked me up with a great photo of an Everleigh butterfly. Graham Garfield schooled me on the finer points of Chicago's El system. Amy Fitch made my trip to the Rockefeller Archive Center an absolute pleasure. Becky Kennedy and Barbara White, the two-woman crew at the Atlanta Fulton Public Library's interlibrary loan department, handled my many requests with efficiency and grace.

Much love to the members of my Atlanta writing group, Joshilyn Jackson (who always goes the extra mile *plus* thirty feet) and Anna Schachner, two immensely gifted writers, discerning critics, and invaluable friends. They kicked this book (and me) along on a daily basis, and made a die-hard Yankee girl feel entirely at home.

I would have quit years ago were it not for my online critique partner, Sara Gruen, who in short order became one of the most vital people in my universe. She read several versions of this book, let me rant, made me laugh, and fed me her famous martinis (huge thanks also to Bob, Benjamin, Thomas, and Daniel for their hospitality toward "Cam'ryn").

My friends and family offered editorial advice, a place to crash, and camaraderie, and otherwise supported me and this book in countless ways. The amazing team of Gilbert King and Nick Barose lugged equipment across New York City in a torrential downpour and spent a day taking my picture. Elisa Ludwig gave an astute critique of this book and talked me off the ledge at regular intervals. Melisa Monastero knows all and loves me anyway. Renée Rosen is my sounding board and an absolute doll. Jennifer Fales and Greg Morris put me up (and put up with me) during several visits to Chicago. Susan Keyock always shows me a good time. The immensely talented Adrian Kinloch designed my website. Thanks also to Gayle McCool (still my M.B.), Maggie Dana, Mary Agnew, Laura and Erik and Nate Kutina, Gwen

Dittmar, Roberta Livingston, Darienne Russell, Lauren Vega, Franky Vivid, Meenoo Mishra, Maija Pelly, Kelly Pattillo, Jill Patrick, and all the folks at Backspace.

A special thank you to Clara C. Boffer, a woman every bit as fascinating as the Everleigh sisters, for saving Minna and Aida's correspondence, books, and photographs; to Clara's nephew, William Reis, for giving these treasures to Clara's great-niece, Patricia Algiers; and to Patricia Algiers, for her help, support, and generosity, and for believing that the Everleigh sisters' greatest lie was that they wished to be forgotten.

Kathy Abbott helped me double-dip on interlibrary loans, accompanied me on a few trips to Chicago at her own expense, and never once complained when I made her stay until the library closed. Anne Scarborough gave me holy-water blessings and scrumptious *potica*. Ron Abbott picked me up from the Philly airport at ungodly hours. Paul Abbott, John Sabatina, and Mark Sabatina coddled me and toughened me up in equal measure. Judy Sabatina is still the Queen of Hearts. Sandy Kahler is unequivocally the kindest human being I know.

Chuck Kahler, my sweetheart and greatest champion, should remind me every day how lucky I am to have him.

And finally, to the great, inimitable city of Chicago: Thank you for having so many fabulous old secrets, and for being so willing to share them.

Every girl who entered the "sporting life" did so intending to abandon her old one, and only in later years did the Everleigh sisters speak of their past—albeit, of course, in largely apocryphal terms. Minna never published her novel, *Poets, Prophets and Gods* (which purportedly included a chapter based on deceased sister Lula), and in 1938 she told Theodore Dreiser that she and Ada had written a book about their madam careers. This, too, went unpublished, but it's curious that the sisters penned a book at all—or at least claimed to—considering the fact that Charles Washburn's biography, *Come into My Parlor*, had been released two years earlier.

"There have been three books written about the Everleigh sisters," Minna told Irving Wallace in 1945. "One is *Come into My Parlor*. It should have been called *The Club*. Another is the *Gem of the Prairie*. And there is also *Lords of the Levee*. Most of all this is a bunch of untruths and lies. But *Come into My Parlor* is the best."

Minna's creative interpretation of "untruths and lies" notwithstanding, she was right: of the three, Washburn's book was the most complete and detailed account of the Scarlet Sisters and their times. (*Gem of the Prairie*—republished as *The Gangs of Chicago*—and *Lords of the Levee* devote considerably less space to the Everleighs.) Although Washburn's biography is an invaluable resource—I could not have written this book without it—*Come into My Parlor* is slightly flawed as source material.

For one thing, Washburn's nonlinear style obscures the sequence of events and conversations; whenever possible, I checked his account against others to determine the most accurate chronology. Washburn's work is also compromised by the fact that the author was close friends with—and very protective of—his subjects. He repeats the misinformation about their ages and upbringings (assuming he was privy to the truth in the first place) and omits certain crucial events altogether. There's an entire chapter in *Come into My Parlor* devoted to Big Jim Colosimo, for instance, but no mention of his threatening the sisters' lives during the final days of the war against the Levee. Likewise, the *Chicago Daily Socialist*'s 1909 attack on the sisters and their resulting trip to Europe are skipped altogether, but corroborated by one of Minna's late interviews with Irving Wallace.

Jane Addams declared in 1911 that "no great wrong has ever risen more clearly to the social consciousness of a generation than that of commercialized vice," yet the national angst over the "social evil" has been overshadowed by other Progressive Era hallmarks: the push for women's suffrage; Ida Tarbell's scathing exposé of the Standard Oil Company; Carrie Nation and her renegade hatchet posse. (One historian suggests that the vice crusade's "schizophrenic" nature is to blame; "admirable people" like Addams and Lillian Wald vied with "people who did not like sex.") Luckily, the red-light district reformers believed both in their mission and in using publicity to achieve it, and documented their efforts—both legitimate and exaggerated—thoroughly.

I spent three years researching this book and relied often on two local libraries. Emory University's Woodruff Library has every issue of the purity journal *The Philanthropist* (and its successor, *Vigilance*) as well as an excellent women's studies section containing many old and rare books about prostitution and white slavery. I first came across the Chicago Vice Commission report and the works of Ernest Bell and Clifford Roe at the University of Georgia's main library, and spent many productive (if dizzying) hours there perusing *Chicago Tribune* archives on microfilm. A number of contemporary books and studies also proved immensely helpful: *The Encyclopedia of Chicago,* edited by James R. Grossman, Ann Durkin Keating, and Janice L. Reiff; Perry Duis's *Challenging Chicago;* David J. Langum's *Crossing over the Line;* Ruth Rosen's *The Lost Sisterhood;* Mark Thomas Connelly's *The Response to Prostitution in the Progressive Era;* and Amy R. Lagler's doctoral thesis, "For God's Sake Do Something: White Slavery Narratives and Moral Panic in Turn-of-the-Century American Cities."

I hesitate to classify my numerous trips to Chicago as work. The people I met were unfailingly helpful, always willing to explain the intricacies of each El line or bus route (often more than once, thanks to my nonexistent sense of direction and utter lack of map skills). The city feels relentlessly vibrant and alive even inside the hushed research room of the Chicago History Museum or the basement of the gorgeous Harold Washington Public Library. At the latter I again logged countless hours in front of microfilm machines, cross-checking articles from the *Tribune* with those from a half dozen other prominent newspapers from the era (and becoming distracted, on occasion, by odd but charming glimpses of American popular culture at the turn of the last century: girls popped pills to gain weight; acne medicine not only promised to clear up "scabby crusts" but to produce a "new supply of rich, red blood"; and a widespread fetish for "lovely arms" contests). The Harold Washington Library is as generous as it is stunning: every single photocopy was free. On several occasions I left the city with an extra suitcase, crammed full of research.

During my last excursion to Chicago I took a cab down to the Near South Side and spent an hour or so walking through the neighborhood that, one hundred years ago, was known throughout the world as the Levee district. Twenty-second Street was renamed Cermak Road in honor of Mayor Anton Cermak, who was fatally shot in 1933, and entire blocks of South Dearborn Street no longer exist. The exact location of 2131–2133 is somewhere on twelve and a half acres of property now owned by the Chicago Housing Authority, the current site of the Raymond Hilliard Homes. The complex, designed in 1966 by renowned Chicago architect Bertrand Goldberg, is lauded for its aesthetic properties: two tall, curving towers laced with honeycomb-shaped windows. In 1999, Hilliard Homes was named to the National Register of Historic Places, the first and only time a Chicago public housing structure has achieved such distinction.

Citations for quotes and more obscure facts follow:

xiii. "Chicago, a gaudy circus": Lindberg, *Quotable Chicago,* 110.

PROLOGUE: ANGELS OF THE LINE

xix. only son and heir: *Chicago American,* November 23, 1905.

xix. "Give the lady": *Chicago Daily Herald,* August 25, 1982.

xix. Tore through: *Chicago Tribune,* November 23, 1905.

xix. "I shot myself": Ibid.

xix. A reporter at the *Chicago Daily News:* Madsen, 158.

xx. breakdown in 1904: *Chicago American,* November 23, 1905.

xx. "We are a funeral parlor": Washburn, *Come into My Parlor,* 99. The author didn't specify exactly which incident provoked Ada's quip.

xxi. "brought a girl around": Kimball, 87.

xxi. dab of gasoline: Duis, *Challenging Chicago*, 51.

xxi. She had an odd walk: Edgar Lee Masters, "The Everleigh Club," *Town & Country*, April 1944.

xxi. "King and Queen of the Cokies": Asbury, 246.

xxii. Mickey Finn: Ibid., 176.

xxii. Merry Widdo Kiddo: Ibid., 246.

xxii. "professors": Washburn, *Come into My Parlor*, 167; Asbury, 266.

xxii. "How *is* my boy?": Edgar Lee Masters, "The Everleigh Club," *Town & Country*, April 1944.

xxii. Frank Carson: Washburn, *Come into My Parlor*, 84.

xxii. "Beau Night": Ibid., 187.

xxiii. "to pleasure what Christ": Ibid., 28.

xxiii. Edmund, the butler: Ibid., 36.

xxiv. Bucket of Blood and Bed Bug Row: Asbury, 264 and 246.

xxiv. a teenage girl from a good family: *Chicago Record Herald*, January 9, 1905.

xxiv. "They were the Angels": Washburn, *Come into My Parlor*, 89.

PART ONE: THE SCARLET SISTERS EVERLEIGH, 1899–1905

STRIPED SKUNK AND WILD ONIONS

3. "An amusing city, Chicago": Ibid., 45.

3. "vestibules": Miller, 180.

3. "wonderful cure": *Sporting and Club House Directory*, 36.

3. "at will through space": Cleveland Moffett, "Marconi's Wireless Telegraph," *McClure's Magazine*, June 1899.

3. first major automobile show: Musselman, 76.

4. "individual shortcomings of dress": Dreiser, 27.

4. Eight years before *New York Sun:* Grossman, Keating, and Reiff, 882.

4. "Go to Chicago now!": Miller, 169.

4. "She outgrows her prophecies": Quoted in Miller, 188.

5. "Respectable women": *Chicago Tribune*, January 19, 1936.

5. "most celebrated banging shop": Longstreet, 119.

5. "A drunk is no good": Kimball, Quoted in *Fille de Joie*, various contributors, 22.

6. Big Matilda: Ibid., 388.

6. "Nowhere in this country": Ibid., 19.

6. Ignace Paderewski and Republican politicians: Wallace, 30.

7. Rosie Hertz, the so-called godmother: Jackson, 947.

7. Rose Hicks, "Lucky" Warren, Annie Chambers: Washburn, *Come into My Parlor*, 18.

7. "wick dipping": *Fille de Joie*, 20.

7. Carrie Watson, had retired: Asbury, 243.

7. "See Effie": *Come into My Parlor*, Washburn, 19.

7. "She-caw-go!": Miller, 181.

8. "It's home to me": *Come into My Parlor*, Washburn, 19–20.

8. "We have catered": Ibid., 20.

9. "Chicagoua": Grossman, Keating, and Reiff, 130.

9. A twenty-eight-mile-long canal: Ibid., 864.

9. "Walking in Dearborn Street": Pierce, 409.

10. The town's board of trustees: Asbury, 37.

10. The Great Fire of 1871: Miller, 159.

10. 2,218 saloon licenses: Asbury, 89.

10. "Black-eyed Amy": Dedmon, 146.

11. "Little Chicago": Asbury, 108.

11. "everybody knows what a 'French' house is": *Sporting and Club House Directory,* 39.

11. "least public colored house": Ibid.

11. "Carrie Watson": Asbury, 137.

11. "Miss Carrie Watson": Dedmon, 145.

11. "Terror of State Street": Asbury, 122.

12. Mayor Carter Harrison II: Asbury, 243. Harrison was actually the fourth namesake in his lineage, but due to the popularity of his father, he was often called "Junior."

13. "Pick a baby": Lindberg, *Chicago by Gaslight,* 127.

ANOTHER *UNCLE TOM'S CABIN*

15. "Stead was a man": Washburn, *Come into My Parlor,* 120.

15. its own *Uncle Tom's Cabin*: Walkowitz, 96.

15. "The slavery of black women": Butler, 13.

15. "The poor child": Stead, *The Maiden Tribute of Modern Babylon: The Report of the* Pall Mall Gazette*'s Secret Commission.* London: Richard Lambert, from the July 6, 1885, issue.

GETTING EVERLEIGHED

18. February 1, 1900: Washburn, *Come into My Parlor,* 21.

18. Several homeless people froze: *Chicago Daily News,* January 31, 1900.

19. "I talk with each applicant": Washburn, *Come into My Parlor,* 110.

19. "Pleasure": Quoted in ibid., 31.

19. Valerie, a doctor's daughter: Ibid., 35.

20. "Every girl, if only": Kimball, 33.

20. "I ain't ashamed": Quoted in Rosen, 101.

20. "It is not adequate": Ellis, *Studies in the Psychology of Sex,* vol. 4, 225.

20. "I got to get out": Quoted in Rosen, 158.

21. "I spent 3 days": Quoted in ibid., 159.

21. Julia Yancy, Etta Wright, Dr. Maurice Rosenberg: *Chicago Tribune,* March 6, 1925.

21. red mouthwash: Lindberg, *Chicago by Gaslight,* 128.

21. "private conservatory of music": Gerald Carson, "The Piano in the Parlor," *American Heritage* 17, no. 1 (December 1965).

21. Vanderpool Vanderpool: Washburn, *Come into My Parlor,* 167.

22. Two private suites: Lait and Mortimer, 33–34.

22. Everly: Longstreet, 294.

22. just like Sir Walter: Washburn, *Come into My Parlor*, 21.

22. "I have always considered": Letter from Evelyn Diment to Irving Wallace, January 20, 1989, courtesy of the Irving Wallace Family Trust.

22. "The double entendre": Boehm, 84.

23. Such relationships were common: Rosen, 104, 171.

23. harlot folklore: Ibid., 105; *Madeleine: An Autobiography*, 144; Winick and Kinsie, 44.

24. Everleigh Club operations: Washburn, *Come into My Parlor*, 29–30; Asbury, 253; Johnson and Sautter, 75–76.

24. "Utopia Novelty Company": Hibbeler, 48. Hibbeler's book is a racy (for 1960) account of the Everleigh Club based on interviews with the former butterfly named Doll. He was the piano professor at Freiberg's Hall, and familiar enough with the sisters to merit a mention in *Come into My Parlor*.

24. "Be polite, patient": Washburn, *Come into My Parlor*, 24.

25. "butterflies": Ibid., 41.

25. "Just a bluff": Ibid., 23.

26. "the King of the Brothels": Wendt and Kogan, 369.

26. RITES FOR P. D. ARMOUR, JR.: *Chicago Daily News*, February 1, 1900.

26. "We've got her all wrong": Washburn, *Come into My Parlor*, 25.

27. pocket more than $100: Asbury, 254.

THE DEMON OF LUST LIES IN WAIT

29. "You may believe it or not": *The Philanthropist*, January 1886.

29. "an organized agency": Ibid., November 1886.

29. authorities raided a Michigan lumber camp: Lagler, 58–59.

30. "These atrocities": *The Philanthropist*, November 1888.

LOVELY LITTLE LIES

32. "Everyone wants to be": Wallace, 54.

32. Ada and Minna Everleigh were born: U.S. census, 1870.

32. "ninety-nine percent more worthy": Wallace, 54.

32. "I am absolutely": Ibid., 52.

32. "No nursery stories": Ibid.

33. "a voice much younger": Ibid., 54.

33. The sisters' forebears: Woods Hampton, 1–39.

33. The sisters' father: Ibid., 68.

33. Twenty slaves cultivated: Slave Schedule 2, Slave Inhabitants in the County of Greene, State of Virginia, 1850.

33. At age twenty: January 2006 e-mail exchange with Allison White, special collections librarian and archivist, University of Virginia Law Library.

33. married his first cousin: Woods Hampton, 24.

34. Jennie gave birth: I followed the evolution of the Simms family through the 1870 and 1880 census.

34. "a grim reality": Woodward, 187–190.
34. baby brother George was handed over: The 1880 census lists George W. Simms, age four, as a nephew living with W. B. Ward and Sarah Ward (née Sarah Simms, sister of Minna and Ada's father).
34. family of five: Wallace, 54.
34. Their neighbors included: 1880 census.
34. Confederate general: Kemper was general of the 7th Virginia, which included many Simms men.
35. letter from Minna to Irving Wallace: Wallace, 47–49, 7; Irving Wallace Papers, Robert D. Farber University Archives & Special Collections Department, Brandeis University.
37. "I was strangely moved": Ibid., 49–50.
37. "The Catholics": Ibid., 51.
37. "I had a sister": Ibid., 58.
38. the sisters moved from Madison County: Woods Hampton, 24.
38. "wealthy devil of a man": Wallace, 56.
38. They hailed not: Washburn, *Come into My Parlor*, 11–13.
38. "Do you know I'm related": Wallace, 58.
39. "southern gentleman" and wedding details: Washburn, *Come into My Parlor*, 14. I hired a private researcher to search marriage records throughout the state of Virginia, and none were found. I also checked every county in Missouri where the sisters lived or had family, also to no avail.
39. "No other man": Ibid., 15.
40. "It is doubtful": Ibid., 148–149.
40. "I love men": Wallace, 59.
40. "estates in the South": Washburn, *Come into My Parlor*, 16.
41. run of bad luck: Woods Hampton, 23.
41. "My mother would": Washburn, *Come into My Parlor*, 16.
41. letter from Evelyn Diment to Irving Wallace, January 20, 1989, courtesy of the Irving Wallace Family Trust, Los Angeles, CA.
42. "lied about their background": Phone conversation with Evelyn Diment, January 2006. When I spoke to her, the Everleigh sisters' great-niece was eighty years old and living in Colorado.
43. In Omaha by 1895: Research conducted by a University of Nebraska at Omaha School of Criminology and Criminal Justice class in October 1992 revealed that a Minnie and Rae Everly are listed in the 1890 city directory, boarding at 822 Dodge.
43. "It is hardly conceivable": Carl Uhlarik, "The Sin Sisters Who Made Millions," *Real West*, December 1968.
43. The town's Trans-Mississippi Exposition: I confirmed facts about the exposition with Gary Rosenberg, a research specialist with the Douglas County Historical Society.
44. "They were some punkins": *Real West*, December 1968.
44. "They were some lookers": *Omaha World Herald*, September 17, 1948.
44. Many courtesans suffered: Rosen, 80.
45. "It is claimed that this disease": Washburn, *The Underworld Sewer*, 303.

45. "wet, flabby sheep's gut": Green, 91.
45. condom names: Ibid., 95.
45. "You wouldn't believe": Quoted in Rosen, 96–97.

THE STORIES EVERYONE KNEW

48. "All civilization has from time to time": Ellis, *Little Essays of Love and Virtue,* 165.
48. "Never before in civilization": Addams, *The Spirit of Youth and the City Streets,* 5.
48. "agony column": Quoted in *The Philanthropist,* January 1888.
49. "organized, systematized traffic": Quoted in Lagler, 86.
49. "We have used facts": Edholm, 3.
49. "false employment snare": Ibid., 13–14.
49. "There are men": Ibid., 26–27.
49. "When I was a bartender": Ibid., 34–35.

LORDS AND LADIES OF THE LEVEE

52. "Laws should be like": Lindberg, *Quotable Chicago,* 112.
52. Isaac Gitelson: *Chicago Tribune,* June 11, 1904.
53. a label marked "HONEY": *Chicago Tribune,* October 13, 1904.
53. "make arrangements": Asbury, 276.
53. the scale of prices: Wendt and Kogan, 322.
54. "Positively" Asbury, 276.
54. "Now see what they done": Washburn, *Come into My Parlor,* 60–61.
55. "paper suits": Ibid., 136.
56. "red ink" and following quotes: Ibid., 137.
56. Big Jim biographical information: Asbury, 312–314.
57. one of thirty-five in the city: Grossman, Keating, and Reiff, 857.
58. "I have watched men": Washburn, *Come into My Parlor,* 148; Lindberg, *Quotable Chicago,* 110.
58. "Everywhere the names": Wendt and Kogan, 285.
58. "largest and coolest": Ibid., 170.
58. Hinky Dink biographical information: Ibid., 73–76. One editor of the *Tribune,* Robert Lee, doubted that Medill gave Hinky Dink his nickname.
59. "Whatever difficulties arose": Washburn, *Come into My Parlor,* 53.
59. "I formed my philosophy": Wendt and Kogan, 17.
59. "Ode to a Bath-tub": Washburn, *Come into My Parlor,* 49.
61. One brothel owner, Ed Weiss: Asbury, 262–263; Washburn, *Come into My Parlor,* 101.
61. Friendly Friends: Asbury, 261; Hibbeler, 46.
61. "Come look out the window": *Chicago Tribune,* March 15, 1949.
62. Vic Shaw biographical information: Ibid.
62. "strip-whip" matches, Gladys Martin, "Lill the Whipper": From the "Vic Shaw Family Album," Lawrence J. Gutter Collection of Chicagoana, Special Collections Department, University of Illinois at Chicago.
63. "Queer ducks, our neighbors": Washburn, *Come into My Parlor,* 30.

GREAT IN RELIGION, GREAT IN SIN

65. "We discovered that the scrupulously strict": Ibid., 146.

65. "one in language, one in God": *Chicago Tribune*, October 9, 1901.

66. "Precisely the same conditions": Ibid.

66. "lowering the tone of the human race": *Chicago Tribune*, October 10, 1901.

66. "purity in thought, word, and deed": *Chicago Tribune*, October 11, 1901.

66. "active experience with vice": Ibid.

KNOWING YOUR BALZAC

68. "If it weren't for the married men": Washburn, *Come into My Parlor*, 241.

68. They came to see: Asbury provides an excellent description of the Everleigh Club, 247–258; Room of 1,000 Mirrors is cited in the December 1968 issue of *Real West*.

68. menu items: Washburn, *Come into My Parlor*, 156–157.

69. *Apollo and Daphne:* Ibid., 149–150.

70. "By comparison": Asbury, 249–250.

70. "a harlot's dream": *Chicago Tribune*, January 19, 1936.

70. "Next week": Washburn, *Come into My Parlor*, 29; Hibbeler, 11.

70. "It was a happy day": Washburn, *Come into My Parlor*, 148.

70. "bringing a glass of water to a lake": Ibid., 153.

71. "Your letter to him": Ibid.

71. $18,000 per year in renovations: Asbury, 250.

72. "Come, I'll show you": Ibid., 145.

72. "wrong end of a whore": Longstreet, 298.

72. round-trip race from Chicago: Grossman, Keating, and Reiff, 55.

73. Crowds cheered as New York drivers: Jackson, 67.

73. the men retired en masse: Musselman, 84–85.

74. "England's only chance": *Chicago Daily News*, February 28, 1902.

74. lunched at Sherry's: *Chicago Daily News*, February 26, 1902.

74. "representative men": *Chicago Tribune*, March 2, 1902.

74. "Prince Henry probably will brush": *Chicago Daily News*, February 28, 1902.

74. "It won't hurt the prince": *Chicago Inter Ocean*, February 26, 1902.

75. Around midnight on March 3: Hibbeler, 52.

75. "smoked up the room": Washburn, *Come into My Parlor*, 78.

76. cast a mild insult: Johnson and Sautter, 76; Longstreet, 300.

76. "fräuleins": Washburn, *Come into My Parlor*, 78.

76. Vidette: *Nevada State Journal*, September 7, 1948.

76. "Boot liquor": Dedmon, 255.

77. "On with the dance!": Washburn, *Come into My Parlor*, 79.

77. "In New York millionaires": Ibid., 80.

77. "depraved blue nosers": Ibid., 147.

78. "Honesty is its own reward": Ibid., 74.

78. "Send for either one": Ibid., 75.

78. "No knockout powders": Ibid.

79. "I do not know": Ibid., 76.

79. "of the slapping kind": Ibid., 37.

79. "I think I'd be the happiest": Ibid.

79. "Fight over me": Ibid., 38.

80. "Gentlemen," she cried: Ibid.

80. "As we were returning toward town": *Chicago Inter Ocean*, May 27, 1903.

80. "one of the most gorgeous": *Chicago Chronicle*, May 27, 1903.

80. "I found myself ": *Chicago Inter Ocean*, May 27, 1903.

81. "traveling incognito": *Chicago Chronicle*, May 27, 1903.

81. "I was sitting at the piano": *Chicago Inter Ocean*, May 27, 1903.

82. "too weak": *Chicago Chronicle*, May 27, 1903.

82. "wild midnight orgies," "resort of considerable notoriety": *Chicago Record Herald*, May 27, 1903.

82. "The police show little interest": *Chicago Daily News*, May 26, 1903.

82. "Silence is louder": Washburn, *Come into My Parlor*, 193.

INVOCATION

84. "When I see a reformer": Lindberg, *Quotable Chicago*, 127.

84. "lambs": Letter to Mary Greer Bell, November 3, 1903, Ernest Bell Papers, Chicago History Museum, box 2, folder 2-10.

84. "Deal bountifully": Ernest Bell Papers, box 4, folder 4.

84. "Lord, help me": Ibid.

84. The salary was $50 to $75: Bell Daniels, 34.

84. his mother named him: Ibid., 3.

84. "My son, I am building": Ibid., 5.

85. "I believe that no greater work": Ibid., 29.

85. "no rich American": Letter to Stanley McCormick, March 9, 1904, Ernest Bell Papers, box 1, folder 11.

85. "If it be thy will": Bell Daniels, 32–33.

85. "It startled him": Ibid., 30.

86. "Good women are a thousand": Ibid., 45.

86. Carrie Watson, who in her prime: quoted in Longstreet, 118–119.

87. "saints": Bell Daniels, 36.

87. "The wages of sin": Ibid., 39.

MILLIONAIRE PLAYBOY SHOT—ACCIDENT OR MURDER?

89. "The Everleighs, as always": Washburn, *Come into My Parlor*, 86.

89. "I desire to make a statement": *Chicago Tribune*, December 2, 1905.

89. "When young Marshall Field was shot": Creel, 3.

90. "the ravings": Madsen, 173.

90. "If that vase could speak": *Chicago Tribune*, March 6, 1925.

90. "If you've come to inquire": Ibid.

90. "stopped to speak to our nurse": Madsen, 158.

90. "There was no foundation": Washburn, *Come into My Parlor*, 87.

91. "I'm in trouble": Dan Rottenberg, "Good Rumors Never Die," *Chicago* magazine, February 1984.

91. "It is not unlikely": Ibid.

92. "Mayor of the Tenderloin": Asbury, 257.

92. Chicago's black population: F. B. Williams, "Social Bonds in the Black Belt of Chicago," *Charities* 15 (October 7, 1905).

92. *Chicago Defender:* Grossman, Keating, and Reiff, 134.

92. "Negro Gambling King of Chicago": Robert M. Lombardo, "The Black Mafia: African-American Organized Crime in Chicago: 1890–1960," *Crime, Law and Social Change* 38 (2002).

93. "Dance halls killed my child": *Chicago Daily Journal*, January 9, 1905.

93. "When vice is segregated": *Chicago Tribune*, June 1, 1905.

93. "fine colored lady": *Broad Ax*, September 30, 1905.

94. "It is the plague": *Chicago American*, December 24, 1905.

95. "Come right over": Washburn, *Come into My Parlor*, 90. Washburn reported that the Pony Moore/Vic Shaw plot occurred about a month after Marshall Field Jr.'s death.

96. "What do you want": Ibid., 91.

96. "We didn't do anything": Ibid.

98. Chief Collins unequivocally declined: Bell Daniels, 42.

98. cost madams in Custom House Place: Ibid., 41.

98. "Throw out the lifeline": Ibid., 39.

PART TWO: FLESH AND BONE, BODY AND SOUL, 1906–1909

MIDNIGHT TOIL AND PERIL

101. "The ministers thundered": *Chicago Tribune*, January 19, 1936.

101. Bell knew politics, too: Duis, *The Saloon*, 258–259.

101. "Mr. Bell": Bell Daniels, 42.

102. "ADA, MINNA": Ernest Bell Papers, box 3, folder 3-13.

102. "Many thanks": Bell Daniels, 41.

102. "Sin Gone to Seed": Ernest Bell Papers, box 5, folder 5-2.

103. "Imagine yourself": Ibid., box 5, folder 5-3.

103. "Young men, where are your heads?": Bell Daniels, 44.

104. "visiting firemen": Washburn, *Come into My Parlor*, 104.

104. "Truthfully, we were open": Ibid., 187.

104. Vernon Shaw Kennedy: *Chicago Tribune*, October 5, 1906. This article discusses Kennedy's divorce, including the revelation that he spent the night of August 26, 1906, at the Everleigh Club. Ernest Bell never offered specific dates about his many encounters with the egg tossers, but he did spend extra-long hours in the Levee district on Saturday and Sunday nights (Bell Daniels, 44). August 26, 1906, was a Sunday, and I took the liberty of selecting this date.

105. "large holder": Ibid.

105. "You bring your money": Bell Daniels, 44.

106. "Thus saith the Lord": Ibid., 46.

106. "tap the resources of God": Ibid., 49.

ULTRA DÉCOLLETÉ AND OTHER EVILS

108. "In Chicago our God": Lindberg, *Quotable Chicago*, 160.

108. "any form of state, local, or police": *Chicago Tribune*, October 10, 1906.

108. "what is deemed objectionable": *Chicago Tribune*, October 11, 1906.

108. "If there is one person": *Chicago Record Herald*, October 11, 1906.

109. "[Kendall's] whole soul": Bell, *War on the White Slave Trade*, 192.

109. "so aroused the friends": Roe, *The Great War on White Slavery*, 447.

109. purity workers' trip to the Levee district: *Chicago Tribune*, October 12, 1906. This article is the source for all names and quotes in this scene.

112. "We have an interesting case": Bell Daniels, 53.

113. Harrison Street court of Judge John Newcomer: Ibid.

113. "God loves your soul": Ibid., 56.

113. He hung a portrait: Ibid., 57.

THE BRILLIANT ENTRANCE TO HELL ITSELF

115. "The next worst thing": Ernest Bell Papers, box 2, folder 2-14.

115. Newbro's Herpicide: *Chicago Tribune* advertisement, January 3, 1907.

116. "These [mission workers]": Asbury, 254.

116. It is a penitentiary offense: Bell, *War*, 406–407.

116. "Theologians in the inspiration": Masters, *The Tale of Chicago*, 281.

116. "The girls may have been vulgar": Washburn, *Come into My Parlor*, 104.

117. "two sisters from Virginia": Bell Daniels, 43.

117. "It was in this canvass": Bell, *War*, 408.

117. "A Virginia woman": *The Philanthropist*, October 1907.

117. "There's enough of them little ones": *Chicago Tribune*, June 14, 1907.

118. "draw a chalk line": *Chicago Tribune*, February 27, 1907.

118. "As long as this evil": *Chicago Tribune*, October 4, 1906.

118. In 1880, only 3,800 women: Meyerowitz, 5, 29; Lagler, 103.

THE TRAGEDY OF MONA MARSHALL

120. "There is not a life": Roe, *The Great War*, preface.

120. "Mr. Roe takes life": *Chicago Tribune*, September 27, 1908.

120. "imperatively": Roe, *Panders and Their White Slaves*, 40.

120. "This is Captain McCann": Ibid.

121. A graft investigation in April: Ibid., 177–179.

121. "useful and upright citizen": Goodspeed and Healy, 748.

121. "The day of Mr. Roe's birth": *Chicago Tribune*, September 27, 1908.

121. "Not a marrying man": Ibid.

122. "tall, broad-shouldered": Roe, *The Prosecutor*, 5.

122. "best and dearest": Roe, *Panders*, 38.

122. "I am a white slave": Lait and Mortimer, 195.

123. *The Thaw-White Case* and *A Husband Murdering His Wife: Chicago Tribune*, May 6, 1907.

123. "Chicago has come to be known": Quoted in *McClure's Magazine*, May 1907.

123. "a company of men": Ibid., April 1907.

123. "The effect of this single article": Quoted in Eric Anderson, "Prostitution and Social Justice: Chicago, 1910–1915" *Social Service Review*, June 1974.

124. "Instead of receiving their support": Roe, *Panders*, 36.

124. "The walls of this musty old room": Ibid., 41–42.

125. The poor woman had been bereft: *Chicago Tribune*, May 27, 1907.

125. "I was working": *Chicago American*, May 27, 1907.

125. "Then what happened to you?": Ibid.

126. "Did they keep you": Roe, *Panders*, 43.

127. one of Harry's co-defendants, William McNamara: *Chicago Tribune*, May 27, 1907; *Chicago Daily News*, May 27, 1907.

127. "severe cross-fire of questions": *Chicago American*, May 27, 1907.

127. "associates in the procuring business": Roe, *Panders*, 44.

127. "I do not know why": *Chicago American*, May 27, 1907.

127. "Don't you think": Roe, *Panders*, 45.

127. "Yes, sir": Ibid.

MEN AND THEIR BASER MISCHIEFS

129. "Upon what meat": Washburn, *Come into My Parlor*, 187.

129. a year in the Chicago House of Correction: *Chicago Inter Ocean*, June 2, 1907.

129. "Half the disorder": *Chicago Inter Ocean*, June 3, 1907.

129. "I have learned to love you": Bell, *War*, 225–226; *Chicago American* and *Chicago Inter Ocean*, June 1, 1907.

130. "Don't speak to me": *Chicago Daily Journal*, August 3, 1907.

130. "happy, care-free life": *Chicago Daily Journal*, June 3, 1907.

130. "There is undoubtedly more actual physical restraint": *Chicago Record Herald*, June 3, 1907.

130. "into pieces" and "send him to the hospital": Bell Daniels, 57.

131. heat wave: *Chicago Daily Journal*, June 17, 1907.

131. "just like rotten eggs": *Chicago Daily News*, June 19, 1907.

132. "I wish I had you in a closet": Ibid.

132. "I hope you like me": Washburn, *Come into My Parlor*, 32.

133. "When Phyllis finally showed up": Hibbeler, 106.

133. "toboggan slide": Ibid., 108.

133. "What are you going to do": Washburn, *Come into My Parlor*, 161.

135. "How much for a little": Ibid., 105.

135. "crusader . . . noted for his good works": Asbury, 255.

135. "well-publicized muck-raker": Washburn, *Come into My Parlor*, 104.

135. "flexible moralists": Masters, "The Everleigh Club," *Town & Country,* April 1944.

135. "star actor": *Chicago Daily News,* June 19, 1907.

135. allegations about blackmail: *Chicago Daily Journal,* June 27, 1907.

136. "Would it surprise you much to learn": *Chicago Daily Journal,* June 26, 1907.

136. "Of all the evil characters": *Chicago Tribune,* June 28, 1907.

136. "It is a lie": *Chicago Record Herald,* June 29, 1907.

136. "vague" causes in India: *Chicago Daily Journal,* June 27, 1907.

136. "work of enemies": *Chicago Tribune,* June 21, 1907.

136. "We were glad to receive": Bell Daniels, 57.

136. "The market for white slaves": *The Philanthropist,* October 1907.

136. "gladly quit" and "honest man": Ibid.

137. Ben Reitman: *Chicago Tribune,* June 9, 1907.

137. "arch-enemies to society": Roe, *The Great War,* preface.

137. the United States government: U.S. Congress, Senate, *Importing Women for Immoral Purposes: A Partial Report from the Immigration Commission,* 3.

DISPATCH FROM THE U.S. IMMIGRATION COMMISSION

140. Memo from Marcus Braun, September 28, 1908, folder 38, box 6, page 5, series 3, Bureau of Social Hygiene Records, Rockefeller Archive Center.

MORE IMMORAL THAN HEATHEN CHINA

142. "The Shanghai is nothing like this": Hibbeler, 69.

142. Gaston: Washburn, *Come into My Parlor,* 57.

142. "The weed": Duis, *Challenging Chicago,* 194.

142. Ethel: Washburn, *Come into My Parlor,* 36.

142. "sloe-eyed": Hibbeler, 59.

143. "There is something": Washburn, *Come into My Parlor,* 58; Dedmon, 268.

143. For months now: Hibbeler, 59. Hibbeler recounted the story of Suzy Poon Tang but did not specify exactly when she came to work for the Everleigh Club.

143. "We've just received": Ibid., 70.

144. "It's better than looking at the original": Ibid., 80–81.

144. he'd lectured representatives from: Lagler, 114–115.

145. "A great many persons": Wilson, *Chicago and Its Cess Pools,* 42.

145. "All of the fellows around there": *Chicago Daily News,* February 10, 1908.

145. Mona's return to the flats: *Chicago Daily News,* May 27, 1907.

145. allegation about Mona's stepfather: *Chicago Daily Journal,* June 29, 1907.

145. A contradictory version: Roe, *Panders,* 40.

145. "There is a remedy": *Chicago Daily News,* February 10, 1908.

146. "more openly vicious": *Chicago Tribune,* February 11, 1908.

146. "We have come": Ibid.

146. Arthur Burrage Farwell spoke last: Minutes from the directors meeting of the Midnight Mission, February 11, 1908, Ernest Bell Papers, box 4, folder 4-9.

146. "Three times": *Chicago Tribune,* February 12, 1908.

147. The Shanghai was: Hibbeler, 60–65.

148. "I've always found it fun": Ibid., 102.

148. "What a beautiful ladder": Ibid., 25.

149. the Swinger: Ibid., 35.

148. the Gold Coin Kid: Ibid., 100–104.

150. "If I pay you well": Ibid., 64.

151. clear that Doll loved women: Ibid., 89–90.

151. "archaic" and "moss covered": Roe, *Panders*, 144–145.

151. his people constituted: Bristow, 177.

151. Between 1880 and 1900: Irving Cutler, "The Jews of Chicago: From Shtetl to Suburb," in Holli and Jones, *Ethnic Chicago*, 133.

152. "If Jews are the chief sinners": Quoted in Bell, *War*, 188.

152. "The Jew has been taught": Bristow, 165.

152. The House passed: *Chicago Record Herald*, May 6, 1908.

152. "elated . . . pioneer state": Roe, *Panders*, 153.

THE ORGANIZER

154. "I know it is repugnant": Memo from Marcus Braun, September 28, 1908, folder 38, box 6, page 4, series 3, Bureau of Social Hygiene Records, Rockefeller Archive Center.

154. federal Immigration Act: U.S. Congress, Senate, *Reports of the Immigration Commission: Importation and Harboring of Women for Immoral Purposes*, 58.

154. "Curiously enough": *Chicago Tribune*, August 2, 1908.

155. "I am determined": *Chicago Tribune*, June 20, 1908.

155. "I am one of those": Letter to Clifford Barnes, December 28, 1906, Clifford Barnes Collection, Chicago History Museum, box 1, folder 1904–1909.

155. feeding their babies beer: Duis, *Challenging Chicago*, 137.

155. Italian population was approaching: Dominic Candeloro, "Chicago's Italians: A Survey of the Ethnic Factor, 1850–1900," in Holli and Jones, *Ethnic Chicago*, 230.

155. "We no longer draw": Francis E. Hamilton, "Restriction on Immigration," *Forum* 42 (December 1908).

155. "syndicate of Frenchmen": *Chicago Tribune*, June 24, 1908.

155. "French Em": Asbury, 269.

156. The French had introduced: Langum, 18.

156. Alphonse and Eva Dufour: Bell Daniels, 62.

156. "They show that they have been drilled": *Chicago Tribune*, June 24, 1908.

156. spies in Sims's office: *Chicago Daily News*, June 20, 1908.

156. Springfield race riot: *Chicago American*, August 17, 1908. This riot prompted the formation of the NAACP.

157. William Donegan: Ibid.

157. His sixty-nine-year-old mother: *Chicago American*, August 18, 1908.

158. "unavoidable": *Chicago American*, August 19, 1908.

158. lived with his mother: *Chicago Tribune*, September 27, 1908.

158. Madam Eva Dufour posted bail: *Chicago Daily News*, October 31, 1908.

158. "It is only necessary": Edwin Sims, "The White Slave Trade of Today," *Woman's World* 24, no. 9 (September 1908).

159. "the roses he found blooming": Hibbeler, 90.

159. "I've made mistakes all my life": Washburn, *Come into My Parlor*, 162.

IT DON'T NEVER GET GOOD UNTIL THREE IN THE MORNING

161. "The *Tribune* has come out": Lindberg, *Quotable Chicago*, 198.

161. "Let's all go": Hibbeler, 29; Washburn, *Come into My Parlor*, 73.

161. "Entertaining most men": Dedmon, 253.

162. "the Derby": Asbury, 278.

162. "the party for Lame Jimmy": Wendt and Kogan, 153.

162. "reign unrefined": Ibid., 154.

162. "Give it to me": *Chicago Tribune*, February 1, 1894.

163. "We take it over": Wendt and Kogan, 154.

163. "a Saturnalian orgy," etc.: Ibid.

164. "don't never get good": *Chicago Tribune*, February 15, 1900.

164. "screecher": *Chicago Tribune*, December 22, 1902.

164. "It is the best": *Chicago Tribune*, January 7, 1903.

164. "charity, education": *Chicago Tribune*, December 12, 1906.

164. "God bless all the little": *Chicago Tribune*, May 16, 1909.

164. quit his job: *Chicago Daily News*, June 21, 1907.

164. "Mr. Farwell is the generally recognized type": Ibid.

164. "*Garbage* Farwell": Wendt and Kogan, 268.

165. "a little of the bunk": *Chicago Tribune*, December 10, 1907.

165. "The annual orgy": *Chicago Tribune*, December 2, 1908.

165. "A real description": Wendt and Kogan, 269.

165. "They don't need anyone sleuthing around after me": quoted in Duis, *The Saloon*, 129.

166. OUR PAL: From the Vic Shaw Family Album.

166. "The gents with whiskers": *Chicago American*, December 5, 1908.

167. "There's a 4-11 fire": Washburn, *Come into My Parlor*, 161.

167. "Mercy, a hundred": Will Irwin, "The First Ward Ball," *Collier's*, February 6, 1909.

167. "Seventy-five tickets?": Ibid.

167. "nightly duty": *Chicago Tribune*, December 9, 1908.

168. "If you dare to go": *Chicago American*, December 8, 1908.

168. newly elected state's attorney John Wayman: *Chicago Daily News*, December 2, 1908.

168. "We won't let parents": Wendt and Kogan, 272.

168. At 8:20 on the evening: *Chicago American*, December 14, 1908; *Chicago Tribune*, December 14, 1908.

169. "You can draw your own": *Chicago Tribune*, December 14, 1908.

169. "tone": Ibid.

169. "Mariutch, she danca": Wendt and Kogan, 273.

169. "Seems to me": Ibid.

170. "feminine element": *Chicago Tribune*, December 14, 1908.

170. "They're here!": Richard T. Griffin, "Sin Drenched Revels at the Infamous First Ward Ball," *Smithsonian*, November 1976.

170. Al Capone's first job: *Chicago Tribune*, March 16, 1949.

170. "too old and feeble": *Chicago Tribune*, July 20, 1952.

171. "So close was the press": Wendt and Kogan, 276.

171. "Gangway": *Chicago Tribune*, December 15, 1908.

171. "mighty little suit": Ibid.

172. "It was usually me": *Chicago Tribune*, March 15, 1949.

172. "I intend to stay": *Chicago Tribune*, December 15, 1908.

172. She winked and beckoned: Ibid.

172. "Why, it's great": Wendt and Kogan, 280.

173. "The Hon. Bathhouse Coughlin": *Chicago Tribune*, December 15, 1908.

173. "Pour champagne, cul": Wendt and Kogan, 279.

173. Another woman, dressed as: Will Irwin, "The First Ward Ball," *Collier's*, February 6, 1909.

173. Courtesans lay facedown: *Chicago American*, December 15, 1908.

173. A harlot swung a whip: Ibid.

174. "We saw as many": *Chicago Daily News*, December 15, 1908.

174. "Keep it up, Minnie!": Wendt and Kogan, 279.

DISPATCH FROM THE U.S. IMMIGRATION COMMISSION

176. U.S. Congress, Senate, *Importing Women for Immoral Purposes: A Partial Report from the Immigration Commission on the Importation and Harboring of Women for Immoral Purposes*, 15, 40; U.S. Congress, Senate, *Reports of the Immigration Commission: Final Report on the Importation and Harboring of Women for Immoral Purposes*, 123; U.S. Congress, Senate, *Importing Women for Immoral Purposes: A Partial Report from the Immigration Commission on the Importation and Harboring of Women for Immoral Purposes*, 59.

JUDGMENT DAYS

178. "I am not a reformer": *Chicago Tribune*, May 16, 1909.

178. Minna's court date: *Chicago Tribune*, March 14, 1909.

178. "trade in rum": *Chicago Tribune*, February 1, 1909.

178. "spitting evil": *Chicago Tribune*, February 17, 1909.

178. Stick to the "small stuff": Asbury, 277.

179. "They have us in the middle": Washburn, *Come into My Parlor*, 101.

179. One night in April: *U.S. v. Johnson*, General Records of the Department of Justice, File Number 16421, Record Group 60; Ward, 146–148.

180. "Even if I am a Virginian": Wallace, 60; 57–58.

180. Inviting Scott Joplin: Rudi Blesh, "Maple Leaf Rag," *American Heritage* 26, no. 4 (June 1975).

180. When Jack Johnson invited five of them: Ward, 148.

181. He traveled to Iowa: *Iowa City Daily Press*, February 18, 1909.

181. Pennsylvania State Legislature: *Pennsylvania Daily Gazette and Bulletin*, February 26, 1909.

181. "That there is a systematic traffic": *Fort Wayne Journal Gazette*, March 21, 1909.

182. "whole thing looks queer": *Chicago Tribune*, February 18, 1909.

183. William Lloyd Garrison: Roe, *The Great War*, 19.

HAVE YOU A GIRL TO SPARE?

185. "It is a conceded fact": Goldman, 4.

185. "keep books": Roe, *The Great War*, 119.

185. "know what kind of a place": Ibid.

185. "Madam Maurice": *Chicago Tribune*, November 28, 1909.

185. "bad place": Roe, *The Great War*, 115.

185. Fern: Ibid., 196.

186. "Now, when you go": Ibid., 126.

186. "It was discovered": *Chicago Daily Socialist*, June 30, 1909.

187. "The story printed about Miss Barrette": *Chicago Tribune*, June 30, 1909.

187. Mark A. Foote agreed: *Chicago Daily Socialist*, July 3, 1909.

187. "servant girl": Roe, *The Great War*, 119.

188. fifteen-foot snake: *Chicago Tribune*, June 17, 1909.

188. As Mollie had promised: Roe, *The Great War*, 120.

188. "I realized that Van Bever's": Ibid., 121.

188. "that Jew girl": *Chicago Tribune*, November 10, 1909.

188. "You're a good-looking": Ibid.

188. "I want to go": Ibid.

188. "You'll like it": Ibid.

189. "I believe Inspector": *Chicago American*, July 22, 1909.

189. both men were members: *Chicago Tribune*, September 1, 1909.

189. "The revelations made at": *Chicago Tribune*, October 4, 1909.

189. Commercial Club of Chicago: Roe, *The Great War*, 192; *Chicago Tribune*, September 26, 1909.

189. the architect's City Beautiful movement: Grossman, Keating, and Reiff, 30–32.

190. "There is nothing political": *Chicago Tribune*, September 1, 1909.

190. Roe had an initial: Roe, *The Great War*, 193.

190. private secretary: *Chicago Tribune*, September 29, 1909.

190. "Well, dear": Roe, *The Great War*, 112; *Panders*, 189.

DISPATCH FROM THE U.S. IMMIGRATION COMMISSION

192. U.S. Congress, Senate, *Importing Women for Immoral Purposes: A Partial Report from the Immigration Commission*, 23.

SO MANY NICE YOUNG MEN

194. "We have struck a blow": Lewis and Smith, 342.

194. "it is not always the fault": Roe, *Panders*, 180.

194. "Now rest as long": Letter to Mary, October 11, 1909, Ernest Bell Papers, box 2, folder 2-11.

194. "Gracious God": Ernest Bell Papers, box 6, folder 6-13.

194. $400 advance: Letter to Mary, October 11, 1909, Ernest Bell Papers, box 2, folder 2-11.

195. "score of resorts": Bell, *War*, 261–262.

195. "When Mollie and Mike": Roe, *The Great War*, 113.

195. Roe's best sleuth: Ibid.

196. "Your name is": Ibid., 113–114.

196. "If the Hart woman": *Chicago Inter Ocean*, October 14, 1909.

196. "underground railway": *Chicago Tribune*, October 17, 1909.

197. consult with Congressman James R. Mann: Duis, *The Saloon*, 264.

197. "Chicago at last": Ibid.

197. Chicago's chief of police, Leroy Steward: Lewis and Smith, 340; Lindberg, *Chicago by Gaslight*, 139.

197. "primal topics": *Chicago American*, August 17, 1909.

197. "inherently vicious": Asbury, 281; "huge slumming party" and "sensational advertising scheme": *Chicago Inter Ocean*, October 17, 1909.

198. "If you show yourself": *Chicago American*, October 18, 1909.

198. "decentize": *Chicago American*, October 12, 1909.

198. "The women have to": Wendt and Kogan, 288.

198. "A girl in our establishment": Washburn, *Come into My Parlor*, 104. Washburn didn't specify when Minna made this speech.

199. propose a raucous toast: Ibid., 107.

199. "A man who visits": Ibid.

199. "To Evangelist Smith's young crusaders": Ibid.

200. Colonel MacDuff: Masters, "The Everleigh Club," *Town & Country*, April 1944.

200. "Dear Sir": Roe, *Panders*, 170.

201. "How a woman": Roe, *The Great War*, 111.

201. "sphinx like and brazen": Ibid., 125.

201. "He kills his victims": *Chicago Tribune*, November 11, 1909.

201. Van Bever's attorney, Daniel Donahoe: *Chicago Tribune*, November 10, 1909.

201. "Sarah came to Chicago": Roe, *The Great War*, 135.

202. "Van Bever's lawyer": Ibid., 141.

202. "Gentlemen": Ibid., 142.

202. "thousands of dollars": Ibid., 124.

202. "We have positive evidence": *Chicago Tribune*, November 28, 1909.

202. "could not be reached": Asbury, 268.

203. "Time will show that": Ibid., 283.

203. "I haven't done as much": *Chicago Daily News*, October 19, 1909.

203. "We had to shut our doors": Ibid.

203. "Greatest business": Ibid.

203. "You'da thought": *Chicago Tribune*, March 15, 1949.

203. "We were certainly glad": Wendt and Kogan, 287–288.

IMMORAL PURPOSES, WHATEVER THOSE ARE

205. "I deplore the Mann Act": Nabokov, *Lolita,* 150.

205. "You are leading yourself": Lewis and Smith, 341.

205. "hoodoo" of the number 13: *Chicago Tribune,* December 14, 1909.

206. "the head form": U.S. Congress, Senate, *Reports of the Immigration Commission: Changes in Bodily Form of the Descendants of Immigrants,* 7.

206. "In explanation of the act": *Oakland Tribune,* December 10, 1909.

207. "I greatly regret to have to say": *Washington Post,* December 8, 1909.

207. A new branch: Langum, 49.

207. Sims drafted the bill: Ernest A. Bell, "New and Pending Laws," *Light,* May 1910.

208. "purpose of prostitution": Langum, 261.

208. "Personally I feel that": Bell Daniels, 72.

208. seventy thousand copies: Donovan, 63.

PART THREE:
FIGHTING FOR THE PROTECTION OF OUR GIRLS, 1910–1912

MILLIONAIRE PLAYBOY DEAD—MORPHINE OR MADAM?

211. "I was the pet of Chicago": *Chicago Tribune,* March 14, 1949.

211. "I know it will mean": *Chicago Tribune,* January 10, 1910.

211. The boy was a drunk and an addict: *Chicago Tribune,* January 11, 1910.

211. It was Nat's birthday: *Chicago Tribune,* January 10, 1910.

212. a Levee morphine salesman: Washburn, *Come into My Parlor,* 91.

212. Diamond Bertha: Ibid., 165.

213. "So damned suspicious": Ibid., 92.

214. "Nat was the biggest": *Chicago Tribune,* January 11, 1910.

214. "Hattie, you're tired": Ibid.

214. "They're framing you": Washburn, *Come into My Parlor,* 92.

215. "What's going on": Ibid., 93.

216. "to China": *Chicago Tribune,* January 10, 1910.

216. long purple robe: *Chicago Tribune,* January 11, 1910.

216. "I was at the Studebaker": *Chicago Tribune,* January 10, 1910.

216. "I have been here": Ibid.

217. "In the afternoon I was told": *Chicago Tribune,* January 11, 1910.

217. "apparently under the influence": Washburn, *Come into My Parlor,* 96.

217. "bound to be blamed": Ibid., 98.

GIRLS GOING WRONG

219. "Many a working girl": Addams, *A New Conscience and an Ancient Evil,* ix, 72–73.

219. Mrs. Emily Hill: Asbury, 284.

219. "determination": *Chicago American,* January 28, 1910.

219. "Let the men take": *Chicago Tribune,* January 25, 1910.

220. "Mr. Busse, you are the mayor": Wendt and Kogan, 289.

220. "I may pray": *Chicago Tribune,* January 28, 1910.

220. "vice problem is exactly like that": Vice Commission of Chicago, *The Social Evil in Chicago,* 3.

220. "Now Lord": Bell Daniels, 78.

221. On March 7, he would wed: *Chicago Tribune,* March 8, 1910.

221. four hundred thousand people had bought: Bell Daniels, 63.

221. George Kibbe Turner: Turner, "The Daughters of the Poor," *McClure's Magazine,* November 1909.

221. "You owe it as a duty to the city": Chernow, 552.

222. The arrangement was a setup: Ibid.

222. "I never worked harder": Ibid.

222. Roe cut out several newspaper clippings: John D. Rockefeller Jr. to Clifford Roe, March 8, 1910, reel 314, series 3, Bureau of Social Hygiene Records, Rockefeller Archive Center.

222. "admired the ostrich": *Washington Post,* February 16, 1909.

222. Clifford Roe push successfully: *Vigilance* 24, no. 5 (May 1911).

223. "The white slave traffic": Quoted in Langum, 43.

223. "a thousand times worse": Ibid.

223. "headquarters and distributing": Ibid., 44.

223. "a beautiful girl taken": Ibid.

223. "every pure woman": Ibid.

223. "Now let's hope": Bell Daniels, 74.

223. "a tower of strength": *Mansfield* (Ohio) *News,* October 1, 1910.

224. "segregation provides the best": Letter from the Midnight Mission to the Chicago Vice Commission, October 15, 1910, Ernest Bell Papers, box 5, folder 5-1.

A LOST SOUL

226. "I do not mind": Wallace, 56.

226. "A Republican is a man": Miller, 445.

226. Roy Jones . . . was back in business: *Chicago American,* July 11, 1910.

226. Clifford Roe had tried to implicate: *Chicago Tribune,* July 8, 1910.

227. donations to reformers: Asbury, 254.

227. Brick Top: *Sheboygan Press Telegram,* September 27, 1923.

227. twelve of whom had syphilis: Vice Commission of Chicago, *The Social Evil in Chicago,* 77.

227. "too vile and disgusting": Ibid., 71.

227. "highest-grade resort": Taylor, *Pioneering on Social Frontiers,* 88.

228. "I found the twenty or more": Ibid., 88–89.

228. The call from one: *Chicago Tribune,* November 20, 1910.

229. eleven printings: Langum, 33.

229. "I am sorry not to comply": John D. Rockefeller Jr. to Clifford Roe, October 26, 1910, reel 353, series 3, Bureau of Social Hygiene Records, Rockefeller Archive Center.

229. "I propose": John D. Rockefeller Jr. to Clifford Roe, January 26, 1911, reel 24, series 3, Bureau of Social Hygiene Records, Rockefeller Archive Center.

230. "The Everleigh Club, Illustrated": Lawrence J. Gutter Collection of Chicagoana, Department of Special Collections, University of Illinois at Chicago.

THE SOCIAL EVIL IN CHICAGO

232. "Here's the difference between us": Lindberg, *Quotable Chicago*, 81.

232. campaign flyer: Grossman, Keating, and Reiff, 633, 650.

232. "I have never been afflicted": Harrison, 308.

232. prompting Hinky Dink to remark: Wendt and Kogan, 291.

233. Hyde Park reformer Charles Merriam: Duis, *The Saloon*, 281.

233. "Hinky Dink has put aside": Wendt and Kogan, 292.

233. CARTER HARRISON ELECTED: Ibid., 293.

233. another $5,000: Vice Commission of Chicago, *The Social Evil in Chicago*, 9.

233. detailed every facet: Ibid., 13–17.

234. $16 million: Ibid., 32.

234. "The (X523), at (X524), (X524a)": Ibid., 152.

234. "gregarious" men: Ibid., 297.

234. "These women": Ibid., 169.

234. "It is undoubtedly true": Ibid.

235. "Nine were seduced": Ibid., 170.

235. "One madame testified": Ibid., 97.

235. "A Dearborn Street resort": Ibid., 78.

235. "Pervert methods": Ibid., 73.

236. "absolute annihilation": Asbury, 289.

236. "Praise God": Bell Daniels, 81.

236. When Edwin Sims and Dean Sumner: Ibid.

236. "enthusiastically looking forward": Roe to Rockefeller, January 30, 1911, folder 42, box 7, series 3, Bureau of Social Hygiene Records, Rockefeller Archive Center.

236. "If the methods": Rockefeller to Roe, February 4, 1911, reel 206, series 3, Bureau of Social Hygiene Records, Rockefeller Archive Center.

237. They had an ingenious: Clifford Barnes Papers, Chicago History Museum, box 1, folder 1910–1915.

237. "[Roe] himself does not care": Heydt to Rockefeller, May 12, 1911, folder 42, box 7, series 3, Bureau of Social Hygiene Records, Rockefeller Archive Center.

238. "They had little fountains": Washburn, *Come into My Parlor*, 188.

238. "all of the rules issued": *Chicago Tribune*, June 17, 1911.

238. "Those women have got to": Ibid.

238. Time to update: Washburn, *Come into My Parlor*, 191.

PAINTED, PEROXIDED, BEDIZENED

240. "Girls will be": Ibid., 31.

240. "sudden longing": Harrison, 307.

240. "with all attendant privileges": Ibid.

241. "lit up like": Ibid., 308.

241. so that one breast escaped: Nash, *Look for the Woman,* 152.

241. "Vic Shaw": Harrison, 308.

241. "notorious brothel keeper": Ibid.

241. "serve merely to gratify": Connelly, 107.

242. "sex must be confined": Ibid., 110.

242. Dean Sumner was at it again: *Chicago Record Herald,* October 15, 1911.

242. "far from my ideas": Harrison, 308.

242. Move all disreputable women: Lindberg, *Chicago by Gaslight,* 140.

243. Death of Herbert Swift: *Chicago Tribune,* October 20, 1911.

243. "Women have no minds": Washburn, *Come into My Parlor,* 151.

243. "Did one of your girls": Ibid., 194.

244. The Hawkeye State had passed: Roe, *The Great War,* 358.

245. "an unpleasant happening": Washburn, *Come into My Parlor,* 194.

245. "Mind your own business": Ibid.

245. "I'm afraid": Ibid.

246. "Pretty snappy town": Ibid., 193.

246. "terrible pair of sisters": Harrison, 309.

246. "painted, peroxided, bedizened": Ibid., 307.

246. "truly historic": Ibid., 309.

246. "Close the Everleigh Club": Wendt and Kogan, 297.

YOU GET EVERYTHING IN A LIFETIME

248. "How dear to my heart": Edgar Lee Masters to Carter Harrison, April 14, 1939, Carter Harrison IV Papers, Newberry Library.

248. "On the square": Wendt and Kogan, 297.

248. "rather sharp language": Harrison, 310.

248. "The most persistent gossip": Ibid., 311.

248. "infamy, the audacious advertising": Asbury, 259.

249. "well known as Chicago itself": *Chicago American,* October 25, 1911.

249. "cool and comical": Washburn, *Come into My Parlor,* 151.

249. "You mustn't believe": Ibid., 195.

249. "Is the report": *Chicago Tribune,* October 25, 1911.

250. Dearborn Street was alive: *Chicago American,* October 25, 1911.

250. "Gibraltar": Bell Daniels, 85.

250. at the Hotel Vendome in Columbus: Bell to Mary, October 24, 1911, Ernest Bell Papers, box 2, folder 1909–1928 (correspondence with wife).

250. "speaking partner": *Chicago Tribune,* October 25, 1911.

250. "I know the mayor's order": Ibid.

250. "I don't worry": Ibid.

251. "If they don't want me": *Chicago American,* October 25, 1911.

251. "Well, boys": Washburn, *Come into My Parlor,* 202.

251. "It may be": Ibid.

251. "It's only 10": *Chicago Tribune,* October 25, 1911.

252. "Sorry, girls": Wendt and Kogan, 297.

252. "We've been expecting": Washburn, *Come into My Parlor,* 203.

252. "Clear out": Ibid.

252. "You'll be going strong": Ibid.

253. "Go away for a few": Ibid., 204.

253. "What do you think": Ibid.

253. "We're going from bawd": Hibbeler, 121.

253. "Let's go to Europe": Washburn, *Come into My Parlor,* 204.

253. "What about us": Ibid.

253. "I'm afraid there never will": Ibid., 204–205.

254. "And neither of you did": Ibid.

254. "Poor kid": Ibid., 206.

254. "We're all nervous": Ibid.

255. about $1 million: Ibid.

255. Chief McWeeny telephoned: *Chicago American,* October 25, 1911.

255. "Vice in Chicago": *Chicago Record Herald,* October 25, 1911.

255. close "a score": *Chicago American,* October 25, 1911.

256. "Two French blondes": Washburn, *Come into My Parlor,* 207.

256. "Until I get": Ibid.

256. Delft Candy Shop: Viskochil, 53. This book aided me in describing several Chicago street scenes.

256. "Don't you recognize": Harrison, 313–314.

257. visit from Taft: *Chicago Inter Ocean,* October 25, 1911.

258. "going strong": Washburn, *Come into My Parlor,* 212.

258. "You ain't got a thing": Wendt and Kogan, 298.

258. "Do the best you can": Washburn, *Come into My Parlor,* 212.

DANGEROUS ELEMENTS

260. "It is the code of honor": Lindberg, *Quotable Chicago,* 30.

260. "known to reside": Langum, 50.

260. Congress . . . played stingy: Ibid., 52.

260. Bell in Europe: "Some Observations in Europe," Ernest Bell Papers, box 4, folder 4-8.

260. "I note that special action": Ibid., box 4, folder 4-8.

260. the Office of the Special Commissioner: Langum, 52.

261. "Mayor Harrison deserves": *Chicago Tribune,* October 31, 1911.

261. "My dear Mr. Mayor": Boynton to Harrison, March 1912, Ernest Bell Papers, box 4, folder 4-8.

261. "even Salt Lake City": Boynton to Mann and Taft, March 23, 1912, ibid.

261. In March 1912, he ordered: Duis, *The Saloon,* 269–270.

261. "I am instructed to advise you": Starr Murphy to Roe, January 5, 1912, folder 42, box 7, series 3, Bureau of Social Hygiene Records, Rockefeller Archive Center.

262. a "pretended" disorderly house: *Chicago Tribune*, August 8, 1912.

262. DANGER!: Hepburn, 4–5.

262. Cincinnati Vigilance Society: *Vigilance*, May 1911.

262. "cordial congratulations": Rockefeller to Roe, April 26, 1912, reel 3, series 3, Bureau of Social Hygiene Records, Rockefeller Archive Center.

263. "wealthiest men in this country": *Chicago Tribune*, March 3, 1912.

263. "Until the public conscience": Roe to Rockefeller, January 5, 1912, box 7, folder 42, series 3, Bureau of Social Hygiene Records, Rockefeller Archive Center.

263. "The Greeks construed Apollo's loss": Washburn, *Come into My Parlor*, 150.

264. 5536 W. Washington Boulevard: *Chicago Tribune*, December 16, 1973.

264. "final stab": Washburn, *Come into My Parlor*, 213.

264. Freiberg's Dance Hall was bombed: *Chicago Tribune*, November 17, 1911.

264. "This home of vice": Dillion and Lytle, 9.

265. "In the days": Wendt and Kogan, 320–322.

266. "acting on orders": Washburn, *Come into My Parlor*, 213.

267. "What's up": Ibid., 137–138.

268. "Take it or leave it": Ibid., 138.

268. "all under the age of eighteen": Annual Report of the Committee of Fifteen, 1912, page 2, Graham Taylor papers, Newberry Library.

268. "I beg to acknowledge the receipt": Ibid.

268. Within the week, Dago Frank: *Chicago Tribune*, August 31, 1912.

269. "If there had been no Everleigh Club": Washburn, *Come into My Parlor*, 213.

269. Two of them were rampaging: Ibid.

JUST HOW WICKED

271. "You can get much farther": Lindberg, *Quotable Chicago*, 115.

271. "We're getting nowhere": Washburn, *Come into My Parlor*, 214.

271. blackened both her eyes: Ibid., 213.

271. shutting down the madam's brothel: *Chicago Record Herald*, September 5, 1912.

271. "Pikers": Washburn, *Come into My Parlor*, 214.

271. "The Levee has it": Ibid.

272. "going to rip off": *Chicago Tribune*, September 27, 1912.

273. "The man who takes": *Chicago Tribune*, October 31, 1908.

273. "handsomest man in Chicago": Lindberg, *Chicago by Gaslight*, 141.

273. "This grand jury": *Chicago Tribune*, September 27, 1912.

273. "most pretentious street parade": *Chicago Record Herald*, September 27, 1912.

273. stated purpose: *Chicago American*, September 27, 1912.

273. "the aim of the crusaders": Quoted in Asbury, 298.

273. "subject of ridicule": *Chicago Daily Socialist*, September 28, 1912.

273. float signs and banners: *Chicago Record Herald*, September 27, 1912.

274. Chief Justice Harry Olson: Wendt and Kogan, 320.

275. she and that sister of hers: Ibid.

275. "they aren't worth the paper": *Chicago Record Herald,* September 29, 1912.

275. "half-naked sirens": Duis, *The Saloon,* 270.

275. "One might expect": *Chicago American,* September 28, 1912.

275. "The South Side Levee is rejoicing": *Chicago Daily News,* September 30, 1912.

275. "it was not generally known": *Chicago Tribune,* October 1, 1912.

277. "Minnie and Ada Everleigh were called": *Chicago American,* October 1, 1912.

277. The order left prominent Atlanta madam: *Chicago Evening World,* October 1, 1912.

277. "Gentlemen, I am through": *Chicago American,* October 1, 1912.

278. "furious passion": Asbury, 299.

278. "There is an apparent effort": Wendt and Kogan, 300.

278. "Wayman's out to pinch": *Chicago American,* October 5, 1912.

278. "Looks like we saved": Washburn, *Come into My Parlor,* 216.

FALLEN IS BABYLON

280. "Have patience, my friend": Ibid., 213.

280. "Another Johnstown flood": *Chicago American,* October 5, 1912; *Chicago Record Herald,* October 6, 1912.

280. valerianate of ammonia, etc.: Bell to Carter Harrison, November 29, 1912, Ernest Bell Papers, box 4, folder 4-8.

280. "Brother Bell, your prayers": Bell Daniels, 84.

281. Officers found twenty harlots: *Chicago Tribune,* October 5, 1912.

281. "It is rather extraordinary": Longstreet, 471–472.

282. the men issued the following: Asbury, 301.

282. The invasion of the harlots: Ibid.

283. "I'll take care of any of them": *Chicago Daily News,* October 7, 1912.

283. But not one harlot applied: *Chicago Evening Post,* October 8, 1912.

283. waving handkerchiefs: *Chicago Record Herald,* October 7, 1912.

283. "Fallen is Babylon!": Bell to Midnight Mission board, October 8, 1912, Ernest Bell Papers, box 4, folder 4-8.

LITTLE LOST SISTER

286. "I suppose we all": Wallace, 55.

286. "fight to the death": Asbury, 302.

286. "We'll make everything clean": Washburn, *Come into My Parlor,* 225.

286. "scattering of evil": *Chicago Record Herald,* October 28, 1912.

286. "Who is that guy": Washburn, *Come into My Parlor,* 225.

286. "It can't be done": Ibid., 226.

287. "Five minutes of real": *Chicago Record Herald,* November 21, 1912.

287. "former queen of Chicago's underworld": Quoted in Washburn, *Come into My Parlor,* 244.

287. Freiberg's Dance Hall celebrated: Asbury, 275.

288. "It surely wasn't a disappointed": Washburn, *Come into My Parlor,* 142.

288. "death bed confession": *Chicago Record Herald,* October 6, 1912.

288. "I am sorry": *Chicago Tribune,* April 18, 1913.

288. "He was an outcast": Washburn, *Come into My Parlor,* 239.

289. letter from Chauncey to Bell, January 8, 1916, Ernest Bell Papers, box 2, folder 2-7.

289. "Our Father Who Art in Heaven": November 16, 1919, Ernest Bell Papers, box 2, folder 2-2.

289. "The song you sung at me": Taylor to Bell, February 27, 1927, Ernest Bell Papers, box 1, folder 11.

289. genre of films: Lagler, 135.

290. *Little Lost Sister:* Washburn, *Come into My Parlor,* 242.

290. "A wave of sex hysteria": *Current Opinion,* August 1913.

290. In the spring of 1913: Lagler, 231–240.

290. boxer Jack Johnson: Ward, 314–315.

290. arrested in the fall of 1912: Langum, 181.

291. "We now went": Ibid., 95.

291. J. Edgar Hoover: Ibid., 190–194.

291. "It owed its passage": *New York Times,* June 25, 1916.

291. "there never was a joke": Langum, 35.

291. "a sort of pornography": Ibid., 34.

291. Sociologist Walter Reckless: Reckless, *Vice in Chicago,* 43–46.

292. another young Chicago girl: *Chicago Tribune,* December 25, 1913.

292. "There has been too much hysteria": *Intermountain Herald-Republican,* January 30, 1914.

292. Roe died of heart disease: *New York Times,* June 29, 1934.

293. Only one major newspaper: Langum, 248.

293. "street of the stately few": Madsen, 223.

293. "bad heart": *Chicago Tribune,* December 2, 1943.

293. "I can't stand to see": *Chicago Tribune,* March 14, 1949.

294. "My God! A man!": Ibid.

294. When Vic Shaw died: *Chicago Tribune,* November 13, 1951.

294. 20 W. 71st Street: Wallace, 48.

294. "former plantation home in the South": *Chicago Tribune,* November 1, 1953.

295. "If you're all decked out": Ibid.

295. "How come your poetry": Ibid.

295. in 1933, the Everleigh Club: *Chicago Tribune,* July 25, 1933. The Hilliard Homes, a public housing project, now stands on the former site of the Everleigh Club.

296. In the early 1940s, Theodore Dreiser: E-mail from Hilary Masters, son of Edgar Lee Masters, December 2005.

296. "Someday if I no longer": Wallace, 59.

296. "She seemed like my own grandmother": *Chicago Tribune,* November 1, 1953.

296. "We never hurt anybody": Ibid.

296. Minna died: Death certificate #20750 for Minna Lester Simms, issued by the Department of Health, Borough of Manhattan. Her nephew, William Simms, filled out the death certificate and listed "Lester" as Minna's middle name. He also indicated that she had never been married or divorced, and listed her former occupation as "housework."

296. Ada was stuck home: *Elyria* (Ohio) *Chronicle Telegram,* September 17, 1948.

296. Ada followed Minna: *Charlottesville* (Virginia) *Daily Progress,* January 4, 1960.

297. "Best Wishes for a Happy": Wallace, 65–66.

BIBLIOGRAPHY

ARCHIVAL COLLECTIONS

Chicago History Museum, Chicago, Illinois:
   Clifford Barnes Papers
   Ernest Bell Papers
   Church Federation of Greater Chicago Papers

University of Chicago, Joseph Regenstein Library, Chicago, Illinois:
   Chicago Committee of Fifteen Papers

University of Illinois at Chicago, Chicago, Illinois:
   Lawrence J. Gutter Collection of Chicagoana, Department of Special Collections

Newberry Library, Chicago, Illinois:
   Carter H. Harrison IV Papers, Roger and Julie Baskes Department of Special Collections
   Graham Taylor Papers, Roger and Julie Baskes Department of Special Collections

The Rockefeller Archive Center, Sleepy Hollow, New York:
   Bureau of Social Hygiene Records

GOVERNMENT ARCHIVAL COLLECTIONS AND REPORTS

Records of the Immigration and Naturalization Service, Series A: Subject Correspondence Files, Part 5: Prostitution and "White Slavery," 1902–1933.

U.S. v. Johnson, General Records of the Department of Justice, File Number 16421, Record Group 60.

U.S. Congress. Senate. Committee on Immigration. *White-Slave Traffic Report to Accompany H.R. 12315.*

———. *Reports of the Immigration Commission. A Partial Report from the Immigration Commission on the Importation and Harboring of Women for Immoral Purposes.* S. Doc. 196, 61st Cong., 2d sess., 1909.

———. *Reports of the Immigration Commission. A Partial Report from the Immigration Commis-*

sion on Changes in Bodily Form of the Descendants of Immigrants. S. Doc. 208, 61st Cong., 2d sess., 1909.

U.S. Congress. Senate. *Reports of the Immigration Commission*. 61st Cong., 3d sess., 1910. Vol. 19. *Importation and Harboring of Women for Immoral Purposes*.

———. *Reports of the Immigration Commission. Changes in Bodily Form of the Descendants of Immigrants*. 61st Cong., 2d sess., 1911. Vol. 38.

———. *Reports of the Immigration Commission. Statements and Recommendations Submitted by Societies and Organizations Interested in the Subject of Immigration*. Washington, DC: Government Printing Office, 1911.

———. *Reports of the Immigration Commission*. (final). Washington, D.C.: Governement Printing Office, 1911.

BOOKS, ARTICLES, DISSERTATIONS

Addams, Jane. *A New Conscience and an Ancient Evil*. New York: Macmillan Co., 1913.

———. *The Spirit of Youth and the City Streets*. New York: Macmillan Co., 1909.

Algren, Nelson. *Chicago: City on the Make*. Garden City, NY: Doubleday: 1951.

Anderson, Eric. "Prostitution and Social Justice: Chicago, 1910–1915." *Social Service Review* (June 1974).

Anonymous. *Twenty Tales by Twenty Women: From Real Life in Chicago*. Chicago: Novelty Publishing Co., 1903.

Asbury, Herbert. *The Gangs of Chicago*. New York: Knopf, 1940.

Bailey, Beth L. *From Front Porch to Back Seat: Courtship in Twentieth Century America*. Baltimore: Johns Hopkins University Press, 1988.

Barker-Benfield, G. J. *The Horrors of the Half-Known Life: Male Attitudes Toward Women and Sexuality in Nineteenth-Century America*. New York: Harper & Row, 1976.

Barnes, Clifford. "The Story of the Committee of Fifteen of Chicago." *Social Hygiene* (April 1918).

Barry, Kathleen. *Female Sexual Slavery*. New York: Avon Books, 1979.

Beaton, Ralph. *The Anti-Vice Crusader and the Social Reformer*. Dallas: Southwestern Printing Co., 1918.

Bell, Ernest. "New and Pending Laws." *Light* (May 1910).

———, ed. *War on the White Slave Trade: Fighting the Traffic in Young Girls*. Chicago: G. S. Ball, 1910.

Bell Daniels, Olive. *From the Epic of Chicago: A Biography, Ernest A. Bell, 1865–1928*. Menasha: George Banta Publishing Co., 1932.

Bingham, Theodore. *The Girl That Disappears: The Real Facts About the White Slave Traffic*. Boston: Gorham Press, 1911.

Bird, Caroline. *Enterprising Women*. New York: W. W. Norton, 1976.

Blair, Cynthia Maria. "Vicious Commerce: African-American Women's Sex Work and the Transformation of Urban Space in Chicago, 1850–1915." PhD dissertation, University of Michigan, 1999.

Blesh, Rudi. "Maple Leaf Rag." *American Heritage* (June 1975).

Blum, Marjorie Christine. "Prostitution and the Progressive Vice Crusade." Master's thesis, University of Wisconsin, 1967.

Boehm, Lisa Beth Krissoff. *Popular Culture and the Enduring Myth of Chicago: 1871–1968*. New York: Routledge, 2004.

Bowen, Louise de Koven. "Dance Halls." *The Survey*, June 3, 1911.

———. *The Department Store Girl*. Chicago: Juvenile Protective Association, 1911.

———. *Five and Ten Cent Theaters: Two Investigations*. Chicago: Juvenile Protective Association, 1911.

Boyer, Paul. *Urban Masses and Moral Order in America, 1820–1920*. Cambridge: Harvard University Press, 1978.

Brandt, Allan. *No Magic Bullet: A Social History of Venereal Disease in the United States Since 1880*. New York: Oxford University Press, 1987.

Bristow, Edward J. *Prostitution and Prejudice: The Jewish Fight Against White Slavery, 1870–1939*. New York: Schocken Books, 1983.

Brooks, Virginia. *Little Lost Sister*. New York: Macaulay Co., 1914.

———. *My Battle with Vice*. New York: Macaulay Co., 1915.

Butler, Josephine. *Personal Reminiscences of a Great Crusade*. Westport, CT: Hyperion Press, 1911.

Carson, Gerald. "The Piano in the Parlor," *American Heritage* (December 1965).

Chernow, Ron. *Titan: The Life of John D. Rockefeller Sr*. New York: Random House, 1998.

"Chicago Committee Against Vice." *The Survey*, July 27, 1912.

"Conference on the White Slave Trade." *The Survey*, August 20, 1910.

Connelly, Mark Thomas. *The Response to Prostitution in the Progressive Era*. University of North Carolina Press, 1980.

Cordasco, Francesco, and Thomas Monroe Pitkin. *The White Slave Trade and the Immigrants: A Chapter in American Social History*. Detroit: Blaine Ethridge Books, 1981.

Creel, Herr G. *Prostitution for Profit: A Police Reporter's View of the White Slave Traffic*. St. Louis, MO: n.p., 1911.

Dedmon, Emmett. *Fabulous Chicago*. New York: Random House, 1953.

D'Emilio, John, and Estelle B. Freedman. *Intimate Matters: A History of Sexuality in America*. New York: Harper & Row, 1988.

de Young, Mary. "Help, I'm Being Held Captive!: The White Slave Fairy Tale of the Progressive Era." *Journal of American Culture* 6 (1983).

Dillon, John, and H. M. Lytle. *From Dance Hall to White Slavery*. Chicago: Stanton & Van Vuet, 1912.

Donovan, Brian. *White Slave Crusades: Race, Gender, and Anti-Vice Activism, 1887–1917*. Urbana and Chicago: University of Illinois Press, 2005.

Dreiser, Theodore. *Sister Carrie*. New York: Penguin, 1994 (1900).

Duis, Perry R. *Challenging Chicago: Coping with Everyday Life, 1837–1920*. Urbana: University of Illinois Press, 1998.

———. *The Saloon: Public Drinking in Chicago and Boston, 1880–1920*. Urbana: University of Illinois Press, 1983.

———. "Whose City: Public and Private Spaces in Nineteenth Century Chicago." Part I, *Chicago History* (Spring 1983). Part II, *Chicago History* (Summer 1983).

Edholm, Charlton. *Traffic in Girls and Work of Rescue Missions.* Chicago: Charlton Edholm, 1899.

Ellis, Havelock. *Little Essays of Love and Virtue.* New York: George H. Doran Co., 1922.

———. *Studies in the Psychology of Sex: Sex in Relation to Society* (vol. 4). New York: Random House, 1936 (1906).

Feldman, Egal. "Prostitution, the Alien Woman and the Progressive Imagination, 1910–1915." *American Quarterly* 19 (1967).

Fille de Joie: The Book of Courtesans, Sporting Girls, Ladies of the Evening, Madams, a Few Occasionals & Some Royal Favorites. Various contributors. New York: Grove Press, 1967.

Filler, Louis. *The Muckrakers.* University Park: Pennsylvania State University Press, 1976.

Fine, Lisa. *Souls of the Skyscraper: Female Clerical Workers in Chicago, 1870–1930.* Philadelphia: Temple University Press, 1990.

Fishbein, Leslie. "Harlot or Heroine?: Changing Views of Prostitution, 1870–1920." *Historian* (November 1980).

"Five White Slave Trade Investigations." Editorial. *McClure's Magazine* (July 1910).

"The Futility of the White Slave Agitation as Brand Whitlock Sees It." Editorial. *Current Opinion* (April 1914).

Gilfoyle, Timothy. *City of Eros: New York City, Prostitution and the Commercialization of Sex, 1790–1920.* New York: W. W. Norton & Co., 1992.

Goldman, Emma. *The White Slave Traffic.* New York: Mother Earth Publishing Association, 1910.

Goodspeed, Weston A., and Daniel D. Healy, eds. *History of Cook County, Illinois.* Chicago: Goodspeed Historical Association, 1909.

Green, Shirley. *The Curious History of Contraception.* New York: St. Martin's Press, 1972.

Greer, Joseph H. *The Social Evil: Its Cause, Effect and Cure.* Chicago: n.p., 1909.

Griffin, Richard T. "Sin Drenched Revels at the Infamous First Ward Ball." *Smithsonian* 7 (November 1976).

Grittner, Frederick K. *White Slavery: Myth, Ideology, and American Law.* New York: Garland Publishing, 1990.

Groetzinger, Leona. *The City's Perils.* Chicago: n.p., 1910.

Grossman, James R., Ann Durkin Keating, and Janice L. Reiff, eds. *The Encyclopedia of Chicago.* University of Chicago Press, 2004.

Haller, Mark. "Urban Vice and Civic Reform: Chicago in the Early Twentieth Century." In *Cities in American History,* edited by Kenneth T. Jackson and Stanley Schultz. New York: Knopf, 1972.

Hamilton, Francis E. "Restriction of Immigration." *Forum* 42 (December 1908).

Harland, Robert O. *The Vice Bondage of a Great City; or, The Wickedest City in the World.* Chicago: Young People's Civic League, 1912.

Harrison, Carter Henry. *Stormy Years: The Autobiography of Carter H. Harrison, Five Times Mayor of Chicago.* Indianapolis: Bobbs-Merrill, 1935.

Hecht, Ben. *Gaily, Gaily.* New York: Doubleday, 1963.

Hepburn, Katharine Houghton. *Women Suffrage and the Social Evil.* New York: National Woman Suffrage Pub., 1914.

Hibbeler, Ray. *Upstairs at the Everleigh Club*. New York: Volitant Books, 1960.

Holli, Melvin G., and Peter d'A. Jones, eds. *Ethnic Chicago: A Multicultural Portrait*. Grand Rapids, MI: William B. Eerdmans, 1995.

Hyde Park Protective Association and Chicago Law and Order League. *A Quarter of a Century of War on Vice in the City of Chicago*. Chicago: Hyde Park Protective Association and Chicago Law and Order League, 1918.

Irwin, Will. "The First Ward Ball." *Collier's*, February 6, 1909.

"Is White Slavery Nothing More Than a Myth?" *Current Opinion* (November 1913).

Jackson, Kenneth T., ed. *The Encyclopedia of New York City*. New Haven: Yale University Press, 1995.

Janney, Edward O. *The White Slave Traffic in America*. New York: National Vigilance Committee, 1911.

"Jews and the White Slave Trade." Editorial. *Literary Digest*, December 4, 1909.

Johnson, Curt, and Craig R. Sautter. *The Wicked City: Chicago from Kenna to Capone*. New York: Da Capo Press, 1998.

Joseph, Judith Lee Vaupen. "The Nafkeh and the Lady: Jews, Prostitutes and Progressives in New York City, 1900–1930." PhD dissertation, State University of New York at Stony Brook, 1986.

Kauffman, Reginald Wright. *The House of Bondage*. New York: Moffat, Yard and Company, 1910.

Kavounas, Margaret J. "Feeblemindedness and Prostitution: The Laboratory of Social Hygiene's Influence on Progressive Era Prostitution Reform." Master's thesis, Sarah Lawrence College, 1992.

Keire, Mara L. "The Vice Trust: A Reinterpretation of the White Slavery Scare in the United States, 1907–1917." *Journal of Social History* (Fall 2001).

Kimball, Nell. *Her Life as an American Madam*. New York: Macmillan, 1970.

Kneeland, George J. *Commercialized Prostitution in New York*. New York: Century Co., 1913.

Kogan, Herman, and Rick Kogan. *Yesterday's Chicago*. Miami: E. A. Seeman Publishing, 1976.

Kraus, Adolf. *Reminiscences and Comment: The Immigrant, the Citizen, a Public Office, the Jew*. Chicago: Toby Rubovits, 1925.

Kwolek-Folland, Angel. *Incorporating Women: A History of Women and Business in the United States*. Woodbridge, CT: Twayne Publishers, 1998.

Lagler, Amy R. "For God's Sake Do Something: White Slavery Narratives and Moral Panic in Turn-of-the-Century American Cities." PhD dissertation, Michigan State University, 2000.

Lait, Jack, and Lee Mortimer. *Chicago Confidential*. New York: Crown, 1950.

Langum, David J. *Crossing over the Line: Legislating Morality and the Mann Act*. University of Chicago Press, 1994.

Larson, Erik. *The Devil in the White City: Murder, Magic and Madness at the Fair That Changed America*. New York: Crown, 2003.

Lehman, Frederick Martin. *The White Slave Hell; or, With Christ at Midnight in the Slums of Chicago*. Chicago: Christian Witness Co., 1910.

Lewis, Lloyd, and Henry Justin Smith. *Chicago: The History of Its Reputation*. New York: Harcourt, Brace, 1929.

Lindberg, Richard C. *Chicago by Gaslight: A History of Chicago's Netherworld 1880–1920.* Chicago: Academy Chicago Publishers, 1996.

———. *Quotable Chicago.* Chicago: Loyola Press, 1996.

Lindsey, Ben B. "Why Girls Go Wrong." *Ladies' Home Journal* (January 1907).

Linehan, Mary. "Vicious Circle: Prostitution, Reform and Public Policy in Chicago, 1830–1930." PhD dissertation, University of Notre Dame, 1991.

Lombardo, Robert M. "The Black Mafia: African-American Organized Crime in Chicago: 1890–1960." *Crime, Law and Social Change* 38, no. 1 (2002).

Longstreet, Stephen. *Chicago: 1860–1919.* New York: David McKay, 1973.

Lowe, David. *Lost Chicago.* New York: Houghton Mifflin, 1975.

Lowry, Thomas P. *The Civil War Bawdy Houses of Washington, D.C.* Fredericksburg, VA: Sergeant Kirkland's, 1997.

Lubove, Roy. "The Progressive and the Prostitute." *The Historian* (May 1962).

Lundberg, Ferdinand. *America's 60 Families.* New York: Vanguard, 1937.

Lytle, H. M. *The Tragedies of the White Slaves.* Chicago: Charles C. Thompson, 1909.

Madeleine: An Autobiography. With an Introduction by Judge Ben Lindsey. New York: Harper & Brothers, 1919.

Madsen, Axel. *The Marshall Fields.* New York: John Wiley & Sons, 2002.

Mark, Norman. *Mayors, Madams and Madmen.* Chicago: Chicago Review Press, 1979.

Masters, Edgar Lee. "The Everleigh Club." *Town & Country* (April 1944).

———. *The Tale of Chicago.* New York: G. P. Putnam's Sons, 1933.

McClure, S. S., "Chicago as Seen by Herself." *McClure's Magazine* (May 1907).

———. "The Tammanyizing of a Civilization." *McClure's Magazine* (November 1909).

Meis Knupfer, Anne. *Reform and Resistance: Gender, Delinquency, and America's First Juvenile Court.* New York: Routledge, 2001.

Meyerowitz, Joanna J. *Women Adrift: Independent Wage Earners in Chicago, 1880–1930.* University of Chicago Press, 1991.

Mickish, Janet. "Legal Control of Socio-Sexual Relationships: Creation of the Mann White Slave Traffic Act of 1910." PhD dissertation, Southern Illinois University, 1980.

Miller, Donald L. *City of the Century.* New York: Simon & Schuster, 1996.

Moffett, Cleveland. "Marconi's Wireless Telegraph." *McClure's Magazine* (June 1899).

Mumford, Kevin J. *Interzones: Black/White Sex Districts in Chicago and New York in the Early Twentieth Century.* New York: Columbia University Press, 1997.

Musselman, M. M. *Get a Horse!: The Story of the Automobile in America.* Philadelphia: Lippincott, 1950.

Nabokov, Vladimir. *Lolita.* New York: Vintage, 1989 (1955).

Nash, Jay Robert. *Look for the Woman.* New York: M. Evans & Co., 1981.

———. *People to See: An Anecdotal History of Chicago's Makers and Breakers.* Piscataway, NJ: New Century Publishers, 1981.

New York Committee of Fifteen, Syracuse Moral Survey Committee, and Massachusetts Commission for Investigation of White Slave Traffic. *Prostitution in America: Three Investigations, 1902–1914.* New York: Arno Press, 1976.

Odem, Mary. *Delinquent Daughters: Protecting and Policing Adolescent Female Sexuality in the United States, 1885–1920*. Chapel Hill: University of North Carolina Press, 1995.

Pierce, Bessie Louise, ed. *As Others See Chicago: Impressions of Visitors, 1673–1933*. Chicago: University of Chicago Press, 1933.

Pivar, David. *Purity Crusade: Sexual Morality and Social Control, 1868–1900*. Westport, CT: Greenwood Press, 1973.

"Popular Gullibility as Exhibited in the New White Slave Hysteria." Editorial. *Current Opinion* (February 1914).

Reagan, Leslie J. *When Abortion Was a Crime: Women, Medicine and Law in the United States, 1867–1973*. Berkeley: University of California Press, 1997.

Reckless, Walter. *The Natural History of Vice Areas in Chicago*. PhD dissertation, University of Chicago, 1925.

———. *Vice in Chicago*. Chicago: University of Chicago Press, 1933.

Reitman, Benjamin. *The Second Oldest Profession*. New York: Vanguard, 1931.

Roberts, Nicki. *Whores in History*. London: HarperCollins, 1992.

Roe, Clifford G. *The Girl Who Disappeared*. Chicago: American Bureau of Moral Education, 1914.

———. *Panders and Their White Slaves*. Chicago: Fleming H. Revell Co., 1910.

———. *What Women Might Do with the Ballot: The Abolition of White Slave Traffic*. New York: National American Woman Suffrage Association, n.d.

———, ed. *The Great War on White Slavery; or, Fighting for the Protection of Our Girls*. Chicago: n.p., 1911.

Roe, Clifford, and Clare Teal Wiseman. *The Prosecutor: A Four Act Drama*. Chicago: Clifford Roe, 1914.

Rosen, Ruth. *The Lost Sisterhood: Prostitution in America, 1900–1918*. Baltimore: Johns Hopkins University Press, 1982.

Rottenberg, Dan. "Good Rumors Never Die." *Chicago* (February 1984).

Sanger, William. *The History of Prostitution: Its Extent, Causes and Effects Throughout the World*. New York: Harper, 1859.

Schlereth, Thomas J. *Victorian America: Transformations in Everyday Life, 1876–1915*. New York: HarperCollins, 1991.

"Sex o'Clock in America." *Current Opinion*, August 1913.

Sims, Edwin. "Slave Traffic in America." *Outlook*, May 29, 1909.

———. "The White Slave Trade of Today." *Woman's World* (September 1908).

———. "Why Girls Go Astray." *Woman's World* (December 1909).

Sinclair, Upton. *The Jungle*. New York: Bantam Classics, 1981 (1906).

Smashing the White Slave Trade. Various contributors. Chicago: Currier Publishing Co., 1909.

Sporting and Club House Directory. Chicago: n.p., 1889.

Stead, William T. *If Christ Came to Chicago: A Plea for the Union of All Who Love in the Service of All Who Suffer*. Chicago: Laird & Lee, 1894.

———. *The Maiden Tribute of Modern Babylon: The Report of the Pall Mall Gazette's Secret Commission*. London: Richard Lambert, 1885.

Steffens, Lincoln. *The Shame of the Cities.* New York: Hill & Wang, 1957 (1904).

Stelzer, Patricia Jacobs. "Prohibition and Organized Crime: A Case Study: An Examination of the Life of John Torrio." Master's thesis, Wright State University, 1997.

"Tammany and the White Slaves." Editorial. *Literary Digest,* November 6, 1909.

Taylor, Graham. *Chicago Commons Through Forty Years.* Chicago: Chicago Commons Association, 1936.

———. "Chicago Vice Commission." *The Survey,* May 6, 1911.

———. "Chicago Vice Report." *Literary Digest,* April 22, 1911.

———. "Chicago Vice Report Barred from the Mails." *The Survey,* October 7, 1911.

———. *Pioneering on Social Frontiers.* Chicago: University of Chicago Press, 1930.

———. "Routing the Segregationists in Chicago." *The Survey,* November 20, 1912.

Thomas, Dana Lee. *The Money Crowd.* New York: Putnam, 1972.

Tingley, Ralph Russell. "From Carter Harrison II to Fred Busse: A Study of Chicago Political Parties and Personages from 1896–1907." Master's thesis, University of Chicago, 1950.

Turner, George Kibbe. "The City of Chicago: A Study of the Great Immoralities." *McClure's Magazine* (April 1907).

———. "The Daughters of the Poor: A Plain Story of the Development of New York City as a Leading Center of the White Slave Trade of the World, Under Tammany Hall." *McClure's Magazine* (November 1909).

Turner-Zimmerman, Jean. *America's Black Traffic in White Girls.* Chicago: n.p., 1912.

———. *Chicago's Black Traffic in White Girls.* Chicago: Chicago Rescue Mission, 1911.

Uhlarik, Carl. "The Sin Sisters Who Made Millions." *Real West* (December 1968).

Vice Commission of Chicago. *The Social Evil in Chicago: A Study of Existing Conditions.* Chicago: Gunthorp-Warren, 1911.

Viskochil, Larry A. *Chicago at the Turn of the Century in Photographs.* Chicago: Chicago Historical Society, 1984.

"Wages and Sin." Editorial. *Literary Digest,* March 22, 1913.

Walkowitz, Judith. *City of Dreadful Delight: Narratives of Sexual Danger in Late-Victorian London.* Chicago: University of Chicago Press, 1992.

Wallace, Irving. *The Sunday Gentleman.* New York: Simon & Schuster, 1965.

Ward, Geoffrey C. *Unforgivable Blackness: The Rise and Fall of Jack Johnson.* New York: Knopf, 2004.

Washburn, Charles. *Come into My Parlor: A Biography of the Aristocratic Everleigh Sisters of Chicago.* New York: Knickerbocker Publishing, 1936.

Washburn, Josie. *The Underworld Sewer: A Prostitute Reflects on Life in the Trade, 1871–1909.* Omaha, NE: Washburn Publishing Co., 1909.

Weinberg, Arthur, and Lila Weinberg, eds. *The Muckrakers.* Urbana: University of Illinois Press, 1961.

Wendt, Lloyd, and Herman Kogan. *Lords of the Levee: The Story of Bathhouse John and Hinky Dink.* Indianapolis, IN: Bobbs-Merrill, 1943.

Whitlock, Brand. *Forty Years of It.* New York: D. Appleton & Co., 1913.

———. "The White Slave." *Forum* (February 1914).

Williams, F. B. "Social Bonds in the Black Belt of Chicago." *Charities* 15, October 7, 1905.

Wilson, Samuel Paynter. *Chicago and Its Cess Pools of Infamy.* Chicago: n.p., 1911.

———. *The Story of Lena Murphy, the White Slave.* Chicago: n.p., 1910.

Winick, Charles, and Paul Kinsie. *The Lively Commerce: Prostitution in the United States.* Chicago: Quadrangle Books, 1971.

Woods Hampton, Margaret. *Descendants of John Early of Virginia (1729–1774).* Larchmont, NY: n.p., 1973.

Woodward, Harold R. *Major General James Lawson Kemper, C.S.A.: The Confederacy's Forgotten Son.* Natural Bridge Station, VA: Rockbridge Publishing, 1993.

"World Wide War on Vice." Editorial. *The Survey,* July 27, 1912.

INDEX

Page numbers in *italics* refer to illustrations.

ILLUSTRATION AND PHOTOGRAPH CREDITS

Sin in the Second City

Karen Abbott

A READER'S GUIDE

1. The Everleigh sisters were technically criminals, yet they genuinely believed they were helping the girls in the Club. What do you think about the Everleigh sisters' business practices? Why were they so successful?

2. How are Minna and Ada alike, and how are they different? Who was the stronger sister, in your opinion? How were they able to perpetuate so many lies for so long?

3. In what ways does Abbott's portrait of turn-of-the-century America mirror the present day?

4. At the time the Everleighs ruled Chicago, what other choices did women have? Do you judge the women who became "sporting girls"? Do you judge the madams? What path do you think you would have chosen if you'd been alive and facing similar circumstances during the turn of the century?

5. On the surface it seems that there are only two sides in *Sin in the Second City*—the reformers and the sisters—but there are actually a few more: the politicians, the Levee gangsters, and the rival madams. Are there heroes in *Sin in the Second City*, and are there villains? Who did you sympathize with? Did you find your loyalties shifting at any point along the way?

6. Do you think the reformers exaggerated or accurately represented the "white slavery" situation?

7. At one point, the African American boxing champion Jack Johnson shows up at the Club, and his presence causes quite a commotion. What does his visit tell you in terms of race and America at the turn of the century?

8. How did America's sexual culture change during the Everleighs' reign? Who was primarily responsible for these changes, the reformers or the underworld?

9. Chicago is as much a character in *Sin in the Second City* as the gangsters and the madams. Why do you think the Everleigh sisters chose to settle in Chicago? Would they have been as successful in another city, or was Chicago particularly conducive to their success?

10. Many reformers cited strong religious convictions as a reason for fighting the red-light districts. How do you think the religious tenor of the times compares to that of today?

11. What was your favorite Everleigh Club anecdote?

12. What satisfaction can be derived from a nonfiction book like *Sin in the Second City* that can't be from novels? In what ways is the book like a novel?

13. Abbott stumbled upon the story of the Everleigh sisters while researching a long-lost relative. How much do you know about your own family's history and ancestry? Do you know where they were and what they were doing from 1900 to 1911, when the Everleigh Club was in business?

PHOTO: GILBERT KING

KAREN ABBOTT is a native of Philadelphia, where she worked as a journalist for several years. Her next book is a portrait of Gypsy Rose Lee and Depression-era New York City. Visit her online at www.sininthesecondcity.com.

ABOUT THE TYPE

This book is set in Fournier, a typeface named for Pierre Simon
Fournier, the youngest son of a French printing family. He started
out engraving woodblocks and large capitals, then moved on to
fonts of type. In 1736 he began his own foundry and made several
important contributions in the field of type design; he is said to have
cut 147 alphabets of his own creation. Fournier is probably best remembered as the designer of St. Augustine Ordinaire, a face that
served as the model for Monotype's Fournier, which was released
in 1925.